LUST FOR BLOOD

Also by Olga Hoyt:
  Witches
  Exorcism
  Demons, Devils, and Djinn
  and many other books

LUST FOR BLOOD

The Consuming Story of Vampires

Olga Hoyt

Scarborough House/Publishers

Scarborough House/*Publishers*
Chelsea, MI 48118

FIRST SCARBOROUGH HOUSE TRADE PAPERBACK EDITION 1990

Lust For Blood was originally published in hardcover
by Stein and Day/*Publishers.*

Library of Congress Cataloging in Publication Data

Hoyt, Olga.
  Lust for blood.

  Bibliography: p.
  Includes index.
  1. Vampires. I. Title.
GR830.V3H69 1984   398'.45   83-17994
ISBN 0-8128-8511-2

Contents

ILLUSTRATIONS

Woodcut of the real Dracula
Vlad Tepes
Countess Elizabeth Báthory, "Vampire Lady of the Carpathians"
Countess Báthory's Csejthe Castle
The Iron Maiden
Max Schreck in *Nosferatu*
Hammer poster for *Dracula*
Hollywood poster for Lugosi movie
Advertisement for London stage production of *Dracula*
Bela Lugosi in title role of *Dracula*
Lugosi as the Count
A Transylvanian castle movie set
Otto Kruger burns on a pyre in *Dracula's Daughter*
The resuscitated corpse
Film version of "un-dead" family members rising
The count prepares to slake his thirst
Modern surrogates for horse-drawn hearse and howling wolf
An up-to-date film vampire
The impaling of a female film vampire
Christopher Lee demonstrates typical vampire fangs
Frank Langella in New York stage play
Frank Langella, sexiest of Draculas
Dr. Jeanne Youngson, president of the Count Dracula Fan Club
Application form to join the Count Dracula Society
London's Highgate Cemetery, reputed home of a vampire (3 photos)

1

THE RED BEVERAGE

FIRST HE SHOT HER IN THE BACK OF THE head.

"Then I went out to the car and fetched a drinking glass and made an incision, I think with a pen knife, in the side of the throat, and collected a glass of blood, which I then drank."

After that he removed her Persian lamb coat and jewelry—rings and necklace, earrings and crucifix—from the body, hauled the corpse over to an empty oil drum in the warehouse, and dumped it in. Then he looked at his watch and saw that it was time for tea. He went "round to the Ancient's Prior's for a cup of tea" to refresh himself after his exertions. Soon, he returned to the warehouse and pumped the oil drum full of enough acid to cover the body. Then he left, and nature took its course, the acid destroying the evidence.

THE VAMPIRE KILLER

He was John George Haigh, a dapper thirty-nine-year-old Englishman. This was the latest of a series of crimes that were unknown to the British police, so clever had John George Haigh been in his bloody efforts.

He had the veneer of a completely respectable man, and indeed he came from a respectable family of Yorkshiremen. His father had worked in a colliery and, except for a bad time during the depression, had

worked steadily and faithfully for the same employer all his life. So John
George Haigh spent the first twenty-four years of his life in Outwood, a
suburb of Wakefield. They were unexciting but unsettling years for the
youth. His mother and father were ardent members of the Plymouth
Brethren, the "Peculiar People" whose religion was a harsh and unforgiving instrument. John George Haigh was bedeviled by the Devil all
during his youth. Join the church choir? Yes. Read Robert Louis Stevenson's *Treasure Island*? No. His father rejected the book—any book
about pirates was ungodly, and there would be no ungodly books in the
Haigh house. No radio, no films, no magazines, no newspapers entered
the Haigh house. The Bible and *Pilgrim's Progress* were quite enough to
supplement his schoolbooks.

No friends from school ever entered the Haigh house; they were not
allowed. Childhood friends might be bad influences. So John George
Haigh had no friends. Alone, lonely, he turned inward. At the age of
eleven, he began drinking his own urine, and from that time onward did
so every day, he said. Did not the Bible say (Prov. 5:15) "Drink waters
out of thine own cistern and running waters out of thine own well"?

Spare the rod and spoil the child was the parenting philosophy of the
elder Haighs; and so young John George often felt the smart of a strap.
One day his mother slapped his hand with a hairbrush for some misdeed,
and the bristles drew blood. He sucked the wound and found the blood
tasty and desirable. It was so good that later he deliberately cut his finger,
in order to experience again the pleasant sensation of drinking blood.

John George attended the Wakefield Grammar School, and there he
began to rebel against the strictures of his family life. The rebellion
brought him into open conflict with his father, and that meant more
punishment. His revenge was sweet: he became a choirboy—for the
Church of England's Wakefield Cathedral Choir! Hardly anything he
could have done would have hurt his family's feelings more.

But they could not fault him for being religious, could they? And he
was a devout believer. Every Sunday morning, he left home at 5:30 to
walk three miles to serve at the Wakefield Cathedral altar for three holy
communion services in a row. He would stay at the cathedral all day—
for matins, Sunday school, and evensong—then he would walk the three
miles home again. He spent many hours in the cathedral during school
days, before the figure of Christ bleeding on the Cross. The thought of
Christ nailed to a cross, dying slowly, filled him with extreme pain. Why
didn't they kill him and be done with it? He had other painful thoughts—
and dreams. Actually it was one dream, repeated over and over again.

"I saw a forest of crucifixes which gradually turned into trees. At first I seemed to see dew or rain running from the branches. But when I came nearer I knew it was blood. All of a sudden the whole forest began to twist about and the trees streamed with blood. Blood ran from the trunks. Blood ran from the branches, all red and shiny. I felt weak and seemed to faint. I saw a man going around the trees, gathering blood. When the cup he was holding in hand was full he came up to me and said 'drink.' But I was paralyzed. . . . The dream vanished, but I still felt faint and stretched out with all my strength towards the cup. . . . I woke up. I always kept on seeing those hands holding out a cup to me that I couldn't quite reach . . . and that terrible thirst . . . never left me. For three or four days I always had the same dream and each time I woke up, my horrible desire always became stronger."

Generally, Haigh managed to sublimate this terrible desire. He became assistant organist at the church, and that took his mind off his dreams. He was a strange young man, not much of a student, and no athlete, but music was his life. The loneliness of the early years wore off. He left school at seventeen to take a job with a firm of motor engineers. He did not like the mechanical work, it was too dirty, so he quit and got a white-collar job. When he was twenty, friends introduced him to sex, and he sowed some wild oats. He also showed business promise and made quite a lot of money promoting insurance purchases on such projects as the construction of a dam in Egypt. He also floated a company, Northern Electric Newspapers Ltd., which was an advertising agency, and for a time it was quite successful. When he was twenty-four years old, in order to get out of the family house, he married a beautiful girl. Not long afterward, Haigh discovered crime.

His first venture outside the law seemed ridiculously easy. He contracted for cars on a hire-purchase plan and then sold them off for cash. This enterprise involved defrauding an auto dealer and a manufacturer and also committing forgery. He was caught, convicted, and, in November 1934, sentenced to fifteen months in prison. He never saw his beautiful bride again.

After less than a year, he was released for good behavior. He got into a legitimate partnership in the drycleaning business and did well until his partner died. The business had to be sold to meet the widow's taxes. He went to London to find work and got a job as a chauffeur and secretary to a Mr. McSwan, owner of an amusement arcade. But that was not lucrative enough, and he soon left to go into another scam, which involved fraudulent stock sales. He was caught again and this time sent to prison for four years. He was paroled in the summer of 1940 and joined the civilian war service as a firewatcher. After some petty criminality, for which he was jailed briefly, he found a job with an engineering firm and building supply house, located at Crawley in Sussex county, as a commission salesman. He also secured the use of a part of a warehouse owned by the company as a "workshop."

During all this time, the blood lust seemed to have been forgotten. But on March 26, 1944, Haigh suffered a scalp wound in an auto accident. "Blood poured from my head down my face and into my mouth. This revived in me the taste, and that night I experienced another awful dream. I saw before me a forest of crucifixes."

Yes, it was the same old horror.

In 1944, Haigh rented a basement at 79 Gloucester Road in London as a workshop. He set up as an inventor. At the same time, in a pub in Kensington, he happened to meet William Donald McSwan, the son of his old employer of the amusement arcade. The arcade was long gone, but the McSwans had prospered and now lived at No. 45 Claverton Street. Young McSwan brought Haigh around to the house, and soon he was a frequent visitor. He and young McSwan hit it off beautifully, perhaps because the latter had a bit of the crook in him, too: he was just then considering a plan to go underground to avoid serving in the armed forces.

On September 9, 1944, McSwan got his wish. The National Service people would never come after him again. Haigh tells the story.

"I got the feeling I must get some blood somewhere. . . . [McSwan] brought a pin-table [pinball machine] to Gloucester Road for repair. The idea came to me to kill him and take some blood. I hit him over the head and he was unconscious. I got a mug and took some blood from his neck slicing it with a penknife, I poured it in the mug and drank it. Then I realized I must do something about him. I left him there dead. . . . I had acid and sheet metal for pickling. . . . I found a water butt [barrel] and took it on a cart and put McSwan in acid. I put the body in a tub and poured the acid on it. I did it with a bucket. I went to see McSwan's parents and told them he had gone away because of his callup. I sent them a letter from Glasgow." He marked a big red cross in his diary on that date, September 9. When the flesh and bones had been reduced by the acid to sludge, Haigh poured the mess down a manhole in the basement shop.

Because the senior McSwans feared that their son was breaking the law and asked no questions, Haigh's first murder went completely unnoticed by the authorities.

The war produced many dislocations and pushed many people out of their usual environment. London was full of strangers. In the next few months, Haigh claimed to have murdered three more people, two women and a man, whom he encountered casually in pubs or at bus stops. The girls he pretended he wanted to make love to, the man he pretended to befriend; but all ended up in John George Haigh's pickle barrel. The murders were carried out for blood and profit, but there was mighty little of the latter: Haigh complained that the man had less than a pound on him and no jewelry at all; the women had little more.

He did much better with the McSwans, younger and elder. By exercising his talent for forgery, he managed to sell off various properties that young McSwan had owned. He also managed to keep the friendship of the senior McSwans by occasionally giving them "news" of their vanished son.

Then one day in July 1945, Haigh persuaded the father, Donald McSwan, to come to the basement workroom at 79 Gloucester Road, and there he killed the old man the same way he had killed the son, by knocking him on the head. "The corpse did not produce enough blood," he complained, so he went back to the McSwan house and brought the mother, Amy McSwan. She, too, got a blow on the head and a knife in the throat. Haigh dissolved both bodies in acid.

No one seemed to notice the disappearance of the senior McSwans, and Haigh had plenty of time to dispose of the old man's securities and, by forgery, of his other property.

All this while, Haigh was more or less commuting between London and Crawley, where he had the use of that storeroom in a warehouse of the engineering company for his "experiments." His lodgings were in Crawley, and he merely "bunked" at the Gloucester Road address. But with all the profit from the McSwan murders, he felt able to extend himself, so he moved up to London into the Onslow Court Hotel, a small place frequented by retired colonels and middle-class widows. He made quite a hit there, and why not? He was a pleasant-looking man, about five feet six inches tall, with glossy black hair and a small clipped mustache and clean-shaven face. At thirty-nine he was considerably younger than the run of the hotel guests. He was the epitome of charm to the ladies. He passed himself off as a factory owner and inventor and spoke expansively but casually of his enterprises. He dressed neatly, and with a certain flair. One of his favorite outfits was a green hopsacking suit, which he wore with a cream-colored shirt, red necktie, green socks, and shiny brown brogue shoes.

The McSwan fortune served John George Haigh well for two years, but eventually it began to run out and he looked around for new opportunities. At Christmas 1947, he gave himself a present: three carboys of sulfuric acid, which he stored in the warehouse "factory" at Crawley. He also ordered two forty-four-gallon steel drums, with tops removed, to be delivered to the warehouse.

Then he set about finding a new source of revenue. He found it in the newspapers.

Dr. Archie Henderson and his wife had decided to sell their house at 22 Ladbroke Square, because the doctor wanted to give up his practice. Dr. Henderson came from an old Scottish family, but he was not precisely the quietest of the clan. He had cut quite a figure in London in the prewar years. When his first wife died and left him quite a lot of money, he ran through it rapidly. He married again, this time a sultry brunette of the beauty-queen type named Rose. When the war began he joined the service. For her part, Rose turned their house at 22 Ladbroke Square into a guesthouse to help meet the need caused by the housing shortage. Dr. Henderson was invalided out of the service in 1945, came home to live at 22 Ladbroke Square, and practiced medicine there. He and Rose also carried on an intense social life; it was said that the good doctor put away a bottle of Scotch whisky every day. Eventually, times got hard for them and they decided to sell the big house on Ladbroke Square and look for smaller quarters. They advertised the house for sale in the London newspapers. John George Haigh, looking for opportunity, saw the advertisement.

The property was put up for sale at about £9,000. Haigh insisted on offering £10,000. Mrs. Henderson was delighted with his stupidity, but when she told her brother about it, he observed that if you met someone like that the best thing to do was run for your life. Mrs. Henderson did not take his advice; in the end Haigh did not buy the house because he could not raise the money, but he realized that he had found his opportunity, and he spent the next few months cultivating the Hendersons.

The Hendersons moved into a much cheaper district and a much cheaper house on Dawes Road in Fulham. They lived in rooms above a shop where they sold toys. Haigh visited them often there. He had the run of the house and even the trust of the Henderson's red setter, Pat.

Waiting for his opportunity, he stole Dr. Henderson's revolver and put it aside for future use.

Haigh's opportunity came just in time. February 1948 found Haigh very near the end of his financial rope. His overdraft at the bank had reached nearly £250. He owed a finance company £400. He was behind in his rent at the Onslow Court Hotel.

Just then, the Hendersons took a trip that ended at Brighton, the seaside resort, where they stayed at the Hotel Metropole.

On February 12, Haigh visited them there and invited Dr. Henderson to drive with him to Crawley to see his factory. When Haigh had lured the doctor inside, he immediately shot him in the head with his own revolver, cut his throat with the penknife, and drank the blood. Then he drove back to Brighton, told Rose Henderson that her husband had been taken ill and needed her, and drove her to the factory, where he repeated the performance.

Both Hendersons were then stripped, their belongings were confiscated, and they were treated to an acid bath. Haigh went home and wrote in his diary "A.H." and "R.H." and the sign of the cross. Realizing that the dog, Pat, had been left behind at the hotel in Brighton and might begin to make a fuss, Haigh telephoned the night porter and, pretending to be Mrs. Henderson, asked him to take the dog for a few days since they were called away.

He returned to the "factory" after two days to empty the sludge out of the acid drums. He noticed that one of Dr. Henderson's feet was still almost completely intact, but he was in a hurry—there was so much to be done to settle the Henderson affairs. So he dumped out the foot with the rest of the gooey remains. Dr. Henderson had been carrying a considerable sum of money: on February 15, Haigh deposited £565 to his own London account. That was enough to satisfy his creditors for the moment and keep up his good name at the Onslow Court Hotel. Then he drove to Brighton, showed the assistant manager a letter purportedly written by Dr. Henderson, paid up the Henderson hotel bill, collected the dog, four suitcases, four coats, and two golf bags, and drove off. The Hendersons had checked out.

Back at the Onslow Court, Haigh sat down to do some complicated forgery. He was well prepared. He had picked up a number of sheets of stationery from the Metropole Hotel in Brighton. He used one of them to write a letter to the housekeeper, saying that the Hendersons were migrating to South Africa and Haigh was looking after their affairs. A few days later, when Mrs. Henderson's brother telephoned, the housekeeper gave him this information. He phoned Haigh, who confirmed the statement and said he had lent Dr. Henderson several thousand pounds, if it was not repaid, he was to have the Henderson house and car. Mrs. Henderson's brother was puzzled, but when he received a letter from his "sister" explaining it all, he was temporarily satisfied. After all, he knew the Henderson living style, and Haigh's forgery of Rose Henderson's handwriting was excellent.

John George Haigh devoted the next few weeks to business. He sold off all the Henderson personal property to jewelers and clothiers. He retained the toy shop on Dawes Road for his own business and kept careful accounts of income and disbursements.

Over the next few months, Haigh disposed of all the Henderson property, the car, and the Fulham house by forging the necessary documents. It should have been enough to keep him for several years, but he spent it all by the end of 1948. In January 1949 all the money was gone. He was behind in his rent at the Onslow Court Hotel. His bank was pressing for payment of his overdraft. Something had to be done. What he needed was a new opportunity.

It arose right there at the Onslow Court Hotel, one evening when he went into the dining room for dinner.

Haigh's single dining table was placed next to that of a sixty-nine-year-old widow named Olive Henrietta Roberts Durand-Deacon. They had been nodding acquaintances for three years; but in the English fashion, although their elbows nearly touched at meals, they had not intruded on one another's privacy. But in recent months they had exchanged a few pleasantries, and, in fact, Haigh had sold Mrs. Durand-Deacon the expensive handbag that had belonged to Rose Henderson, passing it off as an unwanted inheritance. Thus a measure of intimacy had been created, and nowadays they usually exchanged a few polite words at meals.

One evening, Mrs. Durand-Deacon complained about the state of her fingernails. She had often thought, she said, of making plastic nails for women who had such deplorable stubby nails as her own.

What a capital idea! said her friend John George Haigh, the inventor. Oh, there was nothing new about it, said Mrs. Durand-Deacon. In fact, she had some upstairs, but she did not like them and believed they could be made in a better way.

Haigh expressed serious interest, and Mrs. Durand-Deacon promised to show him the nails.

Monday, February 14, 1948. Haigh's bank manager told him he had an overdraft of nearly £85, and the bank refused to honor more checks. He owed the Onslow Court Hotel about £50. He had given them a check and it had bounced. The management was not pleased. He would have to do something immediately to raise some money. He saw Mrs. Durand-Deacon and brought up the matter of the plastic fingernails. She promised to show them to him that day at lunch, and she did.

Haigh agreed with everything she said about the nails. Perhaps they could go into business together, to bring out a superior line? Why didn't Mrs. Durand-Deacon drive with him down to the factory he owned in Sussex, and they could seriously consider the possibilities?

Mrs. Durand-Deacon was pleased and flattered and she agreed. They made an engagement to drive to Sussex on Friday afternoon. Why such a long wait? Haigh needed a little time.

Tuesday, February 15. He drove to Crawley and suggested the plastic fingernail idea to Mr. Jones, the managing director of Hurstlea Products Ltd. Jones was not enthusiastic. He did lend Haigh £50, with the proviso that it be paid back at the end of the week. He did not know it, but he had just set the date for Mrs. Durand-Deacon's death.

Wednesday, February 16. Haigh paid his bill at the Onslow Court Hotel. He also drove to Crawley and ordered more acid.

Thursday, February 17. The acid arrived at Crawley. Haigh appeared with a new pump—the old one had worn out.

Friday, February 18. Haigh and Mrs. Durand-Deacon lunched at the Onslow Court Hotel. At 2:30 they set out for Crawley. They stopped briefly at the George Hotel there and then drove to the warehouse. Haigh took her in and showed her some paper he said would be suitable for treatment to make artificial fingernails. While she was examining it, Haigh shot her in the back of the head. Then he cut her throat with the penknife and drank some blood. He removed Mrs. Durand-Deacon's jewelry and fur coat from the corpse, undressed it, and put the lady's body and her clothing into a forty-four gallon tank. Then he went out for his tea. After that, as darkness fell, Haigh was very busy, moving the valuables into the car and filling the tank up with sulfuric acid. The exercise gave him an appetite. He went to the dining room of the George Hotel for dinner.

Saturday, February 19. Haigh appeared at breakfast in the dining room of the Onslow Court Hotel. He asked the waitress if she had seen Mrs. Durand-Deacon, because she had failed to keep an appointment with him on Friday afternoon. He also posed the same question to Mrs. Lane, a good friend of Mrs. Durand-Deacon's.

Mrs. Lane replied that she had not seen her. As a matter of fact, she had noticed that her friend had not been at the dining table the evening before. She, in turn, asked Haigh if *he* knew where Mrs. Durand-Deacon was, for Mrs. Durand-Deacon had told her she was going out to Crawley with him. Yes, said Haigh, but Mrs. Durand-Deacon did not keep the appointment.

Mrs. Lane was distressed. She checked with the maid upstairs and found that Mrs. Durand-Deacon had not returned the night before.

Sunday was a busy day. At breakfast the scenario with Mrs. Lane was repeated. She said she still had no news and would go to the Chelsea Police Station after lunch to ask them to investigate. Haigh left. A short time later he went looking for Mrs. Lane again. He found her in a sitting room and told her he thought they ought to go together to the Chelsea Police Station. They did and made their statements that afternoon.

Haigh, of course, told the police he did not know where Mrs. Durand-Deacon was. What an inveterate liar! He knew very well where she was—she was having an acid bath.

Monday, February 21. Haigh went to Crawley to check the tank and found that the chemical reaction wasn't complete yet. He drove back to London and went around to several jewelers' shops to dispose of Mrs. Durand-Deacon's jewelry. He sent her Persian lamb coat to a cleaners. Then he went back to Crawley "to find the reaction almost complete, but a piece of fat and bone was still floating on the sludge. I emptied off the sludge with a bucket and tipped it out on the ground opposite the shed, and pumped a further quantity of acid into the tank to decompose the remaining fat and bone. I then left that to work until the following day."

The police were also busy. The Chelsea station sent a woman sergeant to interview people at the Onslow Court Hotel. The manageress did not have a very good opinion of John George Haigh, she discovered. She learned little else. No one had seen Mrs. Durand-Deacon since Friday lunch.

The Chelsea station called the Criminal Records Office for a routine check and struck gold on the name John George Haigh. His criminal past of the war years was revealed. This was enough to prompt the police to send two detectives to the hotel to interview Haigh. Again, he denied any knowledge of Mrs. Durand-Deacon's activities on Friday.

Tuesday, February 22 was another busy day. The press called on Haigh at the hotel. They had learned that he had a criminal record, and that interested them. He fobbed them off with his standard story of ignorance of Mrs. Durand-Deacon's affairs.

"I am just as anxious as you or anyone else is," he said.

After the reporters left the hotel, Haigh went to his bank and paid off part of his overdraft. He then drove to Crawley and paid off Mr. Jones. He tipped the rest of Mrs. Durand-Deacon's sludge out to join the first batch.

The police kept busy, and by February 26 they had enough evidence to break into the Crawley warehouse. There they found plenty more, including the cleaners' receipt for the fur coat, traces of blood, and bits of substance identified as animal fat. They went around to the jewelry establishments and found Mrs. Durand-Deacon's jewelry. When all this was identified, they confronted Haigh and arrested him.

Haigh remained cool. He denied everything. But the police brought up the matter of the Persian lamb coat and the jewelry, and finally he saw that they had him.

"Tell me," he asked a detective inspector, "what are the chances of anyone being released from Broadmoor?"*

The inspector said he could not discuss such matters.

"Well," said Haigh. "If I told you the truth you would not believe me; it sounds too fantastic for belief."

Then Haigh confessed everything, in the most lurid terms. It took him two hours to tell it all.

"It was not their money but their blood that I was after," he said. "The thing I am really conscious of is the cup of blood. . . . I made a small cut, usually in the right side of the neck, and drank the blood for three to five minutes and . . . afterwards I felt better. Before each of the killings I have detailed in my confession, I had a series of dreams."

The London press, of course, relished the new "vampire" to the fullest.

Drinking blood! "Vampire" screamed the headlines:

> Vampire!!! A Man Held. . . .
> The Vampire Confesses. . . .
> The Vampire Will Never Strike Again. . . .

The public was not only horrified, but it could hardly wait for the next horrid installment of the story. There had been murders before, but blood drinking—that was something else!

Haigh was remarkably eloquent in his descriptions of the murders and of his obsession with blood. Four days after his original statement, he

---

*The institution for the criminally insane.

offered the fact that he had murdered those three lonely souls during the war. The police were never convinced of these murders, for Haigh had aroused their suspicions with his talk about Broadmoor, and they believed he was just preparing a defense of such excess as to show insanity.

After much legal maneuvering, in July 1949, Haigh was brought to trial at Lewes, England. The trial was held in the court that had jurisdiction over Crawley, where the murder of Mrs. Durand-Deacon had taken place. The defense pleaded not guilty, by reason of insanity. The evidence was presented, and the corollary evidence of the murders of the McSwans and the Hendersons and of the question of blood was raised.

After both sides had presented their evidence and their statements, the jury took only fifteen minutes to decide that John George Haigh was not insane, but guilty of plain, old-fashioned murder.

On July 19, the white-wigged old justice put on the black hat and announced to the prisoner that he was "to be hanged by the neck until dead."

Haigh was taken to Wandsworth Prison to wait. The press had its field day. Haigh gave interviews and his life story to the press, embellishing it all with talk of blood.

But finally came the day of reckoning. On August 9, 1949, the journalist Stafford Somerfield of the *News of the World* went to Wandsworth to see Haigh. One of his last requests was that the wax figure of him that was being prepared for the Chamber of Horrors at Madame Tussaud's wax museum in London should wear his favorite green hopsacking suit, with a red tie and green socks. "He still sticks to his frequently expressed view that he was not responsible for what he had done, but that he was moved and guided by some power outside himself."

"What is, is, and what is to be, will be," he said, quoting the book of Ecclesiastes.

Haigh was so right. The next morning they hanged John George Haigh, the man the press called the Acid Bath Vampire.

2

Man, Spirit, or Devil?

WHAT IS A VAMPIRE?

Is it a tall, gaunt figure with piercing eyes and fanglike teeth, dressed in evening clothes with a long black cape sweeping across its shoulders?

Is it the "reanimated" body of a dead person, emerging from the grave to terrorize the populace as it seeks living blood to revitalize itself?

Is it a corpse that has been reassembled outside the grave, changed into a creature of blazing red eyes, razor-sharp talons, covered entirely by pale hair of a greenish tint, a beast that sucks the blood and eats the flesh of its living victims?

Is a vampire a demon, a monster with snarling head, the breasts of a woman, the scaly body of a winged serpent, which flies around at night, attacking children to suck their blood?

Or is a vampire a mist that floats through the air, an ectoplasmic mass that can pass through the walls of a house, and float through graveyards, seeking the life substance, blood?

Or, more prosaically, is a vampire an apparently ordinary human being who sinks his or her teeth into a "donor's" flesh and sucks blood—an act that produces a sexual explosion that excites and satisfies?

The vampire has been all these things to peoples across the world throughout history. Although films and television have popularized a picture of a cape-clad vampire (based on Bram Stoker's immortal Count Dracula), in some parts of the world, the belief in vampires as real creatures continues today.

Each age, and each part of the world, has had a differing view of the vampire, but each of them fits more or less into one of three categories:

First is the astral or ectoplasmic vampire—the mass that floats around in the air. Perhaps it is luminescent, perhaps not. Perhaps the vampire leaves bite marks, perhaps not. But always the person who is under attack by the vampire languishes, grows pale from loss of blood, and often dies.

Second is the "un-dead," a creature that is neither dead and decomposing in the grave where it is supposed to be, nor living on the earth as a person. This vampire is a corpse that has risen from the grave—at night—either powered by the Devil (a Christian concept) or by its own past misdeeds or even misfortunes. It wanders about in search of victims to secure blood to revitalize itself, to keep itself alive for the next few days in the grave until the dreadful need for blood comes on it again. "A Pariah even among demons . . . foul are his ravages. . . . He is neither dead nor alive but living in death." Thus wrote Montague Summers, the foremost student of the history of the vampire in Europe.

The third type of "vampire" is the human being, apparently live and well, who seeks blood from other humans, usually on a transactional basis. He or she may be a member of a cult, or a loner. That these beings conform to the traditional beliefs in vampires is questionable, but there have been notable proved cases of vampirism. The common thread of all three types is the need or craving for blood, either to sustain the vampire's life or, as in many modern cases, an erotic experience.

The word *vampire* comes from the part of the world most famous in literature and history as the home of the vampire: Transylvania. The Magyar (Hungarian) word is *vampyr,* but there are many variations in that part of the world: Russian, *upyr*; Polish, *upier*; Turkish, *obour.* The Danes and the Swedes adopted the Magyar *vampyr*; the French put their own stamp on it: *le vampire*; and the Dutch called it *vampir.* But the Greeks had a vampire tradition of their own, and their word for the creature is *vrykolakas.*

The first known English use of the word occurred in 1734 in a travel book published in London, *The Travels of Three English Gentlemen,* whose authors said that *vampyres* found in central Europe were supposed to be "bodies of deceased persons, animated by evil spirits, which come out of the graves in the night-time, suck the blood of many of the living and thereby destroy them." Following the publication of that book, the word gained circulation throughout England, just as it was doing on the European continent. But the concept, if not the word, was centuries old in England, as it was everywhere.

Even in the earliest of times, primitive men believed in such creatures. That belief stemmed from their separation of the entity of "soul" from that of "body." Primitive man did not employ such terms, but he believed that the soul continued to be powerful after death and must be propitiated so that it would not wreak evil on the living. Accordingly, in virtually all regions of the world the dead were treated with respect. Sometimes they were worshiped and given worldly goods to make their repose in the tomb satisfying and tranquil.

For example, the nomads of ancient Scythia said that the soul continued to live after the physical body died. They prepared carefully to satisfy that soul, according to the rank of the person. When a king died, at least one of his concubines was killed and put into the royal grave mound to provide him with joy. His cupbearers, cook, groom, valet, and messenger were also killed and put into the grave to serve their master. To make sure that the king remained "safe" and quiet, a year after his death fifty of his former servants and fifty of his finest horses were strangled. Then servants and animals were disemboweled, the bodies stuffed with straw and sewn up, and each man was placed astride a propped-up horse in full riding regalia to stand guard around the king's grave.

The Egyptians followed the same general practice. Indeed, such reverence was usual throughout Africa, even among the primitive peoples of the south. They built temples for each departed king, and on his ceremonial day crowds of worshipers were called to the temple gates by the beating of sacred tom-toms. They came bearing baskets of food for the king and the followers who had been buried with him; for if the dead were not given enough by the living, then they might arise and take vengeance on the tribe. This led to another unusual burial practice: when the dead were buried, a hole was created in the soil above the grave, and at regular intervals food and drink were dropped through the hole toward the mouths of the corpses.

Such practices seem to have arisen spontaneously in many parts of the world, all prompted by this same fear of the wrath of the dead against the living. The Mongols took great care to see that their princes had all the worldly appurtenances to keep them happy after death. So that the dead prince would have a place to live, milk to drink, and a horse to ride, the Mongol tribesmen buried him with his tents around him, with a horse at the ready, along with a mare and her foal to assure continuity. When the Mongols conquered China they imposed such customs on the people. In fourteenth-century China, when the Ming Emperor Hui Ti died, four young female slaves were buried with him, along with six guards. Again, as in Scythia, a mound was made over the burial spot, but nothing as imposing as the Egyptian pyramids, which were properly numbered among the wonders of the world. Mourners brought four horses to the tomb of Hui Ti and ran them around the hillock until they dropped from exhaustion. The soldiers then killed the horses, impaled them, and set them up as guards beside their emperor.

So it was elsewhere, too: the history of the world shows that the living took care of the dead, who to them were not really dead but only in repose. Nor did the state of civilization have a great deal of effect over such belief. Some prehistoric men cut off their index fingers as a sign of respect for the dead. Australian aboriginal mourners mutilated themselves, slashing their faces and bodies at funerals, to spill the blood that would be needed by the dead. Far better to offer it than have the ghost of the dead one come out of his grave seeking sustenance. The aborigines believed that the spirit of the dead one actually drank the blood. Elsewhere, animal blood could be substituted for the human; a goat or cow was sacrificed to the dead. All such customs, of course, had the same purpose: to propitiate the dead and protect the living.

In most of these places, the soul was believed to be capable of escaping from the body through one of the orifices, usually the nose, mouth, or ears, and precautions were taken to prevent it. The aborigines put hot coals into the mouth and ears of the corpse to prevent the ghost from escaping before the mourners left the burial place. In the Marquesas, the Polynesian priest would hold the mouth and nose of the dying one shut, to prevent the soul from fleeing. In South America, the Itonama Indians actually sealed up the mouth, nose, and eyes of a dying person so that the ghost could not escape. In other areas, even more drastic measures were taken, all to protect the living. The Ovambu tribe of the Bantu nation in southwest Africa cut the arms and legs off the torso of the dead one, and tore out the tongue.

The Oraons of India pegged down the body so it could not become a vampire. The South American Chiriguonos buried the corpse head down so it could not escape the grave. All these customs of "worship" were of a piece: caused by fear of the dead and what they might do. Life was complicated by the fact that the body might decay, but the soul lived on.

Early men also worried about the behavior of their gods, who had miraculous power over the living. In pre-Christian Rome, the animal worship of the god Attis, the Roman god of vegetation, brought a violent bloodbath designed to revitalize the god (and the soil) for the coming year. On one day each March, the priests cut a pine tree, wrapped it in woolen bands, and covered it with violets (which were supposed to have sprung from the blood of Attis). An effigy of the god was attached to the tree trunk, which was then mounted on a dais. Two days after this ceremony, on the Day of Blood, the high priest cut himself deeply and offered the god his blood in a ghastly ceremony. Then the lesser priests—surrounded by the worshipers and urged on by the wild beat of drums, clash of cymbals, screech of horns, and squeal of flutes— danced and whirled and leaped until all the worshipers were in a frenzy. They slashed their bodies and let the blood spill on the sacred tree and on the altar.

Similarly, each autumn, halfway across the world, the Aztecs held a ceremony, just as uninhibited and even more bloody, for the resuscitation of their maize goddess, Chicomecohuatl. The ceremony signified the marriage of the people with nature, and it began with a week-long fast. On the appointed day, a young virgin was dressed in bridal costume, with a wreath on her head and a long necklace of corncobs. She danced through the streets all day. When evening came, she was taken to the temple of Chicomecohuatl to dance some more. There the scene was almost a reflection of that of the Roman worshipers of Attis: drums, flutes, cymbals, and wild abandon. The girl danced through the whole night, by torchlight amidst the heavy smell of incense, on ground covered with roses and corncobs, the crowd praying and cavorting around her. At the first light of dawn, the music stopped. The worshipers came forward one by one to kneel before the virgin. Each had cut himself and collected blood in a small basin, and these were now offered to her. When every worshiper had made his offering, the high priest suddenly lunged at the girl, grabbed her, threw her onto the ground and, with a swift motion of a long knife, cut off her head. As the blood gushed, the lesser priests hurried up with containers to catch it and took it off to fertilize the fields. The high priest skinned the girl's body, put the skin around himself, and then joined the frenzied crowd in more ritual dancing. Thus each year, with blood and death, was resurrected the maize goddess. Were this not done, the Aztecs believed the most horrid consequences might befall them. The sacrifice, in both cases, had to be blood, because blood has always seemed to man the very essence of life.

Blood and its implications have aroused the most stupefying results in man. The Romans literally dripped it. In the springtime, the worshipers of the cult of agriculture held their baptismal ceremonies. The supplicants were first crowned with crowns of gilt and then descended into a pit over which a wooden grating was placed. A bull decked out in flowers was driven onto the grating by the priests, who then stabbed the animal to death. The blood that spurted out fell through the grating onto the faces of the worshipers, who cupped the blood in their hands, poured it over their faces, smeared their lips, nostrils, ears, and eyes with it, and drank a bit. When these initiates emerged from the pit, they were considered to be born again and from that point on to have eternal life.

In Rome, the reverence for blood transcended all other religious cultism. Some Roman gentlemen, feeling languid, were said by the writer Ornella Volta to revitalize their bodies by going down into the arena after the games and drinking the blood of the fallen gladiators before the corpses were hauled away for burial.

Elsewhere in the world, this reverence for blood often produced diametrically opposite viewpoints. Some peoples considered blood to be sacred and thus taboo. The Romans, for example, never used the blood of animals for food in normal life. Nor would the New Guinea tribesmen, the Arabs, or North American Indians. To them the blood *was* the soul of the animal. Africans had two attitudes toward blood: if human blood was spilled, it was disastrous for it to touch the ground. If a tribesman cut himself, his fellows gathered around and let the blood fall onto them. If blood did spill, the men immediately tramped it into the earth or covered it with soil. But these same African tribesmen had no such feeling about animal blood; the Masai, for example, drink the blood of cattle as a part of their normal diet.

In some societies where blood was recognized as the essence of and sustenance of life human blood was valued for its religious properties. Warriors in many parts of the world sought the blood of the brave and the strong, especially from defeated enemies. After killing his first enemy in battle, the young men of the Bering Strait would drink some of the blood and eat a small piece of the heart of the vanquished one. By doing so, they believed they would increase their fighting courage and prowess. So did the Hawaiians. The Thedora and Ngarigo tribes of Australia ate the hands and feet of dead enemies, believing that the flesh and blood would transfer to them the strengths of the dead. To become brave, the head-hunting tribes of the central Celebes, the Tokalaki, drank the blood and ate the brains of their slain foes. The Efugaos, a Philippine tribe, sucked out the brains of a dead enemy. Tribes in the Torres Strait would suck the fingernails of warriors returned from battle, believing that the dried human blood would make them "strong like stone." One can go on and on: the Carthaginians, the ancient Gauls, the Sioux Indians all believed that if they drank the blood of enemies they would absorb their heroic qualities.

Taking matters a step further, the Australian aborigines regarded blood as essential in the curing of the sick and the strengthening of the weak. The sick person's family would find a donor of blood, preferably a strong young warrior. The priest would open a vein in the donor's forearm, and the blood would run into a wooden bowl. When it was half-hardened, the sick person would lift it "to his mouth like jelly between his fingers and his thumb." Again, blood as the essence of life and strength.

Blood brothers—how many times has one heard that expression? A friendship sealed with a bond of blood. A blood letter? A letter of the utmost gravity. A blood vow? A promise made with the essence of life.

The Germans celebrated friendship by drinking a few drops of their friends' blood. So did the Irish. A Frenchman began his honeymoon by making a small cut under his bride's left breast and sucking the blood from it. What greater demonstration of devotion?

Old-fashioned ideas? Myths? Relics of the past? Perhaps.

But come now to a night in the 1970s in California. The night is dark, and only a faint sliver of moon lights the scene. A motorcycle gang of about thirty young men stand in a circle around a fire. They are beginning the ritual that will lead one of them into the "brotherhood of courage." A slender young girl stands on a blanket in the center of the circle. Slowly she unbuttons her blouse and lets it fall to the ground.

Soon only panties cover her nakedness. Then, still slowly, she pulls the panties off. The moment has come. The supplicant steps forward to the girl, reaches between her legs, and pulls a tampon from her vagina. It is red with blood. She lies down on the blanket, raises her knees, and opens her thighs. The night is still, only the crackling of the fire is heard. The youth kneels down, puts his head between the girl's legs and begins to drink the blood from her vagina. He gets up and his blood-smeared face is proof: he has earned his badge of brotherhood.

Violence, blood, strong emotion. Blood is strength, blood is life, blood can be everything. Today, as in the past, some people believe in the overwhelming power of blood. Why could not a corpse reanimate itself if it could secure the rich red blood of the living?

Why, indeed?

3

FOREFATHERS OF THE VAMPIRES

THOUSANDS OF YEARS AGO THE SUMERIANS recognized that the spirit and the body are separate entities. When the Babylonians and Assyrians emerged in Mesopotamia they built on this Sumerian belief. The Babylonians believed in seven evil spirits; one was the *ekimmu,* the soul of a dead person, who could not rest and wandered over the earth, a ghost or specter that lay in wait for men in the desert, in the mountains, on the sea, or in a graveyard. Another was the ghoulish Lilitu, later called by the Hebrews Lilith. She was Adam's wife before Eve, and she gave birth to demons and spirits. These spirits were supposed to be able to wreak all sorts of horrors on people:

> They are the children of the Underworld.
> > Loudly roaring above, bickering below,
> > They are the bitter venom of the gods.
> > They are the great storms directed from Heaven,
> > They are the owls which hoot over a city. . . .

And, they were also vampires:

> Knowing no care, they grind the land like corn,
> > Knowing no mercy, they rage against mankind,

They spill their blood like rain,
Devouring their flesh and sucking their veins.
They are demons full of violence,
Ceaselessly devouring blood.

To combat these evil forces, charms, amulets, incantations, exorcism, and magic were needed. For if the *ekimmu* was forgotten—no offerings made at the tomb—hunger and thirst would drive him up out of the Underworld, and his fury at the neglect would know no bounds.

From these beginnings came derivations. The Arabs had their *ghoul,* a female demon who fed upon dead bodies and wandered in cemeteries at night to suck the dead dry in their graves. She also would lie quietly in a lonely area and if a traveler came by she would leap onto him and suck his blood.

The ancient Greeks had their *empusa,* a vampire demonic spirit that could enter a body. It had no shape of its own, but appeared as "a foul phantom . . . in a thousand loathly shapes." Aristophanes wrote about the *empusa*:

Second Hag:	Come hither.
Youth (to the girl):	O, my darling, don't stand by
	And see this creature drag
	me!
Second Hag:	Tis not I,
	Tis the Law drags you.
	Tis a hellish vampire,
	Clothed all about with blood,
	and boils and blisters.

Sometimes the *empusa* vampire appeared in the form of an enticing woman. One of the most famous tales of this vampire is that told by Philostratus in his *Life of Apollonius of Tyana,* written in about A.D. 217.

Apollonius is seen as a magician and a "Pythagorean philosopher with power over genii." He was credited with many miracles, and once the people of Byzantium asked him to come and help them out of deep trouble. He must have found a real mare's nest, for Philostratus described the journey thus:

He charmed snakes and scorpions not to strike, mosquitoes totally to disappear, horses to be quiet and not to be vicious either toward each other or toward man. The river Lycus also he charmed not to flood and do damage to Byzantium.

And in the case of one of his pupils, Menippus, Apollonius dealt with a vampire.

Menippus was a handsome youth of twenty-five with the body and beauty of an athlete. One day, as he was walking along a road, he met a lovely woman, who surprised him by clasping his hands and telling him that she had been in love with him for a long, long time. Menippus was startled, yet delighted. He soon learned that the woman lived in a suburb of Corinth, and she invited him to come and see her there that very evening.

"When you reach the place this evening, you will hear my voice as I sing to you, and you shall have wine such as you never before drank, and there will be no rival to disturb you, and we two beautiful beings will live together."

So Menippus visited the lady that night and for many other nights. He fell head over heels in love. Apollonius watched his pupil with alarm and finally spoke to him. "You are," he said, "cherishing a serpent and a serpent cherishes you. . . . This lady is of a kind you cannot marry."

Menippus was naturally taken aback. He swore that he loved the lady and the lady loved him. What more could one ask in a marriage?

When Apollonius continued to press him to abandon the woman, Menippus grew angry and said he would be married the very next day. In the morning the lady gave a wedding breakfast for the party, and Apollonius attended. The long tables of the banquet hall were set with golden goblets and fine silver service. Wine bearers and waiters clustered around the tables, and in the kitchen the cooks were preparing a banquet. But this was all illusion, said Apollonius. He charged that the lady was not only a serpent, she was also a vampire. What Menippus saw was not reality but the semblance of reality. She was one of those beings "who fall in love and are devoted to the delights of Aphrodite, but especially to the flesh of human beings." She was luring Menippus only to devour him.

The lady protested, but suddenly Menippus and his guests saw the golden goblets and fine silver flutter into the air and vanish. So did the servants.

The lady continued to protest, but Apollonius sternly pressed her to tell the truth. Finally she admitted that she was "a vampire and was fattening up Menippus with pleasures before devouring his body"; she loved young, beautiful bodies because "their blood was pure and strong."

Thus, wrote Philostratus, Menippus was saved from the *empusa.*

After the *Life of Apollonius* came to the attention of the public, a Greek writer charged that Apollonius only achieved what he did for Menippus through black magic. "The youth," said this writer, "was clearly the victim of an indwelling demon; and both it and the Empusa and the Lamia which is said to have played off its mad pranks on Menippus, were probably driven out of him with the help of a more important demon."

So it was demons, demons, demons.

Some ancient Greek and Roman writers believed that the *lamia* was that sort of demon, a serpent that assumed the guise of a lovely courtesan, then used enticing wiles to clasp handsome young men to its bosom with the intent of devouring them and drinking their blood. All this came from the tale of Lamia, the queen of Libya, dearly loved by the king of gods, Zeus. She bore him a large number of beautiful children, which so aroused the jealousy of the goddess Hera, the wife of Zeus, that she snatched all the children away. Distraught, the queen left Zeus and went to live in a cave in the rocks by the sea, and there her beauty faded. She became an ugly monster, who from that time onward preyed on young children, so overwhelming was her jealousy at being deprived of her own.

Based on this legend, the poet John Keats, hundreds of years later, wrote his poem *Lamia,* which ended thus:

> "A serpent!" echoed he. No sooner said,
> Than with a frightful scream she vanished;
> And Lysius' arms were empty of delight,
> As were his limbs of life, from that same night.
> On the high couch he lay!—his friends came round—
> Supported him, no pulse or breath they found,
> And, in its marriage robe, the heavy body wound.

There was, however, another sort of *lamia* that was altogether monstrous all the time and was said to feed on man's flesh. These were grotesque women with deformities usually of the lower parts of the body.

One was said to be a scaly, winged serpent that flew about at night sucking the blood of children. Somebody else saw a *lamia* that had feet of bronze, shaped like the hooves of an ox. One Macedonian legend described the *lamia* as "a great marvelous monster with crooked claws and a pair of wings, each of which reached down to yonder plain"—a winged serpent.

Again, there were many derivations on the theme; the chief characteristic of the *lamia* was its lust for blood. As a group, they were also stupid, gluttonous, and filthy. They married dragons, but their sloppiness was so awful they were terrible housekeepers: from this, came a Greek figure of speech referring to a slothful housewife as one who "sweeps like Lamia." They lived in caves and in the desert. They were so stupid that they would "put their dough in a cold oven and heap the fire on top of it; they give their dogs hay to eat, and bones to their horses."

The *lamiae* were terrible, but they could be overcome. One rich *lamia,* married to a wealthy dragon, kept guard over his treasure. She was vicious and stupid, but she had one admirable trait: she was a monster of her word. She walked about at night, "seizing and crushing men whom she met until they roared like bulls." But if an intended victim kept his wits and was able to snatch off her headdress, in order to get it back he could extract a promise from her of life and wealth, and it was said that she always delivered.

Akin to the *lamiae* in Greek legend were the *striges,* a term adopted from the Italians, for they knew the *strix,* a "bloodthirsty monster in bird form." The poet Ovid in the first century A.D. wrote of them:

"Voracious birds there are . . . that fly forth by night and assail children who still need a nurse's care, and seize them out of their cradles, and do them mischief. With their beaks they are said to pick out the child's milk-fed bowels, and their throat is full of the blood they drink. Striges they are called."

At first these *striges* were believed to be old women who, with the help of the Devil, could take the shape of a bird. They were attracted primarily to newborn babies, whose blood they sucked until the infants died. But later legend gave them greater power and range.

One Greek legend tells of a traveler who stopped overnight in Messenia, with a friend who was going to accompany him on a journey. Unable to sleep in a strange bed, he was tossing and turning when he heard two female voices whispering in the next room. The women were his friend's wife and her mother. The visitor listened and was able to catch the tenor of the conversation: the women were planning to devour one of the men, and they were arguing over which was the fattest. Soon they entered his room. He pretended to be fast asleep, but as they raised his foot to estimate his weight, he lifted as they raised. His foot seemed so light of weight that the woman dropped it in disgust. They went then to the next room, where his friend lay, and were delighted when he seemed to be very heavy. They attacked the poor man: "they ripped open the wretched man's breast, pulled out his liver and other parts and threw them among the hot ashes on the hearth to cook." While the meat was cooking, the women looked around and found there was nothing to drink. So, "they flew to the wine-shop and took what they wanted and returned." But before they got back, the visitor went to the fire, pulled out his friend's viscera, and substituted animal dung. The two monsters came back and sat down to drink and enjoy their feast. They did not notice what they were eating except that it seemed "somewhat overdone."

Next morning the two friends woke up. He who had been attacked, the husband, seemed no worse for the experience, except that he was paler than usual and complained of hunger. He had no marks on him. After they had set out on their journey, the friend gave the husband his own liver and other parts to eat. Having eaten them, the husband revived fully. Then the friend told the husband what had happened the night before, and together the friends went back to the house and killed the two *striges.*

These *striges* were kin to the later *vrykolakes,* the true vampires or living dead, and just as terrifying in their time as the *vrykolakes* were to be to later generations of Greeks.

This apparition of a woman as a vampire was not confined to the Mediterranean world. Asia had its *penanggalan,* which was seen as only the face and neck of a woman, with intestines hanging down in strings. This creature flew about "with its entrails dangling down and shining at night like fireflies." According to Malayan legend, the first *penanggalan* was a woman who was sitting in a vinegar vat doing penance for her sins, when a stranger came by and asked her what she was doing. She was so indignant at the invasion of her privacy by a total stranger that she kicked her own chin—with so much strength that her head flew off. But the stomach sac stayed attached to the gullet. She flew up into a tree, and from that time on sought the blood of children and women at childbirth. The Malayans had one protection against her: if they hung *jeruju* (thistle) leaves at the doors and windows of the houses of pregnant women and nursing babies, they were safe, because the *Penanggalan* was afraid that her intestines would catch on the thorns of the *jeruju* if she tried to enter the house.

The Malays had another vampire, the *langsuir*. Again it was female, transformed from a beautiful woman who had died of grief when her child was stillborn. "She had clapped her hands and flew whinnying away to a tree, upon which she perched." She retained her beauty, particularly her beautiful black hair, but under the locks was a hole in the neck through which the vampire sucked the blood of children.

To deal with the *langsuir,* the villagers had first to catch the creature, then cut off her black hair and stuff it into the hole in her neck. Once that was done she disappeared and bothered them no more. To protect women who died in childbirth from the horror of becoming *langsuirs,* the mouth of the corpse was filled with glass beads, a hen's egg was placed under each armpit, and needles were stuck into the palms of the hands. Thus the dead could not shriek, nor use her arms as wings to fly, and was safe from becoming a vampire. The corpses of stillborn babies were similarly treated, for the same reason.

The vampire is not a common horror in Japan, although certain demons were known to eat human flesh and drink human blood; but China has its own vampire tradition, in many ways quite like that of Europe, but with differences based on their unique society.

The ancient Chinese believed that the body had two souls, one called the *hun* (higher) and the other the *po* (lower). Either might remain in the body until the corpse turned to dust, but the *po* was the potentially evil spirit. It could become a vampire. As the Chinese still say "The *po* is capable of anything."

If the *po* does become a vampire, that creature is the *xiang shi.* It lives inside the corpse and keeps the corpse from decaying by preying on other fresh corpses or on living people. It has "red staring eyes, huge sharp talons or crooked nails" and its body is covered by greenish white hair. Note the similarities, quite coincidental, with the European vampires.

The Chinese love tales and they have many about the vampires. Here is one:

One night, long ago, a man went out for a leisurely walk down a lonely country road. He had not paid much attention to his surroundings; but when a shadow loomed up in the dark, he slowed down and approached cautiously. To his amazement he saw that the shape was that of a coffin. Startled to see a single coffin so out of place in the middle of the road, he held back.

Should he proceed or should he turn away?

As he stared at the coffin, surprise turned to horror: the lid of the coffin was pushed up from within, and a corpse climbed out and walked away!

The stroller knew of the *xiang shi,* who left their graves to attack the living, and he was sure he had just seen one. After a few moments, looking stealthily around to see that the corpse had truly disappeared, the man hastily filled the coffin with stones and broken pieces of pots that he found along the roadside. Then, curiosity drawing him, he walked to a farmhouse not far away. He saw a ladder that led into an attic. He climbed up, peered out the window, watching the shadows playing on the empty coffin, and waited.

The night wore on, but nothing happened until about one o'clock in the morning. Then he saw movement, the corpse was returning, and it was carrying something. The corpse tried to climb back into the coffin, but found it full of debris. Its eyes began to blaze with an anger so terrible the man in the farmhouse could sense it. Slowly, the corpse looked all around the countryside, trying to discover who had been tampering with its coffin. In the moonlight, it saw the man in the attic and began to run toward the farmhouse.

The man began to fear that he was done for. What if the vampire got him?

He cowered in the darkness beside the window. He heard the vampire come up and shake the ladder. His fear turned to terror. But for some reason the vampire seemed unable to climb up. It fumed and shook and rattled, and finally cast the ladder aside and disappeared.

At first the man feared that he was trapped. His eyes went longingly to the ladder on the ground. There was no way to get it back up. But there was a tree near the window. He climbed out, jumped over to the tree, caught a branch, climbed onto the trunk, and made his way down. Then he started back for the road.

The vampire, however, had not gone far. It was waiting in the shadows and it began to chase the man. Soon he heard the creature's footsteps hot on his heels. Just when he feared all was lost, his eye caught sight of a stream ahead. He knew that vampires could not cross running water, so he headed for the stream and plunged in. He swam across and looked back. There was the vampire, standing on the far side of the stream, screaming and gesticulating after its lost prey. Finally it jumped up into the air three times, turned into a wolf, and ran off!

The man then regained his spirits and his curiosity. He had seen the vampire carrying something, so he crossed the river again, and made his way back to the coffin. There on the ground, next to the coffin, lay the body of a newly dead baby, the flesh half-gnawed away and the corpse sucked quite dry of blood.

Another tale concerns the artist Liu I Shen, who lived at Hangxou. When Liu's neighbor's father died, the son stopped by the artist's house on his way to buy a coffin, to ask Liu to paint a memorial portrait. The artist agreed, gathered up his materials, then set out for the house. When he reached there, all the family had left on various errands, and he had to search around for an open door. He entered and looked about for the body he was to honor with a portrait.

Finally he mounted the stairs and discovered the corpse laid out on a bed in a second-floor room.

Liu arranged his paints, sat down, and began to sketch. He worked for a time in the silence of the room. But suddenly the dead father sat bolt upright and yawned.

In a flash of intuition, Liu realized that he was in the presence of a vampire. If he tried to run away, the vampire would attack. If he even moved from his spot and his work, the vampire might come after him. So, summoning his courage, he continued to draw, assuming an air of indifference to the corpse. This was not easy, particularly because the vampire mimicked every move Liu made, pretending to draw on imaginary paper. But the artist kept on with his work.

Meanwhile, the son, having located the undertaker who could supply a coffin for his father's body, returned to the house. He climbed the stairs and entered the room of the dead man. As he passed through the doorway and saw his father sitting bolt upright, the shock was so great that the son fainted dead away and fell to the floor. The vampire sat, uncaring. Liu sat, drawing.

Soon a neighbor came to help with the arrangements. When he passed through the door and saw the corpse upright, he, too, fainted. The vampire sat, and Liu sat, and both worked at their drawings, one in the air, one on paper. The two who had fainted lay unconscious on the floor.

Finally, along came the men from the undertaker's establishment, carrying the coffin. They entered the courtyard, and called out to discover where to find the corpse. Only then did artist Liu dare to act to save himself.

"Quickly, quickly," he shouted at the men below. "Get some brooms and come up as fast as you can."

The undertaker's men were old hands at dealing with such situations, and in a trice they had grabbed brooms from the kitchen area, and two of them rushed upstairs flailing them. They came into the laying-out room, saw the corpse sitting upright, and began hitting it with the brooms. Meanwhile, the other two undertaker's men brought up the coffin, and then all four grasped the corpse and stuffed it into the box and slammed the lid tight. Thus they put the vampire where it belonged. Only then was there time to go down below and prepare some ginger tea to revive the unfortunates who had fainted. All drank the tea, and everyone praised artist Liu for his cleverness in dealing with the vampire.

Yet another famous tale concerns a vampire who lived in Nanking, the old southern capital of China.

Chang and Li, two dear friends, also lived in that city, and one season they discovered that their separate affairs demanded that each make a trip to Canton, which was several thousand *li* to the south. They agreed to travel together for safety and comfort. When they reached Canton, Chang finished his business first. He learned that Li would be long delayed, so he decided to go on home alone. Li gave Chang a special letter to deliver to his family, and of course Chang did not refuse to take it.

When Chang arrived back in Nanking, his first act was to go to the Li house to deliver the important message. He was appalled to learn that Li's father had just died. Nevertheless he delivered the letter to the widow, extended his sympathies, and performed the ritual offerings for the dead. The widow was touched by his kindness. Since he lived across the city and it was late, she extended him the hospitality of the house for the night and offered to prepare dinner for him.

Chang was tired from the journey. He ate, and shortly after dinner he retired for the night. But after he had gotten into bed, he found he could not sleep. He knew that the body of the old man was lying in a room just across the courtyard, but that didn't bother Chang. He had no fear of the dead. What did bother him was someone moving around the house, making a great deal of noise. He got out of bed and went to the window. He peeked through a crack in the paper window. To his surprise he saw that Mrs. Li was standing beside the bier of her dead husband, holding an incense stick.

Poor woman, he thought. But then he heard her footsteps approaching his room. He sensed that she was doing something to the door, but he did not call out. After a very short time he heard her footsteps retreating. He tried the door. Somehow she had locked it. But why?

Chang turned away from the door and back to the crack in the paper window. To his amazement, he soon saw the coffin lid lift up and the body of the dead man sit up. What he saw was ghastly: "the face of the corpse was black, its eyes were hollow and glaring, and its whole appearance was fierce and horrible to behold."

Then, the corpse jumped out of the coffin and made straight for Chang's door with a strange whistling sound.

Chang rushed to the door and leaned with all his weight as the creature battered at it. Suddenly, the door gave way. Chang jumped behind a clothes chest, and, just as the vampire rushed in to pounce on him, he turned the clothes chest over on the creature. Then he fainted and remembered no more until he awakened to find the Widow Li leaning over him, holding out a cup of ginger tea. The monster was nowhere to be seen.

As Chang drank his tea, the widow told him of the night's events.

Her husband, old Mr. Li, she said, had been a very wicked man, always up to one scheme or another to make a profit. Even after death, his bad habits had continued. He had come to her the night before Chang arrived and told her that Chang would come with a letter. He also said that he knew Chang had a lot of money with him from his Canton trip. So, Li would kill Chang, she would steal the money, and they would share the profits.

The widow had been distraught. She had gone to her husband's bier and found the body back inside. She had prayed, to try to dissuade him from this wicked plan, but the corpse had remained silent. She knew she had failed.

So that night, after Chang had delivered the letter, eaten, and gone to bed, she had removed her girdle, and used it to tie the two handles of the doors to Chang's room together, to try to prevent the monster from getting at him. That was the noise Chang had heard early in the evening. She had never expected her dead husband's corpse to have such unholy strength. When it had broken through the door, she thought Chang was about to be killed, until the heavy clothes chest had felled the vampire and pinned it down. Now it was daylight and the corpse was quiet. She called on the servants to come and put it back into the coffin. She apologized to Chang and said she hoped her husband's corpse would no longer bother anyone.

But Chang knew better than she. He knew that the body of old Mr. Li would become a public scourge unless the soul could be released. He went to the Buddhist monastery nearby and sought the help of the abbot. The monks came and performed a service of exorcism over the body so that the soul of Mr. Li could rest in peace. Then they burned the body. And sure enough, neither Mrs. Li nor anyone else was ever again bothered by that vampire.

But there were other, more vicious, creatures walking the night. In the province of Chihli, near one of the mountain villages, there lived a horrible vampire which scoured the village night after night. This creature was particularly fond of devouring children but would attack any human being it found. Almost wild with desperation, the people of the village sought the help of a learned Taoist priest who lived nearby. They brought him many presents and at last he agreed to come.

When the priest arrived in the village, he prepared for his work. He was empowered, he said, to provide the magic nets and snares that would keep the vampire from flying through the air. But he needed a fearless man to help him kill the vampire. He called for volunteers.

No one spoke up.

He repeated his statement. Finally one young man volunteered to help him.

The priest set up an altar outside the cave where the vampire was known to dwell during the daylight hours. He gave the young man two copper bells and told him that when the vampire emerged from the cave, the young man was to dart inside and begin ringing the bells. He was to ring constantly, never stopping for a moment. This noise would prevent the vampire from returning to the cave, for, as the priest said, "the sound of copper instruments renders specters powerless."

The villagers, meanwhile, were to form a semicircle outside the cave. Their circle and the priest's magic nets would keep the vampire from escaping into the village, and the young man's bells would keep the vampire from escaping back into his cave.

Night approached. All the villagers gathered around the cave at a safe distance, and the young man crept up to the edge of the cave. The priest stood at his altar making his incantations. As usual, as the last ray of light failed, the vampire came out. The young man ducked into the cave and began ringing his bells.

"The vampire turned and glared at me with eyes like lightning, but could not seize me," said the young man later. He continued to ring, and the vampire continued to glare until "the first streak of dawn, when the vampire fell dead."

The villagers cheered and burned the body. The vampire never came back. But thereafter the young man could not stop the bell-ringing motion of his hands. When people asked him why his wrists moved constantly as if he were ringing bells, he would tell them the story of the vampire that had threatened his village.

4

Heartland: The Vampire in Eastern Europe

THE CHINESE WERE ALWAYS VERY CAREFUL in their handling of the bodies of the newly dead, for it was well known that a corpse might become a vampire if not scrupulously attended. One of the greatest threats in this regard was that common creature, the cat. A cat was never let into a room where a dead body lay, for if the cat jumped over the corpse, it would certainly transfer to the body—still housing the lower soul or *po*—a tiger nature so that the dead one would almost certainly become a vampire.

This dread of the cat was inherent in the beliefs of many other societies, including the early Greek. The body of the dead person was watched all night by relatives and friends to make sure that a cat did not leap over the corpse as it lay awaiting burial. If by some chance a cat *did* jump over the corpse, the body was immediately stuck with two large needles, and this action alone could prevent the dead one from being turned into a *vrykolakas*.

But the cat was not the only source of danger. The family scattered mustard seed over the tiles of the roof of the house. The seed was highly prized by vampires, and the vampire who might come in across the roof would be so busy counting his seeds that he would pass the body by. Also, the family barricaded the doors with brambles and thornbushes, so that no roaming vampire could enter the body of the dead one. Vampires had a deadly fear of thorns.

The early Greek Christians were under no illusions about the sanctity of death, they *knew* when their dead became vampires. The funeral was always held as soon as possible, usually the day after the death. When the coffin left the house it was accompanied by mourners, who wailed and lamented all the way to the cemetery. The funeral was followed by a feast and then by more mourning and by offerings to the dead of parboiled wheat mixed with pounded walnuts and other edibles that would be easy for a corpse to manage. On certain days, dedicated as "Souls' Sabbaths" in honor of the dead, sweets, parboiled corn, small loaves of bread stamped with the sign of the cross, and cakes were laid on the graves. These offerings were made on the premise that the dead actually came back to the world to visit the living and partook of the food and drink.

The next ritual concerning the dead confirmed to the Greeks the true nature of the corpse. Three years after the burial, the body was dug up. If it had disintegrated, the soul of the dead one was at rest. The bones were washed with wine, put into a bag or box, and taken back to the cemetery for reinterment in the "sleeping place."

But if the body had not disintegrated, tragedy had struck! The corpse had turned into a *vrykolakas,* "a corpse imbued with a kind of half-life, and actuated by murderous impulses and by an unquenchable thirst for blood." The only thing to do was to get the corpse out of the coffin, scald it with boiling oil, and drive a long nail through the navel. Then the body was returned to the coffin, placed into the grave, the dirt piled over, and millet scattered over the burial place so that if the vampire came out at night it would be so busy picking up grains that dawn would come before it finished, and with dawn the vampire must vanish.

There were all sorts of religious reasons a corpse might become a vampire. Sin in earthly life, curses by the Church or by parents, excommunication (which was common), a cat leaping over the grave, all these would produce vampires. The chance of a body's remaining "inflated like drums and black for a thousand years" was very real to the Greeks. On such a body, they said, the skin was stretched "like parchment on a drum, and when struck gives out the same sound." That sound gave the creature its name, for in Greek *vrykolakas* means drumlike.

One such body was described thus:

A corpse perfectly whole; it was unusually tall of stature; clothes it had none, time or moisture having caused them to perish; the skin was distended, hard, and livid, and so swollen everywhere that the body had no flat surfaces but was round like a full sack. The face was covered with hair dark and curly; on the head there was little hair, as also on the rest of the body, which appeared smooth all over; the arms by reason of the swelling of the corpse were stretched out on each side like the arms of a cross; the hands were open, the eyelids closed, the mouth gaping, and the teeth white.

Such a corpse, the people believed, was the work of demons.

Early beliefs about the dead were little altered in Christian times except that the demons became the Devil. The early church was often preoccupied with problems of vampirism, but the priests were sometimes able to exorcise the evil, whereupon the body would fall to dust.

One tale is told of the Archbishop of Salonika, who had once in anger cursed a man in his diocese. "May the earth refuse to receive thee," he had shouted. He forgot the incident. The cursed man died and, when his body was dug up three years later, it looked as it had on the day of the funeral, not decayed at all. Prayers were said and the body was reburied. Three more years passed, and again the body was exhumed. Again, it was found to be intact.

The man's widow was now distraught, and she sought out the archbishop and reminded him of his curse. He was conscience-stricken; he came to the gravesite, lifted his hands, and prayed.

"He had hardly risen to his feet when, wondrous to relate, the flesh of the corpse crumbled away from the bones, and the skeleton remained bare and clean as if it had never known pollution."

Another story tells of a wanton woman who was excommunicated. (After that she even accused the church patriarch as one of her lovers.) She died and was buried in unhallowed ground. Many years later her body was exhumed and found to be fully intact; not even a hair had fallen off. But the corpse was black and swollen like a drum. The patriarch was summoned and promised a letter of forgiveness for the unfortunate woman. As he read the letter by the graveside, the people could hear the hands and feet beginning to disintegrate. After the religious ceremony, the body was put into a sealed chapel. Three days later, when the people opened the chapel and looked at the body, they found the corpse had crumbled into dust.

Sometimes, however, the church's exorcisms failed to dislodge the

Devil. Then the heart of the body was torn out, cut to pieces, and the whole body burned to ashes.

Balkan peasants lived by superstitions, and among these was the belief that the old and malicious turned into vampires.

And what did such a vampire do?

"[It] steals into cottages, chokes the people who are sleeping, and drinks their blood. These unfortunate people not only die from it, they themselves become vampires."

The Balkan vampires got around easily, either coming up out of their graves in white shrouds and flying about or roaming the neighborhood on horses. They could assume the guise of a man or they could be ectoplasmic, squeezing through cracks in a door more easily than a bat.

The Balkan vampires, for some reason, favored the haunting of grain mills. Here is the tale of one who did:

There once was a very rich man who owned a mill, and he had many servants working for him, especially to guard the mill at night. But one after another the servants disappeared, after spending only one night at the mill. Soon no one in the district would accept the mill owner's offers of employment. The owner grew desperate for help but finally found a young man who was willing to work for him, if he would pay "as much as a man's head is worth." The owner agreed to these stiff terms, and the new servant prepared to spend his first night in the mill. He did not really believe in vampires, obviously, but thought that some human intruders were causing the trouble. When he arrived, he put a wooden trunk on the bed, and covered it to look as though a man were sleeping there. Then he went up to the attic, to see what would happen.

He did not have long to wait. The vampire, "wearing a long beard like a clergyman," came in and approached the bed. With enormous disgust it discovered that the "man" in the bed was only a trunk. "Woe is me," the vampire cried. "How hungry I must remain!"

When the young man in the attic realized that this really was a vampire, he nearly fainted, but he continued to hide in the attic until cockcrow. Then the vampire went out of the mill. The young man followed, caught up with the vampire, which had lost its powers at dawn, and drove a nail through its forehead. He went back to tell the tale to the owner of the mill but was so overcome with his story that, at the end of it, he fell down dead. So he never collected his reward. But, then, neither did the vampire: it never appeared in the district again.

The Russians of those days also believed in vampires that left the grave for the sole purpose of preying on the living. As in other countries, the vampire was created by a cat jumping over the grave, or the flight of a bird, a curse by priest or parents, by suicide, by wizardry, or witchery, or victimization by a vampire. Russian folklore is full of vampires who preyed on the *moujik,* the peasant; so full that W. R. S. Ralston collected hundreds of songs and tales in his *Russian Folk Tales,* many of them featuring vampires. Here is one:

One night a peasant was driving along with a load of pots. It was late, and his horse was growing tired from the long day's journey. Finally he stopped to rest. Although it was night, and the horse had halted in front of a graveyard, the *moujik* thought it would be perfectly fine to take a nap there. He let the horse out to graze and walked over to a nearby grave and lay down. But he did not sleep. He just lay there quietly looking up into the night. Suddenly he felt something move beneath him. The grave he was lying on began to open. The *moujik* jumped up with a start and ran a short distance away. His eyes widened as he saw a corpse come out of the grave. The corpse was dressed in a white shroud, and it carried its coffin lid. The peasant was thunderstruck and could not speak. He watched the corpse as it raced off to the church at the edge of the cemetery, clasping the coffin lid. When the corpse reached the door of the church, it put the coffin lid down carefully, and then went running off in the direction of the village.

By this time the *moujik* had recovered from his surprise. Being a very daring fellow, he went over to the church, picked up the coffin lid, then waited to see what would happen when the corpse returned.

He did not have to wait long. The corpse came back from the village and went to the church for its lid. Not finding it, the corpse began to look around. It saw the *moujik.* As the corpse approached him, the *moujik* staunchly held his ground.

"Give me my lid," the corpse demanded. "If you don't, I'll tear you into little pieces."

"Aha," said the *moujik,* "and my hatchet, how about that? It's I who will be chopping you into small pieces."

The corpse then began to beg for its coffin lid. The peasant finally agreed to give it back if the corpse would tell him what mischief it had been up to in the village.

Reluctantly the corpse admitted it had killed "a couple of youngsters."

The *moujik* demanded that the corpse tell him how the children could be brought back to life before he would hand over the coffin lid.

"Cut off the left skirt of my shroud," the corpse told him, "and take it with you. When you come to the house where the youngsters were killed, pour some live coals into a pot and put the pieces of the shroud in with them, and then lock the door. The lads will be revived by the smoke immediately."

The *moujik* cut off a piece of the corpse's shroud and returned the lid. The corpse took the lid and ran off to its grave, which opened before it, and began to climb in, pulling the lid after it. Suddenly a cock crowed, and although the corpse had managed to get itself into the grave, it had not gotten the coffin lid properly settled. One corner remained sticking out of the earth. The *moujik* saw this, but at the moment he was preoccupied with the problem of the vampire's victims, so he put the matter in the back of his mind.

The *moujik* harnessed up his horse and, as the dawn was breaking, drove into the village. It did not take long to find a house where he could hear cries and wailing. It must be the right house, the peasant thought. He went inside. He was right, there lay the bodies of two young boys. The relatives were mourning, but the *moujik* comforted them, saying that he knew how to bring the boys back to life. Then he began to follow the vampire's instructions to the letter. The children revived, to be greeted with great joy.

But suddenly the relatives seized the *moujik*. "Trickster!" they charged. "We'll hand you over to the authorities. Since you knew how to bring them back to life, maybe it was you who killed them."

"What are you thinking about, true believers?" the peasant cried. "Have fear of God before your eyes."

Then he told them all about his encounter with the corpse. The family and the villagers gathered together, and they all marched straight up the graveyard, where they found the grave with the coffin lid protruding. They dug up the grave, raised the coffin lid, and "drove an aspen stake right into the heart of the corpse, so that it might no more rise up and slay." Then they gave the *moujik* a reward and sent him on his way home.

The Russians tell another tale, about two corpses:

One dark night a soldier, who had been given leave to go home to visit his parents, was walking along a road leading to his village when he passed a graveyard. He quickened his pace for he knew that graveyards were not the place to be during the night. As he did so, he heard the sound of running footsteps coming after him, and then he heard someone call out.

"Stop. You can't escape."

The soldier whirled around and saw that a corpse was running after him, gnashing its teeth. It was a fearful sight, but as the soldier looked at the corpse in fear, he also spotted a little chapel nearby, ran to it, and entered, hopeful that there he would be safe.

However, as his eyes got used to the gloom of the chapel, which was lighted only by two tapers, he saw another corpse laid out on a table. There was no one else around. The soldier quickly hid in a corner, fearing the first corpse might have followed him.

Indeed it had. When the first corpse rushed in, the corpse on the table jumped up and cried, "What hast thou come here for?"

"I've chased a soldier in here, so I'm going to eat him."

"Come now, brother, he's run into my house," said the second corpse. "I shall eat him myself."

"No, I shall."

"No, I shall."

The soldier quaked in his hiding place.

The two corpses began to fight. "The dust flew like anything. They'd have gone on fighting ever so much longer, only the cocks began to crow. Then both corpses fell lifeless to the ground and the soldier went on his way in peace, saying 'Glory be to thee, O Lord, I am saved.'"

The religious overtone of such stories was unmistakable. The Slavs of eastern Europe believed in the existence of the soul after death, and the priests spoke often of the Devil, so it was not hard for them to be convinced of the power of vampires. The vampire took different forms in different parts of the Slavic empire, although there were many similarities. Poles, Slovaks, Bulgars, Ukrainians, and Byelorussians all had their own versions of the vampire. Sometimes the creature was a reanimated body, sometimes a werewolf, witch, sorcerer, dog, cat, toad, hog, louse, flea, or bedbug. All these vampires came out at night and prowled, sucking the blood of both infants and adults. Cockcrow always ended the depradations.

Here is one popular tale:

One night a peasant was out riding and had to pass a cemetery. As he did a stranger came up and asked if the peasant would give him a ride. The peasant did not want to stay around the graveyard, for it was well known that the cemetery was full of vampires, but he was an obliging fellow, and he stopped the cart and the stranger climbed in. They drove along until they came to a village; the stranger indicated he wanted to get off there. Not at the first house, the rider said; and not at the second house, because it was locked up, the rider said. The driver saw that the gate to that house was open, which seemed odd if it was locked up. He also saw that crosses had been burned into the gate.

The stranger gestured onward, and the peasant drove until he came to the very last house in the village. The gate to this house, the peasant saw, was secured by a large lock, but there were no crosses. Still it looked as though the stranger would have a hard time getting inside, when suddenly, in spite of the padlock, the gate swung open. The stranger motioned the peasant to drive up to the house. There the stranger got down. He gestured to the peasant to do likewise. Obviously under a spell, the peasant got down too. The stranger opened the door of the house and entered.

They found themselves in a rude cottage. The furnishings were sparse, but on a bench in the single room they saw an old man and a young boy, both fast asleep.

Without a word, the stranger found a bucket. He put the bucket directly behind the back of the young boy and hit the boy on the back with one hand. The boy's back opened up wide, and blood spurted into the pail. The stranger drank the bucket of blood without a word, then turned to the old man, placed the bucket behind him, and hit him. The blood flowed and once again the stranger drank the blood in the bucket. Then he spoke up.

"Let's go to my place now."

The words had hardly left the stranger's lips when the peasant found himself in the cemetery again, with the horse and cart and his unpleasant rider. The vampire was just reaching out his arm to grab the peasant when the cocks began to crow, and the vampire vanished. The peasant returned to the village and sought out the authorities, who immediately went to the house where they found the old man and the boy—dead.

The Slavs subscribed to most of the beliefs about vampires current in central Europe. They also had some special ones of their own. In the Ukraine and Byelorussia, the following persons were certain to become vampires after death: sorcerers; werewolves; the excommunicated; drunkards; heretics; apostates.

The Ukrainians also believed that werewolves and devils liked to have sexual intercourse with women, and the result was always a child who would become a vampire.

The peasants believed that those who suffered violent death would also become vampires, as would those who in life showed signs of vampirism: thick eyebrows that met in the middle, or double rows of teeth. Pity the poor unfortunates born that way. Their fellow villagers did not.

In Kiev, if the relatives suspected that a body was going to turn into a vampire after it was placed in the grave, they sometimes carried the body out to a swamp and left it there to rot in the open. Sometimes they buried the body at a crossroads, which would make it more difficult for the vampire to find its way back to the village. And they took further precautions. "Onto the grave was piled a heap of stones. The body was turned around face down, so that it would gnaw into the ground." The fingers of the corpse were tied behind the body, the tendons under the knees were cut so that the corpse could not walk, and the head was cut off and put between the legs, which made for a certain disorientation.

If, after all this, the vampire was determined enough, it might reassemble itself as a mouse or a lizard and crawl out of the grave and through the cracks in houses. If plugging up the cracks did not stop the vampire from getting in, then there was nothing to do but go back to the body, buried in the cemetery, swamp, or crossroads, and burn it. This tale is about the burning of a known sorcerer who had obviously become a vampire after death:

> They hauled aspen logs to the cemetery, heaped a pile, dragged the sorcerer from the grave, placed him on the pyre, and lit it. The people gathered around with brooms [remember the Chinese?], spades, and pokers. Flames poured over the pyre. The sorcerer also began to burn. His belly burst open and from it there crawled vipers, maggots, and various vermin. Crows, magpies, and jackdaws also flew out. The men beat them and threw them into the fire, so that even as a worm the sorcerer cannot escape the punishment due him.

The people of Kiev believed that burning was the only sure way to break off the connection of soul with body. The soul became "free only when its body" was "strewn with dust," and if the body became a vampire instead of disintegrating decently, the only solution was fire.

As in the Balkans, when members of a family in Kiev became ill and died one after the other, graves were dug up. The first to die was the first suspected of being a vampire. But if the first body was disintegrating properly, then the diggers continued to dig, until the villagers were certain they had found the vampire. And how did they know him (or her)? Simple enough: "Well-preserved, unspoiled body, reddish lips, and especially blood coming out of the mouth."

The Slavic vampire was particularly obnoxious. Not only did it drink the blood of the victims, but the male vampires would come back after death to have intercourse with their wives. That was the explanation when a widow gave birth more than nine months after the death of the husband. No one blamed her. How could a mere woman resist a vampire, particularly when it was her own husband? In fact, in certain areas of what is now the southern USSR, the vampire's main occupation was not drinking blood but inseminating widows. It was a useful idea for lonely—and careless—widows, but not so good for the children thought to have been thus conceived. Such children were called *vampijerovic,* or sometimes *vampir* or *dhampir.* When they grew up, they were obviously not regarded highly by the marriage brokers.

Some attributed to these children the power to recognize other vampires on sight. Some attributed stillbirths to sexual intercourse between a human and a vampire; the thing born was supposedly "slippery like jelly" and died immediately.

The Kashubian tribe held vampires responsible for many illnesses. If members of a family sickened, particularly when several fell ill, the villagers knew that a vampire was at work. For the Kashubian vampire, after awakening from the sleep of the dead, began to gnaw at its arms and legs, and while it gnawed, one after another of its relatives and their neighbors fell and died. After the vampire had devoured its own body, it would go to the houses of the villagers night after night, drink their blood, and then return to the grave.

Most common of all the Slav practices, however, was to pierce the body with sharpened stakes and drive thorns into the flesh under the tongue and toenails and into the abdomen near the navel. Aspen was the preferred type of stake, usually driven into the heart. Sometimes the relatives would also drive a nail into the base of the skull.

All this was done to keep the vampire from coming out of the grave, for it was inherent that if it did emerge, the vampire would victimize the villagers.

One of the preferred ways for a village to get rid of vampires was to hire a magician to do the job. Ukrainians, Albanians, and Serbs were among those who shared this faith in magicians. They would pay the magician's expenses to come to the village and then give him a settlement in cash or kind after he had done the job. They never quibbled over the magician's fee. Sometimes it was an ox or a cow. Sometimes, in addition to money and "a good dinner, a whole suit of underwear (shirt, underpants, socks, and a shawl or towel)," was demanded by the magician, which tells us a good deal about the home lives of magicians, if not much about vampires.

The Moravians, in particular, honored magicians as vampire exterminators. The magician's exorcism of a vampire was dramatic.

"He enters a village and says that the air smells. In somewhat of a trance he looks about as if he can see something. The cattle have all been driven down to the water, where they stay until the magician is finished. After the magician has looked about him for some time, a gun is given to him and he fires it into the air. A scream is heard. It is believed that this gun shot has killed the vampire; it must have been the vampire's mortal cry." The villagers then pour a bucket of water "over the spot where it is supposed to have fallen, and thus to wash away blood that appeared as a sign of its actual destruction."

Some Slavic people used to offer sacrifices to appease their vampires. At night they would put out bread and cheese, or sometimes sweet halvah—but, secretly, in the next village, so that the vampire would be enticed away from their own homes. As they passed the graveyard between villages (graveyards were usually placed outside the village bounds), they would call out to the vampire by name and say "Come along, let's go to ——— for a visit and have a meal. I am bringing your food. Dine there and come no more to me."

From that time on, they expected to see no more of the vampire.

Nobody said what the people of ——— village thought about all that.

5

CHRISTIAN UNBURIAL: OF PRIESTS AND VAMPIRES

THE FOLKTALES ABOUT VAMPIRES REFLECT a universal dread of the creature and also a remarkable similarity across the world in the methods of ridding the community of these monsters. Talismans, plants to which magical properties were attributed, and sharp instruments were common everywhere. The Chinese, for example, used garlic to keep vampires away. So did the people of Transylvania. The Chinese also used leeks, and the Slavs used juniper wood. But the principle was the same: vampires had the power to move through any door or through tiny cracks in the walls, and the magical plant would protect the family from harm if it did not keep the monster out altogether. Some Slavs put hawthorn and acacia thorns on the windowsills of their houses, to stab the vampire and discourage it from coming in. They also put thorns in holes in the grave of the dead, traps for the vampire: if it tried to come out a hole, it would prick itself on the thorns and die immediately.

These ideas antedated Christianity, but persisted after the coming of the Church to Europe. Indeed, the Church saw in vampirism a means of extending its power over the people and let the beliefs bloom, so that the priests could exorcize the demons and save the people. The spread of the beliefs, however, was greater than the Church could have managed on its own, for two reasons. One was the frequency of excommunication from the Roman Catholic church, which was struggling for its life against all sorts of heresies. Among the threats made by Church authorities was that an excommunicated soul was in danger of becoming a vampire.

A more cogent reason for the spread of vampirism throughout Europe, beginning in the Middle Ages, however, was the terrible plague that began in the thirteenth century and lasted until the eighteenth.

Still another factor, which certainly burgeoned during the plague decades, was premature burial. That is, the burial of the still-living. In warm climates, it had always been wise to bury the dead quickly. When the plague came along, the people were so frightened of it, and of other diseases and fevers, that when the sick person stopped moving, it was presumed that he or she was dead. No time was lost in getting the "corpse" out of the house and into the ground. Almost always the burial was held within twenty-four hours of "death," sometimes much sooner. As the plague spread, people simply put their dead out into the street, where they were picked up by official gravediggers and taken to the burial ground during the night. No one wanted to touch the dead any more than necessary, and thus thousands of poor unfortunates who might have survived were buried alive. Imagine the plight of the sick one who awakens, fever gone, perhaps cured of his illness, to find himself encased in a coffin in a tomb. The unfortunate would claw, would writhe, would gnaw at whatever it could reach, including its shroud, and, if the coffin was opened within a reasonable length of time, it would be found with full and ruddy lips. These attributes of the buried-alive were also attributes of the living dead—the vampires.

There was nothing new about this phenomenon. It had begun early in the Christian era with reports of bodies which moved after "death." Pliny wrote about the evils of premature burial in the first century A.D. "Such is the condition of humanity," he said, "and so uncertain is men's judgment that they cannot determine even death itself."

From Pliny's time on, the phenomenon persisted. For example, in September of 1895, a young boy was found lying on the grass in Regent's Park, London, apparently stone dead. He was taken to the St. Marylebone mortuary nearby for preparation for burial. Fortunately, the morticians had not begun their grisly work before the boy showed signs of life. They called a doctor. By the time a doctor arrived, he was breathing normally. When he was taken to a hospital the medical verdict was that the boy was "recovering from a fit." He was lucky enough to live for many years thereafter.

But Mademoiselle Rachel, a French actress, was not so lucky. One day she "died" in a village near Cannes, and was taken off to the undertaker's establishment. The undertakers opened her veins and shot them full of whatever preserving fluid they were then using, and prepared to eliminate the viscera. Suddenly, under the knife, Mlle. Rachel revived. But the undertakers had gone too far, and ten hours later she was truly dead, a victim of shock and the wounds made by the embalmers.

During the centuries, many skeletons were found with their bones in positions different from those of burial. Thus grew the belief that the dead could be reanimated, and that belief strengthened the belief in vampirism.

The inability to know when death actually occurs lasted into the twentieth century, and even now the media occasionally report on some person who seemed to have died and then revived on the lip of burial. So, even in the twentieth century there is much uncertainty about the moment of death, and some authorities insist that the only true indication of death is decomposition of the body.

With the growth of journalism in the nineteenth and twentieth centuries, the "living-dead" phenomenon was given continual exposure in newspapers and "the penny dreadfuls"—magazines devoted to sensation.

But the fear of the living dead is much, much older, as noted, and by the twelfth century it had spread to England. There Walter Map, the Archdeacon of Oxford, told several tales to illustrate the very real danger he saw of the revitalized dead coming among the living to molest them. One such story concerned the Bishop of Hereford:

The bishop was visited one day by William Laudun, an English soldier who asked for help in combating a dead man who kept coming night after night to the house where Laudun lodged. Laudun had known this man and he recognized him without a doubt. But the man was safely buried, there was no doubt of that either.

The night-visitor would arrive at the house, and in sepulchral tones call out three times the names of one or more of the lodgers. Every man called fell ill and within three days died. So many had died that Laudun, an intelligent fellow, realized that he had to be high on the list, and he had better get help. So he had come to the bishop.

The bishop considered the problem and concluded that the trouble was caused by "an evil angel of that accursed wretch, so that he is able to rouse himself and walk abroad in his dead body." The bishop advised that "the corpse be exhumed, and then do you cut through its neck, sprinkling both the body and the grave throughout with Holy Water, and so rebury it."

Laudun and the handful of remaining lodgers did as the bishop said, but the dead man kept reappearing. One night, Laudun's name was called three times by the corpse. Laudun did not answer. He knew who was calling and why. He jumped up, grabbing his sword as he went, and pursued the corpse all the way to the grave. There he "clave its head clean through from the neck" and the head fell off. That was the end of that vampire.

Also in the twelfth century, the church's Canon William of Newburgh wrote of a number of amazing occurrences involving dead men who came out of their graves. These reports, he said, came from "unimpeachable testimony of responsible persons." They testified to the fact "that bodies of the dead may arise from their tombs and that vitalized by some supernatural power, they speed hither and thither, either greatly alarming or in some cases actually slaying the living."

One of William's examples came from the monks of the Abbey of Melrose:

One of the monks at the monastery had been appointed chaplain to a wealthy lady in the district, and he took to living a most dissolute life. In fact, he took to "hunting with horses and hounds" with such fervor that his fellows referred to him mockingly as *Hundeprest*—dog priest. These and his other activities were not approved by the Church. When the monk died and was buried at the abbey, strange things began to happen. The Hundeprest was seen around the grounds, destroying the monks' crops and causing all sorts of mischief. Domestic animals disappeared or were found dead with terrible wounds. These monks were so pious and Godly that they were not bothered by the appearance of the corpse but accepted it as a visitation from on high.

But the vampire was not content. It began to appear at the manor house of the great lady the monk had served as chaplain. Her ordeal began one night when the corpse suddenly appeared in her bedroom, moaning and shrieking, and gave her a terrible fright. It kept coming back, and she feared that the apparition was going to attack her; so she went to the abbey and appealed to the monks for help. Tearfully, she begged them to say prayers that would make the corpse stay in its grave and torture her no longer. The lady had been an extremely generous benefactor to the monastery so the abbot was most solicitous, and he promised that the monks would do something to end the trouble.

Four of them gathered one night by the grave of the chaplain and set up watch. Midnight passed, but they saw nothing unusual. Finally, since the night was cold, three of the monks took respite from the vigil and went inside the abbey to warm themselves in front of the fire in the great hall. One monk was left to keep watch. It was then, William wrote, that "the devil, thinking that he had found a fine opportunity to break down that pious man's courage and constancy, aroused from his grave that instrument of his which apparently he had for once allowed to slumber a longer time than usual."

The monk on duty saw the corpse rise but was not afraid. "As the horrible creature rushed at him with the most hideous yell, he firmly stood his ground, dealing it a terrific blow with a battle axe." The corpse reeled, turned, and rushed back to its grave, which opened for it, and it disappeared inside, leaving the ground untrammeled. The brave monk's companions returned, and he told them what had happened. They decided that the only thing to do was to dig up the corpse the next morning and move it out of the churchyard.

The next morning, when they dug up the body, they found that it was "marked by a terrible wound, whilst the black blood that had flowed from this seemed to swamp the whole tomb." They carted the body to unhallowed ground outside the monastery grounds, made a huge fire, and put the body on it. The body burned, the ashes scattered to the winds, and no one was bothered again by the dissolute Dog Priest.

Another of William of Newburgh's stories came from Alnwick Castle in Northumberland, reported by "a very devout old priest of high authority and most honourable reputation, who dwelt in that district." He had been a witness to the events.

A lesser noble of Yorkshire county amassed a reputation for evil deeds and finally was so unpopular that the only friend he had left was the lord of Alnwick Castle. He moved into the castle. For a time, some people thought the good lord's influence would have a positive effect on the knight, but they were mistaken. Then, when the knight married, everyone said that would straighten him out. They could not have been more wrong. Instead, the knight continued his dissolute ways and even began to accuse his wife of misbehavior. He charged her with carrying on with the servants, among others. Consumed with jealousy, he determined to find out for himself what was happening. He announced that he was going away on a trip. Instead, with the connivance of his wife's maid, he hid in the rafters of their bedchamber, above the bed.

Perhaps the accusation was father to the idea, but sure enough, his wife had hardly gone to bed when she was joined by a young neighbor boy, "a lusty youth."

From his precarious position, the knight watched with fascination and fury. Finally he forgot himself, leaned over to see better, tumbled to the floor on his head, and was knocked unconscious. The lusty youth jumped out of bed and escaped. When the husband recovered consciousness he began to accuse his wife of her infidelity.

"Nonsense," she said, it was all a figment of his imagination. He was having hallucinations caused by his fall from the rafters, coupled with "the result of your own lusts."

The knight had been badly hurt by his fall, and he became very ill. It seemed that he would die. The priest who reported these events to William of Newburgh said that, although he had no use for him, out of compassion he had gone to visit the sick man and counseled him to confess all his sins and be received back into the Church and take communion. The man was still so angry with his wife that he told the priest what had happened and how she had been deceiving him all along. He was in no state of mind to make a confession or accept the sacraments, so all was put off until the next day. But, alas, the next morning found the man dead, and all the priest could do was give him Christian burial, although he was sure the knight did not deserve it.

That was certainly proved soon enough. The recalcitrant nobleman was even more evil in death than he had been in life. "By the power of Satan" he was able to come out of his grave and wander about the town, attacking person after person. The country air "became foul and tainted as this fetid and corrupting body wandered abroad, so that a terrible plague broke out and there was hardly a house which did not mourn its dead." The village below Alnwick Castle became virtually a ghost town, as the people fled to stay with relatives elsewhere.

The priest who had visited the sick nobleman in his hour of need now decided that something had to be done. He called together the leading citizens of the town and neighboring churchmen to come up with a plan to stop this corpse from continuing its destructive ways. After mass on Palm Sunday, he held special prayers, and then the whole group of advisors joined the priest for supper and to devise a plan.

As they were talking and eating, unbeknownst to them two of the young men of the town decided to take action that very night. Their father had been one of the first victims of the vampire. "This monster hath claimed our father, and if we do not look about he will before long slay us too," one of them said. So the two young men found sharp spades and set off for the cemetery.

They went to the grave of the dead nobleman and began to dig. It was not long before they uncovered the coffin. Oddly enough, although it had been buried in the regular way, it had very little earth over it.

When they opened the coffin, what a sight they saw: the body was "gorged and swollen with a frightful corpulence, and its face was florid and chubby, with huge, red, puffed cheeks, and the shroud in which it had been wrapped was all soiled and torn."

This shocking sight did not stop the young men. They slashed the body with their sharp spades, and immediately "there gushed out such a stream of warm red gore that they realized this vampire had fattened on the blood of many poor folk."

They dragged the body out of the cemetery, past the town limits, and built a huge fire. They then went down to the house of the priest to tell all the men there what they had done. The men stopped talking and arose from the table and followed the young men to the site of the fire. They all helped throw the body onto the fire, and soon it was consumed by the flames.

Just as suddenly as the plague had struck the district, it stopped. It was "as if the polluted air was cleansed by the fire, which burned up the hellish brute who had infected the whole atmosphere."

Of course William's tales had a powerful effect on medieval England. They reaffirmed a belief, already strong in the countryside, that vampires did indeed exist and did come out of the grave to suck the blood of the living and destroy them. And of course, as William and the other churchmen so piously pointed out, the vampires existed only because of the power of the Devil, who had entered the body.

So the wicked had better look out.

6

THE BLOODY COUNTESS BÁTHORY

ELIZABETH BATHORY WAS BORN IN 1560 in a great castle in the northwest part of Hungary in the shadows of the Carpathian mountains near Transylvania. Her father, the Count György Báthory, was a famous soldier and her mother, Anna, was the sister of Stephen Báthory, the king of Poland. They were leaders of the Protestant nobility within the empire.

Elizabeth was brought up carefully and lovingly by her parents, who were so far ahead of their time intellectually that she was taught to read and write, a rare accomplishment for young women in those days, even among the nobility. But when she was ten years old, her father died suddenly, and on her mother's shoulders fell all the cares of the family's enormous estates. Also, she alone had to determine the fate of her daughter Elizabeth.

The next year, Anna arranged for the eleven-year-old girl's betrothal to Ferencz Nádasdy, scion of another of the important Protestant families of Hungary. It was decided that Elizabeth should go to live in Léká at the château of the Countess Ursula Nádasdy, her fiancé's mother, to be trained to rule over those great lands. So she moved to that strange environment. She was a precocious girl in every way and was quickly bored by the routine of managing a noble house. For amusement, she took to frolicking with the peasants, which was all right so long as she was eleven. When she became twelve, things began to change; and by the time she was thirteen, she was quite a grown-up young woman. She continued to frolic, however, until she turned up pregnant, a peasant boy the father of her unborn child.

Elizabeth had the good sense to conceal her condition from her future mother-in-law, but she did tell her mother, and Anna came storming down to the Nádasdy château. The poor girl, Anna declared, was in the first throes of a dreadful and very infectious disease. She had detected it just in time to prevent the most dreadful consequences; there was not even opportunity to discuss the matter with the Countess Nádasdy. She rushed Elizabeth away for "treatment." At least part of what she said was true: among the nobility in sixteenth-century Hungary, a young noble-woman could do almost anything to the peasants except sleep with them. Had the Countess Nádasdy even sniffed a hint of the scandal, Elizabeth's betrothal would have been voided. But she did not. Countess Anna took her daughter to one of the more remote of the Báthory castles, and there she remained until the disease had run its course and Elizabeth had given birth to a baby. Without a moment's delay, the child was turned over to a local woman, who was sent out of the country with a generous financial settlement and orders not to reappear in Hungary during Elizabeth's lifetime. That was the last ever heard of the baby.

A few months later, when Elizabeth was not quite fifteen years old, she was married to the young Count Nádasdy. For Hungarians it seemed a marriage blessed by heaven. The soldier-husband was a handsome, dashing young man with a dark beard, and dark eyes and skin. The bride was a beauty with big black eyes, dark hair, the fairest of skin, regular features, and sensual lips. He was the youngest general ever to command the border fortress defenses of Southwest Hungary. She was the image of noble young womanhood, educated, intelligent, apparently shy and virtuous, and beautiful in every way. They were married in Varanno on the edge of the Hungarian plain, between the two remote family castles, on a lovely day, May 8, 1575. The Emperor Maximilian was so pleased with this alliance of two of the greatest houses of Hungary that he sent a letter of approval, along with a large golden jar of rare wine for a wedding present and two hundred thalers in gold, which would keep a common Hungarian citizen for ten years.

In what was a hint of Elizabeth's true character, she chose to settle in one of the smaller of the Nádasdy castles, Csejthe, a dark and foreboding bastion on a rock high on the side of one of the Carpathian foothills, bordered by dense forest where the wolves howled at night. It was a wild and gloomy place, with thick walls, low ceilings, few windows, and a labyrinth of underground passages, cellars, and dungeons, hardly the sort of honeymoon cottage one would expect a sprightly, blushing bride to adopt. But it was just what Elizabeth wanted, so she moved in, with husband, mother-in-law, and a raft of servants.

When the count was about, life was fine for Elizabeth. They began thinking about raising a family and enjoyed themselves. But when the count was off fighting the wars with the Turks, Csejthe was indeed a dark and gloomy place. Also, like many a young bride before and after her, Elizabeth had problems with her mother-in-law. The countess was a somber, puritanical, religious woman. She forced Elizabeth to manage the household in the way of the Nádasdys. As the Turks took more and more of the count's time, it was not long before Elizabeth became thoroughly bored.

She was intelligent enough to leave the peasant boys alone now, but she had to have something to love, so she turned to herself. She painted her face for hours. The servants concocted various cosmetic preparations, and she tried them all. After every application of each new balm, she regarded herself critically to see if it had made her more beautiful and, if so, how much more beautiful. She fussed for hours with her hair—when she was not having headaches. These came often. Small wonder her servants prepared drugs and potions by the score and she took them all in great quantity. These were supposed to bring about the conception of a child, for, in spite of the fact that she and the count tried often when he was at home, no baby came for nearly ten years. It was very frustrating to the young bride, enough to drive her to turn almost anywhere. Elizabeth turned to magic, and that annoyed the Countess Nádasdy. To avoid arguments, Elizabeth took to keeping to her own apartments when the count was not around. That behavior forestalled family arguments, but it did not solve any of her problems, including loneliness. Since peasant boys were off-limits, Elizabeth turned to peasant girls for amusement when the count was soldiering.

But as she grew older, the idea of amusement became something special. She favored beautiful blonde girls with big breasts, and, among other things, she liked to beat them and bite them. The Countess Ursula had some hint of this behavior, but fortunately for her immortal soul she died before she learned too much about what was going on in Elizabeth's rooms.

What was going on stopped, or slowed down, only when the count came home for a respite from the wars. Then he would take Elizabeth to Vienna, to the great balls and parties given by the emperor and his entourage. Elizabeth loved the glitter, but too soon it was time to return to the gloom of the castle, the departure of her husband, and the girls again.

As time went on, she found herself able to relax enough to conceive again, and between 1585 and 1595 she bore four children. But the preoccupation with the girls was an established part of her life. To conceal from her husband what really went on, she was constantly complaining about the help. The sewing girls had to be beaten because they were slow in their work. The maids had to be beaten because they were stupid and insolent. The serving girls had to be beaten because . . .

The count heard these litanies with half an ear. He had other things on his mind, such as figuring out how to overcome the Turks, and raising that family.

One day when they were walking in the garden, the count and countess came across one of the servant girls, naked, tied to a tree, smeared with honey, with insects crawling all over her body. The count looked and made no objection. In fact, he taught his wife a few new tricks: for example, how to put paper between the girls' toes and then light it. That particular torture was called "star-kicking," because it was said the pain would make the victims see stars.

When the children began coming along, from Elizabeth's letters to Ferencz one would think that she was a totally devoted mother with no thought for anything but her children. But the fact was that the children were in the hands of nurses and governesses, and Elizabeth was dabbling in black magic these days, under the guidance of Dorottya Szentes, known as Dorkó. Dorkó had been the wet nurse for Elizabeth's daughter Anna until Anna was weaned. When Elizabeth learned the Dorkó was adept in the black arts, the witch's future was assured. She taught the countess chants and incantations and the ways of magic. One day Elizabeth wrote delightedly to Ferencz at the front:

> Dorkó has taught me something new: Beat a small black fowl to death with a white cane. Put a drop of its blood on your enemy's person, or, if you cannot reach him, on a piece of his clothing. Then he will be unable to harm you.

This was the faithful helpmeet, offering her soldier-husband the very latest wrinkle in self-protection from his Turkish enemies. He needed it.

The wars went on for years and he was away from home for months at a time. Elizabeth had nothing to do but refine her own amusements.

Often, she went to visit her aunt, the Countess Klara Báthory, who was among Hungary's foremost lesbians of her day. It was said that she raped all her ladies-in-waiting. What a time the two of them had! Beating up naked, big-bosomed serving girls was apparently the principal amusement of aunt and niece during these visits. Elizabeth learned a lot. And so did her two personal maids, Barsovny and Otvos. They were young, beautiful lesbians. "Elizabeth abandoned herself to all the possible pleasure one woman may know in the arms of another," it was said.

Back at home, Elizabeth put into practice what she had learned. Girls were marched down to the torture chamber in the bowels of the castle. Sometimes they were kept in the dungeon for days without food or water, awaiting their turns to amuse the countess. The nanny Jó Ilona, along with Dorkó took part in some of these tortures. So did Kateline Beniezky, Elizabeth's washerwoman. But Elizabeth was the leader; she was becoming a tiger in the torture game.

In the winter of 1604 when Elizabeth was forty-four years old, her husband took sick and died. All Hungary mourned the death of this great soldier of the realm. To Elizabeth, his death meant an end to her sexual relationships with men and a renewed furious round of torture orgies to keep herself merry in her widowhood.

Her valet, Ujvari János, was the only man in the castle privy to Elizabeth's strange manners of amusement. Ficzkó, as she called him, was her principal procurer. It was his responsibility to search the villages around the castle for big-busted peasant girls and promise their families that they would be taken "into service" at the castle. Then he brought them to Elizabeth, who showed them what their service would be: To begin with, they were starved and beaten bloody. And soon there was to be more.

At forty-four Elizabeth fretted ever more about her beauty. It seemed to be fading. No longer was her skin pristine and unwrinkled. There were lines at her throat and on her forehead, the skin of her neck was not as white and soft as it had once been. The search for potions and lotions grew ever more frantic, and onto the scene came Anna Darvulia, Elizabeth's new house magician, to supervise the transformation of a middle-aged woman back into a girl. Darvulia stayed up half the night writing up incantations and preparing potions, and during the day Elizabeth said the words and drank the draughts. Darvulia made poultices from the leaves of deadly nightshade, henbane, and thorn apple, and Elizabeth applied them to her skin. Ever whiter the skin must be, younger, smoother, lovelier—all in the increasingly frenetic search to restore her failing beauty.

One day, as a maid was arranging Elizabeth's long black hair with a net of pearls, the girl did something that annoyed Elizabeth. The countess turned around and dealt the girl such a blow in the face that blood spurted all over her arms and hands. When the blood had been washed away Elizabeth looked with amazement at her hands and arms.

Where the blood had fallen, her skin looked twenty years younger. It was beautiful and soft once again.

Blood! Blood was the answer to everlasting beauty.

What a dreadful discovery it was! Sorcery and torture for sadistic pleasure would now give way to baths of blood for beauty. The girls in the dungeon would soon know a new sort of service.

Elizabeth now began to revel in blood. Before, it had pleased her enough to see the blood run as she beat the poor servant girls. Now she sucked their wounds and smeared the blood over her body. She had come a long way in a short time.

The new Elizabeth had girls brought up from the cellars to her bedroom and laid stark naked on the floor. Then she tortured them, until the blood ran so deep that the servants had to scoop it up by the cupful and bring up cinders to cover the puddles and stains.

Soon one girl was not enough. So they were brought up in twos and threes, and Elizabeth would run about her room beating one girl after another. The more they pleaded for mercy, the harder she beat them. When she would become covered with blood, everything would stop while the countess changed her dress—and then she would be back at it again. When the girls collapsed from loss of blood and the pain, more girls were brought up from the dungeon to replace them. And when there had been enough blood, it was time for other amusements. If a serving girl "lingered long and lovingly between Elizabeth's ceaselessly voracious thighs, she might gain the Countess' favor." But the favor never lasted long, for Elizabeth cast off her favorites once the novelty each brought to her work had faded.

She would burn their cheeks and breasts with red-hot pokers prepared by her lesbian assistants. When she tired of this activity, she would sit in her chair and watch while Dorkó tortured the girls. Dorkó beat them and burned them, and cut them with razors until the blood spurted. The sight of spurting blood began to give the countess the most extreme sexual pleasure. She would work herself into an almost maniacal state.

She screamed "More, Dorkó, more. Harder, much harder." Then she would get back into the game and take a lighted candle and burn the genitals of the girls. It did not take much of this to turn even a former favorite into something less than beautiful.

Precisely when the first girl was beaten to death is a mystery, but it could not have been long after Elizabeth discovered all the "virtues" of blood. Soon beating to death became a ritual in itself. Darvulia tied the girls' hands and arms, and all the participants beat them, until "their whole bodies were black as charcoal and their skin was rent and torn." Dorkó cut their fingers with shears and then slit the veins of their arms and legs with sewing scissors. Dorkó did the stabbing. The wet nurse, Jó Ilona, graduated from her old duties, now tended the fires in the braziers, heated the pokers, and applied them to faces and noses, sometimes opening the poor victim's mouth and shoving the burning iron inside. One day the countess discovered a new treat: she put her fingers in a girl's mouth, and pulled with all her might until the mouth split wide open. She also liked to tear the skin with white-hot pincers and to cut the skin between their fingers to see the blood run. The blood was saved and became Elizabeth's favorite skin lotion. Day after day, she laved her face and arms and body in blood.

Even with so many diversions, life palled for Elizabeth, and she traveled frequently to one of her other castles or to Vienna where she had a big town house at 12 Augustinerstrasse. Wherever she traveled, she installed a torture chamber. At Beckó Castle, the girls were tortured in an abandoned storeroom; at Sárvár, in a disused wing of the castle; at Kéresztúr, in a little dressing room off Elizabeth's own room. Scarcely a day went by that she did not indulge herself in at least a bit of torture. Even when she was traveling in her coach, she always had a servant girl or two along, so that she could bite them and pinch them and stab them with needles.

In Vienna, the countess learned something new. She acquired an iron cage, which was installed in the cellar of her house on the Augustinerstrasse. Huge pointed metal spikes stuck inward from the edge of the cage, which could be lowered and raised on a pulley. Dorkó would drag a naked girl down the stairs and thrust her into the cage, which was then hoisted up to the ceiling. The countess sat on a stepladder directly beneath the cage and watched as Dorkó stabbed at the girl with a sharp iron stake or a red-hot poker, and as the poor girl writhed about inside the cage, trying to avoid Dorkó's thrusts, she ran into the razor-sharp spikes, which slashed and tore her flesh. The blood would flow down onto Elizabeth and she reveled in it. When the girl had fainted or died, the countess would gather her bloody garments about her lovingly and return to the upstairs world.

Magician Darvulia assured Elizabeth that she would remain beautiful as long as she had plenty of blood, and devised a new method of using it. Elizabeth was to have regular baths in the blood of virgins. The supply of peasant virgins in Hungary in those days seemed limitless. Girls were brought to the upstairs rooms and tied up; then their blood vessels were slit with razors to make the blood flow fast and hot. Dorkó collected the spurting blood in a large earthenware vessel, and, while the girls lay dying, she poured virgins' blood over her mistress.

The therapeutic bloodbaths continued, but they had lost their power to amuse. So had the iron cage in the cellar at 12 Augustinerstrasse. Elizabeth was bored again.

Then she heard of a great clock that had been built for the Duke of Brunswick at his castle at Dolna Krupa. It was a fantastic piece of machinery, and all Vienna talked of its intricate works and chimes. It had taken a clockmaker two years to build it. People came from great distances to see the marvelous machine at the castle. So did Elizabeth.

The countess spent more time at Dolna Krupa than she had expected. She had long talks with the clockmaker. What she wanted, however, was not a duplicate of the Duke of Brunswick's clock but a copy of the famous Iron Virgin, or Iron Maiden, of Nuremberg, which was known throughout Europe as the century's most famous torture machine.

What the countess wanted, the countess got. The clockmaker agreed to build an Iron Maiden. When it was ready, he delivered it to Csejthe Castle, where Elizabeth had it installed in the dungeon. When the Iron Maiden was not in use she lay in an ornate oak chest. Next to the chest was the Iron Maiden's pedestal, where she did her grisly work.

What a maiden!

The machine was a life-size figure of a beautiful woman; it had the long, flowing blonde hair of a woman. The body was painted flesh color; it had red nipples and pubic hair. The mouth opened by clockwork to reveal real human teeth in its cruel smile. The eyes moved. A necklace of semiprecious stones hung down over the big breasts. Certain of these stones activated the clockworks. As Elizabeth sat in a chair and watched, a girl would be brought to stand before the Iron Maiden, and the stones would be moved. The arms would rise to clutch the victim to the iron bosom in a grip that was totally relentless. The painted bosom opened. Five daggers emerged to stab the victim's body, while other hidden spikes appeared below to pierce the genitals. The touch of another stone caused the Maiden's smile to fade, and the eyes closed. The blood flowed down into a catchment, and it was saved to pour over the countess, either then, or later in her bath.

Peasant girl after peasant girl was embraced by the Iron Maiden before Elizabeth, like any child with a mechanical toy, tired of the sameness of it. The blood made the works begin to rust, and finally Elizabeth ordered the Iron Maiden put into her case and retired—but not before the rumors of her performance had begun to move across the countryside.

Beginning in about 1608 talk about the Countess Báthory around Hungary began to take on a definitely unpleasant tone. The monks in the monastery in Vienna, near 12 Augustinerstrasse, complained that when Elizabeth was staying at her town house, they were distressed night after night by shrieks and screams and wailing that rent the quiet of the night. In the inn near the cathedral, people spoke of blood in the streets and murdered girls. Patrons of the inn began to refer sardonically to Elizabeth as *die Blutgrafin,* the Bloody Countess.

They didn't know the half of it.

7

WHEN THE BLOOD RAN OUT

COUNTESS BÁTHORY'S DISCOVERY OF blood's therapeutic qualities created a problem: the girls who bled died, and something had to be done with the bodies.

At home at Csejthe Castle, Elizabeth's chaplain was also the pastor of the village. He found himself called upon to officiate at the burials of a number of girls from the castle who had died of "strange maladies." The Reverend Janos Ponikenus, a devout and moral man, did not much like the strange goings-on at the castle. When Elizabeth announced that, from this point on, all burial services would be held at night, the pastor's suspicions grew. Sometimes the only attendants at a funeral service were the countess's intimates, led by Dorkó. One night he was called upon to bless a spot of earth outside the castle, and no one told him who was buried there or why. He began to hear talk about the cruel treatment of the serving girls and even of sadism and torture. Still, he found these charges hard to believe, for the countess was so beautiful and could exert so much charm. How could she be the monster that some said she was?

So the pastor continued to conduct the burial services, odd as he found them. Then, one night, he was ordered by Elizabeth to bury Ilona Harczy, a girl whom Pastor Ponikenusz knew well. She had been a member of his church and had sung in the choir. Elizabeth gave the pastor some instruction on his sermon: he was to speak of Ilona's death as "punishment for her sins." At this, the pastor balked; he knew the girl was virtually pure as snow. He refused to say what Elizabeth wanted him to, and she conducted the funeral without him.

After that breach, many, many burials were held without the officiation of the pastor. When Elizabeth was staying at the Vienna house, or one of her other castles, she was more careful; there were only a few victims each month, and they could be buried in the cemetery at night. But back at Csejthe, as many as five or six girls were killed in a single week. So many were killed, in fact, that the disposal of their bodies became a real problem. Dorkó and Kateline began carrying the bodies out into the fields outside the castle grounds to bury them.

Except when she was in Vienna, Elizabeth seemed to fear nothing and no one; her unholy depradations were conducted almost openly. One winter's day on a trip from Csejthe to another of her castles at Illava, Elizabeth felt the old boredom seizing her. She called for one of the girl servants in the retinue to come and ride with her in the coach. The girl was pushed into the carriage—she had to be pushed, for by this time the servants knew that to be alone with Elizabeth was sheer torture. Elizabeth began to bite the girl and pinch her all over. Then she took a sharp pin from her hair and began to stab the poor servant in the breasts, thighs—anywhere that would hurt and draw blood. When they arrived at Illava Castle, there was the usual confusion that attended going through the gates, and although night was falling and the temperature was far below freezing, the girl slipped out of the coach and ran for her life across the snow-covered fields. But she did not escape. Elizabeth shouted for a search party of guards and ordered the coach turned back into the fields. The riders quickly found the poor struggling girl and brought her back to her mistress.

Elizabeth sat in her coach and by torchlight watched as Jó Ilona ripped off every shred of the girl's clothing. Then she ordered the servants to bring water from the ice-capped puddles in the ditches along the road. Jó Ilona then poured the buckets of water over the naked girl's head. It was so cold that as the water struck the girl's hair and skin, it froze. The girl tried to escape, but she could not. The torturers poured more water over her, and more, until in the end she became a frozen statue standing in the field. Elizabeth tired of the fun and went back to the castle, and Jó Ilona and the servants buried the girl under the snow in the field.

Wherever Elizabeth traveled now, she had to have her amusements with her. In the late autumn of 1609 Elizabeth decided to sample the famous mudbaths at Pistyan, which were said to have marvelous rejuvenatory powers. She had a castle there, near the river Vag, on whose shores the hot springs rose. She invited a number of ladies and gentlemen to join her, but so great was her blood lust that she also insisted on bringing a large number of serving girls along for her amusement.

Each morning, Elizabeth and her guests left the castle and rode to the baths, where they dressed and undressed in purple and white tents, to protect them from the growing cold, and then went into the mud. Elizabeth always protected her fair skin from the sun with a parasol. She would soak in mud up to her neck for hours, feeling the magical properties of the ooze soothing her body. In the afternoon, all would go back to the castle for feasting and dancing. Late at night, Elizabeth would stage her own private amusements.

As luck would have it, on this occasion, Elizabeth's daughter Anna sent word that she was coming to Pistyan to take the baths with her husband, Miklos Zrinyi. This announcement sent Elizabeth into a fury. Daughter and son-in-law would have to have the run of her apartments, and that meant no more late-night entertainments. Angrily, she ordered Dorkó to confine the serving girls to the cellars where no one would come upon them. The change in plans sent her into a particularly nasty mood, and she told Dorkó to punish the girls, as though they were responsible for depriving Elizabeth of her fun. Then, resigned to it all, Elizabeth went back to her room to make herself more beautiful. When the guests assembled that night, she was at her most charming, the perfect hostess. For the next week, she devoted herself to entertaining Anna, her husband, and her other guests with single-minded attentiveness.

Meanwhile, Dorkó was following Elizabeth's instructions to the letter. She gave the girls no food for eight days; at night, she took them outside their dungeon for airing and poured ice-cold water over their naked bodies. One girl died. With so many strangers about, Dorkó did not know what to do with the body, so she stuffed it under a cot and covered it with furs. The other girls fell ill with colds and fever, and some died. Before the week was out, the cellars began to stink of death and decay.

More girls died. Dorkó persuaded one of the castle footmen to help her bury several of them in the fields outside. Others she put in the tower. One she threw into the moat that surrounded the castle, but the body floated up to the surface and had to be retrieved before the guests saw it.

Burial was difficult. But Dorkó found a piece of ground on which vegetables had been stored and wheedled the footman to bury it there.

How unlucky can a poor countess be? Son-in-law Miklos had brought his favorite dog with him to the outing, and the next day when they were out for a romp in the fields, the dog dug up part of the body and brought it to his master. Miklos was horror-struck. But he had the good sense to say nothing. He had been hearing the dreadful tales about his mother-in-law, but she was still one of the most powerful people in all Hungary and it would be suicidal to go up against her without equally powerful backing.

The Pistyan Castle servants were equally horrified, and when Dorkó came to the footman to bury another body, he refused. Nor would any of the others have anything to do with the grisly project. Dorkó was frantic, the stink was growing by the hour. She found some quicklime and took it up to the tower to solve her problem. But the quicklime only added to the smells, and by this time even the guests must have been growing queasy.

Elizabeth saw that it was time to call off the party, and she announced that she must return to Csejthe. She called Dorkó and told her to get the serving girls ready to go.

Serving girls? Dorkó said she was sorry but most of them were dead because she had followed Elizabeth's orders to punish them, and the others were too sick to travel.

Elizabeth was furious with her favorite torturer for having gone too far. Now she would have no girls to amuse her on the long ride back to Csejthe. Dorkó finally found one girl who could at least walk to the carriage, and she was hustled inside. She did not provide Elizabeth with much amusement, she died before they reached Csejthe.

Dorkó was left at Pistyan Castle to dispose of the bodies. After the others had gone, she spent five nights digging graves in the garden, and into each grave she unceremoniously dumped a body.

Bodies, bodies, bodies! What a nuisance they had become. At Csejthe, Jó Ilona and Kateline were given the task of disposing of bodies. It wasn't like the old days. Old Andras Berthoni, the pastor who had led the Csejthe Protestant flock when Elizabeth came to the castle, had always been accommodating about burials. Of course there had not been so many of them in the early days of Elizabeth's lust—just the occasional mistake of overdoing the torture until the girl died. Pastor Berthoni's days in office were nearly ended when the really bloody time began.

Even Janos had been reasonable until the case of the choir singer aroused his suspicions. Now the situation was impossible; two old women had to bear the full burden of getting rid of the evidence. They spent half their time searching for new places to bury bodies. Sometimes they were not quick enough about it, and that could create new troubles.

One day a woman appeared at the castle and identified herself as the mother of one of the new girls taken "into service." She wanted to see how her daughter was getting along in the castle of the famous countess. Unfortunately, the daughter had succumbed to torture two days earlier, but no one had yet figured out where to bury the body. They had to admit the girl was dead. The mother asked—nay, demanded—to see the body. How could they show it to her, that poor blackened, misshapen hunk of rotting flesh? Elizabeth took recourse in umbrage and locked the woman up in the castle for arrogant behavior. Then the old women quickly buried the daughter's body, and let the woman out with a warning that she must say nothing of what had happened to her. The mother went back to her home, frightened into silence by the powerful countess, but she did not forget.

Pastor Ponikenus had also been frightened enough by Elizabeth to keep quiet about his suspicions after the confrontation over Ilona Harczy. Let him not meddle in the affairs of the castle, and she would not meddle in the affairs of his church, she had said. But the minister was so disturbed about the constant rumors of violence at the castle that he determined to do some investigating. Consulting old church records, he found a document written by old Pastor Berthoni, in which the minister revealed his uneasiness about events at the castle. One terrible night, the old pastor had been called upon by the countess to bury nine girls at once. They had been victims of a mysterious and terrible disease, he was told; so evil that the coffins could not be opened and no one could see the bodies. The old pastor had sensed that he was being told lies. But, in his declining years, he had not the heart to go up against the countess, and he had confined his suspicions to this church paper which he left for someone else to find.

Pastor Ponikenus then went down into the crypt below the church in the village, which, along with the castle, had belonged to Count Christopher Orszagh of Giath before it came into the hands of the Báthorys. The crypt had been reserved for the burial of the Orszaghs, and his body had lain there since his death in 1567. No others had been authorized to lie there. When the minister descended the steep stairs into the crypt, he saw not only the ornate sarcophagus of the count, but also nine plain wooden coffins. These, the pastor was sure, held the bodies of girls who had been killed in the castle, about whom the old pastor had written.

Pastor Ponikenus was now suspicious enough to act. He wrote a letter to the central governor at Presbourg. Somehow the countess intercepted it, and it was never delivered. The pastor spoke up bravely from the pulpit, but who was listening? Only the villagers, whose livelihood for the most part depended on the castle. Elizabeth's power was so enormous that she could simply ignore the pastor, which she did.

Elizabeth's intimates were now having a harder time finding young peasant girls to serve in the castle. Too many of those who entered the castle simply disappeared, and the village folk knew they must have been murdered. But peasants could not speak up against the nobility. And where was the proof?

It was too bad the peasants could not see into Elizabeth's rooms. She spent many hours each day in front of her mirror. Naked, she would stare at her figure critically, looking for the flab of age. She had hundreds of dresses, and the seamstresses steadily made more to adorn her fair body. That was always a dangerous business. For Elizabeth might look at a hem with distaste. Dorkó, noticing her mistress's frown, would send away all the girls except the offenders. Then the fun would begin. Dorkó would cut open the skin between the offending fingers "to punish them for their awkwardness." Then she would begin the ritual of torture. The girls would be stripped, and needles stuck into their nipples—more punishment for incompetence. The play might continue for hours, but the end was always the same: "There would be pools of blood at the foot of the bed. The following day two or three seamstresses would be missing."

Elizabeth did what Elizabeth wanted to do, ever more unrestrained and contemptuous of the world around her. She was haughty, arrogant, sure in her powerful position as a Báthory—and she now had the protection of a magical parchment that she believed would always save her from her enemies. Witch Darvulia had prepared this document, written on the skin of a newborn child of the village with secret ink made from the juices of plants from the fields and forest.

It read:

Isten, give me help; and ye also, O all powerful cloud! Protect me, Elizabeth, and grant me a long life. I am in peril, O cloud! Send me ninety cats, for thou are the supreme lord of cats. Give them their orders and tell them, wherever they may be, to assemble together, to come from the mountains, from the waters, from the rivers, from the rainwater on the roofs, and from the oceans. Tell them to come to me. And to hasten to bite the heart of _____, and also of _____, and of _____. . . . And guard Elizabeth from all evil.

The blanks in the parchment were to be filled in by Elizabeth when she had identified her mortal enemies. Even though the blanks were empty, Elizabeth carried the parchment with her in a red silk bag, sewn into her corsets; she wore it always, even under her gorgeous gowns when attending the glittering balls of Vienna.

In the winter of 1609-1610, Elizabeth was playing the great lady. Sometimes on her visits to Presbourg she would engage an entire floor of rooms at The Wild Man Inn. The innkeeper was always pleased to see Countess Báthory coming, for it meant a busy and profitable time for him. She brought the inn to life with her parties. She feasted and was feasted in return. She demanded services and she paid for them; costly perfumes for her endless baths; many new gowns by new dressmakers in the provincial capital. No finger cutting or hot needles for these dressmakers; they were treated with the utmost courtesy by that great and lovely lady, the Countess Báthory. In her new finery, she would visit the high personages related to her. She was sought after by all for her beauty, and wherever she appeared she caused a sensation.

That was the public Elizabeth.

Back at Csejthe Castle, the darker side of Elizabeth bloomed: red-hot coins for the mouths of serving girls who spoke up too much; sewing up their mouths with needles and threads if their cries annoyed her. Dorkó beat the girls until they were one swollen mass of flesh, then cut them up with a razor, the blood spurting all over Elizabeth's newest gown. Who cared? There were more gowns and more girls. Blood was the thing. Dorkó would cut open the veins of the dying with scissors to get that last drop of blood for the countess's bath.

This was the simple life of the castle, compared to the glitter of the town. Month in, month out, it was blood and torture. Then one day Darvulia the magician died, leaving only her cats and parchment of incantations. Now Elizabeth had no magician to protect her. What was she to do?

She heard about an old woman named Erza Majorova who lived in the forest, and was renowned for magical beauty concoctions. Elizabeth sought her out and soon the castle had a new resident witch, who promised that she would give the countess the secret of eternal youth.

But after a few weeks of magician Majorova's potions and lotions and incantations, Elizabeth, craning in her mirror, noticed a new wrinkle, and she threatened the old witch with death if she did not immediately stop the ravages of time. Erza Majorova must have been beside herself, but she had an answer: of course the blood of all those young peasant girls had not brought eternal youth, because they were of the lower classes. If Elizabeth wanted to keep her youth forever, she must have blue blood. The daughters of the nobility must help her. Thus Elizabeth was enticed further along the road to sure disaster.

Dorkó and Jó Ilona were sent out to find girls of blue blood. Their story was that Elizabeth was lonely and needed company during the long winter, so she would graciously accept some young girls of the lesser aristocracy to come and live with her. In exchange for their companionship, she would teach them languages and court manners.

The ploy worked like a charm. Their first time out, the two crones came back with twenty-five young aspirants of the bluest blood. Two weeks later, even before they could master French irregular verbs, all of them were dead. The countess was happy again, but the girls' bodies created a new problem, one Dorkó and her assistants were not quite able to solve. The ground was frozen and burial was hard. Therefore, four of the bodies were left out in the snow for the wolves.

Unfortunately, they were discovered by peasants of the village, who could not help but see the torture marks on them. Servants who visited the village reported back to the castle that the discovery had created a local uproar, but no one knew if any action was being taken, and Elizabeth's accessories were just then too busy to concern themselves with such details. They were out again, seeking more blue-blooded girls. But the aristocracy had become suspicious, and their mission seemed impossible. But Jó Ilona and Dorkó dared not come back empty-handed; so they found five peasant girls, dressed them in fine clothes gathered up around the castle from the belongings of the first contingent, and passed them off to Elizabeth as a new crop of blue bloods.

Thus was spent the late fall of 1610, and the Christmas holidays approached. The members of the Hungarian parliament were scheduled to go into session at Presbourg at the first of the year. Since Csejthe Castle was on the road to Presbourg for most of them, Elizabeth's connections as usual made plans to stop over at her castle for a few days before beginning the work of government.

This year the visits worried Elizabeth. She was not unmindful of the talk at the inns and in Vienna about the "bloody countess," and although she resolutely ignored the talk in public, in private she was more than a little worried about exposure. King Matthias would come to visit this year, as well as her cousin György Thurzo, the Grand Palatine of Protestant Upper Hungary, whose office was as near that of cardinal as the Protestant church had. Emmerich Megyery, one of the king's councillors, would also be on hand. Elizabeth was apprehensive about what they might find out at Csejthe. To whom if anyone had the peasants of the village gone with their tale of the four dead girls? Most of all Elizabeth worried about Megyery, who was a shrewd and artful man. He was the tutor and guardian of Elizabeth's son Pal Nádasdy. She knew he had heard some of the rumors about her. To dilute the influence and power of these august personages in her castle, and to set up a smoke-screen to cover her secret activities with the noise and pomp of public entertainments, she invited scores of noble lords and ladies from neighboring castles. She would be the beautiful and gracious hostess; there would be music; huge logs would burn in the fireplaces, and all the chandeliers and candelabra would blaze through the night.

But the worries nagged her and she had for the first time a premonition of impending doom. She laid plans to leave the castle and flee to Transylvania, to the castle of her dissolute cousin Gábor. He would take her in, and she would be safe forever.

8

A Devilish End for a Vampire

THE KING ARRIVED, AS DID PALATINE Thurzo and councillor Megyery, and Elizabeth's relatives and guests from castles near and far. The gaiety began. Countess Báthory had never been more scintillating or glamorous than she was this Christmas season. But beneath all the glitter ran sinister undercurrents. Elizabeth sensed that her premonition had been correct: the king, Thurzo, and Megyery were somehow aware of the nature of her secret life at the castle.

She was right. Megyery had discovered the awful truth. A young peasant lad from Csejthe village had arrived in the capital one day and come to Pal Nádasdy's palace, seeking an interview. The servants had diverted him to tutor Megyery, and the boy had told the following story:

He was engaged to a beautiful girl who had been taken into service by the Countess Báthory at Csejthe Castle. Her task was to bring water from the castle to the village each day. One day she had failed to come to the village, and she had never come again. He had gone to the castle to inquire about her, and been told nothing. He knew the grim reputation of the castle, and now he had come to see Elizabeth's son to plead for the return of his love.

Megyery had been hearing terrible tales about the countess and nursing his suspicions. Now he went straight to King Matthias with them, and before the king came to Csejthe he had heard the whole story.

Palatine Thurzo had separately received more than a whiff of blood. In his investigations Pastor Ponikenus had discovered the letter written years earlier by Pastor Berthoni. He had sent it on to the palatine.

The net was closing around Elizabeth, and she knew it. Her main preoccupation now was to protect herself from those who wished her harm. She would defeat them by her magic. When Erza Majorova came next to the castle, Elizabeth had her brought to the bedroom. There she asked the magician to make a large magic cake for her guests. The witch promised. She brought her supplies that day, and that night she went to work in the cellar to prepare the magic concoction. Elizabeth descended to watch—and participate. Erza Majorova undressed the countess's lovely body and poured a thick green brew over it, while circling about, muttering incantations. When Elizabeth had been thoroughly doused, the witch divided the remaining brew in half, part for the magic cake, and part for the spirits of the river. She then made the dough, calling on the evil spirits to attack all those who stood against Elizabeth: the king, the Grand Palatine Thurzo, Councillor Megyery, and Justice Cziraky, judge of the high court. Elizabeth filled in the blanks on her precious parchment prayer.

The next night was Christmas Eve. The countess presided over a great banquet, looking her most beautiful and regal, wearing a black band on her forehead to symbolize the sadness of her widowhood. The guests ate and drank their fill—and those who ate the cake all got sick. But although she touted it to the king, Thurzo, and Megyery, they were all too suspicious of her to sample it.

As Elizabeth had suspected, this visit of these important figures to the castle was not for pleasure but for more serious matters. At the king's prompting, palatine Thurzo confronted Elizabeth with Pastor Berthoni's letter. The palatine's private secretary listened from the adjoining room, as a witness to their confrontation.

The palatine was faced with a delicate question. He could not countenance his cousin's terrible deeds, but he did not want a scandal that would blacken the Báthory and Nádasdy names and weaken the Protestant position in Hungary. He hoped to resolve the problem of his cousin's sadistic deeds discreetly. He showed her the letter in which she was accused of having killed the nine girls buried under the church.

"Mad lies!" Elizabeth screamed. "It's my enemies, to begin with Megyery the Red, who invented that horrid story."

Recovering herself, she explained that the old pastor had not known what he was talking about. There had been a dreadful disease running through the castle. That was all there was to the story.

The palatine Thurzo did not believe a word of what his cousin was saying. The rumors had spread throughout the country, he said.

"They're saying you tortured and killed several girls in particular, and worse, that you bathed in their blood to stop your growing old and to remain beautiful."

Indignantly, Elizabeth denied this, and the interview ended. But before the party at the castle broke up, the palatine Thurzo had arranged for all Elizabeth's relations to come to a family council at Presbourg when the parliament met. The problem of Elizabeth was getting out of hand and threatened them all.

The party over, the guests gone, Elizabeth gave herself up to gloomy forebodings. She was drained and distraught, and she needed amusement. She called in Jó Ilona and demanded that she find a serving girl who had committed some misdemeanor and bring her to the underground chamber within the hour.

The number of serving girls had diminished in recent weeks, but Jó Ilona discovered that a big blonde peasant named Doricza had stolen a pear from the banquet tables. That was crime enough for the punishment ahead. Jó Ilona brought Doricza to the cellar, where she was stripped and her arms tied. Elizabeth began by hitting the girl with a cane. She struck her a hundred times, while Jó Ilona was busy at the forge heating up pokers and red-hot coals. These were used next on the girl, until she fainted. Elizabeth was covered with blood, but she was not yet satisfied. She laughed and shrieked and demanded more girls. Jó Ilona went up to find them. Elizabeth stripped off her bloody dress and put on a fresh gown. Jó Ilona found two more girls and brought them down. They were treated to the same furious torture. The floor of the underground chamber was slippery with blood by the time Elizabeth tired of the excitement. She went upstairs to her apartments and changed clothes again, then prepared to leave the castle forever.

The members of parliament who had left the castle after the entertainments had not been idle. They had gone into the village and heard the complaints of the peasants of Csejthe. They discussed the dreadful doings of the countess in her castle. Now, it seemed, they had proof, not just rumors.

Palatine Thurzo knew that action had to be taken against his cousin;

what action he did not know. He was hoping that the family conclave he had called would help him resolve the problem. But the conclave was never held. While palatine Thurzo was pondering the question, he received an order from King Matthias to go immediately and see for himself what the situation really was within the Csejthe Castle walls. There was no time to warn Elizabeth, although out of family feeling he would have preferred to do so.

Knowing to what fury Elizabeth could rise, the palatine took with him a small delegation, including Pastor Ponikenus and a number of armed soldiers. When they reached the castle gate they found it unmanned. The castle still showed traces of the Christmas festivities, but there was no sign of Elizabeth in the great hall or in her apartments.

Accompanied by Pastor Ponikenus, the palatine descended to the cellar. By the staircase leading to Elizabeth's secret torture room they found the mutilated body of Doricza.

As they looked down in horror at the burned, shredded flesh, the breasts slashed open, one witness shuddered. "Even her own mother wouldn't have recognized her," he said.

Palatine Thurzo and the pastor went on. They found one naked girl lying on the stone floor, not yet dead. They found the other huddled in a corner. Then they found cells of girls who had been specially held in reserve for others of Elizabeth's pleasures. The girls told them they had been starved and forced to eat the cooked flesh of other dead girls.

Palatine Thurzo was aghast. He and the pastor raced up the stairs to the secret room, believing Elizabeth might be there. But Elizabeth had gone to another house on the estate, from which she was preparing to leave for Transylvania. They found her in her jewels and furs, ready to enter the coach.

On confrontation, Elizabeth showed no remorse or sense of guilt. She was full of fire, claiming that her nobility gave her the right to do as she pleased.

The palatine struggled to remain calm.

"Elizabeth," he said, "you are like a wild beast. . . . You don't deserve to breathe the air of this earth, nor to see the light of God; you are no longer worthy to belong to the human race. You are going to disappear from the world and you shall never return. Shadows will surround you for as long as you live to repent of this bestial life. May God forgive you for what you have done. Mistress of Csejthe, I condemn you to perpetual imprisonment in your own castle."

On his orders, Elizabeth was taken to the castle and placed in her private rooms, under guard.

Pastor Ponikenus, that godly man, went to see Elizabeth there, still hoping to make some sense of the tragedy. For his pains he received a tongue-lashing. "I have nothing to say to you," Elizabeth told him. I am your mistress. How could your questions, coming from one so low, so humble, reach me, who am so exalted?"

When Councillor Megyery learned of the palatine's decision to imprison Elizabeth for life instead of having her face trial, he was sure the king would disapprove, for in the search of the castle after her seizure a little notebook had been found that listed the names of 610 girls who had been tortured and killed. Was imprisonment enough punishment for taking 610 young lives? The king had the notebook. What would he think?

Palatine Thurzo was caught in a dreadful dilemma. He realized as well as anyone the gravity of Elizabeth's crimes. But it was his responsibility as a clansman to protect the Nádasdy and Báthory family names. He resisted all efforts to make him change his mind about her fate, and the king did not wish to provoke the Protestants at this point. So it was an impasse.

But the king could show his feelings in another way, by public trial of Elizabeth's accomplices. The trial was begun on January 2, 1611, in the market town of Bicse, near Csejthe Castle. Jó Ilona, Dorkó Szentes, Kateline Beniezky, and the ugly manservant Ficzkó faced the twenty judges. Thirty witnesses appeared, among them the mother who had come to the castle to find her daughter and had been imprisoned briefly there. The king's supporters demanded loudly that Elizabeth also be brought to stand trial, but Thurzo managed to avoid that. He also tried manfully to protect the Báthory name. When Elizabeth's part in the murders and bloodbaths was mentioned, he would object:

"There is no point to that," he would say. "It would simply delay matters, and I am anxious to have this affair over and done with as soon as possible."

So Ficzkó, Jó Ilona, Dorkó and Kateline had to go it alone. They were questioned by the judges, and they told the details of killing after killing. The palatine managed to keep Elizabeth's name out of the proceedings, except for one sentence that slipped through, charging that Elizabeth was a "bloodthirsty, blood-sucking Godless woman caught in the act at the Csejthe Castle."

That was enough to let Hungary know the truth.

As for the others, after a five-day trial, the judges found by their own confessions they were accomplices to "a guilt surpassing all evil and cruelty, that is murder, butcherings, and tortures most horrendous and assorted."

Then sentence was passed on each:

Jó Ilona and Dorottya Szentes were "as the foremost perpetrators of this great blood crime, and in accordance with the lawful punishment of murderers, to have all the fingers on their hands, which they used as instruments in so much torture and butcherings and which they dipped in the blood of Christians, torn out by the public executioner with a pair of red-hot pincers; thereafter they shall be thrown alive on the fire."

As to Ficzkó, "because of his youthful age and complicity in fewer crimes, him we sentence to decapitation. His body, drained of blood, should then be reunited with his two fellow accomplices where we wish that he should be burned."

Jó Ilona and Dorkó had claimed that Kateline had no part in any of the actual killings, so the judges felt they could not sentence her on Ficzkó's testimony that she had killed. She was sent to jail pending further investigation.

The court lost no time in carrying out the sentences at public execution. Jó Ilona fainted when her fourth finger was torn off; she was taken to the bonfire without further ado. Dorkó fainted when she saw Jó Ilona tied to the stake; she was taken to join her. The executioner obviously had no taste for the torture portion of the sentences. Ficzko's head was chopped off with a swoop of the executioner's sword, and his body was put on the fire with those of the other two.

As Councillor Megyery had predicted, the king was anything but satisfied with Palatine Thurzo's sentence for Elizabeth, He wrote that she should be tried and executed. Thurzo replied that she deserved more consideration because she was "the widow of a soldier, noble and of illustrious family, and that her name, one of the oldest in Hungary, ought to be spared."

He was joined by other members of the family. Son-in-law Miklos Zrinyi pleaded that a public trial would bring disgrace to all the family. Elizabeth's son, Pal Nádasdy, begged that his mother be saved from punishment she deserved in accordance with the law. Finally, the king was persuaded that nothing was to be gained by dragging the Nádasdy and Báthory names in the mud by a public trial. He agreed to the palatine's sentence of "imprisonment in perpetuity."

But if Elizabeth believed she had gotten off with a sentence to remain in her apartments in the castle for the rest of her life, she was in for a surprise. The palatine had meant precisely what he said: "you don't deserve to breathe the air of this earth, nor to see the light of God; you are no longer worthy to belong to the human race. You are going to disappear from the world and you shall never return." Putting her under house arrest had been merely a stopgap, while waiting for the outcome of the discussion between king and palatine.

Once the sentence was agreed upon, the palatine sent masons to the castle, and they walled up the windows and doors of Elizabeth's bedroom. She would no longer "breathe the air of this earth"—only the stale air of the castle. They left only a narrow slit through which food could be passed to the condemned woman. "Nor to see the light of God . . ." They erected gibbets at the four corners of the castle, so all the world would know that justice had been done to the woman walled up inside, and would stay away from the castle. "You are no longer worthy to belong to the human race . . ."

Having carried out the spirit and the letter of the palatine's sentence, the masons went away.

Countess Elizabeth Báthory, who had killed more than six hundred serving girls, was left alone, in the dark—"shadows will surround you for as long as you live"—and at the mercy of her serving girls. For a woman of her intellect and vivacity, the palatine's sentence was worse than death. It was—appropriately—torture.

The countess was 50 years old when the sentence was passed. She lingered in the darkness for another three and a half years—"to repent of this bestial life"? On August 21, 1614, she died. As the palatine's secretary noted in his journal, Elizabeth "has gone to appear before the Supreme Judge. She died towards nightfall, abandoned by all."

9

THE COMING OF THE NIGHTSTALKER

BEGINNING IN THE SEVENTEENTH century, the form of the vampire we know best began to take shape. That was the vampire as the "un-dead," the animated corpse that preys upon the living, usually by night, seeking blood to continue its existence. This concept spread across Europe, and prominent writers and men of authority began to write about the vampire as a real being.

In 1653, an English publisher brought out Henry More's history of vampires, which was considered an authoritative work. The title was *An Appeal to the Natural Faculties of the Mind of Man, whether there be not a God.* For contemporary England, the most important aspect of this work was More's contention that any person who committed suicide had to be regarded as a vampire.

Witness the following: It is September 20, 1591. The place is Silesia, in Poland. This morning, to the horror of his family, a shoemaker cut his throat and died. Since the church took a dim view of suicide, "to cover the foulness of the fact" his widow declared that her husband had died of apoplexy. He was dressed in his finest clothes with a high collar to conceal the truth, laid out properly, and given a Christian burial as if nothing untoward had occurred.

But after the body was buried, people began to say they had seen the shoemaker walking the roads in his burial clothes. Some saw him in the daytime, some at night. The whole village was frightened. Then matters grew worse: friends reported that he had attacked them, nearly suffocating them to death. Rumors began to circulate to the effect that the dead man must have "laid violent hands upon himself," that the Devil had his soul and he had been turned into a vampire. The widow and her friends gave public testimony and made protests, trying to preserve the secret. That worked for a few months. But the corpse continued to appear. After several citizens told new horror stories about confrontations with the body, the townspeople became so terrified that they huddled over candle-lit tables during the night instead of going to bed. Soon so many people were involved—and were making all sorts of threats, including desertion of the town—that the local magistrate finally decided he had to take action. He called a town meeting at which it was agreed that the body should be dug up. It was done under the supervision of the magistrate.

By that time nearly eight months had passed since the shoemaker had been buried, but when they brought up the body they found it "entire, not at all putrid, no ill smell about him . . . his joints limber and flexible, as those that are alive, his skin only flaccid . . . the wound of his throat gaping."

There was the proof of the suicide.

The religious and civil authorities took all the proper precautions. Prayers were said over the corpse, and it was laid out for six days so that all the townspeople could come and see it. Then it was reburied.

But did the specter stop its wanderings? Not at all. The shoemaker's corpse came out night after night to plague the living man's old friends and even the widow. Finally she became distraught and went to the authorities. She asked them to take any action they wished, but for God's sake to stop the marauding of her husband's corpse.

The body was dug up again. This time the officials took more severe measures to make sure there would be no recurrence of the horrors.

> They . . . cut off the Head, Arms, and Legs of the Corpse, and opening his Back, took out his Heart, which was as fresh and Intire as a Calf new-killed. These, together with his body, they put on a pile of wood, together, and burnt them to Ashes, which they carefully sweeping together, and putting in a Sack (that none might get them for Wicked uses) poured them into the River, after which the Spectrum was never seen more.

At the end of the seventeenth century, the reports of corpses rising from the grave and visiting the living increased enormously, in Hungary, Czechoslovakia, and Greece. Time after time, the "dead" would reappear, with disastrous results for those who saw them. Almost always, those poor people died shortly after seeing the un-dead.

Many such reports came in from bishops and priests, particularly in Moravia in what is now Czechoslovakia. So disturbed was the Moravian hierarchy that a representative was sent to Rome to secure assistance from the Holy See. But the Vatican dismissed the reports as imaginary and refused to take any official cognizance of this surge of vampirism.

Meanwhile, the Greek Orthodox Church was taking a far more serious interest in the phenomenon of the un-dead. In 1695, the priest Leo Allatius wrote a treatise on the *vrykolakes,* and the position of the Greek Orthodox Church in relation to these creatures. The Church was so concerned about the possibility of a soul's being lost to vampirism that the authorities insisted that all bodies be dug up after three years. If a "drumlike" body was found, then that dead person had obviously become a *vrykolakas* and was now activated by the Devil, who sent the poor corpse about its diabolical deeds.

The church had even issued a *nomocanon* (decree of church law) on the subject:

> If a dead person is found whole and incorrupt it is a *Vrykolakas*:
> It is impossible that a dead man become a *Vrykolakas,* save it be that the Devil, wishing to delude some that they may do things unmeet and incur the wrath of God maketh these portents.

But the Greek hierarchy also deplored the hysteria that was sweeping the villages. When faced with a report that a dead person had turned into a *vrykolakas,* the villagers all too often rushed to dig up the body, and finding that it "appears to them to have flesh and blood and nails and hair . . . they collect wood and set fire to it and burn the body and do away with it altogether."

Instead of acting with such unseemly haste, the church officials advised, the peasants would do much better to involve the church. "When such remains be found, ye must summon the priests to chant an invocation of the Mother of God . . . and to perform memorial services for the dead."

In Leo Allatius's own opinion, the people were not so far wrong. He advocated that the peasants should burn suspect bodies but that the burnings be accompanied by prayers.

The church itself was largely responsible for the panic about vampires, through its process of excommunicating religious deviates. At the end of the service of excommunication, the priest always gave the following curse: "and after death to remain indissoluble." Thus, when the villagers dug up a body and found it virtually undecayed, did they not have the words of the priests themselves to show them they had come upon a *vrykolakas*?

Actually Church and the Slavic influence from the north worked together on the Greeks to bring about this sudden influx of fear. For in the past the Greeks had believed that the *vrykolakas* was not necessarily a creature of evil but might be merely an unfortunate. The un-dead might be merely an "uncorrupt body" that might remain in the grave forever, doing no harm. Sometimes these un-dead were miraculously resuscitated and came back to take their places among the living and lead normal lives. Sometimes they came out of their graves to help friends and relatives and then went back to the grave.

But with the infusion of Slavic influence the notion of the benign *vrykolakas* disappeared. Father François Richard, a Jesuit priest who lived on the island of Santorini, reported on the case of a local shoe-maker who turned into a *vrykolakas* after death. He came out of the grave and went home to his house, not once but many times. He continued to mend his children's shoes. He drew water at the reservoir and carried it to the house. He cut wood for the family's use. He was in every way the epitome of the "good" *vrykolakas*. Had he lived and died a century earlier no one would have bothered the grave. But in the changing view of the times, the good work made no difference, and his body was dug up and burned by fellow villagers.

Another case of a "friendly vampire" was that of a man who worked for a farmer, to whom he was devoted. When the farmhand died, he was so concerned about the farmer's welfare that he came out of his grave at night and continued to work the farm. He would "take out the oxen from the stall, yoke them, and plough three acres while his master slept."

Poor good-hearted vampire! As the farmer continued to work the land by day and the vampire by night, his jealous neighbors became aware that the farmer was outproducing them two to one. They could not understand how he got so much done. They questioned the farmer, but he could not explain to their satisfaction why his farm was the most productive in the area. So the neighbors took up a secret watch on the farm, and, sure enough, one night they spotted the *vrykolakas,* working hard.

The next day the neighbors trooped to the graveyard and dug up the body. There it was—whole—as if buried the day before. They took the body out and burned it to cinders. That was the end of the farm's unnaturally high productivity.

The influence of Slavic culture coming down through Macedonia turned every *vrykolakas* into a "wanton and bloodthirsty" vampire, although the Greeks never did adopt the Slavic name *vampyr*. The *vrykolakes* became objects of horror.

This change in attitude also became an embarrassment to Church authorities. That final excommunication curse, consigning the body forever to the realm of the un-dead, meant the church was creating vampires. Lamely, the priests began to tell the people that just because a body assumed that drumlike aspect did not necessarily mean it would be reanimated. But the priests could not have it both ways; having summoned up the monster, they had to live with it. The Church persuaded the government to pass laws against the digging up and burning of bodies, but the peasants ignored the laws and the haranguing of the priests and continued to dig up the *vrykolakes* anyhow.

In 1700, the French botanist Joseph Pitton de Tournefort visited the Greek islands and a few years later published an eyewitness account of the treatment and cremation of a *vrykolakas*. By this time the Slavic influence was all-pervasive, and the Greeks had come to believe that any person who died violently was potentially a vampire. The subject of the Tournefort story was a peasant on the island of Myconos. One day his body was found in a lonely part of the island. It was obvious that he had been murdered, although no one knew who had killed him. After a funeral service in the local chapel, the body was buried there in the Christian manner. Two nights later, it was out of the grave, entering the houses of its former neighbors, blowing out candles, knocking furniture about, and assaulting people. Or that was what the neighbors said.

At first the educated people of the island scoffed at the reports. But then, one night, a highly respectable citizen was attacked, and their view changed. Even the priests began to say that the murdered man's corpse was prowling the town. The churchmen and the leading citizens held a meeting to decide what course to pursue. On the tenth day after the burial, "a solemn mass was sung in the chapel where the body lay in order to appeal to the demon" who, as they believed, had taken possession of it. The body was exhumed after the mass, and soon everything was ready for the heart to be torn out as had become the custom.

"The town flesher, an old and clumsy-fisted fellow, began by ripping open the belly instead of the breast; he groped a good while amongst the entrails without finding what he sought, and then at last somebody informed him that he must dissever the diaphragm. So the heart was finally extracted . . . but the carrion now stank so foully that they were obliged to burn a large quantity of frankincense." The odors and the horror of the mutilation of the corpse combined with the general air of excitement to arouse the peasant's imaginations. Seeing the smoke from the incense, one said it was coming from the body itself.

"*Vroucolacas,*" one person muttered, and the cry was taken up by the others present. Soon the streets were echoing with the cry "*vroucolacas, vroucolacas.*"

One eyewitness said the blood of the dead man was a rich red; the flesher said the body was still warm. The peasants began to murmur that the dead man ought to be ashamed for not being really dead, letting his "body be reanimated by the Devil, for this is the true idea they have of a *vroucolacas.*"

It was obviously "a most malignant *vroucolacas.* One could hear nothing but that word repeated over and over again," Tournefort said. "I am very certain that if we ourselves had not been actually present these folk would have maintained that there was no stench of corruption, to such an extent were the poor people terrified and amazed and obsessed with the idea that dead men are able to return . . . we were retching and well nigh overcome by the stench of the rotting corpse."

Tournefort and his companions tried to explain to the peasants that the dead man was in fact dead and that it was not unusual for gases to rise, and the flesher was not feeling "bright red blood" but rather "foul-smelling clots of filth and gore!" But it was no use: the peasants were too carried away. They took the heart to the seashore and burned it.

Alas, even that did not stop the nightly visitations of the dead peasant. The corpse, said the villagers, walked again.

"All the people were scared out of their wits and the wisest and best among them were just as terrorized as the rest. It was an epidemic disorder of the brain, as dangerous as a mania or as sheer lunacy. Whole families left their houses and from the furthest suburbs of the town brought little tent-beds and pallets into the public square, in order to pass the night in the open. Each moment somebody was complaining of some fresh vexation or assault; when night fell nothing was to be heard but cries and groans; the better sort of people withdrew into the country."

Tournefort and his group did not speak out; they did not want to be considered fools or "godless atheists" by the peasants. They heard more and more tales of the dead man, each more excited than the last. The village council held meetings, priests fasted and washed the doors of the houses with holy water. The peasants dug up the body three or four times a day to look at the *vroucolacas*; they chanted prayers and they pierced the body with swords. Then one day the rumor started that the only way to get rid of the Devil in the man was to burn the *vroucolacas*. Since the fright had become so general and a number of important townspeople were packing their goods and preparing to leave town, the magistrates decided that this suggestion was a good one.

They ordered the body taken to the island of St. George and burned. It was done. A huge pyre was built there and lit. When the flames rose high, the dead man's carcass was thrown on the fire. Tournefort and his party saw the flames as they sailed past the island, on their way back to France. It was January 1, 1701.

No churchman attended the cremation for fear that the Bishop of Tenos would hear about it and they would be fined for allowing the body to be dug up and burned without his express sanction. But at least now the "dread and the abomination of the whole countryside" was gone.

So the superstitions of the Greeks about vampires evolved in the Slavic manner. Even today, in some areas of Greece, these beliefs persist. Rarer, today, are the scenes of a body being dragged from the grave and dismembered by a panic-stricken mob, the heart torn out and boiled to shreds in vinegar, or the ghastly remains burned on a bonfire. Still, scarcely a year passes in Greece that some village does not deal in the traditional manner with a suspected *vrykolakas*.

Superstitions also flourished unabated north of Greece, in the heart of the mountain country, the domain of the *vampyr*, despite discouragement by the Church at Rome.

So many were the "apparitions" that appeared in this region, that in 1706 Charles Ferdinand de Schertz published *Magia posthuma*, a study of the reanimation of the dead. The work was written in all seriousness and dedicated to the Bishop of Olmutz.

Schertz cited case after case of men and women of the mountainous districts of Silesia and Moravia who had emerged from the grave to attack people. Sometimes the peasants died of fright. Sometimes the corpses seized them by the throat. After such encounters with the "dead," the victims seemed to grow pale and become feeble. Sometimes they died a few days after seeing the specter. The answer was to deal with the specters. Schertz told how they did in one case:

A herdsman of the village of Blau in Bohemia died and was buried. A little while later the corpse was seen walking around at night, attacking people. The villagers dug up the body and drove a stake through the heart, then reburied it. But the herdsman came out again that night and attacked and suffocated more people. The next morning the villagers were frantic. They dug up the body again. It was "bloated and swollen, yelled like a madman, kicking and tearing as if it had been alive, and when they pierced it with sharpened pikes of whitethorn it howled terribly, writhing and champing its blub red lips with the long white teeth whilst streams of warm red blood spurted out in all directions."

The body was handed over to the common executioner, who took it outside the village and, after a pyre was built and flaming, threw the body on it and burned it until only ashes were left. The visitations of the herdsman were over.

Schertz recounted many cases in which the villagers took matters into their own hands, and he backed up his own observations with substantiating quotations from several people regarded as the authorities of the day. This he followed with an outline of procedures to be followed in dealing with the un-dead:

The only way to still forever a troublesome corpse was to dig up the body, cut off the head, and burn the corpse. But this must be done only in an "official manner." Villagers must not panic and take hasty action; first an official inquiry must be held, witnesses must be summoned and questioned, and medical men and theologians must be called to examine the body and check for the attributes of vampirism. Only when all these procedures had been followed and it was determined that the corpse was indeed the one that had been attacking the living, could the body be turned over to an official executioner, who would burn it.

The number of vampire cases in the seventeenth century seemed to increase constantly. By the eighteenth century, scores of learned men were writing dissertations on the subject, such as *Relation von den Vampyren oder Menschensaugern* (The Relationship Among Vampires or Bloodsucking), *Nachricht von denen Vampyren oder sogennanten Blut-Saugern* (An Account of Vampires or So-Called Blood-sucking), *Der Hungarischen Vampyre* (The Hungarian Vampire), *Von Vampyren* (About Vampires). Many of these were published at Leipzig.

As reading and writing spread, these learned tracts became the basis for more popular writings, and stories about vampires circulated widely around Europe.

The belief in vampires was often fostered by official actions. In 1730 the Count de Cadreras published a report of events in a small village near the Hungarian border that had caused an official uproar. A man who had been dead for thirty years was reported to have come out of the grave three times during that period. Each time he came at the supper hour, and each time he sprang upon some person "whose neck he bit fiercely, sucking the blood, and then vanishing with indescribable celerity."

The first victim had been the corpse's brother, who died instantly from the attack. The second time he attacked one of his sons, who also died quickly. The third time, one of the servants on the farm was the victim, and he also died. After that last occasion, the people of the village were so aroused they called on the authorities for help. Officials authorized the digging up of the body, and it was done. The corpse was like many others that had been disinterred in that district in recent years: when a cut was made in the body, red blood rushed out, as if the man were alive. "Orders were given that a great twopenny nail should be driven through the temples," and after that was done the body was put back into the grave where it had been (in and out) for thirty years.

Another singular report emanated from Belgrade. There, two officers of the tribunal of Belgrade and an officer in command of the Imperial Hapsburg army forces stationed at Gradiska investigated the case of a farmer, one Peter Plogojowitz, who, said the people of the village of Kisilova, had become a vampire and had caused the death of nine persons in a single week. Under the supervision of these authorities, the graves of Plogojowitz and his alleged victims were opened. When the diggers came to the body of Plogojowitz, they found that body was not a corpse, but that it "was gently breathing, his eyes wide open and glaring horribly, his complexion ruddy, the flesh plump and full . . . his mouth was all slobbered and stained with fresh blood." The authorities decided that the farmer must be a vampire. The executioner was called to drive a stake through its heart. When this was done, blood gushed out, further indication of vampirism, of course. The bodies of the vampire's victims were restored to their coffins, and garlic and whitethorn were put in with them to protect the people in case the dead had been infected with vampirism. The garlic would freeze their souls, and the whitethorn would prevent them from moving. The corpse of Peter Plogojowitz was taken outside the village area and burned, and the ashes scattered. The village was not bothered thereafter by the vampire or its victims.

As the eighteenth century wore on, a plethora of vampire stories coursed through central Europe. A committee of three army surgeons from Belgrade investigated a number of vampire cases in the winter of 1731-32. Their report found the cases to be all of a pattern: when the corpse of a vampire was dug up, it bore the traits unusually attributed to these creatures—ruddy complexion, hot blood pouring from the body when a stake was driven in. These reports fanned the fires of vampirism in central Europe, and the tales, passed by word of mouth and by publication, spread throughout the Western world. By the end of the eighteenth century, the belief that vampires were real was general in Europe.

10

THE MONK'S INVESTIGATION

AS A RESULT OF ALL THE STORIES OF vampire activity, the early years of the eighteenth century saw vampirism terrifying Prussia, Silesia, Bohemia, and much of northern Europe. The most notable case of all occurred in Austria in 1731, an affair given credibility and importance by the behavior of the Austrian authorities and the aftermath.

In 1726, in the village of Medwegya, a farmer named Arnold Paole fell off a haystack, broke his neck, and died. The accident was cause for concern; but his fellow villagers were more than concerned, they were alarmed. For Arnold Paole had been known to boast that, years earlier, he had been bitten by a vampire near Cossowa in Persia. He always said he had cured himself. He liked to tell how he had eaten earth from the tomb of the vampire and rubbed himself with the blood of the vampire. While Paole was alive his tales were taken with a dose of salt; but after his death, his neighbors suddenly had a chilling thought. What if Paole's cure had not worked? The bite of a vampire, as everyone knew, was certain to turn the victim into a vampire after his own death, unless the effects had been exorcised.

The villagers were half-sure that Paole would come back as a vampire; and, indeed, in the next thirty days, four villagers died under circumstances declared suspicious by their fellows. The village was aroused, certain that all the trouble was caused by the vampire Paole.

The bailiff of the village ordered the body dug up. When this was done, the corpse was found to be the traditional vampire corpse: ruddy-skinned, with blood trickling from a corner of the mouth, fingernails, beard, and hair still growing. As a stake was driven through the heart, a "hideous cry" (escaping gas?) was heard from the body and blood spurted. The body was then reburied.

Paole's four "victims," presumed also to be vampires now, were treated in the same way.

As noted, all this occurred in 1726. For the next four years, the village of Medwegya prospered, but in 1731 a rash of incidents began to trouble the villagers once more. In three months, seventeen villagers died violently. Seeking some reason, the village elders concluded that only a vampire could have caused all these deaths, and the only vampires known to the village were those of Paole and his victims. When their conclusion was spread about, the whole village went into hysteria, and normal life simply came to a halt. The farmers charged that the vampires had been attacking cattle as well. And it was well known that any person who ate meat from an animal attacked by a vampire, became a vampire. Consequently, the people of Medwegya were beside themselves. No family trusted any other; every accident to any person or animal was now attributed to vampires; slaughtered cattle were left to rot, and the whole social structure of the village was in disarray.

The hysteria began to spread to neighboring districts and caused so much concern to the central authorities that they sent the army in to investigate. On December 12, 1731, Dr. Johannes Fluckinger, a regimental field surgeon, came to Medwegya with a company of foot soldiers to conduct a public inquiry.

The surgeon questioned all the villagers. He learned that they believed Paole had not only killed or caused those seventeen people to be killed, but that vampires were responsible for all the ills they suffered. They would not be convinced otherwise, so all the bodies the villagers believed to be affected were dug up. Those that had turned to dust were reburied without concern. Those that had not decomposed properly were given the vampire treatment: heads cut off, bodies burned, ashes scattered.

The village of Medwegya returned to normal for a time, but a few years later it became a celebrated place, visited by vampire hunters. The reason was that the story of Medwegya's vampires was picked up from the official Austrian reports by a popular magazine, and that publication stirred a score of other magazines in a dozen countries to print the tale. Intellectuals became interested, and the study of vampirism spread.

Theories and speculations were the order of the day. Finally, the French monk and Biblical scholar, Dom Augustin Calmet began to study the matter. For years he collected vampire cases like the Paole case, and in 1746 he published the "authoritative" work on vampires of Hungary and Moravia. The work was given great momentum because it was written by a churchman from a Christian point of view. That was the reason for his investigation, Dom Calmet said. In the interests of the Church, he wanted to determine if vampires were real. If so, he must state the truth. If not, the lies had to be refuted and exposed as superstition.

Within weeks, Dom Calmet's tome was a "best-seller," but a most controversial one. Some critics scorned Dom Calmet's findings, some praised his work, some tried to refute him point by point.

Calmet's book was based on hundreds of reports of vampires. "Dead men who have been dead for several months . . . return from the tomb, are heard to speak, walk about, infest hamlets and villages, injure both men and animals, whose blood they drain, thereby making them sick and ill, and at length actually causing death."

Dom Calmet adopted the approach of reason in surveying his subject. First of all, he addressed himself to the matter of the corpse leaving its grave. Could a corpse make its way out of shroud or coffin, through four or five feet of earth, get up and walk around, and then get back into the grave where it would be found whole, not decayed, and full of blood like the living? Or was it the ghost of the corpse that appeared to the living, and if so what energized these ghosts? Was it actually the soul of the dead man or was it a demon "who causes them to be seen in an assumed and phantastical body?" And if the "bodies are spectral, how do they suck the blood of the living?" These were knotty questions. "We are enmeshed in a sad dilemma when we ask if these apparitions are natural or miraculous," wrote Dom Calmet.

Pursuing his studies, the monk turned to the case of a vampire from the village of Liebava, Moravia, reported by a priest "who is recognized as possessing intellectual qualities far beyond the ordinary." This priest had accompanied Monsignor Jeanin, Canon of the Cathedral of Olmutz, on an official Church investigation of the "many well-authenticated reports" concerning a vampire that was causing much trouble in Liebava. The two churchmen had set up in the village and taken testimony from witnesses.

Citizen after citizen told of the prominent villager who had turned into a vampire after he died and plagued the people. This had been going on for four years, they said, when a visiting Hungarian boasted that he knew how to deal with vampires. He could "lay the vampire to rest," he said, but first he had to see it. The villagers engaged him to take on the vampire. His first move was to enlist the sexton of the church to help him. The sexton was to lie in wait with a weapon, at the base of the clock tower, but not to show himself until signaled. The Hungarian would go up into the tower to await sight of the vampire.

As evening came, the two men got into position to await the vampire. Their vigil lasted for several hours before the Hungarian saw the vampire come out of its grave in the cemetery, leaving its shroud behind. The vampire set off in the direction of the village, where the Hungarian was sure it was going to terrify the inhabitants once more.

The Hungarian ran down the stairs of the clock tower, over to the vampire's grave, and snatched up the abandoned shroud. He then went back to the top of the clock tower and waited. Shortly before dawn, the corpse came back to the grave and began moving about, obviously looking for its shroud. When it could not find the shroud, it began to become hysterical and shriek. The Hungarian called out then, taunting the vampire and telling it to come up to the clock tower if it wanted its shroud. The angry vampire ran to the clock tower and started to climb the stairs, but the Hungarian gave it a nasty blow, which sent it tumbling down to the ground. The sexton was waiting there with a sharpened spade. He cut off the head of the vampire, and that was the end of it.

The priest who had told this story to Dom Calmet was not a witness himself to these events, but only to the Church investigation.

Dom Calmet was not convinced. The report of these events he said was typical of the "reports of peasants of that district, a folk who were very ignorant, very credulous, very superstitious, and brimful of all kinds of wonderful stories concerning the aforesaid Vampire."

"For my part," Dom Calmet continued, "I think the whole history vain and utterly without foundation, and the more absurd and contradictory are the various tales which were told, the more strongly am I confirmed in the opinion which I have formed."

But that was only one set of circumstances, not conclusive about vampires in general. Dom Calmet continued his studies. If the apparitions that seemed to appear to people were indeed true apparitions, did they get their power from God or from the Devil, and if from the Devil, how could the Devil make the body come from the grave and pass through earth, doors, and windows? That problem would have to wait.

Dom Calmet turned his attention to the "ruddy and lifelike" quality of the dead bodies that were exhumed on suspicion of vampirism.

"The redness and fluidity of the vampires' blood and the pliability of their limbs are nothing extraordinary," he decided, "nor are the growth of their nails and hair and the failure of their flesh to decay." He knew that such phenomena could occur after a very sudden death without illness, or after certain fatal illnesses. The doctors attested to that. As for the continued growth of hair and nails, these were quite natural.

One logical explanation for some vampire cases was premature burial. "It suffices to explain why vampires have been dragged from the grave and made to speak, shout, scream, and bleed: they were still alive. They were killed by decapitation, perforation or burning . . . innocent beings . . . killed as a result of wild and unproved accusations . . . for the stories told of the apparitions . . . are totally without solid proof."

He lamented the general ignorance of the public on the subject of premature burial and the failure of the authorities of France, in particular, to deal sensibly with the subject. "I am not surprised that the Sorbonne [university doctors] has condemned the bloody and violent retribution wrought on these corpses, but it is astonishing that the magistrates and secular bodies have not employed their authority and legal force to put an end to it."

Calmet dealt with hundreds of cases, some of which he summarized, some of which he only mentioned. In the end, he concluded:

"The particulars which are related are so singular, so detailed, accompanied with circumstances so probable and so likely as well as with the most weighty and well-attested legal depositions that it seems impossible not to subscribe to the belief which prevails in these countries that these apparitions actually do come forth from their graves and that they are able to produce the terrible effects which are so widely and so positively attributed to them."

But he continued to hold his skepticism regarding such cases as that at Liebava.

"This is," he said, "a mysterious and difficult matter, and I leave bolder and more proficient minds to resolve it."

So, in essence, after years of study, Dom Calmet had concluded nothing at all, leaving his readers with a mass of material to digest and evaluate for themselves. He said that by writing his treatise he was laying himself open to criticism from both sides, from those who would flail him for presuming to cast doubt on the authenticity of some of these vampire cases, and from those who would claim he was wasting his time by writing on a frivolous subject.

The good monk never spoke a truer word. His treatise on vampires did elicit a stormy response. The leaders of some of the religious orders scolded Dom Calmet for demeaning himself. Sneeringly, his critics called his vampire tales "bedtime horror stories."

Voltaire called Dom Calmet a "naïve compiler of so many reveries and imbecilities." The French Academy's *Encyclopédie,* the acknowledged font of French knowledge, scoffed at Dom Calmet's study as beneath consideration. But the fact was that Dom Calmet's study of vampirism was the first to take a critical view of the subject, that is, to attempt to rationalize the vampire tales within the sphere of human knowledge and the Christian religion.

In stirring up the intellectual community, Dom Calmet performed more of a service, perhaps, than he had contemplated. In the spring of 1755, the Empress Maria Theresa of Austria sponsored legislation in parliament to fight the growing number of cases of "so-called vampires and posthumous magic." Her action created another big stir in philosophical circles. A stir meant discussion, and discussion meant further inquiry. Some blamed vampirism on disease. The Archbishop of Trania made his own inquiry into the subject, asking, "why is this demon so partial to baseborn plebeians? Why is it always peasants, carters, shoemakers, and innkeepers? Why has the demon never been known to assume the form of a man of quality, a scholar, a philosopher, a theologian, a magnate or a bishop? I will tell you why: learned men and men of quality are not so easily deceived as idiots and men of low birth and therefore do not so easily allow themselves to be taken in by appearances."

If the archbishop was showing a good deal less apostolic charity than might be expected, still his point of view reflected that of the educated men of the times. Small good it did them, for the criticism of the common people as idiots and men of low birth did nothing to allay their fears or to stop the growing belief in the existence of vampires that continued to spread across Europe.

11

THE INSCRUTABLE VAMPIRES

THE SPREAD OF VAMPIRES WAS NOT CONFINED to Europe. The Middle East and Asia had their own bloodsucking demons, as noted. During the middle of the eighteenth century, there was a renewal of vampirism in China. Here is a tale that was well known throughout the Middle Kingdom in those days.

It had been a very hot day in the city, and Su Hsieng-sen was washing himself to cool off before he went to bed. The light of the moon sent a few stray rays through the window. As Su was washing, he became aware of the sound of breathing other than his own quite nearby. He stopped and listened. The breathing grew louder, and a light mist floated into the room. Su got into bed. At that moment, a feather duster lying on a table in the room stood up and began turning around and around with no apparent motivation.

Su rapped sharply on the bedstead and told the feather duster to stop the nonsense. Just then his bath towel and his teacup got up and flew out the window, and he heard the crack of the cup as it broke against the trunk of a tree in the garden.

Su was thoroughly alarmed. What evil spirit was this? Was it a vampire, come to sap his blood and make him wither and wane? He got up from his bed and rushed to the servants' quarters to alarm them. Then all the household went into the garden where the cup had flown. They saw "a black shadow which shrouded the roof of the house," but that was all. They searched the garden, but saw nothing more.

Relieved, Su and his servants went back into the house, and Su returned to his room. As he sat down on the side of his bed, "the feather duster begain turning around again." Su jumped up and seized it. It felt like wet hair, it was as cold as ice, and it exuded a terrible odor. His arm grew numb from the cold but he did not let go. Then he heard a voice, harsh as the cry of a parrot.

"I am Wu Chung," said the voice. "I come from Lake Hung Chai, from which the Spirit of Thunder has banished me. Let me go."

Su would not let go. He was not taken in by this tale of the Spirit of Thunder. He knew that the district of Lake Hung Chai was suffering from a dreadful epidemic of fever in which thousands of people were dying. He spoke sharply to the feather duster.

"Are you not more likely to be the spirit of the plague?" he asked.

Reluctantly, the voice admitted that this was so. It was a vampire. On learning this, Su was determined not to let the vampire go, for then the creature would destroy more people, perhaps even Su himself.

The voice continued to plead for freedom and finally offered to give Su a remedy for the plague that had visited Lake Hung Chai. Su wrote down the words spoken by the voice.

All the commotion had roused the servants again, and they came into the room to see what was happening. They warned Su not to let the vampire go. Instead, they said, "Let us imprison it in a jar."

So Su put the feather duster into a porcelain jar and the servants brought wax and sealed it up. They took the jar to Lake T'ai and flung it far out into the waters, where it sank. Su then distributed the charm he had been given, and in every instance of a sick person it was successful.

This spirit encountered by Master Su was obviously a *po,* one of the lower evil spirits that the Chinese believed could turn into misty vampires to destroy the living. The *po* was powerful enough to take different forms, and it could survive in even a part of a dead body. Many *pos* were known to live in the skulls of the dead, and these were every bit as vicious and blood-animated as the European vampires.

Take the story of the young men who were taking a walk one night near the Hsi Ch'ia lake. After strolling aimlessly for a time, they sat down for a rest. One of them brought out a jar of pickled plums for refreshment. They spotted a skull lying on the ground nearby, and feeling sprightly, they thought it would be a pretty funny trick to stuff the plum stones into the mouth of the skull. They did so, laughing, and then one of them asked the skull if it thought they tasted salty.

They wandered away, thinking nothing more of the incident, strolling slowly homeward through the moonlight. Then they heard a noise and looking back saw the skull rolling toward them calling out "salty, salty."

They all took to their heels and ran about six *li* to the nearest canal, where they hailed a boatman and were taken aboard. The boat drew away from the shore and they were safe from the vampire, which could not cross water.

Here is a more ghoulish tale from eighteenth-century China:

Two young men who were traveling together stopped for the night at a pavilion beside a lake, because the spot had a beautiful view of water and the nearby mountains. They were awakened in the middle of the night by the sounds of singing. They roused themselves to see who was there and finally made out the form of a woman. She was no ordinary woman, they could tell, for she was wearing an ancient costume.

"A ghost," said one young man and would have gone away.

"Ah," said the other, "but if a ghost, a very pretty one." And he was brave enough to call out to the woman outside the pavilion, "Why don't you come in?"

To his surprise, a female voice answered, "Why don't you come out?"

The young men decided to go out. They went into the darkness, but saw no one. They called out. A voice answered, this time from the trees. They looked around them, and suddenly they saw a woman's head hanging down from a tree. They both cried out in terror, knowing a vampire was near, and began to run. The head pursued them. They ran back into the pavilion and barred the door. The head came up by leaps and bounds and crashed against the door. They held the door fast. The head began gnawing at the threshold, and they could hear the wood splintering. But then a cock crowed, and the first rays of the sun appeared on the lake. The head rolled down the slope and disappeared into the water, and the young men were saved. But they were so upset after this experience with the vampire that they both fell ill and were sick for a month.

Folklorists have tried to trace the origins of the Chinese belief in vampires, but they say it goes back so far that they can only guess. One folklorist, G. Willoughby-Meade, suggests that Chinese vampirism is peculiarly associated with religious beliefs. The Chinese believe that the dead carry over into the next life the loves and hates of their life on earth. That is one factor. Another is the concept of "karma." Willoughby-Meade asserts that in Buddhist karma "ghosts undergoing the Buddhist purgatory of hunger and penury may well be imagined as seizing and devouring living bodies to refresh themselves with blood." Buddhism, he says, accepts the belief in monsters as an automatic outcome of karma. Perhaps. Many Buddhists would protest this concept.

Another suggestion was that Chinese belief in vampires originated with fear of fever. China has long been a haven for the anopheles mosquito, which carries malaria. It was no trick for anyone to observe a mosquito drinking blood from a human arm and then noting the coming of sickness to the one bitten. Sometimes people died from the malarial fever, sometimes they became anemic. So the Chinese tended to put two and two together. Willoughby-Meade suggests that the centuries-old belief of Chinese villagers in vampires is due to the "credulous, imaginative nature of the Chinese. A belief in Vampires is not so surprising as it might be in other countries," he said.

Willoughby-Meade obviously knew a lot more about China than he did about eastern Europe, where people were not an iota less "credulous."

12

HOME OF THE MODERN VAMPIRE

GENERALLY SPEAKING, THE MODERN concept of the vampire originates from beliefs of central Europe. Bulgaria, alone among the states of this region, has a slightly different tradition. For hundreds of years the Bulgarians have held that a vampire can be detected in its first stages by the sparks it gives off in the dark and the shadow it casts in the light.

The Bulgarians also believed that the vampire—*obour*—was a result of heredity. Vampire blood, they said, was in the veins. When such a person died and was given the usual burial, at the end of nine days the vampire appeared in its "aeroform" shape, giving off the telltale sparks and shadows. In this condition the vampire was more or less harmless, a jokester that visited the villages, ranting and roaring and running about. But some of the vampires also seemed to want to settle old scores— calling villagers by name and beating them black and blue.

One Bulgarian story:

One night a vampire seized Kodja Keraz, a champion wrestler of the village of Derekuoi. The vampire grabbed the wrestler by the waist and cried, "Now then, old Cherry Tree, see if you can throw me."

The village champion did his best but "the vampire was so heavy that Kodja Keraz broke his own jaw in throwing the invisible being that was crushing him to death."

The story was related by S. G. B. St. Clair and Charles A. Brophy after a twelve-year study of Bulgarian beliefs, and they added this note:

"Of course skeptical persons may be found who would explain this story by the hypothesis of too much wine and a fall over a heap of stones; fortunately our village does not contain any such freethinkers, and old Cherry Tree will be happy to relate his tale, as we have given it, to any inquirer after truth. To prove its accuracy he can call many witnesses who will swear to the fact of his jaw being broken. Old Cherry Tree is alive still, and as great a reprobate in 1876 as he was in 1867."

This incident came to have more than purely local importance because it happened at a time when that village was plagued by assaults of the *obours*. People grew so frightened that they huddled together at night in several houses, burning candles as they waited and watched for the vampires to come. And come they did. They "lit up the streets with their sparkles, and . . . the most enterprising threw their shadows on the walls of the rooms where the peasants were dying of fear; whilst others howled, shrieked, and swore outside the door, entered the abandoned houses, spat blood into the floor, turned everything topsy-turvy, and smeared the whole place, even the pictures of the saints, with cow-dung.

Only by the use of magic were the "supernatural visitations" ended. An old woman who was suspected of practicing witchcraft knew how to do it: she brought herbs and special medicines and conducted a secret ceremony, thus ridding the village and Kodja Keraz of assaults by the *obours*.

When the Bulgarian vampire reached its second stage of existence, after forty days of "apprenticeship to the realm of shadows," it came out of the grave in the dead person's own form and actually passed itself off as a human being. Here is one such case, again from the village of Derekuoi:

A stranger came to the village, settled down there, and married. He was the perfect husband except for one fault—every night he left the house and did not come back until late. Suddenly people in the village began to notice that things were in disarray; objects were turned over as if someone were searching for something. Then they began to find dead horses and cattle, partially eaten, with odd toothmarks on them. Cattle grew sick and died, the blood had been drained out of them. The villagers puzzled over all these signs, and then they learned from the wife of the stranger that her husband left the house every night. They questioned him and discovered that he had only one nostril, a telling note. He must be a vampire! Did they go to the authorities with charges? No. They met and condemned the stranger to death and did not even consult their priest. They "just tied their man hand and foot, led him to a hill a little outside Derekuoi, lit a big fire of wait-a-bit thorns, and burned him alive."

The Bulgarians had another way of disposing of their vampires that the folklorists St. Clair and Brophy thought to be unique.

They bottled them. (Remember the Chinese?) This was done by a sorcerer practicing magic, a common Bulgarian profession in earlier times. The sorcerer first had to discover the favorite food of the vampire; having done this, he procured some of it and then took a picture of one of the saints and his holy treasure, his icon, and set up an ambush for the vampire.

When the sorcerer saw the *obour* emerge from its hiding place, he chased it until, in its efforts to escape, the vampire either climbed a tree or jumped up onto the roof of a building. The sorcerer climbed up after the vampire and kept waving it and chasing it in the direction of the bottle, in which he had placed some of the vampire's favorite food. Eventually, they said, he always got the vampire into the bottle. Inside was not only its favorite food but a piece of the sorcerer's icon. "The bottle was thrown into the fire and the vampire disappears forever."

The people knew, of course, that the sorcerers had not actually trapped the dead body of the suspected vampire in the bottle, but they were also certain that what was in the bottle was the vampire.

The biggest difference, however, between the Bulgarian vampire and that of other eastern European countries was that the Bulgarian *obour* did not necessarily thirst for blood. Only if all its other sources of food were exhausted would the vampire seek human blood. Despite that, the Bulgars feared the vampire as much as anyone; their greatest concern was that if the vampire had not been contained during the magic period of forty days after burial, then it would reappear as flesh and blood and cause all sorts of mischief. To the Bulgars this was as terrifying as the vision of a vampire out searching the roads and fields for blood.

From early times, the Rumanian vampire, more than any other, resembled the modern idea of a vampire. Theirs was called the *strigoi* (male) or *strigoica* (female). Legends about them go back to the villages of pre-Christian times.

The Rumanian vampire went through two stages of existence. The first was that of the living, human vampire. The second was that of the un-dead, living in the grave and emerging from it to dwell among the living. The Rumanians have always believed in a life after death, and to them the dead vampire had merely passed from the first stage of life to the second.

Of course not all Rumanians were vampires. But most of those who were vampires were predestined from birth or even from conception. If a child was born with red hair, it was presumed that the red hair was given the child on the night before birth by the Devil, or that the mother had met the Devil disguised in a red wig. It was a sign of the vampire, the child was marked as a *strigoi*.

If the infant was born with a caul, or was the seventh son or the seventh daughter, or had blue eyes, or penetrating black eyes, it was a *strigoi*. If the mother drank impure water before the birth, it might have been mixed with the saliva of the Devil; then too, the child was destined to be a *strigoi*. If a child was born with a small "tail" on the end of its spinal column, and it grew, this would give the child the power to become a *strigoi* after death.

In its first life, the *strigoi* was not necessarily an evil being. Sometimes it did kill the living but rarely by sucking blood. But it was in contact with the supernatural during this first life. He or she could send the animated spirit out into other objects, such as pots and casseroles. All sorts of mischief was possible.

Another peculiarity of the *strigoi* in its first life form was that at the time of certain special feasts, such as that of St. George, while others slept the *strigoi* souls left their bodies and went to a secret meeting called by the chief *strigoi*. There they danced and sang, and if the peasants happened upon this secret meeting, all they would see would be hundreds of little lights, like those of fireflies, moving through the air. For the souls of the *strigois* were phosphorescent, and they shone in the dark. On such occasions, the *strigois* danced and cavorted all night long. They ran through the villages, entering houses and making a racket. They had the magic power to make the corn grow or to kill it. The *strigois,* said the villagers scornfully, believed they had as much power as God.

The second life of the *strigoi* was a much more serious matter. This came after the death of the person who had been born a *strigoi,* or had become one during his or her lifetime. Many factors could cause a normal person to become a *strigoi*: if one had not been baptized, or if one had been excommunicated, or cursed; or had committed crimes, or done evil in any way; or if black magic had been used against one; or if one was a suicide. Even if a dog, cat, chicken, bird, or other living being that had a liaison with evil passed by the body of the dead person—then the dead one would become a *strigoi.*

Obviously many precautions had to be taken by the living to protect themselves from this fate. The living had to look out for themselves. When a person died, the relatives stuffed up the corpse's nostrils with grains of incense so it could not breathe; the ears so it could not hear; the eyes so it could not see; and the mouth so it could not tell the Devil the name of the family. Millet or tiny stones and oil could be used for this same purpose.

These were general-purpose precautions, taken in the case of all dead persons. But if the person had been known to be a *strigoi* of the first sort during life, then the precautions taken were much more stringent. The same was true for people who had been suspected of being sorcerers, or who had committed suicide.

In these cases, the relatives first cut off the head of the corpse and placed the head at the feet, so it could not easily be put back on the body. The head was also covered with a wreath of rose thorns, or was pierced with a long needle, and anointed with the fat of a pig killed at Christmas. If the dead one was known to be a *strigoi,* then a thorn was driven into the navel or the heart, or a piece of charred wood that had been blessed was driven into the heart until seven spurts of blood came out. The peasants of Rumania believed that a *strigoi* had two hearts. The first heart died with the body, but the second heart continued to live on, and this was the heart that must be pierced.

In the Vrancea district, the peasants took great care to see that no one cried over the dead one, for this was certain to bring bad luck to the corpse. When the body was laid out, the relatives placed a knife at the feet and a spindle at the head, and one member of the family recited a little verse:

> If come the *strigoi* from the East
> Then let him be pricked by the knife.
> If come the *strigoi* from the West
> Then let him be stuck by the spindle.

This ceremony would protect the body from contact with another *strigoi.* All the way to the cemetery the funeral party would sing and dance. If they came to a bridge, the strongest man would take the dead body from the coffin and dance across the bridge with it, thus confusing the evil spirits of the water, showing that everyone in the party was alive. Then the body would be restored to the coffin, with the feet raised, and the eyes carefully closed again. If these precautions were not taken, if the head was raised, if the eyes were open, then the corpse would surely become a *strigoi.*

At the gravesite, the priest would recite prayers to keep the dead person from becoming one of the living dead; and when the party left the cemetery, one of the relatives of the dead person would throw grains of millet in the path and say, "Let the strigoi eat each year a grain of millet and not eat the hearts of its family." For the Rumanians believed that the first persons to be attacked by a *strigoi* would be the family. Thus, the tasks for the relatives did not end with the burial service. They were seemingly endless. Three days after the burial, all the relatives had to gather at the tomb and burn incense. They would place nine spindles in the center of the grave, so that if the dead one tried to get out, it would be stopped by the stakes.

In the district of Banat, several days after the funeral the relative had to go to the tomb with wine and bread. They sprinkled the wine on the tomb and passed the bread around to the living, leaving some for the corpse. Thus, by nourishing the body with earth foods, they would prevent the corpse from developing a taste for human flesh and blood.

Long after the funeral, at specified intervals, special ceremonies were performed so that the dead would not become vampires. At the end of six weeks, a woman was employed to go to the tomb and burn incense there. Seven weeks after the burial was the offering of water. In some districts, a daughter of the house had to get forty-four pots of water from the river and pour them over the grave. This was believed to be enough water to facilitate the decomposition of the body. And decomposition was ardently desired, because an incorrupt body was a sure sign of vampirism.

Holy water was often sprinkled over the grave to ward off evil. In some districts, the water had to be brought from seven different churches in seven different bottles. The holy water was then poured into the grave through a little hole dug in the ground. As this was done, the people said the following prayer: "Let _____ be baptized the servant of God, in the name of the Father, the Son, and the Holy Ghost."

Sometimes torches of linseed oil or hemp were placed around the tomb, and as they were lit, the people prayed, "Let this person not become a *strigoi.*"

The most important ceremony of all came seven years after burial. At that time, the body was dug up and the bones were washed, a religious service was held, and the bones were reburied. This occasion was nerve-racking for the peasants, for if the grave was opened and the body had not turned to dust but was found to be whole, then the soul of the dead had already become a *strigoi.* The occasion was equally difficult for the *strigois.*Sometimes they would flee the grave just before the seventh anniversary of death and fly to another country, where they pretended to be normal human beings.

The mark of the seventh-anniversary *strigoi* was undeniable: a ruddy complexion and body, and change of position were proof of vampirism. Blood on the face meant that the un-dead body had been committing murders. But if the body was damp, that meant it had been out living off the countryside, not bothering humans. If the hair or fingernails had grown, or the feet had taken on a hooflike shape, or if the beard had grown, and the teeth stuck out like fangs these were all proofs positive of vampirism.

If it was not a *strigoi* it might be a *moroi,* another form of vampire, formed by the body of a stillborn child or one that died shortly after birth. The Rumanians often used the term *strigoi* to cover both. Another type of vampire was the *priccolitch,* but it could take only the form of a dog or a wolf and was much less common than the *strigoi.* Of course the Rumanian peasants took careful precautions to protect themselves from all these evils, beyond those mentioned that dealt with the body itself.

The Rumanian peasant belief in several forms of life after death was mixed up with the vampire motif. For example, the most important act of a living person was marriage. If death happened before marriage, the peasants would perform the service of marriage for the unfortunate one after death to enrich the quality of its afterlife. For to them death was only a passage from one stage to another, more perfect life, and a married person was much less likely to become a *strigoi.*

In Moldavia, Walachia, and northern Transylvania, the dead one was married to a living person. In Banat, southern Transylvania, and Olthenia, the dead person was married to a tree or a stick, which symbolized life. These were always ceremonies symbolizing joy and the mating of man with nature. The forest, the mountains, the birds and stars, the sheep in the fields were all considered to be witnesses to the happy event.

The Rumanians believed that when the body descended into the grave it entered two new worlds—the celestial world and the world of the earth. The soul of the vampire unfortunately remained caught between the two worlds. The earth tried to destroy the body, which the vampire part of the soul tried to prevent by seeking nourishment. This meant blood. The vampire might have a hole in its grave (for holy water) or it might make a hole. Then the soul could thread its way out of the grave at night and begin its marauding.

There was some dispute about how long it took before a dead body could become a danger. Some said nine days after burial, some said forty days, some said six weeks—the estimates ranged up to the magic seven-year period. The appearance of the vampires was again a matter of convention. Sometimes they were described as "bestial," with claws of a griffin, feet of a bear, or a chest covered with hair like a gorilla.

These *strigois* were of course out to do evil to mankind. A *strigoi* let loose in the earthly world would attack a sleeping victim and suck the blood without waking the victim. The bite was not usually made in the jugular vein, as popularly cited, because the *strigoi* needed the fresh red blood of the heart, coming through the arteries. Also, it was not just the blood of the victim that the vampire needed, but the human soul of the victim. So the victim became prey in two ways, physically and for the immortal soul, as this "song of the *strigoi*" indicates:

> The loves, the loves,
> The heart comes and cries
> To make you understand
> The judgment that it makes against you.
>
> Rabbits, serpents, bitches;
> Isn't the hunt good?
> Rabbits, serpents, bitches,
> Isn't the hunt good?
>
> The human hearts then, where are they found?
> They are lost.
> It is their blood that soothes me.
> It is their flesh that nourishes me.
> And this is how I live.

As for the *moroi,* it was a more complex vampire. Sometimes it attacked its victims in the form of a fly, a mosquito, or a butterfly. The *moroi* was concerned entirely with absorbing the soul of its victim, while the *strigoi*'s main concern was to get enough nourishment to continue its half-life for a period. If it was able to move into the second phase of *strigoi* existence, it would cease persecuting humans but bother only the animals of the field and domestic creatures such as sheep, cows, horses, and chickens. Finally the *strigoi* would stop taking even the lives of animals and leave that region for another country, where it would take up life as a human being again—marrying, having children, and never killing. But of course the blood was still there, and after death the vampire would still be a vampire, and the new children of the vampire would be vampires.

So the Rumanians considered the vampire to be the most serious of all threats against both life and afterlife, and they made arrangements to protect themselves just as seriously as they did against the plague and other diseases.

The first line of protection was the *hotar,* which surrounded the village and its immediate fields. The *hotar* consisted of stakes placed on the frontier, which had magic properties that prevented evil spirits from entering the place. Next in the ring was the courtyard around each house, which was protected by a ceremony in which a team of oxen was driven around the courtyard three times, while the family members sprinkled incense on the ground behind them. The *strigoi* could not penetrate this ring. Magic signs were also put on the doors of the houses, signs of sun, moon, stars, trees, and—in the Christian era—crosses.

The Rumanian peasant house was (and still is) built with magic specifications designed to ward off evil. (This is also true of the Chinese, whose housebuilding was traditionally to the Funghsueh [wind-water] precepts.) The corners of the central room were marked with grain, silver, or the blood of an animal sacrificed for the purpose. Sometimes the head of an animal was buried in the corners so that the vampire would eat that instead of bothering the people.

The roof of the house always possessed special magical qualities. Three days after burial, the souls of the dead were inclined to come back to the house and move around; at night they would sleep in the roof boards. If they were not discouraged, the souls did this for forty days. They could be discouraged by something white. So the Rumanians adopted the custom of putting little white flags on the roof of the house for forty days after the death of a member of the family.

Normally, once these precautions were undertaken, the family was safe from disturbance by evil spirits. But if, in spite of everything, one member of the family fell ill or died, or the cattle herds fell sick, or a drought came, then it was obvious to the peasants that they had failed and that a *strigoi* was at work.

In order to find the vampire that was causing all the trouble, the peasants had to track it back to the grave. This sometimes meant a careful search of the cemetery. A telltale sign would be a small break in the ground near or on the grave, which would be presumed to have been made by the vampire. One way to trap the vampire was to pour honey into the holes for, like bears, Rumanian vampires loved honey.

But sometimes the vampire was too clever for the humans, and they could not find the vampire's grave. Then a horse—a white horse without a single black hair, or a black horse without a white hair—could be ridden around the area by a relative of the vampire's victim. When the horse reached the right grave, it would refuse to go further. A young black bull could also be employed for this purpose. It would stop at the proper grave and paw the ground. Sometimes a black cock served. It would crow at the proper grave. A gander would hiss.

When the peasants found the proper tomb, they dug up the body. If the body was found to be uncorrupted, that was proof positive to the villagers that they had found a vampire. They drove a stake of ash through the heart, or a great spike, or a knife, and then reburied the body, hoping it would remain, soul and all, in the grave.

In some areas, the peasants took further precautions. They would disembowel the body and boil the viscera in wine. They would remove the heart and liver and burn them over a fire until they were reduced to cinders. The cinders were mixed with water, and all the relatives would drink this potion to get rid of the evil.

In other cases, the peasants chopped up the body, and put it back into the coffin in pieces. They poured in quicklime, threw the funeral garments on top, and reburied the corpse. Then they replaced the cross with the name of the dead person on it, and by this act forgave the vampire its sins. They had defeated the true enemy: the Devil.

Today in Rumania, few stories of vampires surface, because magic and sorcery are crimes against the state. So, too, the search for vampires is frowned upon by the authorities. Even so, some recent stories have come to light, such as the case of a well-to-do family in one village whose members knew they had inherited the capacity to become vampires.

One of the family's members died, and the family was seriously upset because all knew that if the body was not dug up and "killed again" with that stake through the secret heart, there could be only evil to pay. So, secretly, they dug up the body, and ran a stake through the heart, and reburied it. Nine years later, a cousin who had moved to the city died in an accident. His friends did not know of the curse of vampirism on the family and did nothing to prevent him from becoming a *strigoi*. So become a *strigoi* he did. He returned to his native village, and it is said that he caused the death of five people. The family prayed and prayed, and finally the *strigoi* agreed to kill no more humans. But it began attacking the chickens and the family cattle.

One may still hear such tales in Rumania, if one has the proper contacts. There, the vampire definitely still lives.

13

VRYKOLAKES!

ANYONE WHO BELIEVED THAT BY THE nineteenth century, the golden age of vampirism was past, has only to consider Greece. Travelers there found that while practices had changed, the *vrykolakas* occupied as important a position as ever in local belief.

Sometimes the people relied on the Church to exorcise the vampire, sometimes they merely carried the body around to as many as forty churches in turn and then reburied the corpse. And here and there cropped up cases of the old fire treatment—done without the approval of the Church, against the law, and most often in secret.

All in all, the peasant superstition about vampires was as firmly rooted in nineteenth-century Greece as it had been centuries before. As the abbot of a monastery in the district of Sphakia on Crete put it in 1888:

"It is popularly believed that most of the dead, those who have lived bad lives or have been excommunicated by some priest, (or, worse still, by seven priests together) become *vrykolakas*; that is to say that after the separation of the soul from the body there enters into the latter an evil spirit which take the place of the soul and assumes the shape of the dead man and so is transformed into a *vrykolakas* or man-demon."

The familiar phrases were still there: "preserves it from corruption . . . causes men great alarms at night and strikes all with panic . . . makes everyone who dies while it is about like unto itself . . . in a short space of time gets together a large and dangerous train of followers."

Many of the old practices had continued: water was still taken to the gravesite for the first forty days after burial, and presents of food taken regularly for three years to supply the needs of the dead.

Church ritual called for the digging up of bodies three years after burial. By that time, any self-respecting corpse should have turned to bones and dust. Thus the church could determine whether a body had been taken over by the Devil and become a *vrykolakas*. If only the white bones remained, then the soul had joined the body outside the grave and there was no need to worry. The dead one was happy.

But if the body was still incorrupt—then came the old consternation. In *Modern Greek Folklore and Ancient Greek Religions,* the English folklorist John Lawson reports how he witnessed an exhumation ceremony in Leonidi, an event which caused a considerable stir in the area.

"Two graves had just been opened when I arrived, and the utmost anxiety prevailed because in both cases there was only partial decomposition—in one case so little that the general outline of the features could be made out—and it was feared that one or both of the dead peasants had become *vrykolakas*."

The relatives of the dead people and the priest held a meeting at the little chapel by the burying ground to discuss what should be done, because the dissolution of the bodies *had to* occur for the sake of the dead and the safety of the villagers. Someone suggested that since prayer had not been effective, the bodies be burned. That suggestion was discarded because the burning of bodies had been outlawed by the civil authorities. The priest suggested reburial, but the relatives rejected that idea as inadequate. Something more had to be done. The family had already performed all the memorial feasts for the dead for three years, and the thought of continuing their attentions to the dead, not knowing if or when the bodies would dissolve, did not appeal to any of them. Something had to be done to dissolve the bodies in a hurry. The priest could be of no further help. His position was anomalous to say the least. Apart from prayer, he could not help because of the strictures of the civil authorities, and he could not hinder the villagers in their determination to follow the way of the past, lest he offend and lose prestige within the community.

Lawson watched as the relatives took matters into their own hands: "On the floor of the chapel there were two large baskets containing the remains; there were men seated beside them busy with knives; and there were women kneeling at washtubs and scouring the bones that were handed to them with soap and soda. The work continued for two days. At the end of that time the bones were shown white and clean. All else had disappeared—had probably been burnt in secret—but the secret was kept close. It was therefore claimed and allowed that the dissolution was complete." As the village priest knew very well, there was more than one way to get rid of a vampire.

So Greek beliefs continued in the pattern of the past. But there was also something new, adapted to the new times and new technology. The abbot of the monastery in Sphakia wrote that there was "Great danger that the sufferer may expire, and himself be turned into a *vrykolakas* if there is not someone at hand who perceives his torment and fires off a gun, thereby putting the blood-thirsty monster to flight; for fortunately it is afraid of the report of fire-arms and retreats . . . not a few such scenes we have witnessed with our own eyes."

The abbot had made his own study of vampirism and of some local cases and felt drawn to some conclusions: "This monster, as time goes on, becomes more and more audacious and blood-thirsty, so that it is able completely to devastate whole villages." To get rid of the monster, the villagers called in people who were said to be priests, "imposters" the abbot said, who summoned the *vrykolakas* back into the grave, where it was imprisoned by prayer.

The abbot concluded that peasant belief in vampires was "an absurd superstition" but that it was nevertheless "rife and vigorous throughout Crete and especially in the mountainous and secluded parts of the island."

Not only on Crete, as others could attest: "The ignorant peasant of Andros believes to this day that the corpse can rise again to do him hurt; and is not this belief in the *vrykolakas* general throughout Greece?"

John Lawson answered that rhetorical question with an emphatic "yes." His travels had shown him that not only was there a great lore of popular stories about vampires, which he heard everywhere he went, but he also found "a very present and real sense of dread in the villagers on the west slopes of Mount Pelion, the village of Leonidi on the east coast of the Peloponnesos peninsula, at Andros, Tenos, Santorini, and Cephalonia."

In 1898, the Frenchman Henry Hautteweur published a study of the vampire folklore of the island of Kythnos. He discovered that the people there believed such diseases as tuberculosis were caused by vampires. And, although the sightings of the *vrykolakas* had been few during the period he spent on the island, there still were the stories and the fear of them. On Kythnos, the *vrykolakes* were regarded as apparitions, caused by the Devil taking possession of a corpse by entering through the dead man's mouth. To prevent this assault, "a little cross made out of wax" was put in the mouth of the dead for "the devil would never dare to pass over the cross." In spite of such precautions, "apparitions are still seen on the island of Kythnos, not as many perhaps as there used to be in the good old days."

Everybody on Kythnos knew the story of Andilaveris, "the most vexious" *vrykolakas* of all. He had plagued the whole village of Messaria, the capital of Kythnos, for a long time. "He used to walk up and down every street . . . sometimes he would even make his way into a house, he would sit down at table, he would eat like a hungry giant and drink like a fish, and then when he had gorged his fill of wine and swallowed all the dainties he pleased, he used to amuse himself by smashing the plates and the glasses and clattering the pots and the pans, howling horribly all the while like a mad werewolf."

Needless to say, the people of Messaria were panic-stricken. They locked their doors at night and huddled inside. No one ventured out after dusk, so great was their fear of this "vicious devil" Andilaveris. The vampire used to "laugh at everybody and defied even the saints in Heaven. On certain days he would take it in his head to climb up on the roof of the church, and from that height he would drench those who passed underneath with floods of urine."

This was too much. The villagers got together and decided that something, and something drastic, had to be done about this *vrykolakas*. On a Saturday—the only day of the week when, the Greeks believed, the vampire could not leave his grave—the peasants assembled and with the priest went to Andilaveris's grave and opened the tomb.

"They took the body, which was fast asleep, comatose as a snake replete with food, and they bundled it into an old sack which they had brought with them, putting their horrible burden on the back of a sturdy mule." They traveled then to the little seaside spot called Bryocastro, and all got aboard a boat, which took them to a very small islet, Daskaleio. There the priest began to make preparations to bury the body. But, ah, Andilaveris had awakened and he "attacked the good priest with volleys of mud and ordure." It was a struggle, but the priest managed to rebury the corpse, and all the villagers returned to their own island and village, happy, knowing that "they had freed their town from the visitations of this foul spectre, for never can a *vrykolakas* cross the sea."

One favorite practice of the Greeks to rid their own island of *vrykolakes* was to cart the bodies over to another island. Santorini was so popular a repository for the corpses of other islands that it became famous for its vampire population. Aside from the displaced *vrykolakes*, Santorini had a great number of vampires of its own. In *The Vampire in Europe,* Montague Summers describes how, when he visited the island in 1906, he heard many a story about the vampires there, as well as the phrase "sending vampires to Santorini," which was the Greek counterpart of the English "carrying coals to Newcastle." Another English traveler attributed the "many wild superstitions among the peasantry about vampires" to Santorini's geology, "the antiseptic nature of the soil and the frequent discovery of undecayed bodies."

Whatever the cause, the inhabitants of Santorini came to enjoy "so vast a reputation as experts in effectively dealing with vampires and putting an end to them" that several cases were reported of bodies taken from the islands of Myconos and Crete and brought to Santorini for the express purpose of having the Santorinians deal with them. (They burned them.)

One might say, then, that for at least part of the Greek population, the belief in vampires in the 19th and 20th centuries is as strong as ever.

A woodcut of Vlad Tepes, the real Dracula, from the earliest surviving published work about him, which appeared in 1485.

(below left) Vlad Tepes, artist unknown

(below) A contemporary portrait of the beautiful Countess Elizabeth Báthory. This sixteenth-century Hungarian noblewoman was a glamourous figure at the Austrian imperial count, while secretly earning the title of "Vampire Lady of the Carpathinians."

The ruins of Countess Báthory's Csejthe Castle in the foothills of the Carpathian mountains. Here she sated her blood-lust on more than six hundred young women, sucking their blood and bathing in it. When finally brought to justice, she was sealed up alive inside her castle.

A latter-day reproduction of Countess Báthory's "Iron Maiden." The machine would grip a young woman and impale her on hidden spikes. The blood flowed into a cachement to be saved for the countess.

It was inevitable that the entertainment industry would capitalize on the subject of vampirism. This photo shows Max Schreck starring in *Nosferatu*, an early German film that set a standard for all future vampire movies. A modern remake, starring Klaus Kinski, was released in 1979. (*The Museum of Modern Art/Film Stills Archive*)

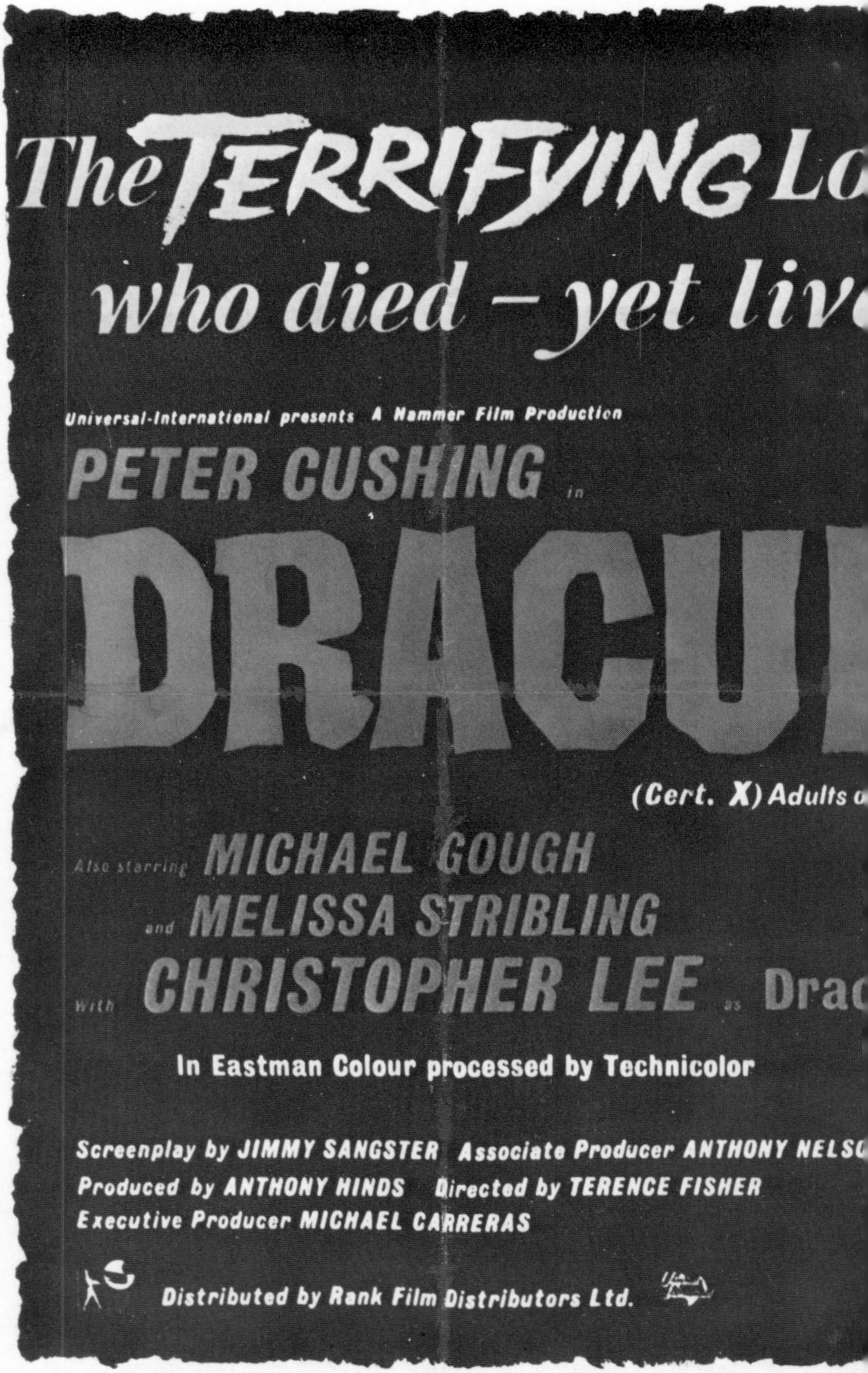

The TERRIFYING Lo
who died – yet liv
Universal-International presents A Hammer Film Production
PETER CUSHING in
DRACU
(Cert. X) Adults o
Also starring MICHAEL GOUGH
and MELISSA STRIBLING
with CHRISTOPHER LEE as Drac
In Eastman Colour processed by Technicolor
Screenplay by JIMMY SANGSTER Associate Producer ANTHONY NELS
Produced by ANTHONY HINDS Directed by TERENCE FISHER
Executive Producer MICHAEL CARRERAS
Distributed by Rank Film Distributors Ltd.

The 1958 Hammer poster for Peter Cushing's film *Dracula.* All the Dracula plays and films took their inspiration from Bram Stoker's novel.

Hollywood's first interpretation of the Dracula myth

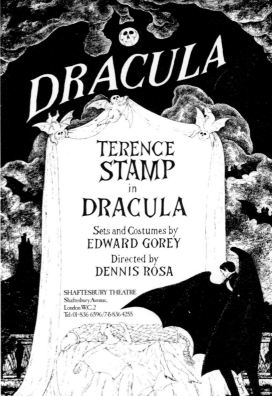

An Edward Gorey advertisement for the London stage production of *Dracula*

Bela Lugosi in the title role of *Dracula*

Lugosi as the Count. *(The Museum of Modern Art/Film Stills Archive)*

(above) A Translyvanian castle setting was *de rigueur* in many early vampire movies. (*The Museum of Modern Art/Film Stills Archive*)

(below) Otto Kruger burns on a pyre as Marguerite Churchill watches, in *Dracula's Daughter*. (*The Museum of Modern Art/Film Stills Archive*)

(above) The resuscitated corpse. *(From the Musée Wiertz, courtesy University Books)*

(below) Un-dead family members rising for a night's stalk in *Dracula's Dog.*

(above)The count prepares to slake his thirst in *Dracula's Dog.*

(below) The traditional horse-drawn hearse and evil-looking wolf have given way to more modern variants in *Dracula's Dog.*

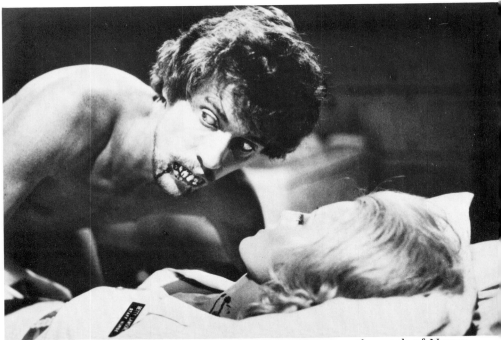

(above) Dr. Stocker (John Holmes) hovering over the neck of Nurse Lawson (Seka) in *Dracula Sucks*.

(below) Blood and sexual excitement have often been combined in vampire lore. The impaling of this vampire in *Dracula Sucks* plays on that theme.

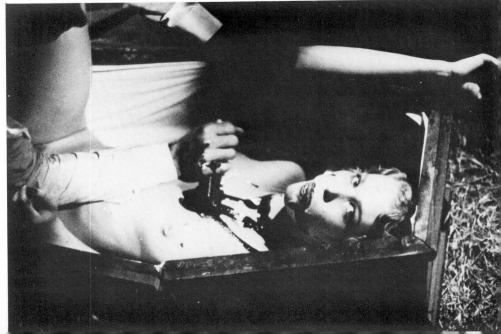

Christopher Lee shows his fangs after feeding in *Dracula A.D. 1972.* *(The Museum of Modern Art/Film Stills Archive)*

Frank Langella and a toothsome morsel in the New York stage play *Dracula.*

Frank Langella has been called the sexiest of Draculas.

Jeanne Youngson, Ph.D., president of the Count Dracula Fan Club, New York City. *(Wing Lee photo)*

YOU ARE INVITED TO JOIN

The Count Dracula Society

DEVOTED TO SERIOUS STUDY OF HORROR FILMS & GOTHIC LITERATURE

APPLICATION FOR MEMBERSHIP FOR ONE FULL YEAR CHECK ONE

LEADER MEMBER . . . . .Donation $50.00 ☐
Benefits: Receives membership card, diploma, bat pin.
 Invited to free film screenings and annual awards program.
 Participates in the selection of the annual awards.

REGULAR MEMBER . . . . .Donation $20.00 ☐
Benefits: Receives membership card, bat pin
 Invited to free film screenings and annual awards program

HONORARY MEMBER . . . .$5 fee required ☐
Benefits: Receives membership card.

NAME_____DATE_____

ADDRESS _____

CITY _____

STATE AND ZIP _____

THE COUNT DRACULA SOCIETY IS A NON PROFIT ASSOCIATION DEVOTED
TO THE SERIOUS STUDY OF HORROR FILMS AND GOTHIC LITERATURE
FOUNDED IN 1962 BY DR. DONALD A. REED

MAIL THIS APPLICATION WITH YOUR CHECK OR MONEY ORDER MADE PAYABLE
TO THE COUNT DRACULA SOCIETY TO
334 WEST 54TH STREET, LOS ANGELES, CALIFORNIA 90037
PHONE (213) 752-5811

Membership available in **THE NOBLE ORDER OF COUNT DRACULA (KNIGHT ORDER)**
Please contact Dr. Reed in this regard

ANNUALLY PRESENTING

DONALD A. REED, National President THE MRS. ANN RADCLIFFE AWARDS

The rundown Highgate Cemetery in the North End of London was alleged to have harbored a vampire in 1970. (*The Count Dracula Fan Club*)

14

THE PARISIAN VAMPIRE

BETRAND THE Ghoul

IN HIS TIME, ALL FRANCE KNEW HIM as The Vampire.

In the early months of 1849, his mysterious form was seen often in cemeteries, gliding at midnight among the tombstones. Graves were ripped open. Bodies were found horribly mutilated. Stakeouts were set up to trap The Vampire, but always he managed to elude his pursuers. Was The Vampire real or was he a phantom?

The journals of the day loved the story. They started one rumor after another and then built upon them for their readers. Who was this creature of the night, this Vampire? How could he move in and out of locked cemeteries? First was the cemetery at Père-Lachaise. One night the caretaker thought he saw a shadowy figure in the moonlight. The next morning, he saw the grisly results: tombs desecrated and parts of bodies scattered here and there. He set up a watch, but the intruder never came back. As the months passed, one cemetery after another around Paris was invaded, always with the same results: graves opened, bodies taken out, torn up, and scattered about willy-nilly. The public cemetery at Montparnasse, where unclaimed bodies were buried, was hit a number of times, but the caretakers never spotted anyone in the cemetery who ought not to be there.

One day the body of a seven-year-old girl was found in a remote suburban graveyard. She had been buried at noon the day before; now her coffin was open, and she lay on the ground, dismembered. For some reason this particular crime aroused more public furor than any of the others. Surveillance of the cemeteries was increased, but again no one was caught. The cemetery caretakers set up traps. They brought in dogs to guard the graves. Still, nothing.

The public began to grow hysterical: who but a supernatural vampire or ghoul could enter a cemetery with thick stone walls and iron gates without being seen? But for a little while there were no more outrages, and the public turned to other amusements. Still, the police and cemetery officials continued their close watch.

Then came a report from the public cemetery at Montparnasse: The Vampire was at work again. This time, however, the police had caught a glimpse of the shadowy figure as it moved among the tombstones. They chased the figure and shot at the fleeing form, and they hit it. But the figure disappeared over the wall. When the police came up, they found a trail of blood leading to the cemetery wall and a few scraps of clothing that had been caught in the iron spikes atop the wall. Upon examination, the scraps seemed to be part of a military uniform.

That evening, the duty sergeant of the 74th Infantry Regiment, which was stationed near the cemetery, noted that one man had come to headquarters with wounds so serious he had to be taken to Val-de-Grâce, the military hospital. Following up the lead of the scraps of clothing, the police discovered the duty sergeant's report and checked with the hospital.

There, they found their vampire: a handsome, well-groomed, young blond man named Sergeant Bertrand. He was taken into custody, and an inquiry was held on July 10, 1849. Public interest was enormous, the affair had caught the eyes of high society, and many ladies and gentlemen in their finery attended the hearing, to watch and listen and be shocked. They got their wish. The facts that were revealed at the hearing were enough to make any fair lady swoon. Sergeant Bertrand, The Vampire, was a despicable necrophiliac, a man with an erotic obsession for corpses.

Like an antique hunter haunting auctions, Sergeant Bertrand had a passion for cemeteries. One time he swam across an icy moat in the dead of winter to get into the cemetery of Douai. He was very careful in gaining entrance to his cemeteries; if he found any devices set up to protect the cemetery he would take them apart. Then he would begin his search for bodies. If he heard anyone coming, he would lie still in the grave next to the corpse. When the dogs came looking for him and found him, they did not give him away. Vampirologist Ornella Volta, who studied this case carefully, decided that Bertrand must have had a hypnotic look about him, "because like Dracula's it made animals lower their eyes and tails and slink away in silence."

It was shocking enough that Sergeant Bertrand desecrated graves, but far more shocking was his obsession with the bodies. Mutilation was his game. As he admitted at the inquiry:

"I would never have taken the risk of violating a corpse if I had not had the possibility of cutting it up afterwards." The height of his pleasure was to cut the corpses into pieces: "I threw their limbs in every direction after having cut them off from the body, playing with them like a cat with a mouse, whether they were men or women."

The judges suggested that he was homosexual. Indignantly, he denied it. "If I have sometimes cut some male corpses into pieces, it was only out of rage at not finding one of the female sex."

Some nights he had to dig up a dozen bodies before finding a woman's in the common graveyard at Montparnasse, his favorite cemetery. When he did find a female, his erotic pleasure was intense. After cutting up the body, he might open the belly of the corpse with his penknife and finger the slippery insides with delight. "I put my hands in their bellies in order to pull out their insides," he told the investigators, "and sometimes pushed up even higher inside them to take out the liver."

His mildest activity was to love up the corpses: "I squeezed her so strongly against me that I almost broke her in two," he told the inquiry about one body.

Some said that Sergeant Bertrand was insane and should be locked up forever. But the judges found him guilty only of the violation of graves and sentenced him to a year in prison.

While in prison, the sergeant wrote a full account of his grisly cemetery life, giving dates, times, and details of his dreadful despoliations. This was a seven-day wonder when it was published in Paris. After that, The Vampire turned silent, and when he was released from prison he dropped out of sight and was never again in the public eye.

However, The Vampire did leave his mark: Volta discovered a "disciple" of The Vampire, a tale related by Monsieur Claude, the French Inspector of Public Security during the Second Empire. M. Claude told the story in his memoirs, published in 1857.

This culprit never received the attention from the press that Sergeant Bertrand enjoyed, but the method was the same. Graveyards in the district of Montmartre were desecrated, tombstones knocked about, and the corpses of men and women were found outside their graves, with torn shrouds and mangled limbs. M. Claude and his assistant, M.

Col-de-Zinc (sic) were assigned to find the criminal. After some investigation, M. Claude's suspicion turned to another soldier, this one the nephew of a brigadier who lived near the cemetery.

But how could it be? The brigadier was eminently respectable. The nephew: "this youth, as gentle as a girl, so respectable, so shy, and so timid."

Still, said the policeman, "I was paid to find out what lay hidden beneath the innocuous appearance of these ferocious creatures who only hold out their arm to you to strangle you, and only kiss you to bite you."

M. Claude's suspicions developed when he learned of the young man's inordinate interest in any and all recent burials. He said nothing to Col-de-Zinc about this. In fact, Col-de-Zinc had his own candidate for the vampire: an old man who lived near the cemetery, who spent his nights playing the violin "in a lugubrious, lamenting sound which seemed, in that hour of the night, like an invitation for the dead to take part in a *danse macabre.*"

So, armed with their separate suspicions, the two police officers took up watch one night in the cemetery to await the coming of "the vampire."

Which would come?

A solitary figure appeared. It was the young nephew, the soldier, in his uniform. However, he did not enter the cemetery. Instead he went into the house of the old violinist!

Which one was it? The tension grew.

The answer came in a little while. A single figure came out of the house in workingmen's overalls. And then the violin once more took up its plaintive melody.

It was the young soldier after all. He carried a shovel, and he wandered among the graves for a while, apparently searching. Finally, he stopped at one grave and began to dig. He unearthed a coffin and opened it. M. Claude and M. Col-de-Zinc crept up to a hiding place behind a huge monument, and from there they watched in fascination as the young soldier took up the body of a woman in his arms. They saw him bite it on the cheek—and rushed him. He was so absorbed in the body that he hardly noticed them until M. Claude gave a loud shout. Then, "the vampire started like a sleep walker suddenly awakened on the brink of a window ledge, dropped the corpse, and allowed himself to be taken without any resistance."

As for the poor old man with the violin, he was nothing but an innocent tool. He believed the soldier was his dead son, who had been killed in the Napoleonic wars. The old man believed the soldier came out of his grave at night to visit, drawn by the soulful music of the violin.

15

VAMPIRES SEIZE THE ENGLISH

ONE RAINY SUMMER EVENING IN 1816, the poet Percy Bysshe Shelley, his wife, Mary, her half sister, Lord Byron, and his young companion-physician, Dr. John Polidori, gathered at the Villa Diodoti on the outskirts of Geneva. They sat before a blazing wood fire and began amusing one another by telling German ghost stories. After a spell of exchanging stories, Lord Byron suggested that each one of them write a ghost story. All agreed. From this casual beginning was eventually to come Mary Shelley's famous novel *Frankenstein* and John Polidori's novella *The Vampyre*, the first English vampire tale.

The plot of *The Vampyre* was actually Lord Byron's. He had mentioned it during the Geneva gathering, but he discarded it; Dr. Polidori took it up and wrote *The Vampyre*.

The novella seemed to have been forgotten, but three years after it was written it appeared in the April 1819 issue of *New Monthly* magazine and created quite a stir in English literary circles. At first, the editors of the magazine attributed the story to Lord Byron. Lord Byron finally disclaimed any authorship, but even then some of his admirers demurred, and he continued to be credited with the story, to the annoyance of Dr. Polidori. Only after the tale had gone through several editions was Polidori given full credit for the work.

The Vampyre had created a sensation in England.

Not only in England, but also on the continent, for it came out just when tales of vampirism in central Europe were making their way west. It was translated into German. It was translated into French and published in Paris that same year, 1819. It became a drama by Charles Nodier, a famous French playwright of the period, and was produced in Paris at the Porte-Saint-Martin theater, where it was a roaring success. The theater was packed night after night, and *Le Vampire* was on the lips of everyone in France with literary pretensions.

The proof of success was in the imitations. *Le Vampire* was followed by a spate of vampire plays on the French stage. As a critic wrote in 1820, "There is not a theatre in Paris without its Vampire: at the Porte-Saint-Martin we have *Le Vampire*; at the Vaudeville *Le Vampire* again, at the Variétés *Les Trois Vampires ou Le Clair de la Lune*."

What was this fantastic tale of Polidori's, to create such a furor?

Polidori himself summarized the plot:

"A modern Greek vampire swears his travelling companion to secrecy and then undergoes a mock death. Months later, the travelling companion returns to London, only to discover his old friend the Greek vampire in English guise and indulging in some very dubious activities. But, like any honourable gentleman, the companion is bound by his oath and therefore has to watch these demonic-vampiristic activities without being able to interfere."

Was that all?

Not by far. Polidori's plot summary does not indicate the power of his story. In *The Vampyre*, Polidori created the prototype of the vampire that was to remain with English readers for more than a hundred years, even until today. It would be copied by scores of writers.

The *vampyre* was Lord Ruthven, "a nobleman, more remarkable for his singularities than his rank." His lordship was popular in London society because everyone wanted to see this cold character. "He gazed upon the mirth around him as if he could not participate therein." He had a "dead grey eye, which fixed upon the object's face, did not seem to penetrate; at one glance to pierce through to the inward workings of the heart; but fell upon the cheek with a leaden ray that weighted upon the skin it could not pass." His face had a "deadly hue . . . which never gained a warmer tint, either from the flush of modesty or from the strong emotion of passion."

The hero of the tale "was a young gentleman of the name of Aubrey," an orphan, but rich, handsome, and frank, and the apple of the eye of every mother who had an eligible daughter.

The story:

Lord Ruthven invites young Aubrey to accompany him on a tour of Europe, and the young man is flattered. In their travels, Aubrey notices an odd trait in Lord Ruthven: he is generous, but somehow the recipient of Lord Ruthven's generosity always ends up suffering disaster.

". . . It was not upon the virtuous, reduced to indigence by the misfortunes attendant upon virtue, that he bestowed his alms; these were sent from the door with hardly suppressed sneers; but when the profligate came to ask something, not to relieve his wants, but to allow him to wallow in his lust, or to sink him still deeper in his iniquity, he was sent away with rich charity."

At the gaming table, it was the "rash youthful novice, or the luckless father of a numerous family" who were Ruthven's targets. Aubrey tries to find an opportunity to persuade Lord Ruthven to stop his charities, but there is no way Aubrey can penetrate the coldness of Ruthven's behavior. When Lord Ruthven encountered his prey, then "his eyes sparkled with more fire than that of the cat whilst dallying with the half-dead mouse." The formerly affluent youth would be destroyed, the father with many children would sit "amidst the speaking looks of mute hungry children, without a single farthing of his late immense wealth, wherewith to buy even sufficient to satisfy their present craving."

Lord Ruthven and Aubrey arrive in Rome, where they part temporarily. Luckily for Aubrey, he receives letters from London telling him of the sinister nature of his companion, who has "the possession of irresistible powers of seduction," which make "his licentious habits more dangerous to society." In Rome, Aubrey saves a potential female victim from the clutches of Ruthven, and then goes on to Greece. Here Aubrey falls in love with the beautiful, delicate Ianthe, a creature "floating as it were upon the wind" as she chases butterflies. It is Ianthe who tells Aubrey tales of the "living vampyre" who was "forced every year, by feeding upon the life of a lovely female, to prolong his existence for the ensuing months." When Aubrey proposes to visit a remote spot in his search for antiquities, Ianthe tries to persuade him not to go, for the trip would take him through a forest that was "the resort of vampyres in their nocturnal orgies."

Aubrey promises to return home before dark, but, alas, he does not make it, and is trapped in the forest by a heavy storm. His horse stops at a hut. Aubrey goes inside, only to be attacked by a being of supernatural strength who throws him to the ground. At the same time, he hears female cries "mingling with the stifled, exultant mockery of a laugh, continued in one almost unbroken sound." Aubrey is rescued by a party bearing torches, and in the torchlight he sees the body of beautiful Ianthe, who has followed him. A dagger is found by Ianthe's side, but it has not been used. "There was no colour upon her cheek, not even upon her lip; . . . upon her neck and breast was blood, and upon her throat were the marks of teeth having opened the vein." His rescuers point to the mark and shout, "A Vampyre, a Vampyre."

Ailing, Aubrey lies in a house in Athens, when, by chance, Lord Ruthven arrives there, too. In compassion, he moves in to help nurse Aubrey. All seems to be forgiven between them. Aubrey recovers and together they plan to tour the remoter parts of Greece. They start out, but are set upon by a gang of robbers, one of whom shoots Ruthven. Ruthven says he is dying and evokes a promise from Aubrey not to say a word about his death for a year and a day. Aubrey promises; Ruthven then "dies."

Aubrey goes to bury the corpse, but it seems to be missing. The robbers tell Aubrey that Ruthven had given them instructions that his body "should be exposed to the first cold ray of the moon that rose after his death." Among Ruthven's possessions, Aubrey finds a sheath that fits the dagger found by Ianthe's side. Finally, Aubrey goes home to England, where his sister is waiting to "come out" in society, which she has been delaying until his return.

In the drawing room at the reception, Aubrey is suddenly accosted and "a voice he recognized too well sounded in his ear. 'Remember your oath,'" it said. Of course, there is Ruthven, large as life.

Aubrey is so shocked at seeing Ruthven that he has a relapse. He languishes between life and death for months and recovers only when a year has passed. There is only one more day left in which he has to keep silent about Ruthven.

Aubrey's sister comes to visit and announces that she is about to be married, which pleases Aubrey—until he sees the picture of her fiancé in her locket. He beholds "the features of the monster who had so long influenced his life. He seized the portrait in a paroxysm of rage and trampled it under foot."

Aubrey begs his sister to postpone the ceremony for just one day. She refuses.

At the ceremony, Lord Ruthven again whispers in Aubrey's ear "Remember your oath," and Aubrey, in a rage, breaks a blood vessel and is forced to take to his bed. He becomes weaker and weaker. But the marriage takes place, and Lord Ruthven and his bride leave London.

When the midnight hour strikes, Aubrey calls one of his guardians and tells him the whole story of Ruthven the vampire. Then, immediately, he dies.

"The guardians hastened to protect Miss Aubrey; but when they arrived, it was too late. Lord Ruthven had disappeared, and Aubrey's sister had glutted the thirst of a VAMPYRE."

The enormous success of Polidori's novella did not end in a season or a year, as is the case with most literary works. The concept of the vampire seized England, and after that France and Germany, as noted. In those countries, too, it did not quickly disappear. Vampire story followed story, vampire play followed play. Charles Nodier's *Le Vampire* was revived at the Porte-Saint-Martin in 1823. Alexandre Dumas saw a performance and was so struck by it that, nearly thirty years later, he used the theme for his own drama *Le Vampire,* which was produced at the end of 1851 at the Ambigu-Comique theater.

Dumas followed the line laid down by Polidori but expanded on it. Lord Ruthven dies and is laid upon the mountain; the audience sees the silver light of the moon fall on the body, the eyes open, and the mouth smile evilly. In a few moments "the vampire leaps to his feet, revitalized and with fresh energy for some new demonic enterprise."

Then, later, "It is too late, the vampire seizes his victim and as midnight strikes he destroys his hapless bride and quaffs his fill from her veins." At the end, however, Dumas lets society have its retribution: "the hallowed sword" is plunged into the monster's heart. "The vampire falls back into the grave, howling fearfully, and a heavy stone closing him in fast seals him there in the womb of the earth for ever and ever."

The public, it seemed, could not get enough of vampires. The lengthiest treatment of all (868 published pages) was *Varney the Vampire, or, the Feast of Blood* by James Malcolm Rymer, which was published in 1847. It was even more successful than Polidori's work and was printed time and again, finally appearing, in 1853, as a serial in a popular magazine that reached the laboring classes.

There is all the difference in the world between Polidori's tale and *Varney the Vampire.* The former was written as a lark by an educated man for the amusement of his educated friends. The whole plot depends on the upper-class concept of noblesse oblige—the gentleman keeps his word no matter what.

There was none of that sort of snobbery in *Varney.* It begins with one bang after another, aimed at the titillation of the great unwashed.

Chapter One. "Midnight—The Hail Storm—The dreadful Visitor. The Vampyre": "Oh, how the storm raged! Hail—rain—wind. It was, in very truth, an awful night." And, in "a stately bed" in an antique chamber a young girl, "beautiful as a spring morning," lies half asleep.

"God! how the hail dashes on the old bay window!"

The girl stirs—"that beautiful girl on the antique bed; she opens those eyes of celestial blue, and a faint cry of alarm bursts from her lips. . . . Heavens! What a wild torrent of wind, and rain, and hail!" Then come lightning and thunder, and finally, she sees a form at the window.

"Another flash of lightning—another shriek—there could now be no delusion.

"A tall figure is standing on the ledge immediately outside the window. It is its fingernails upon the glass that produces the sound so like the hail, now that the hail has ceased. . . . The pattering and clattering of the nails continues." The girl tries to scream but only a hoarse whisper comes out:

"Help—help—help—help!"

"A small pane of glass is broken, and the form from without introduces a long gaunt hand, which seems utterly destitute of flesh." One half of the window is swung wide open upon its hinges.

"'Help—help—help!' . . . that look of terror that sat upon her face, it was dreadful.

"The figure turns half round and the light falls upon the face. It is perfectly white—perfectly bloodless. The eyes look like polished tin . . . the teeth . . . projecting like those of some wild animal, hideously, glaringly white, and fang-like."

The girl is terrorized. "But her eyes are fascinated. The glance of a serpent could not have produced a greater effect upon her than did the fixed gaze of those awful, metallic-looking eyes that were bent on her face."

The sexual overtones are enormous.

What does the creature want? The girl slides to the edge of the bed, clutching the covers. "She drew her breath short and thick. Her bosom heaves, and her limbs tremble, yet she cannot withdraw her eyes from that marble-looking face. He holds her with his glittering eye."

The storm has stopped, the figure advances toward the girl. Can she escape? Can her eyes leave those of the intruder? The "young girl lies trembling. Her long hair streams across the entire width of the bed. As she has slowly moved along she has left it streaming across the pillows."

A pause.

"With a sudden rush that could not be foreseen—with a strange howling cry that was enough to awaken terror in every breast, the figure seized the long tresses of her hair, and twining them round his bony hands he held her to the bed. Then she screamed . . . shriek followed shriek . . . she was dragged by her long silken hair. . . . Her beautiful rounded limbs quivered with the agony of her soul."

"The glassy, horrible eyes of the figure ran over that angelic form with a hideous satisfaction—horrible profanation. He drags her head to the bed's edge. He forces it back by the long hair still entwined in his grasp. With a plunge he seizes her neck in his fang-like teeth—a gush of blood, and a hideous sucking noise follows. *The girl has swooned, and the vampyre is at his hideous repast!*"

More of the same, for over eight hundred pages. Until Varney the vampire goes "to the crater of Mount Vesuvius . . . tired and disgusted with a life of horror . . . Varney took one tremendous leap, and disappeared into the burning mouth of the mountain."

It was, as one critic described it, "penny-a-line fiction at the very top of its bent" or "sheer flatulence." Rymer's readers—and there were hundreds of thousands of them—sucked up every word with the gusto of Varney at lunch.

But just because the English lower classes adopted the vampire did not mean that the upper classes gave it up. One of the most outstanding of the vampire stories of the day was *Carmilla* by Sheridan Le Fanu, an Irish editor. The tale was published in the magazine *The Dark Blue* in 1871 in London and was a far more sophisticated work than *Varney the Vampire*.

The setting is a *schloss* (castle) near Graz in Austria. The story is told through the young heroine Laura, who is fascinated—in what would today be suspected as a lesbian relationship—with the vampire Carmilla. There are many dreams and many convolutions of plot, but eventually Carmilla is found to be Mircalla, Countess Karnstein, who was buried 150 years before the time of the story. In the end, the Countess Mircalla is discovered incorrupt in her grave, and dealt with in traditional fashion:

"The grave of the Countess Mircalla was opened . . . the features, though a hundred and fifty years had passed since her funeral, were tinted with the warmth of life. Her eyes were open, no cadaverous smell exhaled from the coffin . . . there was a faint but appreciable respiration, and a corresponding action of the heart. The limbs were perfectly flexible, the flesh elastic, and the leaden coffin floated with blood, in which to a depth of seven inches, the body lay immersed. There, then, were all the admitted signs and proofs of vampirism. The body, therefore, in accordance with the ancient practices, was raised, and a sharp stake driven through the heart of the vampire, who uttered a piercing shriek at the moment, in all respects such as might escape from a living person in the last agony. Then the head was struck off, and a torrent of blood flowed from the severed neck. The body and head were next placed on a pile of wood and reduced to ashes, which were thrown into the river and borne away, and that territory has never since been plagued by the visits of a vampire."

So ended the story of the vampire Countess Mircalla, but classy vampire tales were just hitting their stride.

16

THE MEN WHO CREATED DRACULA

BRAM STOKER WAS BORN IN IRELAND IN November 1847. He suffered from a leg ailment that prevented him from playing with his six brothers and sisters in their row house in Clontarf, north of Dublin Bay. When he was eight years old, he recovered enough use of his legs to play with them in the park across from their house. Despite his slow start, Bram Stoker grew to be a strapping youth. When he was sixteen he entered Trinity College, and, in contrast to his early years, he showed great athletic ability. In two years at Trinity he became the university's athletic champion. He also showed interest in books and the theater, he was a debater and a member of the philosophical society. He also began writing. His first college essay was "Sensationalism in Fiction and Society," a possible indication of the turn his mind would take in later years.

Bram's father, Abraham Stoker, was a senior clerk at Dublin Castle, a highly regarded and responsible post. His mother, Charlotte, was a strong-minded woman who advocated women's rights.

The money required to raise and educate a large family of children was so great that Bram was expected to seek employment on graduation from Trinity, a rude shock to a young man whose peers at the university had mostly been of independent means. Stoker's father found him a full-time clerical job at Dublin Castle that he took reluctantly, and found deadly dull. To alleviate his boredom, Bram began to think up ideas for articles and stories. He started a correspondence with the American poet Walt Whitman. Stoker admired Whitman and kept up correspondence with him when Whitman was attacked by the professors and students at Trinity as a "ridiculous" writer.

The best cure for boredom, Bram found, was going to the theater. When, in the fall of 1871, Stoker took issue with the *Dublin Mail* for failing to give adequate notice to theatrical performance, the paper's editor, Henry Maunsell, employed him to write theatrical reviews— without pay.

Over the years, Stoker made friends with a number of people in the theatrical and literary world. Oscar Wilde, a fellow student at Trinity, was the first. Alfred, Lord Tennyson, was another. Stoker visited America and his idol, Walt Whitman. He continued to write drama reviews for the *Dublin Mail* and became part-time editor at the short-lived Dublin newspaper the *Halfpenny Press*. His income came from the dull work at Dublin Castle, but he wrote more and more. His first serial story, "The Chain," appeared in the magazine *Shamrock*. It was a cliffhanger of what Stoker called "the phantom of the fiend" variety.

The major change in Stoker's life came after he wrote a glowing review of Henry Irving's performance in *Hamlet,* when it was produced in Dublin. The famous Shakespearean actor was so pleased he asked to meet the reviewer, and thus began a long friendship.

At the time, however, it seemed that Stoker was destined to live the life of a clerk. He was promoted to be inspector of petty sessions, which at least got him out of the castle to make regular tours of the courts. Since he was a writer, he was assigned to write a rule book for the clerks of the castle, a task which bored him almost unbearably. But finally he escaped: Henry Irving's success in London was so remarkable that he decided to take over the Lyceum Theatre himself. This would give him a constant showcase for his acting. He needed a manager, and he asked Bram Stoker to come to London and take that job.

Stoker was delighted. A whole new life was now possible. The doors of Dublin society had always been open to Stoker because of his father's position. He had gone to the balls and soirées for years, often with Oscar Wilde. The latter had become enamored of a young woman named Florence Balcombe and was once engaged to her. When that romance died, and Wilde went off to conquer England, Bram Stoker took up with Florence. It seemed unlikely that they could marry for years, given

Bram's pay at the castle, but the offer from Irving changed all that. They were married and arrived in England shortly before Christmas in 1878.

His new career at the Lyceum Theatre was all that Stoker could have asked for. The programs were an immediate success with the London theater-going public. One hit play followed another.

Stoker worked hard for the Lyceum, but he also managed to continue his writing. A collection of allegorical satires written for children, *Under the Sunset,* was published in 1881. Some of the critics said it was rather stern stuff for the young, but *Punch* called it "charming," and the *Daily News* remarked on "the purity and grace" of the author's style.

Stoker's second book *The Snake's Pass,* was very Irish in its content and approach; still it won approval from the London critics in 1890. Stoker was then taken up by Sampson Low Publishers, who also published the novelist Thomas Hardy, the juvenile adventure king G. A. Henty, and the explorer Henry M. Stanley.

However seriously he took his writing, it wasn't his life. The Lyceum Theatre had become that. He spent many long hours with Henry Irving planning the theatrical programs. They virtually lived in the theater. Irving had wanted a place where he could entertain and show off to his friends and admirers. When he took over the Lyceum it had a large storeroom in the basement. He had this converted to a kitchen and dining room that he called the Beefsteak Room. It had paneled walls and a huge fireplace, and a great long table for eating and drinking. Irving hired a celebrated chef and laid in a wine cellar filled with fine vintages. After the performances, Irving held many a triumphal dinner there. He entertained Edward, Prince of Wales, Lord Randolph Churchill, and Sarah Bernhardt, the queen of London's West End theater. Invitations to dine at the Beefsteak Room were much coveted by society. When Irving was not entertaining outsiders, he, Bram Stoker, and Harry J. Loveday, the stage manager, would sit around eating, drinking, and talking about the theater, and planning new productions.

One night in April 1890, a Hungarian professor of oriental languages at the University of Budapest named Arminius Vámbery came to the Lyceum, and after the performance was invited to the Beefsteak Room for supper. Vambery was a strange combination of social lion and scholar. He spoke sixteen languages fluently—wrote twelve and could get along in four more. He had traveled widely in the mysterious parts of the world—central Europe and Asia. He had somehow made himself useful to the British Foreign Office, for two years earlier the Prince of

Wales had singled Vámbery out in Budapest to make him a Commander of the Royal Victorian Order.

Vámbery started talking that night about the history and literature of central Europe. He told tales of "Dracula the Impaler," a famous Hungarian hero in the wars against the Turks. He spoke of such mysterious places as Transylvania.

Later Bram Stoker was to recall this meeting with Vámbery, but just now he was steeped in the problems of the Lyceum Theatre and a busy life, which included a theatrical tour of the United States with Henry Irving. He did find some time to write, and his work now tended toward the grisly and mysterious. "The Man from Shorrox" appeared in *Pall Mall* magazine. He also wrote "The Squaw," which was not about an Indian maiden, but about the Iron Maiden, that famous instrument of torture so admired by the Countess Elizabeth Báthory, which Stoker had seen on a visit to Nuremberg years earlier.

For some inexplicable reason, he then published two works that were regarded by the critics as trashy. One was *The Watter's Mou,* set in Cruden Bay on the east coast of Scotland, a favorite vacation spot for Stoker. The critics panned it. One said "the chief defect of the book, inevitable perhaps from the author's associations, is a tendency to melodramatic and stagey writing in some of the speeches and situations." Stoker's next attempt fared even worse. *The Shoulder of Shasta* was a disastrous attempt to write a story about a young San Francisco girl's dream summer atop Mount Shasta. Since Stoker did not know a lot about western American flora and fauna and even less about young San Francisco girls, the book did not come off. "This story will not increase his literary reputation nor appeal to many readers . . . the book bears the stamp of being roughly and carelessly put together."

That was probably an apt criticism, for Bram Stoker, as he was writing this pulpy story, was already considering something entirely different, something that had suddenly come to him out of the past.

Nearly a quarter-century earlier, Stoker had read Sheridan Le Fanu's vampire tale *Carmilla* with great interest. He had forgotten it, just as he had forgotten the conversation with Professor Vámbery in the Beefsteak Room about Dracula the Impaler. But now both were suddenly recalled to him, and they excited his imagination. He took a trip to the rocks of Cruden Bay, and there "wandered up and down the sandhills thinking out his plot."

The new book was to be *Dracula,* a book that would contain Stoker's vision of "a vampire king rising from the tomb to go about his ghastly business."

Remembering Dracula the Impaler imperfectly, Stoker wrote his old acquaintance Professor Vámbery in Budapest. Vámbery replied with information about this famous Hungarian nobleman. Stoker then went to the British Museum to learn what more he could find out about this figure.

There really was a person called Dracula. He was Vlad, the son of Vlad, a famous soldier. He was born in Sighisoara, Transylvania, around 1431. Sighisoara was then a German settlement called Schassburg, and the house in which Dracula was born was a typical German burgher's house of the fifteenth century, set in a cobbled lane.

But the boy did not long stay in that environment. The family moved often, following the fortunes of the father, who was an ambitious soldier and a good one. In 1431, Vlad the father was given the Order of the Dragon by Emperor Sigismund of Nuremberg; by that honor he was bound to fight against the Turks, who were trying to swallow up eastern Europe. The emblem of the order was a dragon (*dracul*) with spread wings, hanging on a cross. Because of his connection with this symbol, Vlad the elder was nicknamed Dracul, and the nickname Dracula, son of Dracul, passed on to his son.

The elder Dracul soon went to Walachia, where his half brother had taken over the throne. Soon Dracul had the throne. As the new ruler of Walachia, Dracul was directly in the line of the Turkish advance, which had already swallowed up parts of Serbia and Bulgaria. Although Dracul had been in the service of the Holy Roman Emperor, he decided to cast his lot with the Turks; and when the Sultan Murad II invaded Transylvania in 1438, Dracul and his sons Dracula, Mircea, and Radu joined the Turks in plundering Transylvania. But when Dracul let the citizens of the town of Sebes surrender directly to him instead of to the Turks whom they feared more, Murad got suspicious. He must have assumed that Dracul was trying to put something over on him. To deal with the menace, in 1444 the sultan lured Dracul, Dracula, and Radu to a meeting on the Turkish side of the Danube River. At the meeting, Dracul was seized by the sultan's men and put in chains. He was accused of treason. Somehow he managed to convince the sultan of his innocence of the charges. He was released and given back his throne. He renewed his bonds of loyalty to the Turks, and as an indication of his "good faith," when he went back to Walachia, he left his two sons as hostages to his good behavior.

The boys spent four years as hostages to the Turks, and young Dracula learned to hate his captors with a passion he never forgot. The boys were really endangered when their father, back in Walachia, defied the Turks and pledged his fealty to the Holy Roman Emperor once more. He and his son Mircea joined forces with a famous warrior named John Hunyadi against Sultan Murad. The campaign was a disaster for the Christians, and they had to flee back to Transylvania. Mircea tried to have Hunyadi executed by the emperor as the one responsible for the rout, but Hunyadi managed to worm out of the charges. He did not, however, forget them. In 1447, he arranged the assassinations of Mircea and his father Dracul, justifying his action by charging that they were in the pay of the Turks.

The Turks, at least, accepted the charge, which probably saved the lives of Dracula and his younger brother. They were released the next year and fled to Moldavia, where their cousin's father was on the throne. Dracula stayed there for three years and then returned to Transylvania, where for a reason inexplicable to anyone who does not understand the ins and outs of Balkan politics of the period, he sought and was granted the protection of his father's murderer. Soon Dracula was given the duchies of Fagaras and Almas. Later he ruled over Walachia. In fact he ruled Walachia three times, with several years of imprisonment in between. All this was the result of the uncertain loyalties of the Balkans in the period. The politics of Transylvania, above all, was complicated.

When John Hunyadi, who was known as the White Knight, died in 1456, the Christians had no great champion to send against the Turks. As prince of Walachia for the moment, Dracula pledged his allegiance to Ladislaus Posthumous, the young king of Hungary, and began an extended campaign against the Turks, who were encroaching on Walachia and Moldavia.

During this period, Dracula's reputation as a powerful fighter brought him great fame throughout Europe; but it was a fame touched with notoriety, because of the enormous volume of his acts of cruelty, particularly toward the hated Turks. Stories of his inhumane tortures of his enemies spread even wider than did those of his valor. Torture and boiling in oil were two of his pastimes.

In 1461, the Turks were sick of him, and they invited him to come to the port of Giurgiu on the Danube to discuss Walachian-Turkish difficulties. Dracula remembered that last foray into the arms of the Turks, and suspected another ambush. He agreed to the meeting, but made a few extra preparations: he sent a force of cavalry around the flank to surround Giurgiu, and when he arrived his horsemen came up to overpower the Turkish contingent, thus betraying them before they could betray him.

Dracula took the Turks back to the Walachian capital, Targoviste. There the enemies, men and women, were stripped of their clothes and impaled on spikes in a meadow for everyone to see what happened to those who tried to trick Dracula. The bodies were left in place for many months—eaten by blackbirds and baked by the sun. That was not the first time that the process of impaling had been used or that Dracula had impaled an enemy. In fact, Dracula had learned the technique from the Turks, who in turn had learned the skewering process from the Mongol hordes. But so enormous was this particular effort, involving hundreds of bodies, that it gave Dracula the new nickname of Vlad Tepes, or Vlad the Impaler.

Dracula's method of impalement got the most out of the victim. A powerful horse was harnessed to each leg of the unfortunate one, while the stake was driven into the body in such a manner that it did not kill instantly. Then the stakes, which were rounded instead of pointed, so that they tended not to rupture major blood vessels, were put into the ground. Sometimes death took only a few hours; sometimes it took many days. This mass impalement, staged by Dracula, was a sight to behold. "The victims were arranged in concentric circles on the outskirts of the city, where they could be viewed by all." There were high stakes and low stakes; a man was skewered according to his station in life. "There was impalement from above," with feet up, "and impalement from below," with head up. Some were skewered through the chest and some through the navel. Sometimes nails were driven into the victims' heads, sometimes limbs were cut off; some were blinded, other strangled or burned. Still others had their noses and ears cut off. Women had their breasts and sexual organs cut away; some were scalped, others were skinned alive.

So great was the effect of this effort on friend and foe alike that Dracula adopted the punishment as a regular device. It worked wonders with the feudal barons under his suzerainty, ambitious men who sometimes tried to monopolize the trade in their principalities or to cheat the ruler of taxes.

After a few months, Dracula launched his Danube campaign, with an army of twenty thousand men from Walachia. He sent envoys to all the independent countries in eastern and central Europe for help in his crusade against the Turks. He wrote to King Matthias of Hungary and tried to impress him with the importance of wresting from the Turks the lands they had taken along the Danube. The Christians must invade Bulgaria, Serbia, and Greece and take back the lands and free the people.

So Dracula set out on his "holy" crusade. But the Turks countered with an invasion of Walachia, and soon Dracula was in retreat. He used the scorched earth policy, destroying everything behind him. But the Turks followed, and they won victory after victory. The Turks then marched into Walachia, captured the capital of Targoviste, and installed Radu, Dracula's pro-Turkish brother, on the throne. Dracula and a handful of faithful followers were driven to take refuge in his castle on the bank of the Arges River. The Turks followed them there, but Dracula escaped and made his way to Hungary to seek the aid of King Matthias.

Instead, Matthias imprisoned Dracula and kept him in his dungeon for twelve years. Eventually Dracula was released and returned to the throne of Walachia, but the wars continued, and in 1476 he was betrayed by the Hungarians and killed in battle by the Turks.

All in all, Vlad Dracul, son of a famous father, had made quite a reputation for himself, and in modern times he became one of the celebrated heroes of eastern Europe. But the idea that Dracula was a vampire had never occurred to anyone along the Danube until the Irishman Bram Stoker came along.

17

DRACULA: BY THE BOOK

THE STORY OPENS WITH JONATHAN Harker's diary. The entry for May 3,
written from Bistritz, Austria, notes that he is on his way to Count
Dracula's castle, in the midst of the Carpathian Mountains, at a place
which borders on Transylvania, Moldavia, and Bukovina. His mission:
to settle some matters of real estate with Count Dracula.

Harker has prepared himself for this journey by spending time in the
British Museum in London, where he dug into books and maps about
Transylvania and discovered "that every known superstition in the
world is gathered into the horseshoe of the Carpathians, as if it were the
centre of some sort of imaginative whirlpool; if so my stay may be very
interesting."

"Interesting" is certainly an understatement. From the very beginning
of Harker's journey to Transylvania, horror stalks him, and the tension
grows. Stoker devotes page after page in the early chapters to building
the coming terror.

But back to Harker's trip. En route to the castle, Harker stays the
night at the Golden Krone Hotel in Bistritz, as Count Dracula had
advised him to do. There he finds a note from the count:

"My friend. —Welcome to the Carpathians. I am anxiously expecting
you. Sleep well tonight. At three tomorrow the diligence will start from

Bukovina; a place on it is kept for you. At the Borgo Pass, my carriage will await you and bring you to me."

All seems well, but as Harker prepares to get on the coach, things turn mysterious. The hotel's landlady urges him not to go, for this is the eve of St. George's Day. "Do you know that tonight when the clock strikes midnight, all the evil things in the world will have full sway?" she asks Harker. Of course he does not, and her meaning does not sink in. Despite her begging him not to go, he insists, so she takes a rosary from around her neck and presses it into his hand. As Harker departs, he sees all the hotel's people murmuring and crossing themselves. With the aid of his pocket dictionary he deciphers some of their words: "Ordog, pokol, stregoica, vrolok, and vlkoslak"—Satin, hell, witch, werewolf, vampire.

It is unsettling, even to the foolhardy Harker: "I am not feeling nearly as easy in my mind as usual," he notes in his diary.

The coach almost flies along, past orchards in blossom, pine woods, "mighty slopes of forest," and "lofty steeps of the Carpathians," past crags and snowy peaks. Evening comes, and the coach is still racing along the rugged road. Finally it enters Borgo Pass. There it is overtaken by a *calèche* drawn by four coal-black horses.

Harker steps down from the coach, and his arm is grasped by the count's coachman "in a grip of steel." He looks at the man, and sees a "hard-looking mouth, with very red lips and sharp-looking teeth as white as ivory." The coachman helps Harker into the *calèche*, gets up on the box, and away they go.

"I felt a little strangely, and not a little frightened," Harker tells his diary. The carriage races across the wild countryside, past trees, through tunnels, by great rocks; snow begins to fall, wolves howl, their sound grows closer, blue flames appear. Then the wolves, "with white teeth and lolling red tongues, with long sinewy limbs and shaggy hair" circle the carriage.

The driver waves his arm, and they fall back and disappear. The horses pull up into "the courtyard of a vast ruined castle, from whose tall black windows came no ray of light, and whose broken battlements showed a jagged line against the moonlit sky."

Harker is deposited before the castle door, but no one appears immediately. "The time I waited seemed endless, and I felt doubts and fears crowding upon me."

Finally, Harker hears sounds: "rattling chains and the clanking of massive bolts drawn back. A key was turned with the loud grating noise of long disuse, and the great door swung back."

He gets his first look at his host, Count Dracula, "a tall old man, clean shaven, save for a long white moustache, and clad in black from head to foot, without a single speck of colour about him anywhere."

Dracula motions to Harker to come in and then speaks. "Welcome to my house! Enter freely and of your own will!" After that ominous greeting, he grasps Harker's hand "with a strength which made me wince . . . it seemed as cold as ice . . . more like the hand of a dead than a living man."

Harker is settled in at the castle, and finally given supper, at which he is able to observe his host more closely:

"His face was a strong—very strong—aquiline, with high bridge of the thin nose and peculiarly arched nostrils; with lofty domed forehead and hair growing scantily round the temples but profusely elsewhere. His eyebrows were very massive, almost meeting over the nose, and with bushy hair that seemed to curl in its own profusion. The mouth, so far as I could see it under the heavy moustache, was fixed and rather cruel-looking, with peculiarly sharp white teeth; these protruded over the lips, whose remarkable ruddiness showed astonishing vitality in a man of his years. For the rest, his ears were pale, and at the tops extremely pointed; the chin was broad and strong, and the cheeks firm though thin. The general effect was of an extraordinary pallor."

His hands "were rather coarse—broad, with squat fingers. Strange to say, there were hairs in the centre of the palm. The nails were long and fine, and cut to a sharp point. As the Count leaned over me and his hands touched me, I could not repress a shudder. It may have been that his breath was rank, but a horrible feeling of nausea came over me, which, do what I would, I could not conceal. The count, evidently noticing it, drew back, and with a grim sort of smile, which showed more than he had yet done his protuberant teeth, sat down again on his own side of the fireplace."

Harker notes that the count never eats at meals with Harker and seems to appear for conversations only during the night, when he stays until dawn, then jumps up with a start at the cockcrow and excuses himself.

During the course of these conversations, Dracula tells Harker that he may go any place in the old castle, except where the doors are locked. And he is cautioned, "We are in Transylvania; and Transylvania is not England. Our ways are not your ways, and there shall be to you many strange things."

Again, an understatement of the grossest sort.

Harker wanders about the castle, visits the library where there are many books on England, and continues his nocturnal conversations with the count, who elaborates on his country: "It was the ground fought over for centuries by the Wallachian, the Saxon, and the Turk. Why, there is hardly a foot of soil in all this region that has not been enriched by the blood of men, patriots or invaders. . . .

"We Szekelys have a right to be proud, for in our veins flows the blood of many brave races who fought as the lion fights for lordship . . . we were a conquering race . . . when the Magyar, the Lombard, the Avar, the Bulgar or the Turk poured his thousands on our frontiers, we drove them back . . . to us for centuries was trusted the guarding of the frontier of Turkey-land. . . . Who was it but one of my own race who at Voivode crossed the Danube and beat the Turk on his own ground? This was a Dracula indeed! . . . When . . . we threw off the Hungarian yoke, we of the Dracula blood were amongst their leaders, for our spirit would not brook that we were not free. Ah, young sir, the Szekelys—and the Dracula as their heart's blood, their brains, and their swords—can boast a record that mushroom growths like the Hapsburgs and the Romanoffs can never reach."

Harker notes down all the conversations in his diary, and the strange fact that all—whether of the past glories of the Draculas or of England where the count is purchasing property—have to be broken off at cockcrow. Harker finds that most peculiar. Also odd is the fact that there is not a single mirror in the castle, and he has to use a tiny traveling mirror he has brought with him in order to shave. It is an experience with the mirror that changes Harker's feeling of uneasiness to one of fear.

One morning when Harker is shaving, using the little mirror, the count comes up suddenly behind him, but the mirror does not reflect Dracula. Harker is so startled that he cuts his face with the razor, and "blood was trickling over my chin. I laid down the razor, turning as I did so half round to look for some sticking plaster. When the Count saw my face, his eyes blazed up with a sort of demoniac fury, and he suddenly made a grab at my throat. I drew away, and his hand touched the string of beads which held the crucifix. It made an instant change in him, for the fury passed so quickly that I could hardly believe that it was ever there."

The count's calm is restored. "'Take care,' he said. 'Take care how you cut yourself. It is more dangerous than you think in this country.' Then seizing the shaving glass he went on: 'And this is the wretched thing that has done the mischief. It is a foul bauble of man's vanity. Away with it!' and opening the heavy window with one wrench of his terrible hand, he flung out the glass, which was shattered into a thousand pieces on the stones of the courtyard far below."

Jonathan Harker is disconcerted, all the more so when, as he pokes about the castle, he realizes that it is "set on the very edge of a terrible precipice." There are windows and windows, but he finds that door after door is locked. "A stone falling from the window would fall a thousand feet without touching anything!" Suddenly, Harker realizes that he is the prisoner of Count Dracula.

The ambience becomes ever more alarming. Harker seldom sees his host, never before dark, and never does the count eat with his "guest." The count tells Harker to write letters indicating that he will be at the castle for a month. Harker's heart "grew cold at the thought," but he obeys, for there is no alternative. The count warns him about poking about the castle: he must never fall asleep in any room but his own, for only there can he have safe rest.

So there *is* something to fear. But what?

Harker grows more nervous by the day. "I have placed the crucifix over the head of my bed," he writes in his diary, for protection from "the unnatural horrible net of gloom and mystery which seemed closing around me."

One night, as Harker gazes out the window of his room, he sees something in the moonlight—something moving from what he has determined to be the count's room.

"What I saw was the Count's head coming out from the window. I did not see the face, but I knew the man by the neck and the movement of his back and arms. In any case, I could not mistake the hands. . . . My very feelings changed to repulsion and terror when I saw the whole man slowly emerge from the window and begin to crawl down the castle wall over that dreadful abyss, *face down* with his cloak spreading out around him like great wings. . . . I thought it was some trick of the moonlight . . . but . . . it could be no delusion. I saw the fingers and the toes grasp the corners of the stones, worn clear of the mortar by the stress of years, and by thus using every projection and inequality move downwards with considerable speed, just as a lizard moves along a wall."

At that, "I feel the dread of this horrible place overpowering me; I am in fear—in awful fear—and there is no escape for me."

One night, after Harker sees the count leave the castle in his lizard fashion, he begins to explore more of the halls and wings. He finds door after door locked. Finally he discovers one that merely looks locked, because the heavy door has sagged on its hinges. He pushes the door open and goes into the room, which he can see by the light of his lamp was once occupied by ladies of the castle. Harker writes in his journal here, but then he begins to feel sleepy. He remembers the count's warning, but takes perverse pleasure in ignoring it. He falls asleep on a couch. He awakens to find three young women opposite him. They come close and look at him.

Two are dark and have high aquiline noses like the count's. One is fair "with great wavy masses of golden hair.

"All three had brilliant white teeth that shone like pearls against the ruby of their voluptuous lips. . . . I felt in my heart a wicked, burning desire that they would kiss me with those red lips."

They whispered together. Then all three laughed. The other two urged the fair girl:

"Go on! You are first, and we shall follow; yours is the right to begin," said one dark girl.

"He is young and strong; there are kisses for us all," said the other.

Harker lies paralyzed, not with fear, but with delicious anticipation.

"The fair girl advanced and bent over me till I could feel the movement of her breath on me. . . .

". . . The girl went on her knees and bent over me, simply gloating. There was a deliberate voluptuousness which was both thrilling and repulsive, and as she arched her neck she actually licked her lips like an animal, till I could see in the moonlight the moisture shining on the scarlet lips and on the red tongue as it lapped the white sharp teeth. Lower and lower went her head as the lips went below the range of my mouth and chin and seemed about to fasten on my throat. Then she paused, and I could hear the churning sound of her tongue as it licked her teeth and lips, and could feel the hot breath on my neck. Then the skin of my throat began to tingle . . . I could feel the soft, shivering touch of the lips on the supersensitive skin of my throat, and the hard dents of two sharp teeth, just touching and pausing there. I closed my eyes in a languorous ecstasy and waited—waited with beating heart."

Suddenly, Harker becomes aware of the presence of the count, and his eyes open wide as he sees Dracula grab the girl by the neck and hurl her aside.

"Never did I imagine such wrath and fury. . . . His eyes were positively blazing. The red light in them was lurid. . . . His face was deathly pale . . . the thick eyebrows that met over the nose now seemed like a heaving bar of white-hot metal."

In fury the count shouts, "How dare you touch him, any of you? Back, I tell you all. This man belongs to me." Then he relents a little. "I promise you that when I am done with him you shall kiss him at your will. Now go! go! I must awaken him, for there is work to be done."

"'Are we to have nothing tonight?' said one of them with a low laugh as she pointed to the bag which he had thrown upon the floor, and which moved as though there were some living thing within it."

Dracula nods and gestures to the bag. The three women jump forward and open it. "There was a gasp and a low wail, as of a half-smothered child," and then the three women disappear, taking the bag with them, and Jonathan Harker faints.

He awakens the next morning in his own bed, relieved. "I look round this room, although it has been to me so full of fear, it is now a sort of sanctuary, for nothing can be more dreadful than those awful women, who were—who *are*—waiting to suck my blood."

Days pass. Finally in desperation to escape Harker climbs down the castle walls—he has seen the count do it many times—and finds Dracula's room, and then stairs and a passageway to a ruined old chapel. The chapel is full of boxes of dirt, which have been filled by gypsies whom Harker has seen coming to the castle.

"There, in one of the great boxes, of which there were fifty in all, on a pile of newly dug earth, lay the Count! He was either dead or asleep, I could not say which—for the eyes were open and stony, but without the glassiness of death—and the cheeks had the warmth of life through all their pallor; the lips were as red as ever. But there was no sign of movement, no pulse, no breath, no beating of the heart." Harker goes to search the count for keys to the castle, but then, "when I went to search I saw the dead eyes, and in them, dead though they were, such a look of hate though unconscious of me or my presence, that I fled from the place."

Harker writes a letter telling of some of the horrors he has seen and throws it down to men in the courtyard. But instead of posting it, they give it to the count, and the count brings the letter sneeringly to Harker and burns it before him. Harker now knows that he is to be killed. He also overhears a conversation between the count and the three beautiful vampires, in which the count again promises them that they shall have Harker as soon as the count has finished with him. All that is left now is for the count to manage to get off to England without any suspicion. Thus Harker must be kept alive until the count goes.

What Harker does not know at this point is that the count is planning to invade England with his deadly blood lust. All the property he has bought—the dealings that brought Harker to Transylvania—is to create homes away from home. The boxes of earth are to give the count a number of resting places. Of course, all this must be kept secret. Jonathan Harker knows too much, so when the count departs, he must be turned over to the tender mercies of the three female vampires.

Several more days pass. The count announces to Harker that he is leaving and that Harker will be taken by carriage back to Borgo Pass, where the public coach will again meet him. But it is a vain promise. The doors to the castle are all locked. Harker is determined to escape, so he makes his way back to the underground vaults of the old chapel, again in search of keys. This time he finds the great box there, with nails in place, ready to be hammered down.

"I knew," he writes, "I must reach the body for the key, so I raised the lid, and laid it back against the wall; and then I saw something which filled my very soul with horror. There lay the Count, but looking as if his youth had been half renewed, for the white hair and moustache were changed to dark iron-grey; the cheeks were fuller, and the white skin seemed ruby-red underneath; the mouth was redder than ever, for on the lips were gouts of fresh blood, which trickled from the corners of the mouth and ran over the chin and neck. Even the deep, burning eyes seemed set amongst swollen flesh, for the lids and pouches underneath were bloated. It seemed as if the whole awful creature were simply gorged with blood. He lay like a filthy leech, exhausted with his repletion. . . . There was a mocking smile on the bloated face which seemed to drive me mad."

Harker grabs a shovel which the workmen have left nearby and strikes "at the hateful face."

"But as I did so the head turned, and the eyes fell full upon me, with all their blaze of basilisk horror. The sight seemed to paralyse me, and the shovel turned in my hand and glanced from the face, merely making a deep gash above the forehead. The shovel fell from my hand. . . . The last glimpse I had was of the bloated face, blood-stained and fixed with a grin of malice which would have held its own in the nethermost hell."

The gypsies return. There is much trampling in the halls, and then the sounds of doors clanging shut and keys turned in locks. The count has obviously gone away. Harker is alone, locked in the castle with the three dreadful women. "They are devils of the Pit!" he writes, and he is going to climb down the walls and brave the wolves of the forest, to escape this hellish place. This final entry in the journal is dated June 30.

Exeunt Jonathan Harker for the next six weeks.

The scene switches to England, and through letters and journals we become aware of the other characters in the book: Mina Murray, Harker's fiancée; Lucy Westenra, Mina's bosom friend; Dr. John Seward, head of a London mental hospital; R. M. Renfield, his weird patient; Arthur Holmwood, one of Lucy's suitors; a young American from Texas named Quincey Morris; and Dr. Van Helsing, a physician from Amsterdam.

Dracula's fifty boxes (with Dracula in one of them) arrive from the Black Sea by ship. The vampire, having fed on the members of the crew during the trip, arrives with a ghost ship.

Poor Lucy becomes Dracula's next victim. She is bitten and dies from loss of blood. She then becomes a vampire herself, for as Dr. Van Helsing explains, "All that die from the preying of the Un-Dead become themselves Un-Dead, and prey on their kind."

Lucy's corpse starts flitting around the churchyard at night, and her friends decide they must do something to save her soul. They track her down to her coffin, and see a shocking sight: The corpse has somewhere stolen a living child and is now preparing to suck out its life's blood.

"When Lucy—I call the thing that was before us Lucy because it bore her shape—saw us she drew back with an angry snarl, such as a cat gives when taken unawares; then her eyes ranged over us . . . eyes unclean and full of hell-fire. . . . As she looked, her eyes blazed with unholy light, and the face became wreathed with a voluptuous smile. . . . With a careless motion, she flung to the ground, callous as a devil, the child that up to now she had clutched strenuously to her breast, growling over it as a dog growls over a bone."

Arthur Holmwood is chosen to drive a stake into Lucy's body, while Dr. Van Helsing will read a prayer that should forever free her soul from this evil.

Arthur struck at the body "with all his might. The Thing in the coffin writhed; and a hideous, blood-curdling screech came from the opened red lips . . . the sharp white teeth clamped together till the lips were cut, and the mouth was smeared with a crimson foam . . . the blood from the pierced heart welled and spurted up around it. . . . Finally it lay still."

Arthur Holmwood is disconsolate at having to kill the one he loved. But Dr. Van Helsing consoles him: "No longer she is the devil's Un-Dead. She is God's true dead, whose soul is with Him!"

At this point Jonathan Harker reenters. Mina journeys to Budapest, where Jonathan is in a nursing home, under the care of nuns. After escaping from the castle, he obviously has had a terrible time of it. Pursued by wolves, he finally has made his way to a train station, half-crazy and talking gibberish, and has been given a ticket to the city. There he collapses. His case is diagnosed as "brain fever," and he lies comatose for days. Finally he recovers enough to identify himself, and the nuns call Mina to come to him. Under her care, he recovers. He and Mina are married, and they join the others in the search for the count, the vampire who has destroyed Lucy and threatens "many other poor souls."

Among them only Dr. Van Helsing is completely aware of the nature of the enemy they seek, and he enlightens them. Being a foreigner, he speaks a sort of pidgin English:

"There are such beings as vampires . . . this vampire which is amongst us is of himself so strong in person as twenty men . . . his cunning be the growth of ages . . . he is devil in callous, and the heart of him is not; he can, within limitations, appear at will when, and where, and in any of the forms that are to him; he can, within his range, direct the elements; the storm, the fog, the thunder; he can command all the meaner things: the rat, and the owl, and the bat—the moth, and the fox, and the wolf; he can grow and become small; and he can at times vanish and come unknown."

The good doctor also warns his companions in the search that "it is a terrible task that we undertake, and there may be consequence to make the brave shudder."

Again, a great understatement. Van Helsing enlightens them all further, "let me tell you, he is known everywhere that men have been. In old Greece, in old Rome; he flourish in Germany all over, in France, in India, even in the Chernosese; and in China, so far from us in all ways, there even is he, and the peoples fear him at this day. He have follow the wake of the berserker Icelander, the devil-begotten Hun, the Slav, the Saxon, the Magyar. . . . The vampire live on and cannot die by mere passing of the time; he can flourish when that he can fatten on the blood of the living."

But, said the doctor, the vampire also had some limitations:

"His power ceases, as does that of all evil things, at the coming of the day. . . . He can do as he will within his limit, when he have his earth-home, his coffin-home, his hell-home, the place unhallowed. . . . There are things which so afflict him that he has no power, as the garlic that we know of; and as for things sacred, as this symbol, my crucifix. . . . The branch of wild rose on his coffin keep him that he move not from it; a sacred bullet fired into the coffin kill him so that he be true dead; and as for the stake through him, we know already of its peace; or the cut-off head that giveth rest."

Van Helsing then explains how they can destroy the vampire:

"When we find the habitation of this man-that-was, we can confine him to his coffin and destroy him, if we obey what we know. But he is clever."

"I have asked my friend Arminius, of Budapesthe University . . . and he tell me of what he has been. He must indeed have been that Voivoda Dracula who won his name against the Turk, over the great river on the very frontier of Turkey-land. If it be so, then he was no common man; for in that time and for centuries after, he was spoken of as . . . the bravest of the sons of the 'land beyond the forest.' That mighty brain and that iron resolution went with him to his grave, and are even now arrayed against us. The Draculas were, says Arminius, a great and noble race. . . ."

After Professor Van Helsing has explained everything, the friends set out in earnest to search for the boxes of earth and Dracula.

Dracula, however, strikes first. Renfield, the mental patient, is found unconscious, beaten, lying in a pool of blood. He tells the others that Dracula has been after Mina, and then he dies.

Indeed, Mina has been attacked. As she tells the story:

Beside her bed, out of the mist, stepped "a tall thin man, all in black. I knew him at once . . . the waxen face; the high aquiline nose . . . the parted red lips, with sharp white teeth showing between; and the red eyes. . . . With a mocking smile he placed one hand on my shoulder and, holding me tight, bared my throat with the other, saying as he did so, 'First a little refreshment to reward my exertions . . . it is not the first time, or the second, that your veins have appeased my thirst!' . . . He placed his reeking lips upon my throat . . . it seemed that a long time must have passed before he took his foul, awful, sneering mouth away. I saw it drip with fresh blood!"

Mina continues. "Then he spoke to me mockingly: 'You . . . are now to me, flesh of my flesh; blood of my blood, . . . and shall be later on my companion and my helper.' With that he pulled open his shirt, then with his long sharp nails opened a vein in his breast. When the blood began to spurt out, he took my hands in one of his, holding them tight, and with the other seized my neck and pressed my mouth to the wound, so that I must either suffocate or swallow some of the. . . . Oh, my God! my God! what have I done?"

What she had done was become a slave to Dracula, and she could never escape him until the vampire died.

So the chase for the vampire is redoubled, in the knowledge that he must be killed if Mina is to be saved.

Armed with Jonathan Harker's knowledge of the real estate bought by Dracula, the friends go from one estate to another, finding and destroying the boxes of earth laid down by the vampire. Once they confront Dracula himself. Harker makes a slash at him with his great Kukri knife, which does no damage. Dr. Seward rushes forward holding a crucifix and a wafer in his hand. The count retreats, "his waxen hue became greenish-yellow by the contrast of his burning eyes." He dashes across the room and throws himself out the window with no ill effects, hurling these words back at his pursuers:

"You think that you have left me without a place to rest; but I have more. My revenge is just begun! Your girls that you all love are mine already; and through them, you and others shall yet be mine."

Dracula has temporarily foiled them, but the group continues its chase. Mina, who is tainted by the vampire blood, is now hypnotized by Dr. Van Helsing, and in her trance she is able to tell her friends Dracula's thoughts and plans. He is escaping to Transylvania, by ship. The race against time continues. The protagonists swear to follow Dracula "to the jaws of Hell."

Finally, the Castle Dracula again becomes the scene. Dr. Van Helsing goes on ahead, he finds the three beautiful female vampires in their coffins in the castle, and deals with them in the traditional way.

Dracula himself has not yet shown up. The others of the party arrive on the road to the castle, and overtake the gypsies, who are carrying Dracula's coffin in a cart. Harker and Mr. Morris the Texan set upon the box with a frenzy. "Under the effects of both men the lid began to yield, the nails drew with a quick screeching sound, and the top of the box was thrown back."

Through Mina's eyes we see the finale. "The sun was almost down on the mountain tops, and the shadows of the whole group fell long on the snow. I saw the Count lying within the box upon the earth, some of which the rude falling from the cart had scattered over him. He was deathly pale, just like a waxen image, and the red eyes glared with the horrible vindictive look which I knew too well.

"As I looked, the eyes saw the sinking sun, and the look of hate in them turned to triumph." For with darkness the count would come to life, and his power was greater than that of Mina's friends.

"But on the instant, came the sweep and flash of Jonathan's great knife. I shrieked as I saw it sheer through the throat, whilst at the same moment Mr. Morris' bowie knife plunged into the heart.

"It was like a miracle but before our very eyes, and almost in the drawing of a breath, the whole body crumbled into dust and passed from our sight . . . there was in the face a look of peace, such as I never could have imagined might have rested there."

Finis. What a story it is! One that every lover of horror tales must read.

18

A MEATY VAMPIRE STORY

ON WEDNESDAY, APRIL 15, 1925, THE Hanover Vampire was decapitated.
There was no question about his guilt. He admitted his crimes. But was
this scourge of Hanover really a vampire?

His name was Fritz Haarmann. He was an unhappy child because he
hated and feared his father, but he had a solid middle-class education at a
church school. His schooling lasted until World War I broke out. Then
scholar Fritz Haarmann became soldier Fritz Haarmann, and he served
admirably with the celebrated Tenth Jaeger Battalion, at Colmar and
Alsace. When he was mustered out of the service for illness during the
middle of the war, his record was marked "recht gut," high honor from a
demanding service.

But when Fritz Haarmann got home from the war, all the old troubles
with his father resumed. After many quarrels with his family, he left
home. He became a drifter, and then a thief. He was caught, convicted,
and sent to jail briefly.

After his release from jail, he returned to Hanover and took a room.
He opened a small "cook shop," a combination meat market and
delicatessen in the old quarter of the city at 27 Cellarstrasse. Immediately, he was popular with his customers; because in the last years of
the war virtually everything was ersatz, with meat especially very diffi-

cult to find. But butcher Haarmann always seemed to have a supply, when other markets had none.

For some reason Haarmann became a police informer, giving the authorities tips on the whereabouts of wanted men. This activity of his was well known, and his customers began to refer to him as "Detective Haarmann." He could roam the streets of Hanover freely; the authorities paid him no attention.

He liked to hang out around the railroad station where all sorts of vagabonds clustered. Haarmann befriended many of them, especially the younger ones. He would see a down-and-out youngster, approach him sympathetically, and offer help. If the youngster responded to Haarmann's offer to give him a meal, they would go to his room in the Cellarstrasse. While the vagabond ate, Haarmann would praise him for his good looks and pleasant demeanor. One thing usually led to another—but the end was not quite what the youths expected. Haarmann was homosexual, but he was also a psychotic killer.

Haarmann's first victim was a seventeen-year-old boy named Friedel Rothe. He was a runaway, but apparently one who was having some second thoughts, for he sent his mother a postcard from Hanover. It so happened that on the September day in 1918 that she received the card, Rothe's father was discharged from the service. Together, the parents tried to find the boy. From one of Friedel's new friends they learned that the boy had been befriended by "a detective." They went to the Hanover police station. The police put two and two together and went to 27 Cellarstrasse. They did not find young Rothe, but they did find Fritz Haarmann in "an unequivocal situation" with another boy. They arrested Haarmann and carted him off to jail where he was charged with "gross indecency."

If only they had searched Haarmann's place, they would have found Friedel Rothe's head hidden under a newspaper behind the oven. As it was, Haarmann secured bail, came home, and destroyed the evidence of the Rothe murder by jettisoning the head into the river. Eventually, Haarmann was tried and sentenced to nine months in jail for indecency but that was all. The Rothe case remained unsolved. Friedel Rothe was just another missing person in a nation turned topsy-turvy by defeat.

After Haarmann served his time on the morals charge, he immediately went back to his old ways. He joined forces with Hans Grans, a young thief, murderer, police informer, and bully. Even in the rough Hanover underworld, Grans was regarded as a particularly vile fellow. Somehow, he secured complete power in his relationship with Haarmann; there was nothing Hans Grans wanted that Haarmann would not do. Together they carried out many grisly murders, choosing their victims from the riffraff of Hanover.

One day in November 1923, Hans Grans saw a pair of trousers he liked. The only problem was that they were being worn by seventeen-year-old Adolf Hannappel. But that night the trousers changed owners. Dead Adolf Hannappel had no need for them any more.

A few days later Grans and Haarmann went down to a homosexual hangout, a tiny dancing place called Zur Schwulen Guste (Gay Gussie's). There, Hans Grans admired a shirt. There was the same complication: the shirt was on the back of a young man named Ernst Spiecker.

The difficulty was soon overcome. Poor Ernst Spiecker had no use for his shirt after that night.

Grans was the schemer; Haarmann was the killer and the meat cutter. The corpses were kept in a cupboard until they could be disposed of; but business was good in these hard times, when meat was even harder to find than it had been during the war. Fritz Haarmann's excellent sausages were always in demand. He liked them very much himself—and *he* knew what was in them. As for the skulls and bones, they were thrown into the river behind the Cellarstrasse shop.

The affairs of the murderous team progressed nicely until Haarmann decided to befriend a young man named Fromm. For once, he had mistaken the nature of his quarry. Young Fromm was not a homosexual, and he was infuriated by Haarmann's approach. He accused Haarmann loudly of making indecent proposals. Haarmann blustered. The argument grew noisy, and the police came. Both men were arrested. In the investigation that followed, the police again visited 27 Cellarstrasse, and this time they searched the place. Among the sausages they found parts of several different bodies. They arrested Fritz Haarmann again, this time for murder.

The newspapers immediately christened the butcher "the Hanover Vampire." The reason was the way he killed. He admitted to murdering twenty-seven young men—by biting them in the throat.

In the beginning of the investigation, Hans Grans was arrested and charged as an accomplice to "the Vampire"; but, obviously in exchange for information, he was allowed to plead guilty to a lesser charge of "incitement" and receiving stolen goods and was sentenced to prison before Haarmann was tried.

Some people said butcher Haarmann was insane. Haarmann himself said he was not insane but that he had been in a "trance" each time he committed a murder and was thus unaware of what he was doing.

The judge did not believe him. Haarmann knew exactly what he was doing, the judge said. "It was necessary for him to hold down his victim by hand in a peculiar way before it was possible for him to inflict a fatal bite on their throats. Such action often necessarily involved some degree of deliberation and conscious purpose."

So Fritz Haarmann was sentenced to death by decapitation.

The trial and the sentence made a grand story for newspapers throughout western Europe. In London, the *Daily Express* headline writer went into ecstasies:

VAMPIRE BRAIN:
PLAN TO PRESERVE IT FOR SCIENCE

Owing to the exceptional character of the crimes—most of Haarmann's victims were bitten to death—the case aroused tremendous interest among German scientists. It is probable that Haarmann's brain will be removed and preserved by the University [of Goettingen] authorities.

But all the hokum was forgotten on Wednesday, April 15, 1925, when Fritz Haarmann was taken to the execution ground and faced the long sword of the headsman. The sword rose and came down, blood spurted out of the severed neck, and the head rolled into the basket. The seven-year career of the Hanover Vampire had come to an abrupt end.

The question remained: Was Fritz Haarmann really a vampire?

The answer is yes, he was. The biting of the throats of his victims was Haarmann's passport into the realm of vampires of the twentieth century.

There are two questions to which no one who outlived Fritz Haarmann knew the answer: Just how many of Hanover's good burghers had partaken of sausages made from parts of Friedel Rothe, Adolf Hannappel, Ernst Spiecker, and twenty-four other unfortunate young men?

Did that make them cannibals?

19

THE VAMPIRE PRIEST

VAMPIRES HAVE ALWAYS BEEN A RARE phenomenon in Ireland, perhaps because of the strength of the Catholic Church there. But in the 1920s, at least one vampire seems to have showed up in Ireland. "Seems to have" are the key words, because the whole tale is shrouded in mystery and entombed in concealment. But enough details surfaced for R. S. Breene to write an account of the Irish Vampire, which appeared in the October 1925, issue of the *Occult Review*.

The locale of the tale is not revealed, more than to say it was a "remote, wild and mountainous place," which could be virtually anywhere in Ireland outside Dublin. The villagers took their Catholicism seriously. They were poor, honest, brave, hardworking people; they were also crude and superstitious, and leprechauns were not unknown to them. Being so isolated, their concept of seen and unseen, reality and unreality tended to get mixed up. Even so, these factors combined are not enough to account for the Irish Vampire.

The village priest was not a local person, and he had never properly made himself part of the village scene. He was respected, but he was not loved. The people consulted him on matters of faith, but they did not socialize with him. Still, he served the district well enough until just after his fiftieth birthday, when suddenly he died.

His body was laid out at his mother's house, which was some distance from this village, but all the villagers made the trip to help bury their priest.

It was a sad picture when the body was brought home to the aged mother, whose chief pride in her later years had been "her boy in the Church"; and it was sadder still when the coffin set out once more from the whitewashed farmhouse, to carry its occupant to the rocky graveyard in the hills where all his kin had laid their bones for generations.

All the neighbors of the priest's mother joined the villagers in the funeral cortège; but the mother was not feeling up to the strain, so she remained in her house.

It took some time for the burial party to reach the graveyard, and the trip back over the rocky road was equally slow. Shadows were beginning to lengthen over the ground as they returned. As the cortège came down the last hill, the occupants of the first car saw a man approaching. Everyone around the neighborhood was in the funeral party. Who could this stranger be?

As the distance between pedestrian and riders narrowed, two men in the first car "saw at once and quite clearly, that they were face to face with the man whom they had laid in his grave two or three hours before. He passed them with his head slightly averted, but not sufficiently to prevent them from making absolutely certain of his identity, or from noting the intense, livid pallor of his skin, the hard glitter of his wide-open eyes, and the extraordinary length of his strong, white teeth, from which the full red lips seemed to be writhed back till the gums showed themselves. He was wearing, not the grave-clothes in which he had been attired for his burial, but the decent black frock-coat and garments to match in which they had last seen him alive. He passed down the long line of vehicles, and finally disappeared around a turn in the road."

Someone in every vehicle saw the priest. It was unnerving, to say the least, and the villagers hurried their return trip, fearful that night might overtake them on the road.

At last they reached the dead man's mother's house. The leaders consulted among themselves and agreed that they would say nothing to her of what they had seen on the road. They approached the door, but she did not come to greet them. They knocked. There was no answer. They knocked again. And again. Still there was no answer, and they began to worry. Someone peered into a small front window near the door, and was shaken by what he saw: there on the floor lay the crumpled body of the priest's mother. Hastily they broke in the door and gently lifted the mother up. They spoke to her, and she regained consciousness.

The mother told the anxious villagers what had happened to her. Just about a half an hour before they arrived and found her, she had heard a knock on the door. She could not think who it might be, for everyone in the area had gone to the burial. Surely she would have heard the sound of the cars if the funeral cortège had returned. But she knew she was alone. Afraid to open the door, she looked out the window. "There, to her horror, she saw her dead son, standing in the broad daylight much as she had last seen him alive. He was not looking directly at her. But she too noted the extraordinary length of his teeth, the cold blaze of his eyes, the wolfishness of his whole bearing, and the deathly pallor of his skin. . . . Fear swept over her. . . . She felt her limbs giving way under her." She fell to the floor, and that is where the villagers found her on their return.

That was writer Breene's "true vampire story." But had the priest really turned into a vampire?

The principal scholar of vampirology, Montague Summers, answered the question a few years later. "I have," he wrote in his study *The Vampire in Europe*, "seldom met with a more interesting account of a vampire . . . it bears the hall mark of truth in every particular and is indeed most notable and striking."

Montague Summers was an English priest who had been an editor of the Elizabethan and Restoration dramatists when he became interested in vampires. In the second quarter of the twentieth century, he abandoned his other studies to undertake his exhaustive research on vampires. He might be called the principal vampire apologist, for there is no question that after his study he believed in the existence of vampires. Moreover, he had developed "an absolute and complete belief in the supernatural, and hence in Witchcraft."

But of all the phenomena, the most startling to him was the vampire.

"In all the darkest pages of the malign supernatural there is no more terrible tradition than that of the Vampire, a pariah even among demons. Foul are his ravages; gruesome and seemingly barbaric are the ancient and approved methods by which folk must rid themselves of this hideous pest. Even today in certain quarters of the world, in remoter districts of Europe itself, Transylvania, Slavonia, the islands and mountains of Greece, the peasant will take the law into his own hands and utterly destroy the carrion who—as it is yet firmly believed—at night will issue from his unhallowed grave to spread the infection of vampirism throughout the countryside."

Summers spent several years in France and Italy on his studies, and some unfriendly critics have hinted that he became converted to black magic there. The charge has never been proved; it does remain a rumor.

The fact is that Montague Summers started where Dom Calmet left off. He conducted "the first serious study in English of the Vampire, and kindred traditions from a general, as well as from a theological and philosophical point of view." And most critics have agreed that Summers did an admirable job in his study.

In trying to set forth a "philosophy of vampirism," Summers cited many cases, from ancient to modern times, and investigated the beliefs in vampires of many people. He was not afraid to challenge his many known adversaries, those skeptics who did not believe. He refuted Dom Calmet's doubts about the existence of vampires, firm in his own belief that anything—even the vampire—is possible in this world.

Dom Calmet had asked how the vampire could leave its grave without disturbing it. Was it the Devil that reenergized the corpse, Dom Calmet asked?

Summers argued that Dom Calmet was raising the most superficial of issues. One of Dom Calmet's major arguments against the existence of vampires rested on the case of the vampire in the graveyard by the clock tower who tried to retrieve his shroud. That story was a gross exaggeration, of course, said Montague Summers, but "one can hardly brush aside the vast vampire tradition because one instance proves to be overdrawn—the story when divested of these trappings offers nothing impossible."

As to Calmet's question about how the corpse was changed into a vampire, Montague Summers had an answer:

"Three things are necessary, the Vampire, the Devil, and Permission of Almighty God. . . . Whether it be the Demon who is energizing the corpse or whether it be the dead man himself who by some dispensation of Divine Providence has returned is a particular which must be decided severally for each case. So much then for Dom Calmet's question, to whom are the appearances of Vampires to be attributed?

"Can the Devil endow a body with these qualities of subtlety, rarification, increase, and diminishing, so that it may pass through doors and windows? I answer that there is no doubt the Demon can do this, and to deny the proposition is hardly orthodox."

As further explanation of vampirism, Summers offered ectoplasm: "Matter can, then, pass through matter . . . we may, if we will, adopt the ectoplasmic theory to explain the mode whereby the Vampire issues from his grave."

And as for the undisturbed grave from which the vampire may have issued: "Where careful investigation was made, it was generally found that there were discovered four or five little holes or tunnels, not much larger indeed than a man's finger, which pierced through the earth to a very considerable depth. And here, perhaps in this one little detail, we may find the clue to the whole mystery."

Thus Montague Summers put down Dom Calmet: "The good Benedictine has been a little too dogmatic in his assertions."

And, then, Montague Summers's detractors countered his arguments with their own, proving, among other things, the scientific impossibility of vampire existence.

Meanwhile, vampires around the world ignored all the arguments and flourished.

20

THE MONSTER OF DUESSELDORF

THE STORY BEGAN ON SUNDAY EVENING, February 5, 1929. The locale was a lonely scraggly area of half-built development houses in a depressed section on the northern outskirts of Duesseldorf. After a week of hard work, Frau Kuhn had been visiting friends here, and she was walking home. She had turned off the avenue into a side street when she heard footsteps behind her.

A man seized the sleeve of her coat. "Keep quiet. Not a word!" he whispered fiercely. She felt sharp pain as her body was slashed, and then . . . she was in the hospital with twenty-four stab wounds, including deep ones in her temple that apparently had been designed to kill her. She could recall nothing about her assailant.

Five days later, as Frau Kuhn still lay in the hospital, workmen in the same neighborhood found the body of a little girl, covered with her coat, next to the high fence of an unfinished building. She too, had been stabbed, in the temples and her left side—thirteen times. The girl, Rose Ohliger, had been eight years old.

Two vicious crimes in the same neighborhood in the same week! Two crimes of the same sort! The newspapers took up the case. They dubbed the murderer "Jack the Ripper"—after the infamous English killer of some years earlier, who had terrified London. For Duesseldorf was indeed terrified by these seemingly mad attacks.

Worst of all, the papers said gloomily, there seemed to be no clues.

A few days later, the killer struck again. Poor old Rudolf Scheer, a disabled laborer living on a pension, had gone to a local public house. He got a little drunk and left the tavern at 11:30. But he never got home. They found his body the next morning in the same area where they had found Rose Ohliger. He had been attacked from the rear, and he had been stabbed twenty times.

Three vicious crimes and the police still had no clues. This new murder gave a new dimension to the case. It was not just girls and women that the killer sought. He could not be just a sex maniac, for his victims had been a respectable middle-aged working woman, a little girl, and a poor old man. Was anyone in Duesseldorf safe?

The police put out a dragnet, they brought in all known criminals with records of violence. They interviewed hundreds of them. Two months went by, and they were no closer to solving the case than they had been after the attack on Frau Kuhn.

April 2. Erna Pinner, a sixteen-year-old girl who lived in the area where the other crimes had been committed, was on her way home one evening. She heard footsteps behind her, but her only thought was that one of her friends was coming to catch up with her. To fool the friend, Erna suddenly lifted the heavy hood of her coat over her head. Suddenly she was jerked backward and dragged along the ground. The dragging stopped, and someone bent over her. It was a strange man. He put his hands around her throat, and she knew he was trying to strangle her. She could not scream. But she seized his nose and pulled it as hard as she could. She would not give up. Finally, she saw the man loosen a rope with which he had snared her, and grab it and run off. Erna had fought for her life, and she had saved it. But she could not describe the man. It had been dark, and with the hood over her head she had not seen much, anyway.

This time the police had a suspect, a man who had been seen in the area. He was Hans Strausberg, a twenty-one-year-old epileptic. He confessed to all the crimes and described them faithfully. He was sent to an insane asylum for life. All Duesseldorf breathed a collective sigh of relief. The "Ripper" crimes had been solved.

But on July 30, a thirty-five-year-old woman named Erma Gross was found in a shabby hotel room in Duesseldorf, naked and dead. She had been strangled.

That crime did not immediately attract much attention from the police, the papers, or the public, for women found dead in shabby hotel rooms were not so uncommon as all that. But within the next three weeks, more crimes of this nature occurred.

First, on August 21, at the country fair in the Duesseldorf suburb of Lierenfeld, young Frau Mantel was walking along alone when she was accosted by a man. "Fraulein, may I accompany you?" he asked. Frau Mantel had no chance to refuse, for she was immediately stabbed in the back. Her assailant ran away.

That same night, near the same place, Anna Goldhausen was also walking alone. A man came up to her and without a word lunged at her and stabbed her.

Still later that night, Gustav Kornblum was sitting on a bench in the fairgrounds, resting. Without warning, he was suddenly stabbed from behind.

Three crimes in one day! The papers began to wonder if that epileptic Hans Strausberg had really committed those other crimes. Or had he read about them in the papers and obliged the police with a made-up confession? Or could this night's spree be the work of a copycat?

The police announced that they were increasing their surveillance. But surveillance of what? They could not be everywhere. And it seemed that the criminal could.

August 23. Fourteen-year-old Luise Lenzen took her five-year-old foster sister Gertrude Hamacher to the Neuss fair. When they did not come home that evening, the family worried and a police search was started.

August 24. Someone at the fair said he thought he heard a girl's voice cry "Mama, Mama," at about 11:30 that night. That was all. The bodies of the two girls were found in a field of runner beans near the fairgrounds. They had been strangled and their throats cut. As the police reconstructed the crime, they theorized that the little girl had been killed first. When Luise saw what was happening, she had cried out, but it did her no good. She had been stabbed in the back and then killed.

This time, however, the police had a clue. A good shoe print had been left at the scene: the crime had been committed by a man, or someone wearing men's shoes.

But how many thousands of pairs of shoes were there in Duesseldorf?

The day that the bodies of the two girls were found, twenty-six-year-old Gertrude Schulte, a domestic worker, went out for her afternoon off from her employer's house. She was walking in the village of Oberkassel, when she was approached by a nice-looking man, about thirty-five years old. He introduced himself as Fritz Baumgart and asked her if she would like to go to the fair. She accepted his invitation, and they went to the fair. That evening, they went for a walk in the Flingern woods. But once in the woods Fritz began to grow bold, and soon Gertrude knew that his intentions were far from honorable—and most immediate. Not only did he show her in body language what he wanted, but he also suggested it most crudely.

"I'd rather die!" cried Gertrude.

"Well, die then!" said Fritz.

She saw a knife in his hand, then felt blows to her neck and shoulder. Before she could cry out, she felt a terrible pain in the back, and heard Fritz shout, "Now you can die"—and she was flung to the ground.

But then came a welcome noise. Someone had heard her screams and came crashing through the woods. Fritz ran away, and her rescuer ran to her. Gertrude was rushed to the hospital, where the surgeons found part of the knife blade in her back. The only identifying thing she could remember about the man who had tried to kill her was that he had a missing tooth in his upper right jaw.

Who is this madman?

Why can't the police catch him?

All Duesseldorf was asking these questions.

The poor police. What had they to go on? A single footprint. A thirty-five-year-old man, who might have been thirty or forty; "nice-looking"—what did that mean? A name. Fritz Baumgart. They checked all the Baumgarts. There was no Fritz in the thirty-to-forty age group with a missing right upper tooth. Still, one missing tooth was their only real clue. They began looking for men with missing teeth.

The crime wave slowed. A month went by, and there were no more attacks. Duesseldorf's newspapers turned to other matters, and the public began to relax again.

Just as it seemed that the horror was over, in that same wooded area Ida Reuter's body was found on a late September Monday morning. She, too, had been a domestic worker, and she, too, had gone off for her Sunday afternoon and had never been seen again alive. Her body had been dragged from the path through the grass. She had been beaten to death, struck in the head with a blunt instrument.

"Hammer Murderer!" screamed the newspaper headlines.

Was this still another killer, loose in Duesseldorf against an impotent police force?

Ten days later, the newspapers could answer their own question: a girl named Elizabeth Dorrier was found, killed by blows to the temple with a blunt instrument. The marks looked like hammer marks. They were now looking for two men, said the police, one with a knife and a missing tooth, and a complete unknown, who wielded a hammer.

October 25. Frau Meurer was walking home through the Flingern district. A stranger came up alongside her as she walked along this lonely road, and spoke.

"Aren't you frightened? So much has happened here," he said.

Frau Meurer did not even have a chance to consider her answer. When she woke up, she was in the hospital. Her head had been battered by a hammer. She was lucky to be alive.

That same night, Frau Wanders had gone to the park in Duesseldorf, and there she had encountered a man. A promising conversation had sprung up, but before it had progressed very far, the man pulled out a hammer and hit Frau Wanders on the head repeatedly. She collapsed but then managed to pick herself up. The man was gone. She went to the hospital, where doctors and the police agreed that her wounds followed the pattern of the hammer attacks of recent days.

If the police had been given a hard time before by the Duesseldorf public, that was as nothing to the press and public uproar that began now. Even the politicians were threatened. No day went by that some segment of the media did not attack the authorities for their failure to protect the public.

November 7. Five-year-old Gertrude Albermann was reported by her parents to be missing from their home in Flingern. A search was begun in the fields and roads and streets, through the woods and the high grass of the park area. Nothing.

Then came an anonymous letter to one of the newspapers, telling where Gertrude's body could be found—and where another body could be found. Soon the police had the letter, and, following its directions, they discovered Gertrude Albermann's body, "lying against Haniel's Wall," just as the note had advised.

The murderer now had the gall to boast of his crimes, and the arrogance to advertise them to the press. It was monstrous.

And what of that second body, about which no one knew anything at all?

The murderer had written on a piece of gray-white wrapping paper, "Murder at Pappendelle. In the place marked with a cross, a corpse lies buried." A crude map of the Pappendelle area near Duesseldorf had been sketched in, with the X clearly marked.

Detectives went to Pappendelle. The problem was that no one had reported anyone missing in the area. Did the Pappendelle police have no clues at all?

They did have one report of a strange finding, which had been filed away because no one could make anything of it. Several weeks earlier, a Pappendelle farmer had found a bunch of keys, of the sort that house-holders give their trusted servants. He had found them on the ground, next to a man's hat. He had turned them in to the police, but no one had called for them and no one had reported any keys missing. Now, for a change, the police made positive use of the press. The newspapers ran photographs of the bunch of keys, hoping that someone would come forth to identify them.

Sure enough, a wealthy lady of Pappendelle saw the picture and identified the keys as hers. She had entrusted them to her housekeeper, Maria Hahn, and was mildly vexed because Maria had gone off with the keys. Maria's going off was not surprising; she had already been given notice, and everyone believed that out of spite she had left early and taken the keys. This had all happened on Sunday, August 14. Maria had gone out, saying she was taking her half day, and she had never come back.

By now a familiar scenario: Domestic servant goes out for Sunday outing. She meets a man. She does not come back.

The police were certain that they knew what had happened to Maria Hahn, but they could not be sure until they found a body. They tried to locate the place in Pappendelle marked by the X; but the map was too crude, they could not find it.

They turned to the newspapers again.

Finally, as a result of the latest publicity, two women came forward to report that they had seen Maria Hahn on that Sunday, accompanied by a prosperous-looking man in horn-rimmed spectacles. Excited by that information, the police sent out a public appeal for more—and got it by the barrelful. Unfortunately, all the reports of new murders, old bodies, and suspicious persons offered by the public did not lead anywhere. The police ultimately began filing the letters with scarcely a glance.

Berlin's Central Police Bureau was called in to make its expertise available, but still there was nothing. The Berlin Murder Commission entered the case and began at the beginning, reexamining all the bits of "evidence" available. It was precious little. A footprint. A missing tooth that almost undoubtedly had been repaired by this time. One anony-mous letter, telling where to find the body of little Gertrude Albermann and also of another crime. But no real modus operandi, no telling similarity among all the crimes, save that they were brutal, and they always involved many wounds and a great deal of blood. The Berlin police began going through all the letters received as a result of the call to the public.

One anonymous letter received during the public call for information amplified the letter about little Gertrude and the second body in the Pappendelle area. In the spate of useless offerings, this one had been stuffed away. Now it was brought out again and reread. It promised a body, which would be found under a big flat stone in the Pappendelle area. The Berliners went out looking for big flat stones, and they found one that fit the description. They lifted it up and dug. There was the body of a woman, naked, with twenty stab wounds in the temples, throat, and breast. It was identified as that of Maria Hahn.

The "Jack the Ripper" syndrome set in again, this time with a fury fanned by the newspapers, dredging up the old London crimes of 1888. The original Jack the Ripper had also gloated over the police in letters. Here it was, more than forty years later. Couldn't the modern police deal with modern criminals?

Under the guidance of Berlin, the Duesseldorf police brought in every modern method. They made a public offer to the underworld of rewards for information about any of the dead women. In one day, they received two hundred letters, and every one of them was followed up. They fabricated a mannequin that looked like the Dorrier girl and dressed it in her clothes, and took it around to cabarets and dance halls, to see if it awakened any memories, and also to warn the night world of Duesseldorf of the dangers that lay somewhere out there in the darkness.

Still nothing. The days passed, turned into weeks, became months, and there was no progress. But neither were there any more murders. Perhaps the murderer had moved on to some other area. Perhaps he had died. The absence of crimes seemed to satisfy the public, and the hue and cry against the authorities died down once more.

May 14, 1930. It was evening. Maria Buedlick paced up and down the Duesseldorf railroad station platform. She was looking for Frau Brueckner. Maria had just that day come to Duesseldorf from Cologne; on the train, she had met Frau Brueckner, who had promised to help find her a job. More important, Frau Brueckner had told Maria that she would find her a place to stay and had gone off from the station to do so. But she had not come back. It was getting late, and Maria was wondering where she could spend the night. She knew absolutely no one in Duesseldorf. She did not even know where the hotels were located.

As she paced, a man came up and started a conversation. When Maria told him her troubles, he offered to show her the way to a women's hostel. That sounded like the safest of all places to go, and Maria gratefully accepted the man's offer to accompany her. They started off on foot through the streets. Soon they came to the Volksgarten, the tree-lined public park. Beyond, said the man, was the women's hostel. Maria became suspicious. A hostel in the midst of a deserted park? And just now a walk through the dark park with a strange man? She began to voice her suspicions.

Just then, another man came up and Maria turned to him for confirmation. Where was the women's hostel? Was it beyond the park as her companion indicated?

Absolutely not, said the second man. It was in the diametrically opposite direction. Maria turned to give her "friend" a look, but he was already slinking away. Maria's new acquaintance offered to show her the real hostel. She looked him over; he was soft-spoken and ever so kindly and quiet. At least she was in the hands of a respectable man!

As they wandered back through the streets, the man observed that it was late and Maria must be getting hungry. When she admitted that this was so, he offered to take her to his "nice flat" for a bite to eat. They went to 71 Mettmannerstrasse, where Maria was disappointed to discover that the "nice flat" was an attic room on the fourth floor. But she was grateful for the cup of milk and the ham and bread her rescuer provided for her.

Back to the business at hand: she simply had to find a place to stay that night, and now it was past eleven o'clock. Her friend agreed that they must hurry, and they went out into the street again to find the women's hostel. He took her on a short tram ride, and then they started walking. The further they walked, Maria observed, the further they were from the lights of the city. In fact, they were heading for the woods northeast of the city, the Flingern district.

For the first time since she had been with this new friend, Maria became alarmed. They were deep in the woods. Yes, said her friend, the women's hostel was located in the heart of Wolf's Glen.

"I don't believe you," said Maria. She began to protest.

Her friend stopped short. "Do you know now where you are?" he shouted. "I can tell you. You're alone with me in the middle of the woods. Now you can scream as much as you like and nobody will hear you!"

He grabbed her and kissed her. Then his hands sought her throat. Maria struggled. The hands tightened around her throat. She was choking. Suddenly the hands dropped. The man spoke, but calmly and solicitously.

"Do you," he asked in his soft voice, "remember where I live? Just in case you may ever be in need and want my help?"

Maria was no fool. She lied. No, she said, she was so confused she had no idea where he lived. The answer satisfied the man. He guided her back through the woods until the lights of the city were bright on them again; he showed her the tramway, and went off. Maria boarded a tram, received real directions to the women's hostel, and went there for the night.

She was so upset about her adventure, however, that she spent much of the night writing a letter to her errant friend from the train, Frau Brueckner. Apparently, her spelling or her recollection of the address was wrong, for the letter was misdirected to a Frau Bruegmann. Perhaps it was lucky for Maria, for when Frau Bruegmann read the letter, she turned it over to the police. Twenty-four hours afterward, the police found Maria and asked her to help them. Could she remember the house where she had gone for her cup of milk and bread and ham?

She could remember the street, she said, for she had seen the name in the light of the corner lamppost, Mettmannerstrasse. About the number, she was not so sure. The police took her to Mettmannerstrasse, and they walked with her up and down the street. Finally, she recognized the house; she went inside, while two plainclothes policemen stayed outside. Maria walked up the stairs to the attic room. She looked at the door. She was sure this was the place. In the hall, she encountered the landlady and asked her if "a fair-haired and rather sedate gentleman" lived there. Yes, indeed, said the landlady. Together, the women returned to the attic room, and the landlady unlocked the door. Maria recognized the room as the one she had been in two nights earlier. This was the room of a lodger who lived here with his wife, the landlady said. She wrote the name on a piece of paper and gave it to Maria.

The women started down the stairs. On the stairway they passed a man, and Maria recognized him as the man who had "befriended" and then nearly murdered her. As he went by, he had given a visible start. The women continued on downstairs. They heard the attic door open and then close, and shortly later heard it close again. They heard someone go down the stairs, and through a window they saw the man leaving the house, his hat pulled down over his eyes. Maria ran outside and told the police officers that the man who had attacked her two nights before had just left the house. She handed the police the piece of paper the landlady had given her, and they read: Peter Kuerten. After fifteen months of terror, the authorities at last had a description, a sight of the suspect, his place of residence, and a name, all at once.

THE DUESSELDORF VAMPIRE

When Peter Kuerten recognized Maria Buedlick on the stairs, and saw that she recognized him, he knew he was a marked man. He returned to the room after dark and told his wife that he had to hide. He confessed to her the attempted attack on Maria and said that would surely bring him at least fifteen years in prison. Then he went away. The next day he met his wife again, but not at the house. This time he confessed to her that there was more. He was the man who had attacked Gertrude Schulte, he said.

This was all news to Frau Kuerten. She was shocked and distraught. She threatened to kill herself. Kuerten consoled her. No, he said, she should not commit suicide, she should turn him in to the police. That would bring her at least part of the reward.

Later that day, they met again and took a long walk across the Rhine Bridge. Kuerten blurted out the whole truth.

"I've done everything that's been happening here in Duesseldorf," he said.

"What do you mean by that?"

"I mean the murders and the attacks."

"What, those innocent children, too?"

"Yes."

When Frau Kuerten returned to the attic room this time, the police were waiting for her. They took her away. After a night in jail, she agreed to cooperate with them in capturing her husband. It was one more step along the final path for Peter Kuerten.

At their last meeting, she had agreed to bring him some personal supplies; they were to meet outside St. Rochus Church. At the appointed hour she was there, carrying a parcel that contained a towel and soap. Kuerten appeared from the shadows. Four policemen came charging forward with drawn guns.

"I must fly," said Kuerten.

"It won't help."

Kuerten thought it over for a moment. He did not flee. As the policemen took hold of his arms he smiled at them.

Word of the capture of the "Duesseldorf Murderer" spread quickly and caused a sensation. In the movie houses, operators stopped the show to flash the news across the picture screen. In dancehalls and cabarets, performances were interrupted so management could make the big announcement. Newspapers were in wild demand for the details.

The public feeling was, first of all, one of relief. But almost immediately doubts set in. Had the people not gone through all this before? What about Hans Strausberg, the man in the lunatic asylum? Had the police really caught the monster this time? Many people did not believe it.

What about Peter Kuerten? The people who knew him best were loudest among the scoffers. Quiet, refined, a man who did not raise his voice, impeccable of dress, clean in his person, and neat in his demeanor. "He can't be the Duesseldorf Monster," said those who knew him. "He can't be."

But, once arrested, Peter Kuerten admitted all the crimes and said he was guilty of even more. For example, the murder of a little girl back in 1913. His detailed confession convinced even the skeptics. Indeed, the longer Peter Kuerten talked, the more convulsed the public became with the horror of his deeds.

What was Kuerten's motive? It began to come out, a secret that had not even been suspected for fifteen months.

Blood.

Peter Kuerten was a vampire.

This soft-spoken, nattily dressed, forty-seven-year-old man with such mild manners was actually a killer of the most horrible sort. This man who always wore clean clothes, combed his hair, and powdered his face and rouged his cheeks—his delight was to drink the blood of his victims. This friendly fellow, who was generally admired by his acquaintances, was adept at stabbing and hammering, and got sexual gratification from killing and torturing.

Peter Kuerten was kept in jail for almost a year before his trial. While waiting in prison, he made a detailed confession of his crimes. His wife corroborated his testimony by relating what he had told her. By the time the trial came up, it seemed to be an open-and-shut case. Here was a living vampire, a man who killed for pleasure and for blood.

So many sensational details of Kuerten's crimes had been released before the trial that the presiding judge appealed to the journalists to use some restraint in reporting the trial. The result was that most of the journalists suppressed the dreadful truth about Kuerten's vampirism.

During the trial, Kuerten told the gory story of his first murder, of that ten-year-old girl in 1913. "I seized the child's head with my left hand and strangled it for about a minute and a half. It woke up, and struggled, but then lost consciousness. I had a small but very sharp pocket knife with me, and I held the child's head and cut her throat. I heard the blood spurt and drip onto the mat beside the bed. It spurted in an arch, right over my hand."

He drank some of the blood, with great satisfaction.

He had other grisly tales to tell. One day in the fall of 1929, walking in the park, searching for a victim, he was frustrated because no one came along. Finally, he caught a swan asleep beside the lake, cut off its head, and drank the blood.

Kuerten's principal satisfaction in his crimes, wrote one reporter, "was to receive the stream of blood that gushed from his victim's wounds into his mouth." In Kuerten's confessions, suppressed by most newspapers, he said that the murders gave him intense sexual pleasure. "He speaks of his need to kill," said one witness at the trial, "as others talk about their habit of smoking."

At the trial, the prosecutor called Kuerten "the king of Sexual Delinquents" and said he would prove that the true motive of the killer's criminal actions was sexual.

Was that true? Was Peter Kuerten a madman, or was he a vampire? His prison correspondence with the families of his victims indicated the latter. One woman had chided him for his terrible acts. "What do you want, madame," he replied to her, "I need blood as others need alcohol."

Madman or monster?

The judge found him sane. The weapons were produced, two pairs of scissors, the handle and part of the blade from the dagger with which he had stabbed Gertrude Schulte. The judge sentenced Peter Kuerten to death nine different times for nine different murders; plus, in one case, "murder in connection with immoral practices"; and in two cases "murder accompanied by rape." There were seven other attempted murders, but the prison terms for these need not be counted, for Peter Kuerten was to go to the guillotine.

After the sentencing, he was sent back to prison to wait. Since Duesseldorf did not have a guillotine, he had to be moved to Klingelpirtz Prison in Cologne for execution. He was taken there, and at six o'clock on the morning of July 2, 1931, twelve witnesses took their places in a semicircle behind the guillotine in the prison yard. The executioner was ready, and the "poor sinner's bell" was ringing. Peter Kuerten walked to the guillotine unaided and was strapped down to the board. A second later the blade dropped, and with a spurt of the blood Kuerten loved so well, his head dropped into the canvas bag.

The Monster of Duesseldorf was dead. The vampire was finished.

21

Your Neighborhood Vampire

IN NEW YORK CITY, EARLY IN THE 1930s, lived a thin pale girl with flaming red hair named Mary Lensfield. She was an artist and a translator of children's books, and she was certain she had become a vampire. This belief had begun when she was in college and went one day to visit a friend at Vassar for a weekend. Her friend had cut herself on a broken glass, and Mary had bound up the wound and given the friend a sedative. While the girl was asleep, the thought of the blood overwhelmed Mary; she removed the bandage from her deeply sedated friend and sucked her blood.

It had happened at other times, too. In New York she had a roommate who suffered a puncture wound while wielding an ice pick carelessly. Mary found herself irresistibly drawn, and she sucked blood from her roommate, too. As time went on, there were other such occasions.

Mary Lensfield did not want to be a vampire. The idea worried her to the point of obsession. She read everything she could find on the subject, from scholarly tomes to quackery, from the literary to the preposterous. She had read so much, and had absorbed so much, of the superstition and fear of vampires that she was certain she had changed into one. The idea haunted her.

One night, she was invited by a Gramercy Park artist, for whom she was sitting as a model, to an experiment in the occult. A Madame Ludovescu promised that she could stop the flow of blood and heal burns and cuts by supernatural powers. So the artist, who was intrigued by such things, assembled an audience that included Mary, a doctor friend, and the writer William Seabrook. They all assembled around a table, and Madame Ludovescu got ready to perform. The doctor provided the scalpel, the artist provided a saucer and himself as the victim. The doctor made a superficial cut in a vein on the artist's wrist, and the blood dripped slowly into the saucer. Madame Ludovescu mumbled something, then leaned down and pressed her lips to the wound. When she brought her face up, the blood had stopped flowing from the artist's wrist, but her face and lips were covered with shining gore. Mary Lensfield took one startled look and fainted.

The artist had noticed that before Madame Ludovescu had put her mouth to the wound she had palmed a handkerchief, and he accused her of treating the wound with something like tannic acid or adrenalin to stop the blood flow. He turfed her out of the meeting. As for Mary Lensfield, under the doctor's ministrations she recovered promptly, and he assured her and the others that for a person to faint at the sight of blood was not at all uncommon. After that, the witnesses of the experiment went their own way and did not see much of one another.

However, in the summer of 1932, Mary Lensfield and William Seabrook met again, by accident, at a hotel on the French Riviera which catered to artists and writers. One day Seabrook went down to the little cove on the Mediterranean that was the swimming hole for the hotel. He found Mary sitting by a rock, alone. They spoke casually, as acquaintances do, and he went down for his swim. Coming out of the water, he scraped his shoulder on a barnacled rock, but thought nothing of it.

As Seabrook sat down next to Mary in companionable silence, he saw that she was staring at the blood coming from the cut.

"Then she jerked convulsively toward me, and her teeth were in my shoulder, and she was sucking like a leech there—not like a leech either, but more like a greedy half-grown kitten with sharp pointed teeth."

Seabrook was too stunned to move.

"She had deepened the abrasion, and was literally drinking blood."

A truck roared by on the highway above. The sound seemed to jolt Mary, and she suddenly stopped, aware of what she was doing, and she began to sob. She poured out her story then, including her fears and her self-torture. Was she a vampire? Was she going mad? What was going to happen to her?

Seabrook comforted her and advised her to seek medical advice when she got back to New York. She did, he learned later; but, alas, it was too late for Mary Lensfield. She died shortly afterward of pernicious anemia—an irreversible shortage of red blood cells.

As Seabrook put it, Mary Lensfield had a craving for blood for which she was "no more morally responsible . . . than midgets, dwarfs, giants . . . are for their monstrous shapes."

Throughout the twentieth century, a constant body of "cases" of vampirism have come to public attention, usually through the popular and sensational press. If anything, the incidence has grown in the second half of the century.

Headline in the London weekly *News of the World,* October 27, 1974: "BLOODLUST VAMPIRE IS SEIZED IN COFFIN"

The article below tells about a "genuine" vampire who was prowling the streets of Hamburg, Germany, in October 1974. His victim was a burly electrician named Helmut May, who was walking down the street when he saw a tall man dressed all in black. The man approached him, attacked him with a karate chop, and knocked May unconscious. When May awakened, he found himself in a white silk-lined coffin, in a very small room, which was lit only by a candle. The walls of the room were painted white, and the floor (as May saw later) was painted black. A miniature guillotine stood in a corner, and a large motion picture still photo of Count Dracula was on the wall. On a table stood a white enamel bowl. The "vampire" approached the coffin and spoke:

"I'm Count Dracula, also called the Grand Master. I lust for human blood." (Unlikely as it seems that such words ever issued from human or vampire lip, May swore to it.)

With that, the tall man struck the electrician in the face; as the blood flowed, he bent over his victim, collected the blood in the white enamel bowl; and then he drank the blood.

May lay there, stuck tight in the coffin, until the self-styled Count Dracula, with no apparent effort, lifted him out. May was terrified. He got on his knees and begged the vampire for mercy. He would do anything, he said, that the Grand Master ordered. The Grand Master ordered him to kiss his feet and pledge that he would be his servant. May did. After this ritual, "Dracula" forced Helmut May to run half a mile through the streets of Hamburg to a graveyard, which they entered. "Dracula" called a halt at an ivy-covered vault, and said he had to pray.

"Soon," he said, "there will be dawn and the Grand Master must return to his coffin."

As the Grand Master knelt before the vault, May managed to make his escape; he went straight to the police. The police were not at all sure they were not talking to a madman, but they accompanied Helmut May to the house where May had been taken. When they went in, May showed them the tiny room, and there "Dracula" lay, asleep in his coffin. On the table was the white enamel bowl, tinged with dried blood.

The police woke up "Dracula" and arrested him. They charged the twenty-four-year-old man with kidnapping and inflicting bodily harm.

From the *Journal of Vampirism* come the following notes:

1. In September 1975, a tall thin pale woman was arrested in New York City for the murder of her four-year-old daughter. The mother had beaten the child to death and then drained the body almost completely of blood. When questioned by a psychiatrist, Marie Horst said she had been "guided by some dark, demonic, spiritual force."

2. Several homeless tramps in California were found dead during the fall and winter of 1945. Usually the bodies were discovered after a night with a full moon. Each victim's throat had been slashed. Searching for "the Phantom Slasher," on December 29 the police arrested thirty-three-year-old Vaughn Greenwood. He admitted that he was the slasher. He said he had killed nine old men who could not defend themselves. He said he drank the blood of all his victims.

3. The Reverend Ronald Paparesta, formerly a security police lieutenant for the company that provided security service at the Manhattan Hotel in New York City, told a strange story from his past. The Reverend Paparesta is a man of parts. He now identifies himself as "Rev. Dr. Ronald Paparesta, D.D., D.Ed., D.Oc.S., M.S.P.R., M.S.B.S., Pastoral Counselor, and Certified Metaphysical Psychologist, Fifth Ministery of Christ."

In the old days, the Reverend Dr. Papresta was just a private cop.

Here is his story of what began at the Manhattan Hotel on June 3, 1971:

"I guess it was just one of those ordinary rainy nights in New York City. The streets seemed deserted except for the doorways where the prostitutes were conducting business as usual; your friendly drug-dealer was selling his cure-alls; the local muggers were eyeing their next victims; and the poor pimps were getting their orange suits wet trying to drum up business. That night I decided to check on the security patrolmen of the Manhattan Hotel. I arrived . . . at 2:15 A.M. That is when the week of horror began."

A report that something strange was occurring on the eighteenth floor of the hotel sent Lieutenant Paparesta up there. He saw nothing of unusual interest but was irresistibly drawn to room 1810. There was no physical evidence of crime near the room; nor had Paparesta been informed of a complaint by the occupant. Yet he went to the door and, when no one responded, he broke it down. Inside he saw a man lying on the floor, unmoving.

"The room, when I entered it, had a strange odor. The odor was nauseating and although in June, the room was cold. When I got into the room, three girls and two men were standing over the body of the victim—chanting. A cross was hanging upside down and pictures of hideous beings were sprawled all over the room. There were black candles lit all over the place . . . I ordered everyone not to move. One of the men involved, a very lanky and tall fellow with eyes that looked like red marbles, wearing a black robe with XXX in silver across his chest, started to move toward the window; I ordered him to stop but he did not heed my warning and just jumped out the window. I called for assistance, and the rest you can surmise from the logs:

> June 2, 1971. 2:31 A.M.—broke chain off door—Room 1810—five suspects taken into custody—one suspect jumped out of window—had on black robe with three silver Xs—can't find body—victim—dead—taken to St. Vincent's hospital—test tubes full of blood all over the room—suspects seem to be in trance-like state—retrieved one .25 automatic—large quantities of narcotics—suspects' clothes and cranial area smeared with red sticky substance—suspects arrested and incarcerated into the 16th precinct.

> June 2, 1971, 5:10 A.M.—victim pronounced legally dead—coroner's report—victim died of extreme loss of blood caused by multitude of transfusions—police laboratory report—red substance on perpetrators' cranials and clothes—human type blood AB negative—no sign of perpetrator who jumped out of window.

Paparesta went to the police to find out what they were doing. The answer was, nothing. The police wanted nothing to do with this case, he decided. When he pursued the subject, he found himself suddenly suspended from his job for thirty days. Obviously that was a warning to lay off. The Manhattan Hotel even denied that the room had been occupied.

Paparesta decided to investigate on his own. He sought the assistance of a friend who was a detective on the New York City police force and had access to the files. They discovered that this was not an isolated case; and that the cases had several things in common: the victims' bodies were all drained of blood, and those who committed the acts were all discovered in trancelike states. In every case, "a tall lanky man with fiery red eyes escaped under mysterious circumstances."

Paparesta and his friend suspected that black magic rituals were involved in the cases. But that did not give them the answers they needed. Paparesta took to roaming the streets of lower New York, down by the docks, where he knew many of the drug and kook cults hung out. Finally, he found a building in a block on Tenth Avenue where there seemed to be black magic going on. When he saw the man with the red eyes he was sure!

He followed Red-eyes up the stairs of the building to an apartment on the second floor. Then he decided he needed official help.

He left the building, hailed a police car passing by, and told his story: that a murder suspect was on the second story of the building on Tenth Avenue. One policeman went with Paparesta. Detectives were called in, and the authorities prepared to assault the apartment. Paparesta was told to guard the outside of the apartment door.

"The detectives decided to break down the door to gain entrance to the apartment. This is when the horror began! As the door flew off its flimsy hinges, the first wave of detectives rushed in; a commotion followed and shots were fired—and running right out of the apartment was red-eyes. I grabbed at him, but there was nothing to hold onto! He seemed to be transparent. I then realized that he was a metaphysical being. A sense of fear and helplessness came over me as I watched the apparition walk right out of the building into the street and disappear from my view.

"I then entered the apartment and became sick to my stomach. There were four bodies, or what seemed to be bodies, stretched side by side on the bare floor. These bodies were so mutilated that only an expert could identify their sex. All over the living room and bedroom, the same hideous pictures that I had seen in the hotel room were covering the walls. A cross, upside down, was overshadowing a table; three Xs in silver were displayed on a black cloth.

"The detectives took four suspects into custody and made arrangements for the bodies. The next day I reported the facts, just as they happened, to my superiors. They told me I was overworked and needed a vacation."

Lieutenant Paparesta took that vacation, a long one. During his absence from security work, he became convinced of the existence of a metaphysical world. He never went back to his job, but decided to devote the rest of his life to religion and metaphysics.

4. One day in 1978, London's *News of the World* reported, the Reverend Donald Omand, a Church of England minister of Honiton, Devonshire, was called by psychiatrists of a nursing home to talk to a young man, twenty-two years old, who was attacking other patients with his teeth and nails to get their blood. The most worrisome thing was that after he had attacked a person, his victim showed similar signs of vampirism. Earlier, the Reverend Mr. Omand had been called in by those doctors to exorcise some demons. Now he returned.

According to the article, the Rev. Mr. Omand said that "One moment he [the twenty-two-year-old man] was talking quite rationally. The next he had leaped at me—his face was diabolical. He scratched my lips and had to be overpowered. He openly admitted that he got an ecstasy from sucking blood. It might be only a coincidence. But it's curious that the man's mother came from Transylvania—the very place where Dracula is said to have lived."

The day after the attack on the minister, Omand exorcised the young man with salt and water, and with those prayers which are used by the Church in such ceremonies. The next day the young man could remember nothing of his vampire history.

There are, of course, more respectable sources of modern vampire tales, such as Dr. Leonard Wolf, who in the 1970s taught a course in vampirism at San Francisco State College. In 1972, Little, Brown and Co. of Boston published his book *A Dream of Dracula: In Search of the Living Dead.*

Dr. Wolf's book tells of personal encounters with "vampires," which resulted from his public call for vampires to come forward and talk to him.

One day Wolf met with a young man he calls Jay, a poet in his middle thirties, and his young friend, Alex, a twenty-two year old with dark hair and abnormally dark eyes.

Alex was first to broach the subject, wondering aloud if he would measure up to what the professor expected in a vampire. The professor suspected that drugs played a role in these two young men's lives; but Jay, sensing the unsaid, said that Alex was "clean"—he had kicked the heroin habit. Reassured of Wolf's continued interest, Alex began to talk. He wanted to tell the professor about his "vampire trip."

Blood, said Alex, really turned him on, and had since he was thirteen years old. That's when he had begun using drugs, belladonna, speed, uppers, downers, and, finally, heroin. When he got to shooting up, he was always fascinated by the needle. His first experience with blood came when another youth cut a pentagram in his own hand with a razor blade and then cut Alex's chest. He rubbed his bleeding hand into Alex's bleeding chest. Blood to blood, he said. It brought a new excitement, a beautiful feeling.

From that experience, Alex moved on to sex and blood. When he was sixteen, he took a girl to Tijuana and "married her" there. Sex was usual enough for Alex by this time, and he wanted something new. He bit the girl so hard that blood streamed down to her chest and she cried out in pain. Apparently he had gone too far. She jumped up, got away, and he never saw her again.

And where, asked the professor, was Alex getting his blood these days?

All over, said Alex airily. All of San Francisco was one great blood bank for him. Everybody was on some sort of blood kick. He knew lots of people who were eager to have someone suck their blood. The gays and the girls all wanted to join up for the blood-sucking. Passion, said Alex, was blood and sex.

Did Alex ever suck his lovers' throats? Of course, said Alex, but somehow he did not seem to get much of a charge out of others sucking him. His guess was the others did not have the technique perfected as he did. He told the professor how he sucked, in detail, illustrating his technique with lips and gestures: in the throat, the arm, the groin. Each time he sucked he did it for about ten minutes. How much blood did he ingest? He did not know that; a lot of blood, he estimated. And a lot of pleasure.

"I get an erection, man . . . it feels good. Something is being consummated . . . shared blood . . . it goes along real well when you're fucking . . . you might call it blood lust . . . particularly well with sodomy . . . it's a real high. The blood and the balling."

Then, for Dr. Wolf's benefit, Alex demonstrated his technique with Jay, who was obviously his lover. Jay held out his left arm, and Alex lowered his mouth to the vein, on the inner side near the elbow. As Alex sucked the blood, Professor Wolf looked with fascination on the change that came over the youth. He closed his eyes and was "gone, elsewhere."

After about half a minute of this, Alex came out of his trance with a start. He seemed disoriented. Dr. Wolf had a feeling of horror at having been "inside a mystery."

After the bloodsucking, Alex seemed to find it harder to articulate. He admitted that he took blood from about fifty people, including his own mother, and among them he "balled and sucked" thirty or forty men and women.

Dr. Wolf suggested that some of this might be the result of Alex's fear of impotence. Alex denied it. No, he said, it was nothing like that. He was just "very hot" on the idea of sucking blood. And besides, "a lot of guys are on a heavy M [masochist] trip. They have to split it up in some dark corner. And the darkest corner they can find is me."

So what did it all mean? Was there a real element of vampirism in Alex? Was this just another complication of the perversions of the easy society of the 1970s in America? Or was there something operating here that went back to age-old superstitions about blood, to dark corners that even Alex was unaware of?

There must be such dark corners, for the depth and breadth of modern "vampirism" seems to be extending. And not only in the United States. In 1970, the Highgate Cemetery in the north end of London was the scene of a vampire hunt.

Highgate Cemetery is extremely old, disused, and rundown from centuries of neglect. It is a labyrinth of tiny paths, overgrown greenery, and many ancient graves in ruins. For some time, vandals had plagued the cemetery. The gutted old windowless chapel was apparently used by several black magic cults for their rites. Occasionally, someone around the area complained of seeing or hearing or feeling or knowing about "vampires." When more than the usual number of complaints surfaced, the police made it a point to keep an eye on the cemetery. One night they drove by, and saw a man trying to climb the wall. They nabbed him. He was carrying a sharp wooden stake and a rude cross fashioned from two pieces of wood tied together with a shoelace.

Who was he and what was he up to? The police wanted to know.

He was David Farrant, the man said, and further identified himself as a founder of the British Occult Society. There was a vampire haunting the cemetery, he said. It slept in a coffin by day and haunted the cemetery at night. He had seen it himself, a creature about eight feet tall that seemed to float across the ground. It was his intention to search it out.

"I would have gone into the catacomb, searched through the coffins until I recognized the vampire asleep in one and then I would have driven

my wooden stake through the heart," said vampire hunter Farrant, with
the aplomb of a St. George. That was very impressive, but even more so
was his defense attorney's plea that because there were so many breaches
in the walls, Highgate Cemetery could not be legally called an enclosed
area, and therefore, Mr. Farrant had done no wrong.

Magistrate J. D. Purcell found for the defendant, but he did comment
as he dismissed the case that he thought Mr. Farrant "should be seen by a
doctor."

So, apparently should a lot of other people associated with vampires.
Consider the case of the student arrested in 1979 in Frankfurt, Germany,
as a "modern-day vampire." The charges came from his practice of
drinking the blood of girls he seduced and then drugged. Many of these
girls were twelve to fifteen years old. The "vampire" did not just drink
from their bodies, he used syringes and bottles to take and store the
blood for future use. When his apartment was raided, the police found
the equipment, drugs, chemicals, and four large knives. Luckily, the
latter did not look used. Maybe they were being saved for a further
advance in "vampirism." The accused denied that he had made any
"vampire" attacks and asserted that he only took blood for "scientific
research." The girls said otherwise, and the police believed the victims.

In Chicago, Jerry Moore, thirty-five, was arrested for murdering his
girl friend, Mattie Alice Jones, and then drinking her blood. He said he
cut her throat from ear to ear, after she bungled a suicide attempt with a
paring knife. Just to help out, he said, he had finished the job right. And
having exerted all that effort, he needed the blood to repair his strength.

In New Jersey, the police were a little unnerved, one day in December
1979, when they came across the bodies of Howard Green, a fifty-three-
year-old artist and part-time taxi driver and his friend Carol Marron,
thirty-three, a secretary at the Pratt Institute. They were found off Route
80 in West Paterson. The bodies had both been mutilated. What was
really unnerving was the fact that both bodies had been totally drained of
blood. About fifteen and a half pints in all. The police decided the
killings were the work of a satanic cult to which the pair belonged.
Apparently they had broken the rules and so were attacked and killed
ritually, their blood systematically drained. The survivors, according to
the police theory, then drank the blood.

The thoughtful reader will of course say, "But look at the sources," for
nearly all of these reports originate in the more sensational journals: in
London, the *News of the World*; and in the United States, the *National
Enquirer, Weekly World News,* and such periodicals. Every nation has

its sensations, and vampires are a sensation the world over. Yet for a serious student, reports such as that of the Reverend Dr. Paparesta have some serious clues: *Hotel Manhattan, New York 16th Police Precinct.* . . . And the Reverend Mr. Omand has an address: Honiton, Devonshire, England. Dr. Wolf did hold a post at a responsible university.

It is for the reader to judge the merits of these cases, just as it is for the reader to make up his own mind about the more academic studies of the phenomena, which have been with us since Dom Calmet, and include Krafft-Ebing, Montague Summers, and such modern students as Dr. Leonard Wolf.

The question about most of these people, of course, is: are they vampires, or are they sick?

22

THE VAMPIRES' SIDE OF THE STORY

IN THE 1980s, VAMPIROLOGY CERTAINLY runs the gamut—from the Count Dracula Fan Club, a lighthearted organization whose aims are "ethical, social, moral and educational combined with a sense of good fun," to the Count Dracula Society, "devoted to serious study of the horror films and Gothic literature," to the small Vampires Studies Society, to the Vampire Information Exchange, "a pen pal network for persons interested in research into any or all aspects of vampirism." That means folklore, alleged cases, philosophical ramifications, and fiction.

Students of the vampire come in all shapes and sizes. The most ambitious (some say pretentious) is Dr. Stephen Kaplan of Elmhurst, New York, who claims to have discovered seven true vampires and has been in contact with one "Elizabeth" who admits to being 439 years old. Dr. Kaplan has set up a Vampire Research Center and a Vampire Hall of Fame (two members: Dr. Kaplan and Mrs. Kaplan). He also has announced plans to publish a work based on a "serious" survey of vampires, "The Last Official Vampire Evaluation," which "will ascertain and evaluate the vampire population in the world today." The ninety-eight questions seem to be in dead earnest. Examples are:

After you have taken the blood, your victims are left:

Dead _____
Unconscious _____
Satisfied _____
Not seriously harmed _____
and
Can you transform a human being into a vampire? _____

At about the time that Dr. Kaplan was getting ready for his massive survey, the Count Dracula Fan Club put out one of its own: "So You Want to Be a Vampire?" by Eileen Watkins, whose thirteen questions follow:

SO YOU WANT TO BE A VAMPIRE*

This position normally requires a great deal of dedication and perseverance, and is not for the fly-by-night personality. If, however, you have been willing to make the usual Faustian compromises, as well as being willing to die first, you may have what it takes. (Then again, you can probably accomplish it simply by falling in with the wrong crowd.)

1. My favorite music is:
    a. disco
    b. soft rock
    c. Mantovani
    d. Beethoven
    e. the howling of hungry wolves
2. My most embarrassing moments socially tend to occur:
    a. when I speak in front of a group
    b. when I play sports with more athletic opponents
    c. when I try a new dance in public
    d. when I accept an invitation to dinner
3. Fill in the blank: "Only my _____ knows for sure."
    a. hairdresser
    b. mother
    c. best friend
    d. confessor
    e. orthodontist
4. I never drink:
    a. alone
    b. before 5 P.M.

*Copyright © 1982 by Eileen Watkins.

    c. more than two cocktails

    d. . . . wine

    e. Perrier

    f. coffee

    g. diet cola

    h. all of the above

5. When I look in the mirror the first thing I see is:

    a. my crow's feet

    b. my spare tire

    c. my big blue eyes

    d. the mole on my chin

    e. the room behind me

6. Life begins at:

    a. eighteen

    b. twenty-one

    c. thirty

    d. forty

    e. five hundred forty-seven

7. My favorite article of clothing is:

    a. my Levis

    b. my Cardin suit

    c. my silk lounging pajamas

    d. my Diane von Furstenberg wrap dress

    e. my 400-year-old opera cape

8. When I look at Farrah Fawcett, I see:

    a. a great beauty

    b. a flash-in-the-pan

    c. a wholesome American sex symbol

    d. a light snack

9. My dream home would be:

    a. designed by Frank Lloyd Wright

    b. a split-level in the suburbs

    c. a geodesic dome

    d. an A-frame in the Hamptons

    e. a New York penthouse

    f. condemned by the board of health

10. Someday I would like to move to the country and raise:

    a. a brood of children

    b. horses

    c. tomatoes

    d. grapes for wine

    e. rabid bats

11. My greatest fear is:

    a. staying up past my bedtime

    b. gifts from religious relatives

    c. falling on a fencepost

    d. kissing someone who has just eaten in an Italian restaurant

    e. senseless bloodshed

    f. all of the above

12. The best way to respond to a chance meeting with me is:

    a. smiling and nodding

    b. saying hello

    c. stepping aside

    d. cringing behind a crucifix

13. For variety, I sometimes like to date a person:

    a. from a different part of the country

    b. of a different religion

    c. of a different race

    d. with different interests

    e. with blue blood

All good clean fun.

But some of the lighthearted vampirologists turn out to be serious students, too, as Jeanne Youngson, who (1) holds a Ph.D. in Communications from the University of Sussex (England) and (2) is president of the Count Dracula Fan Club. Her doctoral dissertation was a 16mm documentary film dealing with a sex change from male to female. Her most recent work is the current issue of the *Count Dracula Fan Club News,* which features gossip, contests, and cartoons about vampires. Some of her more serious work has been devoted to interviewing transsexuals as part of a scholarly study. Some of her less serious is indicated by her remarkable collection of vampire letterhead stationery. In the middle of the 1960s, Dr. Youngson toured Transylvania and then returned to New York where she founded the fan club.

Today there are many more persons afflicted with blood fetish than one would imagine in a sophisticated society such as ours. In addition to the seekers of blood who make the newspaper headlines, generally because of their criminal actions, there is a subculture which, either in groups or individually, seeks to drink or suck blood—the age-old definition of a vampire. Dr. Wolf's Alex, in the previous chapter, is obviously one of these.

Students of vampirology have investigated many instances of persons who have an inordinate interest in and great attraction to blood. Dr. Youngson has amassed a considerable file of such cases. These people have talked freely with her on condition that she not compromise their anonymity. Here are some examples:

1. K.G. 36 years old. Female.

Lives in a rural community in western New Jersey. Has never married. Was the oldest of four children and had to leave school at age fifteen, when her mother died, to take care of the house. Still tends house and cooks for her father. She buys bloody cuts of meat at supermarkets and drinks the blood. When she heard I was president of a Dracula Society she wanted to know if there were other blood fetishists in her area. Then she said she was only kidding and that she would be too shy to make contact with them. She has guilt feelings about her desire to drink blood but says she has no control over the urges that come upon her suddenly.

2. S.N. 17 years old. Male.

Lives in a small city in New England. Parents are both professionals and are very permissive. S.N. thinks he is Dracula. He doesn't go out during the day if possible, but at night he often takes long walks through the local cemeteries and, in the summer, lies atop graves. He says it is the only time he feels peaceful. He follows "vampire rules" faithfully: has no mirrors in his room, waits to be invited into other people's houses, avoids garlic, etc. His teeth are loose, and he sucks them until his gums bleed and then swallows the blood. He has a large collection of vampire movies he has taped from TV and plays these over and over to himself. He masturbates constantly and has fantasies of self-fellatio.

3. S.G. 26 years old. Female.

Lives in a large midwestern city. Works as secretary for a commercial company. She was orphaned at the age of six and lived in a number of foster homes. She never felt loved. Has continual fantasies about drinking blood from a large goblet. At one time she had a boyfriend who wanted her to spank him before sex. She agreed if he would cut his finger and let her suck some blood. They did this for several years using a variety of techniques for getting blood. He was eventually sent to prison for embezzlement and wrote that when he got out he didn't want to see her any more because she was "sick." (The last time I spoke to her she was definitely suicidal.)

In the summer of 1983, Dr. Youngson had the following interviews:

G.N. Middle forties. Female.

G.N. is a bit overweight, with green eyes and light brown hair. She is five feet four inches tall.

Q. How do you view yourself?

A. I view myself as a basically decent and talented person who was born disadvantaged, who was psychologically orphaned at a very early age, and who is now struggling to survive in a largely hostile world where hard practicality is valued above poetry and the fine arts.

Q. Does the word *vampire* ever occur to you?

A. It did a great deal when I was a teen. But I knew that I didn't have fangs (though I did have protruding teeth, which a dentist filed down), or pointed ears, or the ability to hypnotize people or to fly like a bat. I figured that I was a vampire, a sort of prenatal or halfway vampire. Years later I learned from another blood drinker that the technical term for what I was (and am) is *blood fetishist,* which distinguishes the mortal blood drinkers from the legendary, traditional, supernatural vampires and the SF [science fiction] alien blood drinkers—if such exist.

Q. What would you say if someone called you a vampire?

A. I would yell and holler a lot. My friends and donors (and my donors are my good friends) are too discreet, polite, and sensitive to say anything like that to my face. Although one man wrote me a really gross introductory letter in which he asked me point-blank if I drank blood. The rest of his letter was an invitation to join his cozy gang of vampires (?) and Satanists and S&M [sadism and masochism] creeps. I may be strange, but I am not *that* strange! Satanists and sado types turn me off. Enough is enough! When it comes down to that sort of depraved insanity, then count me out! This obnoxious character gave me his phone number, so I called and burned his ears off. When I get called a vampire, I tend to get a trifle upset.

Q. Do you really feel you have a blood fetish?

A. I think about drinking blood often, and I sometimes even dream about transforming myself into a vampire. I guess I *am* a vampire, since I get rather grumpy when I don't get any. And lately I haven't been getting any, since my donors are getting a bit squeamish. And how much can I nag them? Also, what with hepatitis, herpes, and AIDS—it gives one pause.

Q. Do you think this is unusual?

A. Oh, yes. So few people do it, and there are so few of us around. Let's face it—people like me do not exactly win popularity contests. Even if there are more of us around, I'd like to bet they are all hiding in the closet—or crypt, as the case may be.

Q. How long have you had this craving?

A. Since puberty and the onset of menstruation. About 12 or 13 years of age. That would be about 1949 or so. But I think my fascination with *blood* started *before* I got my periods. Way back in Catholic boarding school, in third through fifth and sixth grades, I was taught by the nuns that the sacred blood of Jesus was very special, and that Christ shed his blood for us because he *loved* us so much. Yet we were only given the Bread (Body) and not the Wine (Blood). We were told that only the priest and specially holy people could have the blood of Christ.

Every classroom had a crucifix, a picture of the heart of Jesus, pierced and crowned with thorns, and a picture of Mary's Immaculate Heart all crowned with roses and pierced with a sword. During Lent we were shown "the Way of the Cross" and pictures of Christ being whipped and tortured. The nuns repeated over and over again that Jesus loved us *so* much that he shed his very own blood for our redemption.

One fresco in the convent school church showed angels collecting the blood of the crucified Christ in golden chalices for martyrs and saints to drink. We kids were told that we were unworthy sinners who scarcely deserved the love and blood of Jesus.

And then there were all the tales of sainted martyrs who bled and died for the Faith and for the Lord. Over and over we children were shown Bleeding Hearts of Jesus, Mary, and the blessed martyrs. All of this made a very powerful impression on my pre-adolescent mind.

From birth I wasn't wanted by my parents (who fought constantly with each other). I was dumped into camps and boarding schools as soon as I was old enough to go. I never knew a settled home life, or the love of parents. I did learn that Jesus' heart was pierced with love, and bled for us. Before I reached the age of 10, my subconscious mind made certain connections and equations, such as: the heart=love; the heart pumps blood; therefore blood=love!

As a child I was absolutely *starved* for love. My father deserted the family when I was 7. My mother was unstable and incapable of caring for a small child. My grandparents were child abusers who tormented their own children as well as their grandchildren. And my godparents were cold, unfeeling people. As I grew toward adolescence, money ran out for boarding school and I was put into the "care" of my grandparents, who did *incalculable* psychological damage to me. From age 12 to 15, I lived in an incredibly hellish nightmare. I began to menstruate during that time. I also started to read escapist horror and SF comics on the sly. And I learned that my maternal ancestors came from Rumania. Three significant factors. I knew that vampires were East European (for the most part) and that they drank blood. I knew, too, that they had certain supernatural powers. How I longed for love and for blood, and for the power to better my life. That is how I became a blood fetishist. The seeds were planted in early childhood, grew during adolescence, and matured in adulthood . . . mostly as a result of child abuse. To escape from the misery of my horrible existence, I'd daydream of being a lovely, faery princess or a powerful werewolf, or a hypnotically seductive and eternally invincible VAMPIRE.

The vampire-lover fantasies were my favorite. I usually dreamed that I would be rescued by an Elfin king, or a mighty vampire who would ravish me and share his powers with me. I'd fly away on black wings to a better life.

Q. Is it a craving or just an idle pastime?

A. Well, seriously—*dead* seriously if you catch my drift—if I did not make light-hearted jokes about vampirism, then my donors and friends would get queasy and upset, and I don't want to upset people by the *intensity* of my needs. . . .

I need love, devotion, and sincere commitment just as much as I need blood. It is hard to find sincere, decent, caring people. Whenever I trusted and/or loved anyone I got the shaft. Now I am back in my protective shell and my defenses are back up. . . .

But I digress. . . . Of *course* I crave blood. But you can buy me off with a rare roast beef sandwich, hot coffee, and a Godiva chocolate bar. Among other things I am a chocoholic and a caffiend. What I really need is a good F R I E N D who will love me in spite of my faults . . . someone who won't tell me I am his "best/special/permanent favorite person," and then callously throw me over after a few precious months of phoney "kindness."

Q. How did you get blood?

A. When I was an adolescent, I pricked myself with pins and rose thorns (green ones are sharper than brown ones), and I drank my own blood. I did not drink the blood of *other* people until after I reached the age of 21, and got my first job. After I was graduated from college, I obtained a position as a first and second grade teacher in a small school. . . . As a teacher I often had to watch over the tots during recess. Frequently the little ones would trip and scrape their knees and elbows. Many times the school nurse would not be in her office, so I would have to take care of the cuts and scrapes myself. The sight of all that blood triggered a certain urge in me. However I was extremely careful *never* to reveal it to the kids. After I cleansed their wounds and dabbed on some iodine I would save the bloody swabs and hide them in my pocket. Later I'd go to the ladies' room and lick the blood off the cotton swabs. No one *ever* saw me do this, or suspected that I was unusual in any way. Midway in my career as a teacher, the TV show "Dark Shadows" became very popular. This program featured a noble and handsome hero who suffered under the curse of vampirism. Unlike the Satanic Dracula, Barnabas Collins was a decent soul who had a conscience and didn't really want to be a vampire. Everyone at school talked about the show, including me. No one thought my interest in "Dark Shadows" was so strange, since nearly *everyone* was watching it to see what all the fuss was about.

My teaching job came to an end in 1972, twelve years after I began. Some time near the middle of my career, certain changes became apparent to the teaching staff. The students gradually got more and more stubborn, antagonistic, and uncooperative in class. Even the parents became argumentative with the teachers and the principal. After all those years as a teacher, I and several other instructors called it quits.

For a year or two I floundered around, wondering what to do. I was the Ivory Tower, bookish, academic type, and definitely not suited to the business world.

After a couple of years I connected with a nice ladies' apparel shop with a fair and honest boss. Things went well until the economy slumped. Business fell off and after five years the shop had to close down. During that time I had to plan a way to get blood without arousing suspicion. My fellow employees were mostly of an ethnic group which believed in magic, sorcery, spells, charms, etc. I too was (still am) fascinated by the occult and the supernatural. I offered to do some magical spells for them in return for a few drops of their blood on a clean piece of paper. I'd take the drops of blood home to "snack" on and I would work the spell. I am happy to say that the spells were 80 percent successful, and most of their wishes came true. I felt like a sort of Dark Faery.

Q. Did this ever interfere with your work?

A. No, since I licked the blood from the swabs or pieces of paper in a private spot, like a bathroom or in my own quiet bedroom. . . . On my sales job no suspicions were aroused when I did magic spells in exchange for blood since most of my fellow workers sincerely believed in magic. If I had done this elsewhere I might have gotten into trouble.

Q. Did you ever exchange blood with another person?

A. Yes. I did this in about 1979 with a fellow blood fetishist, whom I shall call "Dusty." When we first contacted each other, I hoped I'd finally found a kindred soul. Little did I know she was into Lesbianism, Marxism, and the sadist side of S&M. She drove me up the wall with endless and lengthy feminist, leftist harangues. I am bored to *undeath* with politics and I've got a particular distaste for all kinds of extremist radicalism. As for S&M, the idea of hurting others is absolutely horrible and disgusting to me. Unlike Dusty I do not want to torture victims to get my kicks. I want friends and blood brothers (and sisters) to share things in my life.

I finally had to dump Dusty in 1981 for several reasons. She began practicing S&M on me, and she started telling lies about me to the very few and precious friends that I have. Just as I do not want to be a "whipper" so I do not want to be a "whippee." Dusty was destroying me body and soul. Therefore I had to break off my relationship with her, although she was the only one who ever drank my blood and shared her own with me.

Q. How did you do it and where?

A. My friend lived in New York and I visited her there. We shared blood in the privacy of her room. There was no lying on beds or sharing prone embraces in bed, either while sharing blood. One cannot take blood or give it while both partners are prone. You might end up carelessly squashing your donor, or you both might end up having some very NON-vampiric ideas if you try and share blood in bed. The easiest way is for the donor to sit, while the "vampire" stands or leans over the donor. Forget all that "I vant to bite your neck" stuff. I discovered that neck (and facial) skin is bouncier and more flexible than the rest of the body's skin. Contrary to popular belief, we blood fetishists do not have fangs. When you try to bite necks, all you will get is a mouthful of very elastic skin, *no blood.* It is easier to take it from another part of the body, like fingers or toes. And it is safer to use the extremities. I always took blood with a sharp, *sterilized* straight pin or sometimes a green thorn . . . from a rose bush. Fortunately my donors never felt more than a slight prick. Unlike the blood fetishist from New York, I do not want to cause pain. My own idea was to find blood brothers/sisters.

Q. What are your present activities?

A. I wish I had *activities*. At the present time I am unemployed. My hands are full, though, as I have to care for my elderly, half-crippled, half-blind mother (who demands most of my time). My hobbies are reading horror/fantasy books, watching SF programs on TV, and studying tomes on esoteric philosophies.

Q. Do you get blood now? Still have the desire?

A. I only have one or two friends who are willing to donate "snacks" and lately they've gotten squeamish and we are all sort of sensitive about that. I haven't had any "snacks" lately and I hate to nag at my few real friends for that. Desire? Oh, yes, I think of it often. Wanna donate? Nah, I guess not. I'd settle for a sincere, honest, loyal, caring friend.

Q. How do you view your future?

A. I wish that I had a *future* to view. As a friend said, we live in the "eternal now" and the future never comes. There are only probabilities and possibilities, which are determined by past actions. Gautama Buddha could not have said it better. Wish my future would be a good one. My own past (childhood) was horrendous and my present isn't much better. Since I was 21 I've lived in a shell due to the horrible treatment I received as a child. After nearly 20 years of miserable loneliness, three people have pretended to give me love. Those very same characters were the same "pals" who did a real con job on me. The very same people I trusted the most were the ones who hurt me the most. They did incredible psychological damage, which has not healed.

My future looks empty and bleak. I have no money, no job, and few real friends. My skills are nonviable to this computer/high-tech/math-oriented world.

I am a stranger in a strange land, and I am a long, long way from my true home. Some day the exploiters who stomped on me will get the same sort of treatment from others, and then they'll know how it feels. Perhaps some day a crystal ship with silken sails will take me back to Elvenhome.

C.H. 29 years. Female.

Q. Tell me about yourself.

A. I was born October 3, 1954, in Brooklyn, and was the youngest of three children. I have an older brother and sister. My brother was eight years old when I was born and my sister was six.

My mother was in bed for as long as I can remember, although my sister once told me she wasn't really sick but just didn't want to sleep with my father and have more kids.

We lived on the first floor of a two-story house and my grandmother and Uncle Ben lived upstairs. He was my father's brother. He was a truck driver and a very macho guy. I guess I took over some of his mannerisms, like keeping my cigarettes rolled up in the sleeve of my T-shirt. My sister Alice was very pretty and he was always after her. Kidding, he'd say, "The hell with it, kid, let's go to bed." And then he'd laugh. She was scared I knew, because she would never be in the same room alone with him if she could help it.

My father drank a lot but I don't think he was an alcoholic because he kept his job right up to the time he died. He'd come home drunk on Friday night and stay drunk until Sunday night. Sometimes he'd stay home the week end, and watch TV if the ball games were on. Other times he'd come home and change his clothes, and go out again and stay away until Sunday night. He'd always be all right for work on Monday though, and only had beer through the week.

I had a very unhappy childhood. The other kids in school didn't like me. I don't know why. It hurt me a lot. I remember once, though, when I fell down and bled and bled—this was at school—and they stood around and were friendly because I had hurt myself. I guess that may be one of the reasons I like blood now. I remember that experience like it was yesterday.

I had a big thing about my sister, worshiped the ground she walked on. When she started her periods I was really fascinated by it. I used to pull her used Kotex pads out of the wastebasket and smell them. I was sitting next to her one night on the couch watching TV and she was about asleep. I don't remember how old I was at the time. I tried to touch her breast, but she woke up and said it was bad enough she had to be careful about Uncle Ben, but now she had to watch her own sister too. I guess maybe I was ten or so. I didn't realize it was a wrong thing to do, but she looked so pretty I just couldn't help myself. She didn't hold it against me though. I loved her a lot. . . .

I hated school and I hated it at home too. My grandmother was always bitching about something or other and complaining that she had to take care of my mother. She yelled at my father—he was her son—

maybe realizing the real reason why Ma was in bed, maybe not. I don't remember Ma ever kissing me or being loving. Daddy never paid any attention to me at all, and neither did my brother. There were two kids in school who were orphans and I envied them because they didn't have a family to make them unhappy.... The only one who was ever nice to me when I was little was my sister, and she got married and moved out when I was about 12.

As soon as she left, Uncle Ben started going after me. "My little tomgirl," he'd say. One night my mother had some kind of a spell, and Daddy was away. It must have been on a weekend. Uncle Ben was late getting home from bowling, or probably the race track, so Gran had to go with Ma in the ambulance. I was left alone waiting to give Uncle Ben supper Gran had left in the oven warming, and I was upstairs in their place watching TV. He came home and said he had a nice surprise for me in his room, so I went in to see what it was. He locked the door and dropped his pants, and there was this big thing sticking straight out in front of him. I gotta tell you that I had never seen a naked man before. My brother and father always closed the bathroom door, and I wasn't sure just what the fuck this thing was. He laid down on the bed and made me play with it and then told me to put it in my mouth like it was the top of an ice cream cone, and suck. It was so big and round that it hardly went into my mouth, but I really didn't mind playing with it, and it even tasted kind of nice. After a while he got up with the thing still big and got a five dollar bill out of his pants pocket and gave it to me. He patted my shoulder and pushed me out the door of his room. For the very first time, someone in the family besides my sister was nice to me, and the experience, plus the money, hadn't been bad at all. After that we did it a lot, always the same thing, he'd lie on his back and I'd play with his big thing. Sometimes I'd bat it around, you know, back and forth, between my hands like a toy, but most of the time just suck the top of it. One night I was doing it, sucking away, and I saw his eyes roll back in his head, and suddenly stuff squirted out of the end of the thing. I threw up all over his stomach. He got up after a couple of seconds and hit me around the head, some really sharp cuffs you know, and didn't give me no money. I was so dumb I didn't realize what had happened, that he had come, I mean. After that he didn't do that again. Come I mean, and things got back to normal. Ha! His mother was so afraid of him that even if she did suspect what was happening, she didn't say nothing. My own grandmother! Can you believe it? This went on for a couple of years.... I noticed that when I was with Uncle Ben I began to get wet panties while I was playing with him. It started affecting me in other ways, too. There was a kid, Bud, next door, and we played together sometimes after school, although he wouldn't speak to me at school. His mother told him not to. One day we took off our clothes and I sucked his little dick like I did my uncle's. After that we got together almost every afternoon after school. His dick was cute and cold and little, and I really got wet panties when I was with him. . . . One day his mother came home unexpectedly and found us, and I thought she would kill me. She gave me such a beating I was black and blue all over. Just to show you the situation at home, no one even noticed it. . . . A couple of days later, I tried to burn that lady's house down, but nothing happened. . . .

It was about this time I got a crush on a girl at school. Betty. She was kind of dumb, a low IQ I guess, and she was older than the rest of us. She was built like a woman and had a nice set of boobs and a real big ass. I used to take her to the movies with the money my uncle gave me, and all the way through I'd feel her boobs. Sometimes she'd start moaning, and then I'd have to stop because people would turn around and stare. One day she took my hand and put it up under her skirt, and it was then I knew it was women I liked. I don't know, something just clicked into place. Right after that they took her away, though . . . Willowbrook or something. . . . I never did see her again. . . .

There was another girl, Mary, in my class who wore real pretty dresses. She always looked so clean, and she was about the nicest to me of anyone. I got a crush on her, and used to buy her presents and leave them on her desk. I had so much money, it didn't mean nothing to me, whereas most of the other kids had to hustle for their dough. . . . Nothing came of it, the crush I mean, and she never knew who left those presents. Probably thought it was one of the asshole guys. Ha! . . .

I was heavy even then, and wanted to wear my hair short, but my mother cried every time I had it cut off so I finally let it stay shoulder-length to keep her happy. I wore jeans and shirts, though. Always.

I guess it was about this time my uncle got a girl friend, some lady who was the sister to one of his buddies. He didn't have me come in as much as before, so I guess she was putting out for him though she was supposed to be high class. . . .

After I got to high school I met a crazy girl, Flo, who was into almost everything weird. She liked to get hit, and would sit around pinching herself, just to feel the hurt. We got to be friends, social outcasts I guess, 'cause nobody liked her either. After the movies one night we were in her living room and she told me she liked blood. She said if I would give her a little of mine, she would do something fantastic to me that I would never forget. What the fuck, I thought. . . . Well, I let her slice me with a razor and she sucked the cut. Then she went down on me and put her tongue way into my cunt, and I had an orgasm. My first. Jesus!

Well, that's all there was to it. That same something clicked again, and I was hooked. I became her slave, although I would never get really involved in that wanting to get hurt business. Up to a point I'd do almost anything she said. All day and all night all I could think of was her making love to me. I didn't mind cutting my arms and having a little blood. The cuts seemed to heal up right away in those days. And shit, it was worth it. I learned a lot from that horny bitch, believe me.

Later, with Dorothy [CH's present girl friend] we exchanged blood by both cutting our arms one time so we would be, you know, part of each other, intermingled, I guess you would call it. Later I got her into sucking my cuts. I'd make love to her much better than her husband ever did. What an asshole *he* is. I had her in my power just like Flo did me. It's more than that, though. We really love each other. I'd like her to leave her husband and come and live with me. I got a job that pays well and would love to support her. She is my soulmate. I'm not ashamed of my arm scars. They don't bother me at all. People stare when I wear short sleeves or T-shirts. Anyway we—I don't do that any more, because Donna don't like people staring at my arms.

I suppose it sounds terrible but we do drink each other's blood when we have our periods. I read in a magazine it is good clean stuff, and well, what happened was that once I was going down on her and her period was just starting. I liked the taste and then later she did it to me. She said she liked it, too. I—we--don't think there's anything dirty about it at all.

She has to be real careful because her husband is a very jealous person. She'd like to come and live with me, but he would kill us both, I know. . . .

Q. Does the word *vampire* ever occur to you?

A. Yeah, when I go to the movies or see a vampire movie on TV. Then it does. Oh, now I see what you're getting at. No, as far as I'm concerned I don't think of myself as being a vampire. Aren't they supposed to lie in graves and only come out at night? Something like that?

Q. That's the way they're portrayed in the movies, certainly. What would you say if someone called you a vampire?

A. I wouldn't like it.

Q. Do you feel you have a blood fetish, then?

A. Yeah, I guess I do. Among other things.

Q. Do you think this is unusual?

A. Yeah. I guess it is.

Q. How long have you had a craving for blood?

A. Well, it isn't really a craving. No, I lie. It *is* a craving. I just never thought of it that way before, never thought of that word I mean.

Q. Could you elaborate a bit? When did you first . . .

A. Let me just say that at one time in my life I was much more into the blood thing than I am now . . . in high school this friend Flo . . . she got me into that and it was kind of nice after a while. . . . I remember one time we went to a place on the Upper West Side. The people had a Doberman dog, a big scaly-looking mutt, almost bald, and they gave him a lot of booze. He lapped it up like it was milk. Then they slit his throat and everyone had some of his blood in a glass. Later they smeared his blood all over their bodies and everybody fucked each other. Jesus, what a scene! That was the last time I ever got involved in anything that far out. . . .

Q. Now in regard to . . .

A. You know, I really don't like this kind of questioning . . . it's making me nervous. . . .

23

So, What Does It All Mean?

THIS BOOK OPENED WITH A MODERN case of "vampirism." John George Haigh was a self-styled drinker of blood who carried out his dreams over and over again, he said. Blood was the dominating influence in his life—he said—and he had to have it. To get what he wanted he had to murder—he said. It was not a question of whether he knew what he was doing, whether his murderous behavior was right or wrong—he said. A compelling power directed his actions—he said.

But for one driven by compulsion, his activities certainly showed a cool pattern of planning. His preparations before all of his murders were elaborate. His acid baths after the murders were thoroughly planned, even if he was a bit sloppy at the last, when he boiled down Mrs. Durand-Deacon incompletely.

On the night before his execution, Haigh took up pen with a steady hand to write to a journalist acquaintance, Stafford Somerfield:

> I go forward to finish my mission in other form. Has it occurred to you that liberty of religious thought is still not wholly existent in this country: that they still execute their heretics?

All things considered, that seems just a little pompous.

There is something very dubious about John George Haigh's stories.

His defense counsel tried to prove that Haigh's crimes were psychotic, in order to get a verdict of guilty, but insane, and save him from the gibbet. But the whole pattern indicates the murders were cold, calculating, and done for the profit of John George Haigh. Even when he was "assisting the police," the first question Haigh asked was whether it was possible to get out of Broadmoor. What he should have been asking was "How do you get into Broadmoor?" Probably Haigh, and certainly his attorney, thought that if he appeared to be psychotic, a jury would spare his life. He took the big gamble, he told all; he made a big point of his drinking the blood of his victims.

But of all the "vampires" in this book, he was the least convincing to me. He was a very ordinary-looking person. He was dubbed a vampire by the British press, and that may have given him some ideas.

I do not question that he drank blood. What I do question was that he was *compelled* by any external force at all to do so. The real factor is that he profited enormously from all his crimes, in terms of property and cash. The real force that seemed to be driving him was economic need. He had no money, he had the rent to pay at Onslow Court, and there were living expenses and walking-around money. He was a schemer, an inveterate liar, a crook. The evidence brought forth at the trial about his childhood difficulties, conflicting religious training, sensitivity, and confusion, do not bear much weight when balanced against the evidence of his crimes. They were too well planned, he cozened his victims too carefully; his technique of body disposal was too neat to represent the workings of a disorderly mind.

Haigh's motive was cold hard cash.

As noted, differing concepts of the vampire have prevailed at different times, in different parts of the world. Bram Stoker's vampire is the one the Western world has adopted. Ask any youngster what a vampire looks like, and he will reel off a description, culled from films of a man in evening dress, a long black opera cape, with fiery eyes, clutching fingers, and fangs. If he is a little older and a male, he may mention a sleek voluptuous beauty with cherry red lips and a wicked eye.

But as vampire history goes, this is a relatively new concept. Originally, the vampire was a monster, a corpse risen from the grave, or merely a mist. It also was not necessarily bad. All that changed.

But then and now vampires fall into three classifications: the astral, metaphysical, or ectoplasmic vampire, like Detective Lieutenant Paparesta's bony man in the black robe with the Xs, the "un-dead," and the "ordinary" human being who sucks blood.

In spite of Dr. Jeanne Youngson's G.N., who fantasized being carried away by a vampire lover, there are not yet any documented cases of this happening. The dictionary definition of a vampire is: "1. the body of a dead person believed to come from the grave at night and suck the blood of persons asleep," and "2. one who lives by preying on others." The contemporary blood-drinkers' claim to the title has to come in the second category.

The connection of blood, soul, and life has been powerful enough to bring about the propitiation of the dead, both in the past and present. There is not so much difference between the burying grounds of the ancients and our own. There is not so much difference between the floral offerings brought to the graves in the twentieth century and the bread and wine deposited on graves by the ancients. In Asia, particularly, the compulsion to honor the dead lest they become annoyed continues. As far as blood is concerned, either the people felt blood was sacred and thus taboo, or they used blood to celebrate and revitalize themselves. In Haiti and some other places, the people still do. In a sense, we of the "civilized" world do, too, for a blood transfusion is certainly a revitalization. And the refusal to have one (Jehovah's Witnesses) has a very clear relationship to the taboo. One may say that the belief in the importance of blood goes back to prehistoric times; but the above would certainly indicate that it continues today.

The oldest vampires were really interchangeable with gorgons, dragons, and other vile creatures of the imagination. The ancient Greek vampires not only drank blood, but they ate their victims as well. It must have been difficult living in those days, with a monster or a demon around just about every turn. One of the worst aspects was that these beings seemed to be able to take on any shape they wished. Out of this, in several different parts of the world, developed the idea of the corpse that came out of the grave. No matter the description (Malay vampire trailing intestines, or Greek *vrykolakas*) all these vampires had one thing in common: lust for blood. By the time the Chinese tales began to surface, more and more stories concerned the vampire as a reanimated, dangerous corpse, which would attack the living.

That, of course, is why the Chinese took such good care of *their* dead. They did not want anyone rising up out of the grave. It was the same for the Greeks, the Slavs, the eastern Europeans, the Russians. Sometime in the Middle Ages, the monster vampires began to go, replaced by the un-dead. The Christian Church gave a cogency to these beliefs for its own benefit: the excommunicated, the great sinner, the suicide, were all prime candidates to become a vampire.

All this, of course, played right into the superstitions of the peasantry: if a man had sinned, and when they dug him up to check the bones he was ruddy and fleshy, he had become a vampire. The prayers, the stake driving, the burning, all began at about this time.

So many cases of vampirism came to light in Europe, that by the twelfth century "respected authorities" were reporting cases of the un-dead coming out of their graves. Witness the stories of Walter Map and William of Newburgh. These tales reinforced what the people already believed: vampires did indeed exist physically, and they came out of the grave to attack people. The un-dead were to be feared, the Church pointed out, because they were representative of the Devil himself.

The tales of Countess Elizabeth Báthory's bloody years certainly show what can happen to a society in which the powerful are completely unrestricted. The countess's sadistic lust for blood not only indicates the depths of degradation to which a human being can sink when indulging in self-gratification, but it reflects the history of the times. The nobility could do no wrong—except steal the king's revenues—and the peasants were forced to accept what life meted out to them—little enough when ruled by someone like Elizabeth.

Elizabeth was an extreme case. Another was Gilles de Rais, a century earlier, who lived in France and was known as the Marshal of France by those who did not know him as an indecent monster. Gilles de Rais made a real contribution to his world by befriending the Maid of Orléans, Joan of Arc. However, the depth of his depravity might have been even greater than that of Countess Elizabeth Báthory's. Still, try as I might, I could find no real evidence that Gilles de Rais ever drank the blood of his hundreds of juvenile victims, although he did everything else to them, including disembowelling them. He was a homosexual, he dabbled in alchemy and sorcery, and practiced sodomy. Since he didn't drink blood, he cannot be properly classified as a vampire; he was just a human monster. So I left his sordid story out of this compendium.

In one way, at least, Gilles was morally superior to Elizabeth. In the end he repented of his sins and was sorry for his wickedness. Not Elizabeth. When she was hailed up for her crimes she snarled like a cornered wildcat and spewed forth venom at all who dared to question her. She was a Báthory, was she not? Then who had the right to question anything, *anything* she wanted to do?

What set Elizabeth apart from all the other cruel nobles of the time was her insatiable lust. No one in her century could match her torture and appetite. She was bad enough when her husband was around, but after he died, her depravity knew no bounds at all. Bathing her face and her body in blood, letting blood drip all over her fine clothes, sucking blood, wallowing in blood, and getting her sexual excitement from watching big-breasted serving girls squirm under torture, she would shout "More! More! More!" She would certainly have horrified the real Count Dracula. Even Bram Stocker's Dracula would, I think, have been just a little shocked by her.

By the beginning of the seventeenth century, the vampire had become the frequent subject of study by apparently responsible figures. These people were not concerned with writing tales about vampires and other monsters, but in getting at "the truth" of vampirism. Henry More was one of the first. This English churchman suggested that suicide was a basic cause of vampirism, an idea that had not previously occurred to the English church. But something had to be done to explain the appearance of vampires, reported ever more frequently as plagues and fevers coursed across Europe. Various other religious figures wrote about the vampire and the Devil, and suggested that the Devil was responsible in all cases. The Church then got into difficulties because the Church wanted full responsibility for exorcising the Devil out of those vampires, and the people knew that the way to get rid of them was a sharp stake and a fire.

The Church's admission to the possible existence of vampires, along with the dark influence of the Slavs, convinced the Greeks that the *vrykolakas* could never more be benign. From this point on, the only good vampire was a destroyed vampire. All had to be "Devil-inspired." The Church, fearful of losing sway if the people took such practices into their own hands, convinced the government of Greece to pass legislation outlawing the digging up and burning of bodies, but as is seen in the de Tournefort account, the edicts had little effect on the practices of the peasantry.

Such massive works on vampires as de Schertz's merely fanned the flames of the popular belief in vampirism. There was a good deal of such writing in the eighteenth century by scholars, churchmen, and government officials; but where the goal was to lay the ghost of vampires, it failed signally. By the end of the century, the vampire had a solid hold on the imagination of all Europe.

In the third decade of the eighteenth century, had come the celebrated investigation into the "vampire" case of Arnold Paole. Here was a government conducting a "scientific inquiry" into a case of vampirism. The result was that the bodies that had been found to be incorrupt at exhumation were destroyed and the ashes scattered—now officially—but just as the peasants had been doing for years. So the authorities' investigation did nothing to allay fears or remove the problems caused by vampires.

As a result of the notoriety surrounding the Paole case, more and more men of an intellectual turn of mind began to address themselves to the question of vampirism. As noted, the first important work was that of Dom Augustin Calmet, who sought answers to vampirism within the framework of organized religion. Dom Calmet took up the question of the uncorrupted dead body and attempted to offer a convincing "scientific" explanation for it. He called the stories of vampires "vain and without foundation" and said they were nourished by "ignorance, prejudice, and fear"; yet he could only conclude that "this is a mysterious and difficult matter, and I leave bolder and more proficient minds to resolve it." So although his work raised many questions, in the end it did not resolve any of the issues.

The result of Dom Calmet's work was that those who wanted to believe, believed harder than ever, and those who did not believe still did not believe. Nevertheless, to my mind, Calmet deserves great credit for braving the matter of vampires at all. He ran the danger of reaping the scorn of his religious community by questioning certain tenets, and he could be called a fool—he was, by some—for even bothering to pay serious attention to the question of vampires.

The Rumanians, as noted, connected the vampire with predestination and magic. Their *strigoi* lived its first life as a human, its second life as a vampire. It was easy for the Rumanians to accept this concept because they believed in life after death, and everybody has got to be someplace, on earth, in heaven, hell, or limbo. They took the most elaborate precautions to prevent a vampire from getting out of hand. They still do. Because the Communist government has strict laws against magic and sorcery, the vampire in Rumania lives very quietly, and only a few stories of the *strigoi* surface these days; but the fact is that belief in vampires is probably still stronger in Rumania today than anywhere in the world.

With the Greeks it is different. Until the nineteenth century, all the old ways persisted. The big change then was the use of firearms to route vampires. Belief in vampires was called an absurd superstition by the enlightened, but the enlightened did not generally live in Greek villages or on Greek islands. The farmers and fishermen who did live there *believed*. By this time, vampires were the "reanimated" bodies of the dead.

The French added their own touch, with such stories as that of Sergeant Bertrand and his disciple, the brigadier's nephew. In the absence of any body of information about the practices these two followed, prior to Krafft-Ebing's monumental work on sexual aberrations they were lumped together with vampires.

It was inevitable that the European imagination would be roused to create a vampire literature—so many legends, so many "truths" about vampire cases. Some imaginative writer was bound to seize the vampire theme and create a sensation. And so it was: Dr. Polidori was the first, with his *Vampyr*. Once the fictionalization began, it built on and on, until the present day, when if one flips the TV switch late at night, the chances are good of finding a vampire or two lurking on the tube.

The standardization of the vampire brought new sexual overtones to vampirism. The Victorian age was anachronistic: ladies had only limbs, and these heavily veiled under yards of crinoline; but men had mistresses and engaged in some of the most shocking sexual practices. The hearty businessman in mutton chop whiskers and frock coat might well have a fourteen-year-old girl in the closet. Vampire literature was a way for the great unwashed to enjoy a bit of titillation. Varney the Vampire's innocent victim of the hailstorm gave indications of enjoying every minute of what was happening to her, in a morbid sort of way. The story of vampire Carmilla had definite lesbian overtones. As Dr. Youngson's G.N. put it much later: "I dreamed that I would be rescued by . . . a mighty vampire who would ravish me and share his powers with me." But it was left to Bram Stoker to project in about half a page, the image of the female vampire as temptress, seductress, and infinitely desirable being. Probably this was a result of his long years in the theater. There is a scene, in the early chapters of *Dracula,* when the three temptresses descend on Jonathan Harker, and there is no question that Harker loves every moment of it—heady stuff for the Victorian era.

We must credit Bram Stoker, too, with the picture of "our" vampire: Dracula in his impeccable black, his steely red eyes and sharp teeth, and opera cape.

It is a good thing for Bram Stoker that he was never reincarnated as a

Rumanian, for he did a monstrous disservice to the national hero Vlad Dracula, who had battled the Turks so fiercely. In fact, when reverberations of Stoker's Dracula first reached Bucharest, the Rumanians did not know what to make of this foolishness. By now they have learned, and the government tourist officers try to make it quite clear to visitors, that the Dracula of Mr. Stoker is not the Dracula of history. They are quite sensitive about it still.

In 1978, a Rumanian writer named Nicolae Stoicescu published a monograph in *Bibliotheca Historica Romaniae* about the real Vlad Dracula, also called Vlad Tepes (Impaler). The occasion was the five hundredth anniversary of the death of this hero. The monograph was to show "the real picture 'of Vlad,' so highly controversially depicted in scientific literature and fiction."

A Rumanian reviewer praised the work (in the foreword to the book), for "carefully removing the false layer distorting the picture of the Prince and his actions; . . . the author . . . restores Tepes to the image of a statesman of his time." No one could claim that a man who had impaled thousands was just a kindly old ruler, but the reviewer reminded his readers that the "innumerable fiction speculations . . . had nothing in common with the Rumanian Prince except, perhaps, his name *Dracula* taken over from his father—to which the most unbelievable stories were associated." It was, the reviewer wrote a "sad fame . . . due to cheap literature. . . ."

It was a good try by the Socialist Republic of Rumania to set the record straight. But I suspect that if you were to ask anyone, even five hundred years from now, who Dracula was, the answer would be the vampire in black with the red eyes, fangs, and opera cape, not the statesman with his sharp stakes.

The story of Fritz Haarmann, "the Hanover Vampire," was shocking to me, whereas Breene's account of the priest's leaving his grave seemed only eerie. Perhaps that is because Haarmann killed in a very real fashion. Summers considered Breen's priest to be a real vampire, though certainly not a vicious one. Summers, of course, believed in vampires. He was a highly respected authority (and still is) on the history of vampirism and few scholars have done such a vast amount of research on any subject as he did for his two volumes. If Summers were living today, he would most certainly be investigating the most interesting phenomena of modern vampirism: the cases of men and women, not reanimated from the grave but out-and-out alive, who have the basic attribute of the vampire: the lust for blood.

Peter Kuerten was one such. In the 1920s, so horrifying to the public would the news have been that Kuerten drank his victims' blood that the judge cautioned journalists to use care in reporting the trial, and they refrained from mentioning this aspect of the murders. Thus the public missed the whole point. Compare Peter Kuerten and John Haigh—the former killed for blood and for blood alone; there was no calculation of the assets of his victims as there was with the latter.

These twentieth-century "vampire" murder cases might elicit one particular response: that society is on the downgrade. Horror seems to be piled upon horror, and the result is stupefying. But is our society ailing so badly as to create a climate for such inhuman acts?

I would have to say no. In fact, the degree of freedom from horror of human beings is greater now than it has ever been. Don't forget the state of European society in the days of Gilles de Rais and the Countess Elizabeth Báthory and Vlad Dracula. Wholesale torture rarely occurs in the twentieth century; and where it does occur, it is almost always the result of war, or political activity—in other words, official torture by governments, not torture at the whim of individuals. That may say something about governments and power. As for individual monstrosities, they certainly are no worse than in the past.

Consider the case of the Italian Vincenz Verzeni, chosen by Krafft-Ebing for his study *Psychopathia Sexualis,* published nearly a hundred years ago. Verzeni was born in 1849. By the time he was twenty-two years old, he had committed innumerable violent crimes. Only by a stroke of fortune was he captured even then.

One day in December 1870, a fourteen-year-old girl named Johanna Motta left home after seven o'clock to walk to a neighboring village. She never returned. Her body was discovered lying in a field. The corpse was horribly mutilated, the genitals and intestines had been torn out. It appeared that rape had been attempted, and apparently her attacker had stuffed her mouth with earth to stifle her cries. The earth suffocated her, the authorities theorized. Near the body was found flesh torn from the right calf. Had it not been for the stuffing of the mouth, the police would have suspected a wild animal, so beastly was the crime. The police found no clues and had no suspects.

On August 28 of the next year, a twenty-eight-year-old woman from a neighboring village started for the fields early in the morning. She never got there, and after a few hours her husband went out to look for her. He found her body lying naked in a field, with the mark of a thong around her neck. She had been strangled. There were many terrible wounds in the body; the abdomen had been ripped open and the intestines were hanging out. But there were no clues and no suspects.

The next day nineteen-year-old Maria Previtali started out through the fields at noon. She was followed by her cousin, Vincenz Verzeni. He attacked her and started to choke her. She struggled and screamed and he let go. He went to see if there was anyone around before resuming the assault. There was no one. Maria pleaded with him, however, and he let her go. She told her family, and they sent her to the police, and on this charge Verzeni was arrested.

He was sent to prison to await a hearing and was examined by physicians. He was found to have a number of physical abnormalities, oversize cranium, defective ears, overdeveloped penis, and underdeveloped bone structure. A study of his family revealed a good deal of degeneration, including several cretins.

Verzeni finally confessed to the crimes of which he was suspected, and others as well. Earlier, when he was ill, he had tried to strangle his nurse. He had tried to strangle two married women.

Why?

Verzeni said these crimes gave him "an indescribably pleasant (lustful)" feeling, which was accompanied by erection and ejaculation. As soon as he had grasped his victim by the neck, "sexual sensations were experienced." It did not matter to Verzeni whether his victims were young or old, pretty or ugly. Usually the moment of choking gave him the most sexual satisfaction, and then he let his victims go. Thus the nurse, the married women, and his cousin had been saved by orgasm. But if for some reason the sexual pleasure was delayed, he continued choking until the victims died.

The dreadful damage to the Motta girl's body had been made by Verzeni's teeth, "while sucking her blood in most intense lustful pleasure." He had torn out part of the thigh to take the meat home and eat it, but he had been afraid to bring it into the house and had hidden it instead. He had also carried off pieces of his victims' clothing because it gave him pleasure to touch them. But he claimed no interest in normal sex, nor in his victims' genitals. Blood was what he was after.

"I had an unspeakable delight in strangling women, experiencing during the act erections and real sexual pleasure. It was even a pleasure only to smell female clothing. The feeling of pleasure while strangling them was much greater than that which I experienced while masturbating. I took great delight in drinking Motta's blood. . . . I am not crazy, but in the moment of strangling my victims I saw nothing else. . . . It never occurred to me to touch or look at the genitals or such things. It satisfied me to seize the women by the neck and suck their blood."

While awaiting sentencing, Verzeni told an officer that it would be a good thing if he were kept in prison forever, for if he were released he would not be able to resist his impulses. The judge concurred; Verzeni spent the rest of his life behind bars. Krafft-Ebing referred to him as "this modern vampire." It would be hard to disagree with that judgment.

One could not say that Vincenz Verzeni's actions were a result of a sick society; he was simply a deficient member of it. Such psychological deviates have always existed. And so it is with the criminal "vampires" of our time.

Twentieth-century Western society does, however, have something new. The cases of Alex and Jay reported by Dr. Wolf, and the cases reported by Dr. Youngson, indicate another sort of situation. Today, more people seem to be afflicted by blood fetishism than ever before in history. These people are not "abnormal" in the Krafft-Ebing sense. Many of them, like Alex, come from middle-class backgrounds, have college educations, and no apparent physical difficulties, unless you class homosexuality a physical difficulty. Even those who came from a lower stratum of society, such as Dr. Youngson's G.N. and C.H., were raised under conditions that would be regarded luxurious in many parts of the world. Certainly their childhood provides no clue to the reason for their blood lust.

Perhaps it is a question of thrills, in a society that sometimes seems at the point of satiation, where everything possible has been tried to create physical thrill. Is our permissive society, then, responsible for a new wave of "vampirism"? I think so. Is this likely to increase and become truly dangerous? That is for the reader to consider.

CHAPTER NOTES

1.

Most of the material for this chapter is from *The Trial of John George Haigh (The Acid Bath Murder)* edited by Lord Dunboyne. I read with interest *The Authentic and Revealing Story of John George Haigh,* by Stafford Somerfield, who was a reporter covering the case for the *News of the World.* Haigh's note to Somerfield is included here, as are snatches of his conversation with the journalist. Duncan Webb has several chapters on Haigh in *Crime Is My Business*; and there is one short chapter on Haigh and his crimes in *A Book of Trials,* by the Right Honorable Sir Travers Humphreys. *Newsweek* ran a story on Haigh on August 1, 1949; *Time* ran two: one on July 25, 1949 and the other on August 1, 1949.

2.

One of the definitions of a vampire, "A pariah . . . ," is from Montague Summers's *The Vampire: His Kith and Kin,* as is the material on the various names given vampires and the material concerning *The Travels of Three English Gentlemen.* The discussion of the soul and the treatment of kings in the grave comes from Frazer. The information about the African tribal customs comes from Summers's same volume, the material about the Congolese tribes comes from Hill, and the prehistoric and aboriginal material from Volta. The study of the sacrifice of animals is based on material from Summers, and the various treatments of corpses is described by Frazer, Summers, Volta, and Hill. The story of the maize goddess is from Volta, that of getting blood from the bulls is from Frazer and Leonard Wolf. The discussion of the importance of blood is based on material from Frazer, Volta, and Summers. The note about the French custom of drinking blood from the bride's breast is from Volta, and the story about the California initiation is from Leonard Wolf.

3.

The information and verse about the Babylonian and Assyrian evil spirits comes from Thompson. The Arab *ghoul* description is from Summers, as is the material on the *empusa,* and the story of Menippus, and the Keats verse. Some of the material about the *lamia* comes from Summers and Abbott; but most of it is from Lawson. Both Abbott and Lawson have the story of the Queen of Libya. Lawson describes the vampires as grotesque women. The winged serpent description is from Hurwood, and the *lamia* with the feet of bronze is from Lawson. Abbot mentions "the great marvelous monster." Lawson provided the discussion of the lust for blood and the tales of the sloppy, rich *lamias.* The information about the *striges* and *strix* comes from Lawson, as does the legend from Messenia. The material about the Malay vampires is from Skeat. The description of the Chinese vampire comes from Summers and Willoughby-Meade; the Chinese legends are all from Willoughby-Meade.

4.

The material about the Greek treatment of the dead comes from Abbot, as does that about the condition of the corpses. The quotation describing the corpse is contained in Lawson, as a quotation originally from Leo Allatius. The tale of the Archbishop of Salonika is from Abbott, as is the story of the wanton woman. The material about tearing out the heart is from Lawson. The information and quotation regarding the Slavic and Eastern European vampires comes from Perkowski. The stories of Russian vampires are from Ralston.

5.

Basic were Montague Summers's two books. The Pliny quotation is from Summers, as are the Walter Map and William of Newburgh stories.

6.

The blood-lusting Countess Báthory is mentioned in many books, but the ones I used most were those by Penrose and Ronay. The quotation of Elizabeth's letter to her husband about Dorkó's tricks is from Penrose. The material about Elizabeth's visits to her aunt is from Ronay. The notations and quotations about the maids Barsovny and Etvos are from Woodruff. The various tortures described are from the trial records which are contained in Penrose and Ronay. The quotation about girls lying between Elizabeth's thighs is from Woodruff. The quotation "more, Dorkó, more" is from Ronay, as is the report about the burning of the girls' genital organs. Further reports and quotations about the torture of the girls and the places where the torture took place are from the trial records.

7.

I used the same basic sources, including the trial records, for the continuing story of the Countess Báthory. The quotation about the seamstresses is from Penrose. The incantation appears both in Penrose and Ronay.

8.

Again, Penrose and Ronay were basic sources for this third chapter on Countess Elizabeth Báthory. The confrontation of Elizabeth by the Palatine Thurzo and the pertinent quotations come from Penrose. So is Thurzo's comment at the trial. The sentence that Elizabeth was a "blood-thirsty and blood-sucking Godless woman" is from Ronay. The facts of the trial and its results are from the records included in Penrose and Ronay. The Palatine's secretary's note about Countess Báthory's death is from Penrose.

9.

Material and quotations about More and the Polish shoemaker story are from Summers's *The Vampire: His Kith and Kin*. Excellent material on Greek vampires is contained in Lawson. Included is such material as the views and quotations of Leo Allatius, Father Richard's report of vampires at Santorini, and much more about Greek vampires. De Tournefort's account of the *vrykolakas* is from his book *A Voyage to the Levant*, which has been widely quoted by writers on the subject. I found mine in Donald Glut's the *True Vampires of History*. The material contained in Charles Ferdinand de Schertz's *Magia posthuma* can be found in Summers, as can the notation of the learned dissertations on vampires, which began appearing in Europe in the eighteenth century. The other vampire cases in the chapter are also from Summers.

10.

The story of Arnold Paole has been told time and again, and has often been embellished in various books on vampires. I relied on the official report of the Austrian government, published in Belgrade in 1732, as printed in the introduction to Frayling's book, on Dom Augustin Calmet's treatise quoted in Summers (*Kith and Kin*), and on Volta and Riva. The material about Dom Calmet's views of the vampire and his quotations on the subject are from his own work, and a shortened version can be found in Summers. The Liebava story is from Summers. Criticism of Calmet is from Frayling, as is the information about the Empress Maria Theresa of Austria and the Archbishop of Trania's statement about vampires.

11.

The Chinese stories of Mr. Su, the rolling skull, and the woman's head are found in Willoughby-Meade.

12.

The material about the Bulgarian vampires is from St. Clair and Brophy. The information about Rumanian vampires is from Cremene.

13.

Again, Lawson is used as the source of information on the Greek vampires. His work contains the report from the abbot about Sphakia. Lawson also saw an exhumation ceremony himself. The report of Henry Hautteweur about vampires on Kythnos and the story of Andilaveris are from Summers's *The Vampire in Europe,* as is the material on the vampires of Santorini.

14.

Many books on vampires carry the story of Sergeant Bertrand. The reader should remember that in this period little was known about the nature of human sexual abnormalities, and thus Bertrand was widely regarded by the public and press as a "vampire." For the description of his activities and the trial, I relied on Summers. The quotations about Bertrand's "hypnotic look" come from Volta, as do Bertrand's statements at the trial. The Claude vampire case is also from Volta.

15.

Copper, Masters, Frayling, McNally, Farson, and Wolf all discuss the germination of the idea of Polidori's *The Vampyre.* Masters repeats Lord Byron's brief summary of the plot. The story of the novel's life, its popularity and translations and adaptations, is told by Summers in *Kith and Kin.* The quotations from *The Vampyre* are reprinted in Frayling's collection. Notes about Nodier's play *Le Vampire* and Dumas's play of the same name come from Summers, as does much of the material about the fate of *Varney the Vampire,* the first popular vampire book aimed at the masses. That novel was attributed for years to Thomas Presket Prest, a popular writer of the nineteenth century, but it was actually written by Rymer, a fact that became apparent only in 1963 when Louis James was perusing Rymer's scrapbooks. Copper,

Frayling, and others have all made use of the work. Leonard Wolf was the one who described the book as "penny-a-line" fiction, referring to the magazine method of paying authors in those days. Quotations from *Carmilla* are from the work. McNally uses it in his *A Clutch of Vampires.*

16.

Many books mention Bram Stoker, the author of *Dracula.* I used Ludlam's biography and that of Stoker's grandnephew Daniel Farson. The critics' comments on *Under the Sunset* and *The Snake's Pass* come from Ludlam. The description of the Lyceum Theater and the Beefsteak Room, with all its festivities, is from Farson. Farson and Ludlam both indicate the importance of Stoker's chance meeting at the Beefsteak Room with Arminius Vámbery. Farson speculates that "There is good reason to assume that it was the Hungarian professor who told Bram, for the first time, the name of Dracula." Obviously, however, Professor Vámbery, being an expert on Eastern European matters, would not have told Stoker that Vlad Dracula, the Impaler, was a "vampire." The idea had never entered the head of anyone in Rumania. The extension of the feats of the heroic Dracula to an afterlife as one of the un-dead was strictly Stoker's idea, and must have come out of his theatrical experience. He recognized a compelling name when he saw one—probably also a result of his theatrical life.

Ludlam was also the source for my account of Stoker's other writings and the public and critical reaction to them. The material about the "real" Dracula is from Summers, Wolf, Ronay, McNally, and Florescu, and above all from Stoicescu, the author of the official Rumanian government study of Vlad Dracula, written to drive away the vampires forever.

17.

This chapter is based entirely on Bram Stoker's novel *Dracula.* The reason I have included this précis is to give readers unfamiliar with the work a glimpse of the origin of the vampires we now see cavorting on TV. Virtually all of the film vampires are in some way takeoffs from Stoker.

Bram Stoker killed off his Dracula in the end, but the literary Dracula and his kith and kin live on in the hands of hundreds of imitative and innovative writers. The imitations began immediately after *Dracula* was published and continue today in Europe and America.

The first dramatization of *Dracula* was produced in September 1927 at the Shubert Theater in New Haven. After its favorable reception there, it was moved to the Fulton Theater in New York City. Vampirologist Montague Summers must have seen the play. At least he read it. He was not very kind to it. "The striking fact that an indifferent play should prove so successful can, I think, be attributed to the fascination of the theme. Consciously or unconsciously it is realized that the vampire tradition contains far more truth than the ordinary individual cares to appreciate or acknowledge. . . ." That may be the key to the constant stream of vampire theatrics over the years.

18.

The basic source for this true story of the Hanover Vampire is Summers's *Kith and Kin*. The responsible press of Britain has never been very high on vampire stories, so Summers was forced to rely for his press accounts on the *News of the World* and the *Daily Express,* both popular and somewhat lurid publications. One can speculate that perhaps the "responsible" press is not as responsible as all that in ignoring such outrageous but important phenomena as mass murderers.

19.

The vampire story from Ireland, one of the very few to emerge from that island, comes from R. S. Breene's story in the *Occult Review* for October 1925 and was quoted in Summers's *The Vampire in Europe.* Summers was enormously impressed with this story because so many witnesses saw the vampire pass by, and so Summers uses it as one of his bastions in refuting Dom Calmet's views on vampires.

20.

The basic study in English of the Duesseldorf Monster is Margaret Seaton Wagner's book *The Monster of Duesseldorf,* published by Faber and Faber of the United Kingdom. All my quotations are from this work, with two exceptions. I drew from Volta the remark that Kuerten "speaks of his need to kill, as others talk about their habit of smoking" and Kuerten's line in a letter to one of his victim's relatives, "What do you want, Madame? I need blood as others need alcohol."

21.

The story of William Seabrook's encounters with Mary Lensfield comes from his book *Witchcraft,* published by Harcourt Brace and Co. in 1940. McNally uses it in his *Clutch of Vampires.*

The case of Electrician May was described by the *News of The World* of October 27, 1974. I got it from Haining's *The Dracula Scrapbooks.* The cases of Marie Horst and the Vampire Slasher are from the *Journal of Vampirism,* Fall 1978 issue. Paparesta wrote of his New York experience in "The Vampire, Tool of the Devil," which appeared in the *Journal of Vampirism* in the summer of 1978.

The Reverend Omand's story is from the *News of the World,* October 28, 1973, and was found in the Summer 1978 issue of the *Journal of Vampirism.*

Dr. Leonard Wolf's experience with Alex and Jay is from his *A Dream of Dracula: In Search of the Living Dead.* Permission to quote was given by Little, Brown and Co., who published the book in 1972.

The Highgate Cemetery story comes from an article in the *London Evening Standard.* Haining has it in his *Dracula Scrapbooks,* and it also appears in Copper, along with other articles from the *London Daily Mail* and the *London Evening News.*

The case of the Frankfurt student originally was reported in the *Shropshire Star* of January 3, 1937, and later in the *Journal of Vampirism,* Blue Moon issue, 1979.

The case of Jerry Moore comes from the *Vampire Information Exchange Bulletin,* edited by Martin Riccardo.

The case of the murdered couple was described in the New York *Post* of February 21, 1980 and in the *Weekly World News* of December 2, 1979.

22.

All the case descriptions and the interviews contained in the chapter were the result of the research of Dr. Jeanne Youngson of New York, who kindly made her findings available to me.

The information about the Count Dracula Fan Club comes from Dr. Youngson, who is its president; that of the Count Dracula Society from the Society in California, and that of the Vampire Information Society from that organization's headquarters in Illinois. The information about Dr. Sidney Kaplan came from material sent me by Dr. Kaplan, plus a telephone interview. The "quiz" prepared by Eileen Watkins appeared in the newsletter of the Count Dracula Fan Club in the summer of 1982 and is used with the kind permission of the author and the club president.

23.

The Haigh note to journalist Stafford Somerfield is contained in Somerfield's account of Haigh's story. The material about the Rumanian monograph on Vlad Tepes comes from Stoicescu. The case of Vincenz Verzeni is from Krafft-Ebing. The opinions are my own. The reader can understand, and possibly sympathize with, the following conversation I had with an antiquarian bookseller not long ago.

"Do you believe in vampires?" he asked me.

"No. Do you?"

"No," he answered, "but I am afraid of them."

ACKNOWLEDGMENTS

I AM GREATLY INDEBTED TO DR. JEANNE Youngson of the Count Dracula Fan Club of New York City for lending many books from the club's library. I am also grateful to her for the enormous amount of time and energy she spent in support of my book, giving me leads, pictures, and her own interviews with "modern vampires."

Martin Riccardo, publisher of the now defunct *Journal of Vampirism* and president of the Vampire Studies Society, was also very helpful in several ways. He sent me materials and pictures he had collected and directed me to new sources, and granted permission to use various materials.

Bernhardt J. Hurwood, author of a number of books on the occult, shared his views and his books with me. Dr. Wayne de Ashmead also was helpful in suggesting certain books that he felt were important in the study of vampirism. Pisces & Capricorn Books of Albion, Michigan was kind enough to lend me a copy of *The Trial of John George Haigh* until I could find one of my own. Faber and Faber Ltd. of London was kind enough to grant permission to use information from Margaret Seaton Wagner's *The Monster of Duesseldorf,* which they published in 1932.

Little, Brown and Co. granted permission to use material from Leonard Wolf's *A Dream of Dracula*.

I owe Diana Hoyt a great debt for the many hours she spent tracking down books for me without which I could not have finished this book.

I am indebted to my husband, Edwin P. Hoyt, who took time from his own writing to read and edit the manuscript and gave me invaluable suggestions.

Olga Hoyt
Maryland
August 1983.

Bibliography

Abbott, G. F. *Macedonia Folklore*. Cambridge, England: University Press, 1903.

Bourre, Jean Paul. *Le Vampire Aujourd'hui*. Nice: A. LeFeuvre, 1978.

Copper, Basil. *The Vampire in Legend, Fact, and Art*. London: Robert Hale, 1973.

Cremene, Adrien. *Mythologie du Vampire en Roumanie*. Monaco: Editions du Rocher, 1981.

Dunboyne, Lord, ed. *The Trial of John George Haigh: (The Acid Bath Murder)*. London and Edinburgh: William Hodge and Co., 1953.

Eberhard, Wolfram. *Chinese Fairy Tales and Folk Tales*. London: Kegan Paul, Trench, Trubner & Co. Ltd., 1937.

Ennemoser, Joseph. *History of Magic*. 2 vols. Translated by William Howlitte. New Hyde Park, NY: University Books, 1970.

Farson, Daniel. *The Man Who Wrote Dracula, A Biography of Bram Stoker*. London: Michael Joseph, 1975.

————. *Vampires, Zombies, and Monster Men*. Garden City, NY: Doubleday and Co., 1976.

Fitzgerald, C. P. *China: A Short Cultural History*. New York: Praeger, 1950.

Florescu, Radu, and Raymond T. McNally. *Dracula: A Biography of Vlad the Impaler, 1431-1476*. New York: Hawthorn Books, 1973.

Frayling, Christopher, ed. *The Vampyre*. London: Victor Gollancz, 1978.

Frazer, James G. *The Golden Bough*. New York: Macmillan, 1942.

Glut, Donald. *True Vampires of History*. New York: HC Publishers, 1971.

Haining, Peter, ed. *The Dracula Scrapbooks*. New York: Bramhall House (Clarkson Potter), n.d.

Hill, Douglas. *The History of Ghosts, Vampires, and Werewolves*. New York: Harper and Row, 1973.

Humphreys, Sir Travers. *A Book of Trials*. London: Pan Books, 1955.

Hurwood, Bernhardt J. *Vampires*. New York: Quick Fox, 1981.

_____. *The Vampire Papers*. New York: Pinnacle Books, 1976.

Jastrow, Morris. *Religion of Babylonia and Assyria*. Binn and Co., n.p., 1818.

Jones, Ernest. *On the Nightmare*. London: Hogarth Press, 1931.

Krafft-Ebing, Richard. *Psychopathia Sexualis*. New York: G. P. Putnam's Sons, 1965.

Lawson, J. C. *Modern Greek Folklore and Ancient Greek Religions*. New Hyde Park, NY: University Press, 1964.

Lewis, Wyndham. *The Soul of Marshall Gilles de Rais*. London: Eyre and Spottiswoode, 1952.

Ludlam, Harry. *The Biography of Dracula: The Life Story of Bram Stoker*. London: W. Foulsham and Co., 1962.

Masters, Anthony. *The Natural History of the Vampire*. New York: G. P. Putnam's Sons, 1972.

McNally, Raymond T. *A Clutch of Vampires*. Greenwich, CT: New York Graphic Society, 1974.

McNally, Raymond T., and Radu Florescu. *In Search of Dracula*. New York: Warner Books, 1973.

Moncrieff, Ian. *The Blood-Countess: Elizabeth Báthory, The Monster of Csejthe*. London: The Dracula Society, 1977.

Penrose, Valentine. *The Bloody Countess*. Translated from the French by Alexander Trocchi. London: New English Library, 1970.

Perkowski, Jan L. *Vampires of the Slavs*. Cambridge, MA: Slavica Publishers, Inc., 1976.

P'u Sung-ling. *Chinese Ghost and Love Stories*. Translated by Rose Quong. New York: Pantheon Books, 1946.

Ralston, William R. *Russian Folk Tales.* New York: Arno Press, 1977.

Ronay, Gabriel. *The Truth About Dracula.* New York: Stein and Day, 1972.

St. Clair, S. G. B., and Charles A. Brophy. *Twelve Years Study of the Eastern Question in Bulgaria.* London: Chapman and Hall, 1877.

Seabrook, William. *Witchcraft.* New York: Harcourt Brace and Co., 1940.

Senn, Harry A. *Were-Wolf and Vampire in Romania.* East European Monographs, No. xvii. Boulder, CO: 1982.

Skeat, W. W. *Malay Magic.* London: 1900.

Somerfield, Stafford. *The Authentic and Revealing Story of John George Haigh.* Manchester: Hood Pearson, 1950.

Stoicescu, Nicolae. *Vlad Tepes: Prince of Walachia.* Bucharest: Editure Academiei Republicii Socialiste Romania, 1978.

Stoker, Bram. *Dracula.* Garden City, NY: Doubleday and Co., 1970.

Summers, Montague. *The Vampire in Europe.* New Hyde Park, NY: University Books, n.d.

———. *The Vampire: His Kith and Kin.* New Hyde Park, NY: University Books, 1960.

Thompson, R. Campbell. *The Devils and Evil Spirits of Babylonia,* 2 vols. London: Luzac and Co., 1904.

Twitchell, James B. *The Living Dead: A Study of the Vampire in Romantic Literature.* Durham, NC: Duke University Press, 1981.

Volta, Ornella. *The Vampire.* Translated by Raymond Rudorff. London: Tandem Books, 1965.

Volta, Ornella, and Valeria Riva. *The Vampire: An Anthology.* London: Neville Spearman, 1963.

Wagner, Margaret Seaton. *The Monster of Duesseldorf.* London: Faber and Faber, 1932.

Webb, Duncan. *Crime Is My Business.* London: Panther Books, 1956.

Willoughby-Meade, G. *Chinese Ghouls and Goblins.* London: Constable, 1928.

Wilson, Colin. *The Occult.* New York: Vintage Books, 1973.

Winwar, Frances. *The Saint and the Devil: Joan of Arc and Gilles de Rais.* New York: Harper and Bros., 1948.

Wolf, Leonard. *A Dream of Dracula:In Search of the Living Dead.* Boston: Little, Brown & Co., 1972.

Woodruff, J. P. *Infamous Sex Maniacs.* San Diego: Publishers Export Co., 1969.

Magazines, Newspapers, Journals

Count Dracula Fan Club Newsletter, Summer 1981.
Journal of Vampirism, Vampire Studies Society, 1977-1979.
Newsweek, August 1949.
New York Post, February 1980.
TAT Journal, Summer 1979.
Time, July, August, 1949.
Vampire Information Exchange Newsletter, 1983.
Weekly World News, 1980.

INDEX

Also available from
SCARBOROUGH HOUSE

THE TRUTH ABOUT DRACULA
Gabriel Ronay

THE MORNING OF THE MAGICIANS
Louis Pauwels and Jacques Bergier

VOODOO & HOODOO
Jim Haskins

THE BOOK OF GHOST STORIES
M. R. James
Edited by Peter Haining

**THE ONLY ASTROLOGY BOOK
YOU'LL EVER NEED**
Joanna Martine Woolfolk

Robert Louis Balfour Stevenson

Throughout his life, Robert Louis Balfour Stevenson was tormented by poor health. Yet despite frequent physical collapses—mainly due to constant respiratory illness— he was an indefatigable writer of novels, poems, essays, letters, travel books, and children's books. He was born on November 13, 1850, in Edinburgh, of a prosperous family of lighthouse engineers. Though he was expected to enter the family profession, he studied instead for the Scottish bar. By the time he was called to the bar, however, he had already begun writing seriously, and he never actually practiced law. In 1880, against his family's wishes, he married an American divorcée, Fanny Vandegrift Osbourne, who was ten years his senior; but the family was soon reconciled to the match, and the marriage proved a happy one.

All his life Stevenson traveled—often in a desperate quest for health. He and Fanny, having married in California and spent their honeymoon by an abandoned silver mine, traveled back to Scotland, then to Switzerland, to the south of France, to the American Adirondacks, and finally to the South Seas. As a novelist he was intrigued with the genius of place: *Treasure Island* (1883) began as a map to amuse a boy. Indeed, all his works reveal a profound sense of landscape and atmosphere: *Kidnapped* (1886): *The Strange Case of Dr. Jekyll and Mr. Hyde* (1886); *The Master of Ballantrae* (1889).

In 1889 Stevenson's deteriorating health exiled him to the tropics, and he settled in Samoa, where he was given patriarchal status by the natives. His health improved, yet he remained homesick for Scotland, and it was to the "cold old huddle of grey hills" of the Lowlands that he returned in his last, unfinished masterpiece, *Weir of Hermiston* (1896).

Stevenson died suddenly on December 3, 1894, not of the long-feared tuberculosis, but of a cerebral hemorrhage. The kindly author of *Jekyll and Hyde* went down to the cellar to fetch a bottle of his favorite burgundy, uncorked it in the kitchen, abruptly cried out to his wife, "what's the matter with me, what is this strangeness, *has my face changed*?"— and fell to the floor. The brilliant storyteller and master of transformations had been struck down at forty-four, at the height of his creative powers.

Bantam Classics
Ask your bookseller for these other British Classics

THE CANTERBURY TALES by Geoffrey Chaucer

ROBINSON CRUSOE by Daniel Defoe

GULLIVER'S TRAVELS AND OTHER WRITINGS
  by Jonathan Swift

PRIDE AND PREJUDICE by Jane Austen
EMMA by Jane Austen

FRANKENSTEIN by Mary Shelley

JANE EYRE by Charlotte Brontë
WUTHERING HEIGHTS by Emily Brontë

DAVID COPPERFIELD by Charles Dickens
GREAT EXPECTATIONS by Charles Dickens
HARD TIMES by Charles Dickens
OLIVER TWIST by Charles Dickens
A TALE OF TWO CITIES by Charles Dickens

SILAS MARNER by George Eliot

FAR FROM THE MADDING CROWD by Thomas Hardy
TESS OF THE D'URBERVILLES by Thomas Hardy
JUDE THE OBSCURE by Thomas Hardy
THE MAYOR OF CASTERBRIDGE by Thomas Hardy
THE RETURN OF THE NATIVE by Thomas Hardy

HEART OF DARKNESS and THE SECRET SHARER
  by Joseph Conrad
LORD JIM by Joseph Conrad

DR. JEKYLL AND MR. HYDE by Robert Louis Stevenson
TREASURE ISLAND by Robert Louis Stevenson
KIDNAPPED by Robert Louis Stevenson

DRACULA by Bram Stoker

ALICE'S ADVENTURES IN WONDERLAND and THROUGH THE
  LOOKING-GLASS by Lewis Carroll

Kidnapped
by Robert Louis
Stevenson

BANTAM BOOKS
TORONTO · NEW YORK · LONDON · SYDNEY

KIDNAPPED

A Bantam Book

PRINTING HISTORY

Kidnapped *was originally issued serially in* Young Folks, *May 1 to
July 13, 1886. It was published in book form in the same year.*

Bantam Classic edition / February 1982

*Cover painting, ''On the Island of Erraid'' by N. C. Wyeth.
Courtesy of Mr. and Mrs. William V. Sipple, Jr. and the
Brandywine River Museum. (Copyright Charles
Scribner's Sons, 1913).*

Map by David Perry
*The copyrighted portions of this book may not be reproduced
in whole or in part, by mimeograph or any other means, without
permission. For information address: Bantam Books, Inc.*

ISBN 0-553-21067-X

Published simultaneously in the United States and Canada

KIDNAPPED

BEING MEMOIRS OF THE ADVENTURES OF DAVID
BALFOUR IN THE YEAR 1751

HOW HE WAS KIDNAPPED AND CAST AWAY; HIS SUFFER-
INGS IN A DESERT ISLE; HIS JOURNEY IN THE WILD
HIGHLANDS; HIS ACQUAINTANCE WITH ALAN BRECK
STEWART AND OTHER NOTORIOUS HIGHLAND JACOB-
ITES; WITH ALL THAT HE SUFFERED AT THE HANDS OF
HIS UNCLE, EBENEZER BALFOUR OF SHAWS, FALSELY
SO CALLED

WRITTEN BY HIMSELF
AND NOW SET FORTH BY

ROBERT LOUIS STEVENSON

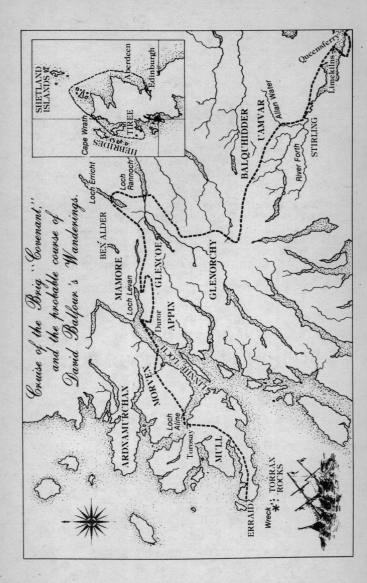

Cruise of the Brig "Covenant," and the probable course of David Balfour's Wanderings.

SHETLAND ISLANDS

Aberdeen

Edinburgh

Cape Wrath

HERBRIDES

TIREE

Loch Errocht

Loch Rannoch

BEN ALDER

Queensferry

Limekilns

L'AMVAR

BALQUHIDDER

Allan Water

STIRLING

River Forth

Loch Leven

MAMORE

GLENCOE

Duror

APPIN

GLENORCHY

ARDNAMURCHAN

MORVEN

LINNHE LOCH

Loch Aline

Torosay

MULL

ERRAID

Wreck

TORRAN
ROCKS

Contents

Prefatory Note

While my husband and Mr. Henley were engaged in writing plays in Bournemouth they made a number of titles, hoping to use them in the future. Dramatic composition was not what my husband preferred, but the torrent of Mr. Henley's enthusiasm swept him off his feet. However, after several plays had been finished, and his health seriously impaired by his endeavours to keep up with Mr. Henley, play writing was abandoned forever, and my husband returned to his legitimate vocation. Having added one of the titles, *The Hanging Judge*, to the list of projected plays, now thrown aside, and emboldened by my husband's offer to give me any help needed, I concluded to try and write it myself.

As I wanted a trial scene in the Old Bailey, I chose the period of 1700 for my purpose; but being shamefully ignorant of my subject, and my husband confessing to little more knowledge than I possessed, a London bookseller was commissioned to send us everything he could procure bearing on Old Bailey trials. A great package came in response to our order, and very soon we were both absorbed, not so much in the trials as in following the brilliant career of a Mr. Garrow, who appeared as counsel in many of the cases. We sent for more books, and yet more, still intent on Mr. Garrow, whose subtle cross-examination of witnesses and masterly, if sometimes startling, methods of arriving at the truth seemed more thrilling to us than any novel.

Occasionally other trials than those of the Old Bailey would be included in the package of books we received

from London; among these my husband found and read
with avidity:—

THE
TRIAL
OF
JAMES STEWART
in Aucharn in Duror of Appin
FOR THE
Murder of COLIN CAMPBELL of *Glenure,* Esq;
Factor for His Majesty on the forfeited
Estate of *Ardshiel.*

My husband was always interested in this period of his
country's history, and had already the intention of writing a story that should turn on the Appin murder. The tale
was to be of a boy, David Balfour, supposed to belong to
my husband's own family, who should travel in Scotland as
though it were a foreign country, meeting with various
adventures and misadventures by the way. From the trial
of James Stewart my husband gleaned much valuable material for his novel, the most important being the character
of Alan Breck. Aside from having described him as "smallish in stature," my husband seems to have taken Alan
Breck's personal appearance, even to his clothing, from
the book.

A letter from James Stewart to Mr. John Macfarlane,
introduced as evidence in the trial, says: "There is one
Alan Stewart, a distant friend of the late Ardshiel's who is
in the French service, and came over in March last, as he
said to some, in order to settle at home; to others, that he
was to go soon back; and was, as I hear, the day that the
murder was committed, seen not far from the place where
it happened, and is not now to be seen; by which it is
believed he was the actor. He is a desperate foolish fellow;
and if he is guilty, came to the country for that very
purpose. He is a tall, pock-pitted lad, very black hair, and
wore a blue coat and metal buttons, an old red vest, and
breeches of the same colour." A second witness testified to
having seen him wearing "a blue coat with silver buttons,
a red waistcoat, black shag breeches, tartan hose, and a

feathered hat, with a big coat, dun coloured," a costume
referred to by one of the counsel as "French cloathes
which were remarkable."

There are many incidents given in the trial that point to
Alan's fiery spirit and Highland quickness to take offence.
One witness "declared also That the said Alan Breck threatened that he would challenge Ballieveolan and his sons to
fight because of his removing the declarant last year from
Glenduror." On another page: "Duncan Campbell, change-
keeper at Annat, aged thirty-five years, married, witness
cited, sworn, purged and examined *ut supra*, depones,
That, in the month of April last, the deponent met with
Alan Breck Stewart, with whom he was not acquainted,
and John Stewart, in Auchnacoan, in the house of the walk
miller of Auchofragan, and went on with them to the
house: Alan Breck Stewart said, that he hated all the name
of Campbell; and the deponent said, he had no reason for
doing so: But Alan said, he had very good reason for it:
that thereafter they left that house; and, after drinking a
dram at another house, came to the deponent's house,
where they went in, and drunk some drams, and Alan
Breck renewed the former conversation; and the deponent, making the same answer, Alan said, that, if the
deponent had any respect for his friends, he would tell
them, that if they offered to turn out the possessors of
Ardshiel's estate, he would make black cocks of them,
before they entered into possession by which the deponent understood shooting them, it being a common phrase
in the country."

Some time after the publication of *Kidnapped* we stopped
for a short while in the Appin country, where we were
surprised and interested to discover that the feeling concerning the murder of Glenure (the "Red Fox", also called
"Colin Roy") was almost as keen as though the tragedy had
taken place the day before. For several years my husband
received letters of expostulation or commendation from
members of the Campbell and Stewart clans. I have in my
possession a paper, yellow with age, that was sent soon
after the novel appeared, containing "The Pedigree of the
Family of Appine," wherein it is said that "Alan 3rd Baron
of Appine was not killed at Flowdoun, tho there, but lived

to a great old age. He married Cameron Daughter to
Ewen Cameron of Lochiel." Following this is a paragraph
stating that "John Stewart 1st of Ardsheall of his descendants Alan Breck had better be omitted. Duncan Baan
Stewart in Achindarroch his father was a Bastard."

One day, while my husband was busily at work, I sat
beside him reading an old cookery book called *The Com-
pleat Housewife: or Accomplish'd Gentlewoman's Companion*. In the midst of receipts for "Rabbits, and Chickens
mumbled, Pickled Samphire, Skirret Pye, Baked Tansy,"
and other forgotten delicacies, there were directions for
the preparation of several lotions for the preservation of
beauty. One of these was so charming that I interrupted
my husband to read it aloud. "Just what I wanted!" he
exclaimed; and the receipt for the "Lilly of the Valley
Water" was instantly incorporated into *Kidnapped*.

F. V. DE G. S.

Dedication

My dear Charles Baxter:

If you ever read this tale, you will likely ask yourself more questions than I should care to answer: as for instance how the Appin murder has come to fall in the year 1751, how the Torran rocks have crept so near to Earraid, or why the printed trial is silent as to all that touches David Balfour. These are nuts beyond my ability to crack. But if you tried me on the point of Alan's guilt or innocence, I think I could defend the reading of the text. To this day you will find the tradition of Appin clear in Alan's favour. If you inquire, you may even hear that the descendants of "the other man" who fired the shot are in the country to this day. But that other man's name, inquire as you please, you shall not hear; for the Highlander values a secret for itself and for the congenial exercise of keeping it. I might go on for long to justify one point and own another indefensible; it is more honest to confess at once how little I am touched by the desire of accuracy. This is no furniture for the scholar's library, but a book for the winter evening school-room when the tasks are over and the hour for bed draws near; and honest Alan, who was a grim old fire-eater in his day, has in this new avatar no more desperate purpose than to steal some young gentleman's attention from his Ovid, carry him awhile into the Highlands and the last century, and pack him to bed with some engaging images to mingle with his dreams.

As for you, my dear Charles, I do not even ask you to like this tale. But perhaps when he is older, your son will; he may then be pleased to find his father's name on the *fly-leaf; and in the meanwhile it pleases me to set it there, in memory of many days that were happy and some (now perhaps as pleasant to remember) that were sad. If it is strange for me to look back from a distance both in time and space on these bygone adventures of our youth, it must be stranger for you who tread the same streets—who may to-morrow open the door of the old Speculative, where we begin to rank with Scott and Robert Emmet and the beloved and inglorious Macbean—or may pass the corner of the close where that great society, the L. J. R., held its meetings and drank its beer, sitting in the seats of Burns and his companions. I think I see you, moving there by plain daylight, beholding with your natural eyes those places that have now become for your companion a part of the scenery of dreams. How, in the intervals of present business, the past must echo in your memory! Let it not echo often without some kind thoughts of your friend,*

R. L. S.

Skerryvore,
   Bournemouth.

Chapter 1

I SET OFF UPON MY JOURNEY TO
THE HOUSE OF SHAWS

I will begin the story of my adventures with a certain morning early in the month of June, the year of grace 1751, when I took the key for the last time out of the door of my father's house. The sun began to shine upon the summit of the hills as I went down the road; and by the time I had come as far as the manse, the blackbirds were whistling in the garden lilacs, and the mist that hung around the valley in the time of the dawn was beginning to arise and die away.

Mr. Campbell, the minister of Essendean, was waiting for me by the garden gate, good man! He asked me if I had breakfasted; and hearing that I lacked for nothing, he took my hand in both of his and clapped it kindly under his arm.

"Well, Davie lad," said he, "I will go with you as far as the ford, to set you on the way."

And we began to walk forward in silence.

"Are ye sorry to leave Essendean?" said he, after a while.

"Why, sir," said I, "if I knew where I was going, or what was likely to become of me, I would tell you candidly. Essendean is a good place indeed, and I have been very happy there; but then I have never been anywhere else. My father and mother, since they are both dead, I shall be no nearer to in Essendean than in the Kingdom of Hungary; and, to speak truth, if I thought I had a chance to better myself where I was going I would go with a good will."

"Ay?" said Mr. Campbell. "Very well, Davie. Then it

behoves me to tell your fortune; or so far as I may. When your mother was gone, and your father (the worthy, Christian man) began to sicken for his end, he gave me in charge a certain letter, which he said was your inheritance. 'So soon,' says he, 'as I am gone, and the house is redd up and the gear disposed of' (all which, Davie, hath been done), 'give my boy this letter into his hand, and start him off to the house of Shaws, not far from Cramond. That is the place I came from,' he said, 'and it's where it befits that my boy should return. He is a steady lad,' your father said, 'and a canny goer; and I doubt not he will come safe, and be well liked where he goes.'"

"The house of Shaws!" I cried. "What had my poor father to do with the house of Shaws?"

"Nay," said Mr. Campbell, "who can tell that for a surety? But the name of that family, Davie boy, is the name you bear—Balfours of Shaws: an ancient, honest, reputable house, peradventure in these latter days decayed. Your father, too, was a man of learning as befitted his position; no man more plausibly conducted school; nor had he the manner or the speech of a common dominie; but (as ye will yourself remember) I took aye a pleasure to have him to the manse to meet the gentry; and those of my own house, Campbell of Kilrennet, Campbell of Dunswire, Campbell of Minch, and others, all well-kenned gentlemen, had pleasure in his society. Lastly, to put all the elements of this affair before you, here is the testamentary letter itself, superscrived by the own hand of our departed brother."

He gave me the letter, which was addressed in these words: "To the hands of Ebenezer Balfour, Esquire, of Shaws, in his house of Shaws, these will be delivered by my son, David Balfour." My heart was beating hard at this great prospect now suddenly opening before a lad of seventeen years of age, the son of a poor country dominie in the Forest of Ettrick.

"Mr. Campbell," I stammered, "and if you were in my shoes, would you go?"

"Of a surety," said the minister, "that would I, and without pause. A pretty lad like you should get to Cramond (which is near in by Edinburgh) in two days of walk. If the worst came to the worst, and your high relations (as I cannot but suppose them to be somewhat of your blood) should put you to the door, ye can but walk the two days back again and risp[1] at the manse door. But I would rather hope that ye shall be well received, as your poor father forecast for you, and for anything that I ken come to be a great man in time. And here, Davie laddie," he resumed, "it lies near upon my conscience to improve this parting, and set you on the right guard against the dangers of the world."

Here he cast about for a comfortable seat, lighted on a big boulder under a birch by the trackside, sate down upon it with a very long, serious upper lip, and, the sun now shining in upon us between two peaks, put his pocket-handkerchief over his cocked hat to shelter him. There, then, with uplifted forefinger, he first put me on my guard against a considerable number of heresies, to which I had no temptation, and urged upon me to be instant in my prayers and reading of the Bible. That done, he drew a picture of the great house that I was bound to, and how I should conduct myself with its inhabitants.

"Be soople, Davie, in things immaterial," said he. "Bear ye this in mind, that, though gentle born, ye have had a country rearing. Dinna shame us, Davie, dinna shame us! In yon great, muckle[2] house, with all these domestics, upper and under, show yourself as nice, as circumspect, as quick at the conception, and as slow of speech as any. As for the laird—remember he's the laird; I say no more: honour to whom honour. It's a pleasure to obey a laird; or should be, to the young."

"Well, sir," said I, "it may be; and I'll promise you I'll try to make it so."

"Why, very well said," replied Mr. Campbell, heartily. "And now to come to the material, or (to make a quibble) to the immaterial. I have here a little packet which contains four things." He tugged it, as he spoke, and with some great difficulty, from the skirt pocket of his coat. "Of these four things, the first is your legal due: the little pickle money for your father's books and plenishing, which

[1] Knock.   [2] Large.

I have bought (as I have explained from the first) in the design of re-selling at a profit to the incoming dominie. The other three are gifties that Mrs. Campbell and myself would be blithe of your acceptance. The first, which is round, will likely please ye best at the first off-go; but, O Davie laddie, it's but a drop of water in the sea; it'll help you but a step, and vanish like the morning. The second, which is flat and square and written upon, will stand by you through life, like a good staff for the road, and a good pillow to your head in sickness. And as for the last, which is cubical, that'll see you, it's my prayerful wish, into a better land."

With that he got upon his feet, took off his hat, and prayed a little while aloud, and in affecting terms, for a young man setting out into the world; then suddenly took me in his arms and embraced me very hard; then held me at arm's-length, looking at me with his face all working with sorrow; and then whipped about, and crying good-bye to me, set off backward by the way that we had come at a sort of jogging run. It might have been laughable to another; but I was in no mind to laugh. I watched him as long as he was in sight; and he never stopped hurrying, nor once looked back. Then it came in upon my mind that this was all his sorrow at my departure; and my conscience smote me hard and fast, because I, for my part, was overjoyed to get away out of that quiet countryside, and go to a great, busy house, among rich and respected gentlefolk of my own name and blood.

"Davie, Davie," I thought, "was ever seen such black ingratitude? Can you forget old favours and old friends at the mere whistle of a name? Fie, fie; think shame!"

And I sat down on the boulder the good man had just left, and opened the parcel to see the nature of my gifts. That which he had called cubical, I had never had much doubt of; sure enough it was a little Bible; to carry in a plaid-neuk.[1] That which he had called round, I found to be a shilling piece; and the third, which was to help me so wonderfully both in health and sickness all the days of my life, was a little piece of coarse yellow paper, written upon thus in red ink:

[1] The sewn-up corner of a plaid used for carrying.

"To Make Lilly of the Valley Water.—Take the flowers of lilly of the valley and distil them in sack, and drink a spoonful or two as there is occasion. It restores speech to those that have the dumb palsey. It is good against the Gout; it comforts the heart and strengthens the memory; and the flowers, put into a Glasse, close stopt, and set into ane hill of ants for a month, then take it out, and you will find a liquor which comes from the flowers, which keep in a vial; it is good, ill or well, and whether man or woman."

And then, in the minister's own hand, was added:

"Likewise for sprains, rub it in; and for the cholic, a great spoonful in the hour."

To be sure, I laughed over this; but it was rather tremulous laughter; and I was glad to get my bundle on my staff's end and set out over the ford and up the hill upon the farther side; till, just as I came on the green drove-road running wide through the heather, I took my last look of Kirk Essendean, the trees about the manse, and the big rowans in the kirkyard where my father and my mother lay.

Chapter 2

I COME TO MY JOURNEY'S END

On the forenoon of the second day, coming to the top of a hill, I saw all the country fall away before me down to the sea; and in the midst of this descent, on a long ridge, the city of Edinburgh smoking like a kiln. There was a flag upon the castle, and ships moving or lying anchored in the firth; both of which, for as far away as they were, I could distinguish clearly; and both brought my country heart into my mouth.

Presently after, I came by a house where a shepherd lived, and got a rough direction for the neighbourhood of Cramond; and so, from one to another, worked my way to the westward of the capital by Colinton, till I came out upon the Glasgow road. And there, to my great pleasure and wonder, I beheld a regiment marching to the fifes, every foot in time; an old redfaced general on a grey horse at the one end, and at the other the company of Grenadiers, with their Pope's-hats. The pride of life seemed to mount into my brain at the sight of the red coats and the hearing of that merry music.

A little farther on, and I was told I was in Cramond parish, and began to substitute in my inquiries the name of the house of Shaws. It was a word that seemed to surprise those of whom I sought my way. At first I thought the plainness of my appearance, in my country habit, and that all dusty from the road, consorted ill with the greatness of the place to which I was bound. But after two, or maybe three, had given me the same look and the same answer, I began to take it in my head there was something strange about the Shaws itself.

The better to set this fear at rest, I changed the form of my inquiries; and spying an honest fellow coming along a lane on the shaft of his cart, I asked him if he had ever heard tell of a house they called the house of Shaws.

He stopped his cart and looked at me, like the others.

"Ay," said he. "What for?"

"It's a great house?" I asked.

"Doubtless," says he. "The house is a big, muckle house."

"Ay," said I, "but the folk that are in it?"

"Folk?" cried he. "Are ye daft? There's nae folk there—to call folk."

"What?" say I; "not Mr. Ebenezer?"

"Ou, ay," says the man; "there's the laird, to be sure, if it's him you're wanting. What'll like be your business, mannie?"

"I was led to think that I would get a situation," I said, looking as modest as I could.

"What?" cries the carter, in so sharp a note that his very horse started; and then, "Well, mannie," he added, "it's nane of my affairs; but ye seem a decent-spoken lad; and if ye'll take a word from me, ye'll keep clear of the Shaws."

The next person I came across was a dapper little man in a beautiful white wig, whom I saw to be a barber on his rounds; and knowing well that barbers were great gossips, I asked him plainly what sort of a man was Mr. Balfour of the Shaws.

"Hoot, hoot, hoot," said the barber, "nae kind of a man, nae kind of a man at all"; and began to ask me very shrewdly what my business was; but I was more than a match for him at that, and he went on to his next customer no wiser than he came.

I cannot well describe the blow this dealt to my illusions. The more indistinct the accusations were, the less I liked them, for they left the wider field to fancy. What kind of a great house was this, that all the parish should start and stare to be asked the way to it? or what sort of a gentleman, that his ill-fame should be thus current on the wayside? If an hour's walking would have brought me back to Essendean, I had left my adventure then and there, and returned to Mr. Campbell's. But when I had come so far a way already, mere shame would not suffer me to desist till I had put the matter to the touch of proof; I was bound, out of mere self-respect, to carry it through; and little as I liked the sound of what I heard, and slow as I began to travel, I still kept asking my way and still kept advancing.

It was drawing on to sundown when I met a stout, dark, sour-looking woman coming trudging down a hill; and she, when I had put my usual question, turned sharp about, accompanied me back to the summit she had just left, and pointed to a great bulk of building standing very bare upon a green in the bottom of the next valley. The country was pleasant round about, running in low hills, pleasantly watered and wooded, and the crops, to my eyes, wonderfully good; but the house itself appeared to be a kind of ruin; no road led up to it; no smoke arose from any of the chimneys; nor was there any semblance of a garden. My heart sank. "That!" I cried.

The woman's face lit up with a malignant anger.

"That is the house of Shaws!" she cried. "Blood built it; blood stopped the building of it; blood shall bring it down. See here!" she cried again—"I spit upon the ground, and crack my thumb at it! Black be its fall! If ye see the laird, tell him what ye hear; tell him this makes the twelve hunner and nineteen time that Jennet Clouston has called down the curse on him and his house, byre and stable, man, guest, and master, wife, miss, or bairn—black, black be their fall!"

And the woman, whose voice had risen to a kind of eldritch[1] sing-song, turned with a skip, and was gone. I stood where she left me, with my hair on end. In those days folk still believed in witches and trembled at a curse; and this one, falling so pat, like a wayside omen, to arrest me ere I carried out my purpose, took the pith out of my legs.

I sat me down and stared at the house of Shaws. The more I looked, the pleasanter that country-side appeared; being all set with hawthorn bushes full of flowers; the fields dotted with sheep; a fine flight of rooks in the sky;

---

[1]Weird, uncanny.

and every sign of a kind soil and climate; and yet the barrack in the midst of it went sore against my fancy.

Country folk went by from the fields as I sat there on the side of the ditch, but I lacked the spirit to give them a good-e'en. At last the sun went down, and then, right up against the yellow sky, I saw a scroll of smoke go mounting, not much thicker, as it seemed to me, than the smoke of a candle; but still there it was, and meant a fire, and warmth, and cookery, and some living inhabitant that must have lit it; and this comforted my heart.

So I set forward by a little faint track in the grass that led in my direction. It was very faint indeed to be the only way to a place of habitation; yet I saw no other. Presently it brought me to stone uprights, with an unroofed lodge beside them, and coats of arms upon the top. A main entrance it was plainly meant to be, but never finished; instead of gates of wrought iron, a pair of hurdles were tied across with a straw rope; and as there were no park walls, nor any sign of avenue, the track that I was following passed on the right hand of the pillars, and went wandering on toward the house.

The nearer I got to that, the drearier it appeared. It seemed like the one wing of a house that had never been finished. What should have been the inner end stood open on the upper floors, and showed against the sky with steps and stairs of uncompleted masonry. Many of the windows were unglazed, and bats flew in and out like doves out of a dove-cote.

The night had begun to fall as I got close; and in three of the lower windows, which were very high up and narrow, and well barred, the changing light of a little fire began to glimmer.

Was this the palace I had been coming to? Was it within these walls that I was to seek new friends and begin great fortunes? Why, in my father's house on Essen-Waterside, the fire and the bright lights would show a mile away, and the door open to a beggar's knock!

I came forward cautiously, and giving ear as I came, heard some one rattling with dishes, and a little dry, eager cough that came in fits; but there was no sound of speech, and not a dog barked.

The door, as well as I could see it in the dim light, was a great piece of wood all studded with nails; and I lifted my hand with a faint heart under my jacket, and knocked once. Then I stood and waited. The house had fallen into a dead silence; a whole minute passed away, and nothing stirred but the bats overhead. I knocked again, and hearkened again. By this time my ears had grown so accustomed to the quiet, that I could hear the ticking of the clock inside as it slowly counted out the seconds; but whoever was in that house kept deadly still, and must have held his breath.

I was in two minds whether to run away; but anger got the upper hand, and I began instead to rain kicks and buffets on the door, and to shout out aloud for Mr. Balfour. I was in full career, when I heard the cough right overhead, and jumping back and looking up, beheld a man's head in a tall nightcap, and the bell mouth of a blunderbuss, at one of the first story windows.

"It's loaded," said a voice.

"I have come here with a letter," I said, "to Mr. Ebenezer Balfour of Shaws. Is he here?"

"From whom is it?" asked the man with the blunderbuss.

"That is neither here nor there," said I, for I was growing very wroth.

"Well," was the reply, "ye can put it down upon the doorstep, and be off with ye."

"I will do no such thing," I cried. "I will deliver it into Mr. Balfour's hands, as it was meant I should. It is a letter of introduction."

"A what?" cried the voice, sharply.

I repeated what I had said.

"Who are ye yourself?" was the next question, after a considerable pause.

"I am not ashamed of my name," said I. "They call me David Balfour."

At that, I made sure the man started, for I heard the blunderbuss rattle on the windowsill; and it was after quite a long pause, and with a curious change of voice, that the next question followed:

"Is your father dead?"

I was so much surprised at this, that I could find no voice to answer, but stood staring.

"Ay," the man resumed, "he'll be dead, no doubt; and that'll be what brings ye chapping to my door." Another pause, and then defiantly, "Well, man," he said, "I'll let ye in"; and he disappeared from the window.

Chapter 3

I MAKE ACQUAINTANCE OF MY UNCLE

Presently there came a great rattling of chains and bolts, and the door was cautiously opened and shut-to again behind me as soon as I had passed.

"Go into the kitchen and touch naething," said the voice; and while the person of the house set himself to replacing the defences of the door, I groped my way forward and entered the kitchen.

The fire had burned up fairly bright, and showed me the barest room I think I ever put my eyes on. Half-a-dozen dishes stood upon the shelves; the table was laid for supper with a bowl of porridge, a horn spoon, and a cup of small beer. Besides what I have named, there was not another thing in that great, stone-vaulted, empty chamber but lock-fast chests arranged along the wall and a corner cupboard with a padlock.

As soon as the last chain was up, the man rejoined me. He was a mean, stooping, narrow-shouldered, clay-faced creature; and his age might have been anything between fifty and seventy. His nightcap was of flannel, and so was the nightgown that he wore, instead of coat and waistcoat, over his ragged shirt. He was long unshaved; but what most distressed and even daunted me, he would neither take his eyes away from me nor look me fairly in the face. What he was, whether by trade or birth, was more than I could fathom; but he seemed most like an old, unprofitable serving-man, who should have been left in charge of that big house upon board wages.

"Are ye sharp-set?" he asked, glancing at about the level of my knee. "Ye can eat that drop parritch?"

I said I feared it was his own supper.

"Oh," said he, "I can do fine wanting it. I'll take the ale, though, for it slockens[1] my cough." He drank the cup about half out, still keeping an eye upon me as he drank; and then suddenly held out his hand. "Let's see the letter," said he.

I told him the letter was for Mr. Balfour; not for him.

"And who do ye think I am?" says he. "Give me Alexander's letter!"

"You know my father's name?"

"It would be strange if I didna," he returned, "for he was my born brother; and little as ye seem to like either me or my house, or my good parritch, I'm your born uncle, Davie my man, and you my born nephew. So give us the letter and sit down and fill your kyte."[2]

If I had been some years younger, what with shame, weariness, and disappointment, I believe I had burst into tears. As it was, I could find no words, neither black nor white, but handed him the letter, and sat down to the porridge with as little appetite for meat as ever a young man had.

Meanwhile, my uncle, stooping over the fire, turned the letter over and over in his hands.

"Do ye ken what's in it?" he asked, suddenly.

"You see for yourself, sir," said I, "that the seal has not been broken."

"Ay," said he, "but what brought you here?"

"To give the letter," said I.

"No," says he, cunningly, "but ye'll have had some hopes, nae doubt?"

"I confess, sir," said I, "when I was told that I had kinsfolk well-to-do, I did indeed indulge the hope that they might help me in my life. But I am no beggar; I look for no favours at your hands, and I want none that are not freely given. For as poor as I appear, I have friends of my own that will be blithe to help me."

"Hoot-toot!" said Uncle Ebenezer, "dinna fly up in the snuff at me. We'll agree fine yet. And, Davie my man, if you're done with that bit parritch, I could just take a sup

---

[1]Moistens.   [2]Stomach.

of it myself. Ay," he continued, as soon as he had ousted me from the stool and spoon, "they're fine, halesome food—they're grand food, parritch." He murmured a little grace to himself and fell-to. "Your father was very fond of his meat, I mind; he was a hearty, if not a great, eater; but as for me, I could never do mair than pyke at food." He took a pull at the small beer, which probably reminded him of hospitable duties, for his next speech ran thus: "If ye're dry, ye'll find water behind the door."

To this I returned no answer, standing stiffly on my two feet, and looking down upon my uncle with a mighty angry heart. He, on his part, continued to eat like a man under some pressure of time, and to throw out little darting glances now at my shoes and now at my homespun stockings. Once only, when he had ventured to look a little higher, our eyes met; and no thief taken with a hand in a man's pocket could have shown more lively signals of distress. This set me in a muse, whether his timidity arose from too long a disuse of any human company; and whether perhaps, upon a little trial, it might pass off, and my uncle change into an altogether different man. From this I was awakened by his sharp voice.

"Your father's been long dead?" he asked.

"Three weeks, sir," said I.

"He was a secret man, Alexander—a secret, silent man," he continued. "He never said muckle when he was young. He'll never have spoken muckle of me?"

"I never knew, sir, till you told it me yourself, that he had any brother."

"Dear me, dear me!" said Ebenezer. "Nor yet of Shaws, I daresay?"

"Not so much as the name, sir," said I.

"To think o' that!" said he. "A strange nature of a man!" For all that, he seemed singularly satisfied, but whether with himself, or me, or with this conduct of my father's, was more than I could read. Certainly, however, he seemed to be outgrowing that distaste, or ill-will, that he had conceived at first against my person; for presently he jumped up, came across the room behind me, and hit me a smack upon the shoulder. "We'll agree fine yet!" he cried. "I'm just as glad I let you in. And now come awa' to your bed."

To my surprise, he lit no lamp or candle, but set forth into the dark passage, groped his way, breathing deeply, up a flight of steps, and paused before a door, which he unlocked. I was close upon his heels, having stumbled after him as best I might; and then he bade me go in, for that was my chamber. I did as he bid, but paused after a few steps, and begged a light to go to bed with.

"Hoot-toot!" said Uncle Ebenezer, "there's a fine moon."

"Neither moon nor star, sir, and pit-mirk,"[1] said I. "I canna see the bed."

"Hoot-toot, hoot-toot!" said he. "Lights in a house is a thing I dinna agree with. I'm unco feared of fires. Good-night to ye, Davie my man." And before I had time to add a further protest, he pulled the door to, and I heard him lock me in from the outside.

I did not know whether to laugh or cry. The room was as cold as a well, and the bed, when I had found my way to it, as damp as a peat-hag;[2] but by good fortune I had caught up my bundle and my plaid, and rolling myself in the latter, I lay down upon the floor under lee of the big bedstead, and fell speedily asleep.

With the first peep of day I opened my eyes, to find myself in a great chamber, hung with stamped leather, furnished with fine embroidered furniture, and lit by three fair windows. Ten years ago, or perhaps twenty, it must have been as pleasant a room to lie down or to awake in, as a man could wish; but damp, dirt, disuse, and the mice and spiders had done their worst since then. Many of the window-panes, besides, were broken; and indeed this was so common a feature in that house, that I believe my uncle must at some time have stood a siege from his indignant neighbours—perhaps with Jennet Clouston at their head.

Meanwhile the sun was shining outside; and being very cold in that miserable room, I knocked and shouted till my gaoler came and let me out. He carried me to the back of

[1]Dark as the pit.   [2]Hole in a peat bog.

the house, where was a draw-well, and told me to "wash my face there, if I wanted"; and when that was done, I made the best of my own way back to the kitchen, where he had lit the fire and was making the porridge. The table was laid with two bowls and two horn spoons, but the same single measure of small beer. Perhaps my eye rested on this particular with some surprise, and perhaps my uncle observed it; for he spoke up as if in answer to my thought, asking me if I would like to drink ale—for so he called it.

I told him such was my habit, but not to put himself about.

"Na, na," said he; "I'll deny you nothing in reason."

He fetched another cup from the shelf; and then, to my great surprise, instead of drawing more beer, he poured an accurate half from one cup to the other. There was a kind of nobleness in this that took my breath away; if my uncle was certainly a miser, he was one of that thorough breed that goes near to make the vice respectable.

When we had made an end of our meal, my uncle Ebenezer unlocked a drawer, and drew out of it a clay pipe and a lump of tobacco, from which he cut one fill before he locked it up again. Then he sat down in the sun at one of the windows and silently smoked. From time to time his eyes came coasting round to me, and he shot out one of his questions. Once it was, "And your mother?" and when I had told him that she, too, was dead, "Ay, she was a bonnie lassie!" Then, after another long pause, "Wha were these friends o' yours?"

I told him they were different gentlemen of the name of Campbell; though, indeed, there was only one, and that the minister, that had ever taken the least note of me; but I began to think my uncle made too light of my position, and finding myself all alone with him, I did not wish him to suppose me helpless.

He seemed to turn this over in his mind; and then, "Davie my man," said he, "ye've come to the right bit when ye came to your Uncle Ebenezer. I've a great notion of the family and I mean to do the right by you; but while I'm taking a bit think to mysel' of what's the best thing to put you to—whether the law, or the meenistry, or maybe the army, whilk[1] is what boys are fondest of—I wouldna like the Balfours to be humbled before a wheen[2] Hieland Campbells, and I'll ask you to keep your tongue within your teeth. Nae letters; nae messages; no kind of word to onybody; or else—there's my door."

"Uncle Ebenezer," said I, "I've no manner of reason to suppose you mean anything but well by me. For all that, I would have you to know that I have a pride of my own. It was by no will of mine that I came seeking you; and if you show me your door again, I'll take you at the word."

He seemed grievously put out. "Hoots-toots," said he, "ca' cannie,[3] man—ca' cannie! Bide a day or two. I'm nae warlock, to find a fortune for you in the bottom of a parritch bowl; but just you give me a day or two, and say naething to naebody, and as sure as sure, I'll do the right by you."

"Very well," said I, "enough said. If you want to help me, there's no doubt but I'll be glad of it, and none but I'll be grateful."

It seemed to me (too soon, I daresay) that I was getting the upper hand of my uncle; and I began next to say that I must have the bed and bedclothes aired and put to sundry; for nothing would make me sleep in such a pickle.

"Is this my house or yours?" said he, in his keen voice, and then all of a sudden broke off. "Na, na," said he, "I didna mean that. What's mine is yours, Davie my man, and what's yours is mine. Blood's thicker than water; and there's naebody but you and me that ought the name." And then on he rambled about the family, and its ancient greatness, and his father that began to enlarge the house, and himself that stopped the building as a sinful waste; and this put it in my head to give him Jennet Clouston's message.

"The limmer!"[4] he cried. "Twelve hunner and fifteen—that's every day since I had the limmer rowpit![5] Dod, David, I'll have her roasted on red peats before I'm by with it! A witch—a proclaimed witch! I'll aff and see the session-clerk."

---

[1]Which.   [2]Few.   [3]Move cautiously.   [4]Hussy.   [5]Sold up.

And with that he opened a chest, and got out a very old and well-preserved blue coat and waistcoat, and a good enough beaver hat, both without lace. These he threw on any way, and taking a staff from the cupboard, locked all up again, and was for setting out, when a thought arrested him.

"I canna leave you by yoursel' in the house," said he. "I'll have to lock you out."

The blood came to my face. "If you lock me out," I said, "it'll be the last you'll see of me in friendship."

He turned very pale, and sucked his mouth in. "This is no' the way," he said, looking wickedly at a corner of the floor—"this is no' the way to win my favour, David."

"Sir," says I, "with a proper reverence for your age and our common blood, I do not value your favour at a bodle's[1] purchase. I was brought up to have a good conceit of myself; and if you were all the uncle, and all the family, I had in the world, ten times over, I wouldn't buy your liking at such prices."

Uncle Ebenezer went and looked out of the window for a while. I could see him all trembling and twitching, like a man with palsy. But when he turned round, he had a smile upon his face.

"Well, well," said he, "we must bear and forbear. I'll no' go; that's all that's to be said of it."

"Uncle Ebenezer," I said, "I can make nothing out of this. You use me like a thief; you hate to have me in this house; you let me see it, every word and every minute: it's not possible that you can like me; and as for me, I've spoken to you as I never thought to speak to any man. Why do you seek to keep me, then? Let me gang back—let me gang back to the friends I have, and that like me!"

"Na, na; na, na," he said, very earnestly. "I like you fine; we'll agree fine yet; and for the honour of the house I couldna let you leave the way ye came. Bide here quiet, there's a good lad; just you bide here quiet a bittie, and ye'll find that we agree."

---

[1] Copper coin worth two Scottish pence.

"Well, sir," said I, after I had thought the matter out in silence, "I'll stay a while. It's more just I should be helped by my own blood than strangers; and if we don't agree, I'll do my best it shall be through no fault of mine."

Chapter 4

I RUN A GREAT DANGER IN THE HOUSE OF SHAWS

For a day that was begun so ill, the day passed fairly well. We had the porridge cold again at noon, and hot porridge at night; porridge and small beer was my uncle's diet. He spoke but little, and that in the same way as before, shooting a question at me after a long silence; and when I sought to lead him in talk about my future, slipped out of it again. In a room next door to the kitchen, where he suffered me to go, I found a great number of books, both Latin and English, in which I took great pleasure all the afternoon. Indeed the time passed so lightly in this good company, that I began to be almost reconciled to my residence at Shaws; and nothing but the sight of my uncle, and his eyes playing hide and seek with mine, revived the force of my distrust.

One thing I discovered, which put me in some doubt. This was an entry on the fly-leaf of a chap-book (one of Patrick Walker's) plainly written by my father's hand and thus conceived: "To my brother Ebenezer on his fifth birthday." Now, what puzzled me was this: that as my father was of course the younger brother, he must either have made some strange error, or he must have written, before he was yet five, an excellent, clear, manly hand of writing.

I tried to get this out of my head; but though I took down many interesting authors, old and new, history, poetry, and story-book, this notion of my father's hand of writing stuck to me; and when at length I went back into the kitchen, and sat down once more to porridge and small beer, the first thing I said to Uncle Ebenezer was to ask him if my father had not been very quick at his book.

"Alexander? No' him!" was the reply. "I was far quicker mysel'; I was a clever chappie when I was young. Why, I could read as soon as he could."

This puzzled me yet more; and a thought coming into my head, I asked if he and my father had been twins.

He jumped upon his stool, and the horn spoon fell out of his hand upon the floor. "What gars ye ask that?" he said, and he caught me by the breast of the jacket, and looked this time straight into my eyes: his own were little and light, and bright like a bird's, blinking and winking strangely.

"What do you mean?" I asked, very calmly, for I was far stronger than he, and not easily frightened. "Take your hand from my jacket. This is no way to behave."

My uncle seemed to make a great effort upon himself. "Dod man, David," he said, "ye shouldna speak to me about your father. That's where the mistake is." He sat a while and shook, blinking in his plate: "He was all the brother that ever I had," he added, but with no heart in his voice; and then he caught up his spoon and fell to supper again, but still shaking.

Now this last passage, this laying of hands upon my person and sudden profession of love for my dead father, went so clean beyond my comprehension that it put me in both fear and hope. On the one hand, I began to think my uncle was perhaps insane and might be dangerous; on the other, there came up into my mind (quite unbidden by me and even discouraged) a story like some ballad I had heard folk singing, of a poor lad that was a rightful heir and a wicked kinsman that tried to keep him from his own. For why should my uncle play a part with a relative that came, almost a beggar, to his door, unless in his heart he had some cause to fear him?

With this notion, all unacknowledged, but nevertheless getting firmly settled in my head, I now began to imitate his covert looks; so that we sat at table like a cat and a mouse, each stealthily observing the other. Not another word had he to say to me, black or white, but was busy turning something secretly over in his mind; and the longer we sat and the more I looked at him the more certain I became that the something was unfriendly to myself.

When he had cleared the platter, he got out a single pipeful of tobacco, just as in the morning, turned round a stool into the chimney-corner, and sat a while smoking, with his back to me.

"Davie," he said, at length, "I've been thinking"; then he paused, and said it again. "There's a wee bit siller[1] that I half promised ye before ye were born," he continued; "promised it to your father. O, naething legal, ye understand; just gentlemen daffing at their wine. Well, I keepit that bit money separate—it was a great expense, but a promise is a promise—and it has grown by now to be a maitter of just precisely—just exactly"—and here he paused and stumbled—"of just exactly forty pounds!" This last he rapped out with a sidelong glance over his shoulder; and the next moment added, almost with a scream, "Scots!"

The pound Scots being the same thing as an English shilling, the difference made by this second thought was considerable; I could see, besides, that the whole story was a lie, invented with some end which it puzzled me to guess; and I made no attempt to conceal the tone of raillery in which I answered—

"O, think again, sir! Pounds sterling, I believe!"

"That's what I said," returned my uncle: "pounds sterling! And if you'll step out-by to the door a minute, just to see what kind of a night it is, I'll get it out to ye and call ye in again."

I did his will, smiling to myself in my contempt that he should think I was so easily to be deceived. It was a dark night, with a few stars low down; and as I stood just outside the door, I heard a hollow moaning of wind far off among the hills. I said to myself there was something thundery and changeful in the weather, and little knew of what a vast importance that should prove to me before the evening passed.

When I was called in again, my uncle counted out into my hand seven and thirty golden guinea pieces; the rest

[1]Money.

was in his hand, in small gold and silver; but his heart failed him there and he crammed the change into his pocket.

"There," said he, "that'll show you! I'm a queer man, and strange wi' strangers; but my word is my bond, and there's the proof of it."

Now, my uncle seemed so miserly that I was struck dumb by this sudden generosity, and could find no words in which to thank him.

"No' a word!" said he. "Nae thanks; I want nae thanks. I do my duty; I'm no' saying that everybody would have done it; but for my part (though I'm a careful body, too) it's a pleasure to me to do the right by my brother's son; and it's a pleasure to me to think that now we'll agree as such near friends should."

I spoke him in return as handsomely as I was able; but all the while I was wondering what would come next, and why he had parted with his precious guineas; for as to the reason he had given, a baby would have refused it.

Presently he looked towards me sideways.

"And see here," says he, "tit for tat."

I told him I was ready to prove my gratitude in any reasonable degree, and then waited, looking for some monstrous demand. And yet, when at last he plucked up courage to speak, it was only to tell me (very properly, as I thought) that he was growing old and a little broken, and that he would expect me to help him with the house and the bit garden.

I answered, and expressed my readiness to serve.

"Well," he said, "let's begin." He pulled out of his pocket a rusty key. "There," says he, "there's the key of the stair-tower at the far end of the house. Ye can only win into it from the outside, for that part of the house is no' finished. Gang ye in there, and up the stairs, and bring me down the chest that's at the top. There's papers in't," he added.

"Can I have a light, sir?" said I.

"Na," said he, very cunningly. "Nae lights in my house."

"Very well, sir," said I. "Are the stairs good?"

"They're grand," said he; and then, as I was going,

"Keep to the wall," he added; "there's nae bannisters. But the stairs are grand underfoot."

Out I went into the night. The wind was still moaning in the distance, though never a breath of it came near the house of Shaws. It had fallen blacker than ever; and I was glad to feel along the wall, till I came the length of the stair-tower door at the far end of the unfinished wing. I had got the key into the keyhole and had just turned it, when all upon a sudden, without sound of wind or thunder, the whole sky lighted up with wildfire and went black again. I had to put my hand over my eyes to get back to the colour of the darkness; and indeed I was already half blinded when I stepped into the tower.

It was so dark inside, it seemed a body could scarce breathe; but I pushed out with foot and hand, and presently struck the wall with the one, and the lowermost round of the stair with the other. The wall, by the touch, was of fine hewn stone; the steps too, though somewhat steep and narrow, were of polished mason-work, and regular and solid underfoot. Minding my uncle's word about the bannisters, I kept close to the tower side, and felt my way in the pitch darkness with a beating heart.

The house of Shaws stood some five full stories high, not counting lofts. Well, as I advanced, it seemed to me the stair grew airier and a thought more lightsome; and I was wondering what might be the cause of this change, when a second blink of the summer lightning came and went. If I did not cry out, it was because fear had me by the throat; and if I did not fall, it was more by Heaven's mercy than my own strength. It was not only that the flash shone in on every side through breaches in the wall, so that I seemed to be clambering aloft upon an open scaffold, but the same passing brightness showed me the steps were of unequal length, and that one of my feet rested that moment within two inches of the well.

This was the grand stair! I thought; and with the thought, a gust of a kind of angry courage came into my heart. My uncle had sent me here, certainly to run great risks, perhaps to die. I swore I would settle that "perhaps," if I should break my neck for it; got me down upon my hands and knees; and as slowly as a snail, feeling before me

every inch, and testing the solidity of every stone, I continued to ascend the stair. The darkness, by contrast with
the flash, appeared to have redoubled; nor was that all, for
my ears were now troubled and my mind confounded by a
great stir of bats in the top part of the tower, and the foul
beasts, flying downwards, sometimes beat about my face
and body.

The tower, I should have said, was square; and in every
corner the step was made of a great stone of a different
shape, to join the flights. Well, I had come close to one of
these turns, when, feeling forward as usual, my hand
slipped upon an edge and found nothing but emptiness
beyond it. The stair had been carried no higher: to set a
stranger mounting it in the darkness was to send him
straight to his death; and (although, thanks to the lightning
and my own precautions, I was safe enough) the mere
thought of the peril in which I might have stood and the
dreadful height I might have fallen from, brought out the
sweat upon my body and relaxed my joints.

But I knew what I wanted now, and turned and groped
my way down again, with a wonderful anger in my heart.
About half way down, the wind sprang up in a clap and
shook the tower, and died again; the rain followed; and
before I had reached the ground level it fell in buckets. I
put out my head into the storm, and looked along towards
the kitchen. The door, which I had shut behind me when
I left, now stood open, and shed a little glimmer of light;
and I thought I could see a figure standing in the rain,
quite still, like a man hearkening. And then there came a
blinding flash, which showed me my uncle plainly, just
where I had fancied him to stand; and hard upon the heels
of it, a great tow-row of thunder.

Now, whether my uncle thought the crash to be the
sound of my fall, or whether he heard in it God's voice
denouncing murder, I will leave you to guess. Certain it
is, at least, that he was seized on by a kind of panic fear,
and that he ran into the house and left the door open
behind him. I followed as softly as I could, and, coming
unheard into the kitchen, stood and watched him.

He had found time to open the corner cupboard and
bring out a great case bottle of aqua vitæ, and now sat

with his back towards me at the table. Ever and again he would be seized with a fit of deadly shuddering and groan aloud, and carrying the bottle to his lips, drink down the raw spirits by the mouthful.

I stepped forward, came close behind him where he sat, and suddenly clapping my two hands down upon his shoulders—"Ah!" cried I.

My uncle gave a kind of broken cry like a sheep's bleat, flung up his arms, and tumbled to the floor like a dead man. I was somewhat shocked at this; but I had myself to look to first of all, and did not hesitate to let him lie as he had fallen. The keys were hanging in the cupboard; and it was my design to furnish myself with arms before my uncle should come again to his senses and the power of devising evil. In the cupboard were a few bottles, some apparently of medicine; a great many bills and other papers, which I should willingly enough have rummaged, had I had the time; and a few necessaries, that were nothing to my purpose. Thence I turned to the chests. The first was full of meal; the second of money-bags and papers tied into sheaves; in the third, with many other things (and these for the most part clothes) I found a rusty, ugly-looking Highland dirk without the scabbard. This, then, I concealed inside my waistcoat, and turned to my uncle.

He lay as he had fallen, all huddled, with one knee up and one arm sprawling abroad; his face had a strange colour of blue, and he seemed to have ceased breathing. Fear came on me that he was dead; then I got water and dashed it in his face; and with that he seemed to come a little to himself, working his mouth and fluttering his eyelids. At last he looked up and saw me, and there came into his eyes a terror that was not of this world.

"Come, come," said I; "sit up."

"Are ye alive?" he sobbed. "O man, are ye alive?"

"That am I," said I. "Small thanks to you!"

He had begun to seek for his breath with deep sighs.

"The blue phial," said he—"in the aumry[1]—the blue phial." His breath came slower still.

I ran to the cupboard, and, sure enough, found there a

___

[1]Cupboard.

blue phial of medicine, with the dose written on it on a paper, and this I administered to him with what speed I might.

"It's the trouble," said he, reviving a little; "I have a trouble, Davie. It's the heart."

I set him on a chair and looked at him. It is true I felt some pity for a man that looked so sick, but I was full besides of righteous anger; and I numbered over before him the points on which I wanted explanation: why he lied to me at every word; why he feared that I should leave him; why he disliked it to be hinted that he and my father were twins—"Is that because it is true?" I asked; why he had given me money to which I was convinced I had no claim; and, last of all, why he had tried to kill me. He heard me all through in silence; and then, in a broken voice, begged me to let him go to bed.

"I'll tell ye the morn," he said, "as sure as death I will."

And so weak was he that I could do nothing but consent. I locked him into his room, however, and pocketed the key; and then returning to the kitchen, made up such a blaze as had not shone there for many a long year, and wrapping myself in my plaid, lay down upon the chests and fell asleep.

Chapter 5

I GO TO THE QUEEN'S FERRY

Much rain fell in the night; and the next morning there blew a bitter wintry wind out of the north-west, driving scattered clouds. For all that, and before the sun began to peep or the last of the stars had vanished, I made my way to the side of the burn,[1] and had a plunge in a deep whirling pool. All aglow from my bath, I sat down once more beside the fire, which I replenished, and began gravely to consider my position.

There was now no doubt about my uncle's enmity; there was no doubt I carried my life in my hand, and he would leave no stone unturned that he might compass my destruction. But I was young and spirited, and like most lads that have been country-bred, I had a great opinion of my shrewdness. I had come to his door no better than a beggar and little more than a child; he had met me with treachery and violence; it would be a fine consummation to take the upper hand, and drive him like a herd of sheep.

I sat there nursing my knee and smiling at the fire; and I saw myself in fancy smell out his secrets one after another, and grow to be that man's king and ruler. The warlock of Essendean, they say, had made a mirror in which men could read the future; it must have been of other stuff than burning coal; for in all the shapes and pictures that I sat and gazed at, there was never a ship, never a seaman with a hairy cap, never a big bludgeon for

[1]Brook.

my silly head, or the least sign of all those tribulations that were ripe to fall on me.

Presently, all swollen with conceit, I went upstairs and gave my prisoner his liberty. He gave me good-morning civilly; and I gave the same to him, smiling down upon him from the heights of my sufficiency. Soon we were set to breakfast, as it might have been the day before.

"Well, sir," said I, with a jeering tone, "have you nothing more to say to me?" And then, as he made no articulate reply, "It will be time, I think, to understand each other," I continued. "You took me for a country Johnnie Raw, with no more mother-wit or courage than a porridge-stick. I took you for a good man, or no worse than others at the least. It seems we were both wrong. What cause you have to fear me, to cheat me, and to attempt my life—"

He murmured something about a jest, and that he liked a bit of fun; and then, seeing me smile, changed his tone, and assured me he would make all clear as soon as we had breakfasted. I saw by his face that he had no lie ready for me, though he was hard at work preparing one; and I think I was about to tell him so, when we were interrupted by a knocking at the door.

Bidding my uncle sit where he was, I went to open it, and found on the doorstep a half-grown boy in sea-clothes. He had no sooner seen me than he began to dance some steps of the sea-hornpipe (which I had never heard of, far less seen), snapping his fingers in the air and footing it right cleverly. For all that, he was blue with the cold; and there was something in his face, a look between tears and laughter, that was highly pathetic and consisted ill with this gaiety of manner.

"What cheer, mate?" says he, with a cracked voice.

I asked him soberly to name his pleasure.

"O, pleasure!" says he; and then began to sing:

"For it's my delight, of a shiny night,
    In the season of the year."

"Well," said I, "if you have no business at all, I will even be so unmannerly as to shut you out."

"Stay, brother!" he cried. "Have you no fun about you? or do you want to get me thrashed? I've brought a letter from old Heasyoasy to Mr. Belflower." He showed me a letter as he spoke. "And I say, mate," he added; "I'm mortal hungry."

"Well," said I, "come into the house, and you shall have a bite if I go empty for it."

With that I brought him in and set him down to my own place, where he fell-to greedily on the remains of breakfast, winking to me between-whiles, and making many faces, which I think the poor soul considered manly. Meanwhile, my uncle had read the letter and sat thinking: then, suddenly, he got to his feet with a great air of liveliness, and pulled me apart into the farthest corner of the room.

"Read that," said he, and put the letter in my hand.

Here it is, lying before me as I write:

"The Hawes Inn, at the Queen's Ferry.

"Sir,—I lie here with my hawser up and down, and send my cabin-boy to informe. If you have any further commands for over-seas, to-day will be the last occasion, as the wind will serve us well out of the firth. I will not seek to deny that I have had crosses with your doer,[1] Mr. Rankeillor; of which, if not speedily redd up, you may looke to see some losses follow. I have drawn a bill upon you, as per margin, and am, sir, your most obedt., humble servant,

"ELIAS HOSEASON."

"You see, Davie," resumed my uncle, as soon as he saw that I had done, "I have a venture with this man Hoseason, the captain of a trading brig, the *Covenant*, of Dysart. Now, if you and me was to walk over with yon lad, I could see the captain at the Hawes, or maybe on board the *Covenant* if there was papers to be signed; and so far from a loss of time, we can jog on to the lawyer, Mr. Rankeillor's. After a' that's come and gone, ye would be sweer[2] to believe me upon my naked word; but ye'll believe Rankeillor. He's factor[3] to half the gentry in these parts;

---

[1]Agent. [2]Unwilling. [3]Manager.

an auld man, forbye[1]: highly respeckit; and he kenned
your father."

I stood a while and thought. I was going to some place
of shipping, which was doubtless populous and, where my
uncle durst attempt no violence and, indeed, even the
society of the cabin-boy so far protected me. Once there, I
believed I could force on the visit to the lawyer, even if
my uncle were now insincere in proposing it; and, perhaps, in the bottom of my heart, I wished a nearer view of
the sea and ships. You are to remember I had lived all my
life in the inland hills, and just two days before had my
first sight of the firth lying like a blue floor, and the sailed
ships moving on the face of it, no bigger than toys. One
thing with another, I made up my mind.

"Very well," says I, "let us go to the Ferry."

My uncle got into his hat and coat, and buckled an old
rusty cutlass on; and then we trod the fire out, locked the
door, and set forth upon our walk.

The wind, being in that cold quarter the northwest,
blew nearly in our faces, as we went. It was the month of
June; the grass was all white with daisies and the trees
with blossom; but, to judge by our blue nails and aching
wrists, the time might have been winter and the white-
ness a December frost.

Uncle Ebenezer trudged in the ditch, jogging from side
to side like an old ploughman coming home from work.
He never said a word the whole way; and I was thrown for
talk on the cabin-boy. He told me his name was Ransome,
and that he had followed the sea since he was nine, but
could not say how old he was, as he had lost his reckoning.
He showed me tattoo marks, baring his breast in the teeth
of the wind and in spite of my remonstrances, for I thought
it was enough to kill him; he swore horribly whenever he
remembered, but more like a silly schoolboy than a man;
and boasted of many wild and bad things that he had
done: stealthy thefts, false accusations, ay, and even murder; but all with such a dearth of likelihood in the details,
and such a weak and crazy swagger in the delivery, as
disposed me rather to pity than to believe him.

[1]Besides.

I asked him of the brig (which he declared was the finest ship that sailed) and of Captain Hoseason, in whose praises he was equally loud. Heasy-oasy (for so he still named the skipper) was a man, by his account, that minded for nothing either in heaven or earth; one that, as people said, would "crack on all sail into the day of judgment"; rough, fierce, unscrupulous, and brutal; and all this my poor cabin-boy had taught himself to admire as something seamanlike and manly. He would only admit one flaw in his idol. "He ain't no seaman," he admitted. "That's Mr. Shuan that navigates the brig; he's the finest seaman in the trade, only for drink; and I tell you I believe it! Why, look 'ere"; and turning down his stocking he showed me a great, raw, red wound that made my blood run cold. "He done that—Mr. Shuan done it," he said, with an air of pride.

"What!" I cried, "do you take such savage usage at his hands? Why, you are no slave, to be so handled!"

"No," said the poor moon-calf, changing his tune at once, "and so he'll find. See 'ere"; and he showed me a great case-knife, which he told me was stolen. "O," says he, "let me see him try; I dare him to; I'll do for him! O, he ain't the first!" And he confirmed it with a poor, silly, ugly oath.

I have never felt such pity for any one in this wide world as I felt for that half-witted creature; and it began to come over me that the brig *Covenant* (for all her pious name) was little better than a hell upon the seas.

"Have you no friends?" said I.

He said he had a father in some English seaport, I forget which. "He was a fine man, too," he said; "but he's dead."

"In Heaven's name," cried I, "can you find no reputable life on shore?"

"O no," says he, winking and looking very sly; "they would put me to a trade. I know a trick worth two of that, I do!"

I asked him what trade could be so dreadful as the one he followed, where he ran the continual peril of his life, not alone from wind and sea, but by the horrid cruelty of those who were his masters. He said it was very true; and then began to praise the life, and tell what a pleasure it was to get on shore with money in his pocket, and spend it like a man, and buy apples and swagger, and surprise what he called stick-in-the-mud boys. "And then it's not all as bad as that," says he; "there's worse off than me: there's the twenty-pounders. O laws! you should see them taking on. Why, I've seen a man as old as you, I dessay" —(to him I seemed old)—"ah, and he had a beard, too— well, and as soon as we cleared out of the river, and he had the drug out of his head—my! how he cried and carried on! I made a fine fool of him, I tell you! And then there's little uns, too: O, little by me! I tell you, I keep them in order. When we carry little uns, I have a rope's end of my own to wollop 'em." And so he ran on, until it came in on me what he meant by twenty-pounders were those unhappy criminals who were sent over-seas to slavery in North America, or the still more unhappy innocents who were kidnapped or trepanned (as the word went) for private interest or vengeance.

Just then we came to the top of the hill, and looked down on the Ferry and the Hope. The Firth of Forth (as is very well known) narrows at this point to the width of a good-sized river, which makes a convenient ferry going north, and turns the upper reach into a land-locked haven for all manner of ships. Right in the midst of the narrows lies an islet with some ruins; on the south shore they have built a pier for the service of the Ferry; and at the end of the pier, on the other side of the road, and backed against a pretty garden of holly-trees and hawthorns, I could see the building which they called the Hawes Inn.

The town of Queensferry lies farther west, and the neighbourhood of the inn looked pretty lonely at that time of day, for the boat had just gone north with passengers. A skiff, however, lay beside the pier, with some seamen sleeping on the thwarts; this, as Ransome told me, was the brig's boat waiting for the captain; and about half a mile off, and all alone in the anchorage, he showed me the *Covenant* herself. There was a sea-going bustle on board; yards were swinging into place; and as the wind blew from that quarter, I could hear the song of the sailors as they pulled upon the ropes. After all I had listened to upon the way, I looked at that ship with an extreme abhorrence; and from the bottom of my heart I pitied all poor souls that were condemned to sail in her.

We had all three pulled up on the brow of the hill; and now I marched across the road and addressed my uncle. "I think it right to tell you, sir," says I, "there's nothing that will bring me on board that *Covenant*."

He seemed to waken from a dream. "Eh?" he said. "What's that?"

I told him over again.

"Well, well," he said, "we'll have to please ye, I suppose. But what are we standing here for? It's perishing cold; and if I'm no' mistaken, they're busking the *Covenant* for sea."

Chapter 6

WHAT BEFELL AT THE QUEEN'S FERRY

As soon as we came to the inn, Ransome led us up the stair to a small room, with a bed in it, and heated like an oven by a great fire of coal. At a table hard by the chimney, a tall, dark, sober-looking man sat writing. In spite of the heat of the room, he wore a thick sea-jacket, buttoned to the neck, and a tall hairy cap drawn down over his ears; yet I never saw any man, not even a judge upon the bench, look cooler, or more studious and self-possessed, than this ship-captain.

He got to his feet at once, and coming forward, offered his large hand to Ebenezer. "I am proud to see you, Mr. Balfour," said he, in a fine deep voice, "and glad that ye are here in time. The wind's fair, and the tide upon the turn; we'll see the old coal-bucket burning on the Isle of May before to-night."

"Captain Hoseason," returned my uncle, "you keep your room unco hot."

"It's a habit I have, Mr. Balfour," said the skipper. "I'm a cold-rife man by my nature; I have a cold blood, sir. There's neither fur, nor flannel—no, sir, nor hot rum, will warm up what they call the temperature. Sir, it's the same with most men that have been carbonadoed, as they call it, in the tropic seas."

"Well, well, captain," replied my uncle, "we must all be the way we're made."

But it chanced that this fancy of the captain's had a great share in my misfortunes. For though I had promised myself not to let my kinsman out of sight, I was both so impatient for a nearer look of the sea, and so sickened by

35

the closeness of the room, that when he told me to "run downstairs and play myself a while," I was fool enough to take him at his word.

Away I went, therefore, leaving the two men sitting down to a bottle and a great mass of papers; and crossing the road in front of the inn, walked down upon the beach. With the wind in that quarter, only little wavelets, not much bigger than I had seen upon a lake, beat upon the shore. But the weeds were new to me—some green, some brown and long, and some with little bladders that crackled between my fingers. Even so far up the firth, the smell of the sea water was exceedingly salt and stirring; the *Covenant*, besides, was beginning to shake out her sails, which hung upon the yards in clusters; and the spirit of all that I beheld put me in thoughts of far voyages and foreign places.

I looked, too, at the seamen with the skiff—big brown fellows, some in shirts, some with jackets, some with coloured handkerchiefs about their throats, one with a brace of pistols stuck into his pockets, two or three with knotty bludgeons, and all with their case-knives. I passed the time of day with one that looked less desperate than his fellows, and asked him of the sailing of the brig. He said they would get under way as soon as the ebb set, and expressed his gladness to be out of a port where there were no taverns and fiddlers; but all with such horrifying oaths, that I made haste to get away from him.

This threw me back on Ransome, who seemed the least wicked of that gang, and who soon came out of the inn and ran to me, crying for a bowl of punch. I told him I would give him no such thing, for neither he nor I was of an age for such indulgences. "But a glass of ale you may have, and welcome," said I. He mopped and mowed at me, and called me names; but he was glad to get the ale, for all that; and presently we were set down at a table in the front room of the inn, and both eating and drinking with a good appetite.

Here it occurred to me that, as the landlord was a man of that county, I might do well to make a friend of him. I offered him a share, as was much the custom in those days; but he was far too great a man to sit with such poor customers as Ransome and myself, and he was leaving the room, when I called him back to ask if he knew Mr. Rankeillor.

"Hoot, ay," says he, "and a very honest man. And, O, by the by," says he, "was it you that came in with Ebenezer?" And when I had told him yes, "Ye'll be no friend of his?" he asked, meaning, in the Scottish way, that I would be no relative.

I told him no, none.

"I thought not," said he, "and yet ye have a kind of gliff[1] of Mr. Alexander."

I said it seemed that Ebenezer was ill-seen in the country.

"Nae doubt," said the landlord. "He's a wicked auld man, and there's many would like to see him girning in the tow:[2] Jennet Clouston and mony mair that he has harried out of house and hame. And yet he was ance a fine young fellow, too. But that was before the sough[3] gaed abroad about Mr. Alexander; that was like the death of him."

"And what was it?" I asked.

"Ou, just that he had killed him," said the landlord. "Did ye never hear that?"

"And what would he kill him for?" said I.

"And what for, but just to get the place," said he.

"The place?" said I. "The Shaws?"

"Nae other place that I ken," said he.

"Ay, man?" said I. "Is that so? Was my—was Alexander the eldest son?"

" 'Deed was he," said the landlord. "What else would he have killed him for?"

And with that he went away, as he had been impatient to do from the beginning.

Of course, I had guessed it a long while ago; but it is one thing to guess, another to know; and I sat stunned with my good fortune, and could scarce grow to believe that the same poor lad who had trudged in the dust from Ettrick Forest not two days ago, was now one of the rich of the earth, and had a house and broad lands, and might mount his horse to-morrow. All these pleasant things, and

[1]Look. [2]Grinning in the rope (hanging). [3]Report.

a thousand others, crowded into my mind, as I sat staring before me out of the inn window, and paying no heed to what I saw; only I remember that my eye lighted on Captain Hoseason down on the pier among his seamen, and speaking with some authority. And presently he came marching back towards the house, with no mark of a sailor's clumsiness, but carrying his fine, tall figure with a manly bearing, and still with the same sober, grave expression on his face. I wondered if it was possible that Ransome's stories could be true, and half disbelieved them; they fitted so ill with the man's looks. But indeed, he was neither so good as I supposed him, nor quite so bad as Ransome did; for, in fact, he was two men, and left the better one behind as soon as he set foot on board his vessel.

The next thing, I heard my uncle calling me, and found the pair in the road together. It was the captain who addressed me, and that with an air (very flattering to a young lad) of grave equality.

"Sir," said he, "Mr. Balfour tells me great things of you; and for my own part, I like your looks. I wish I was for longer here, that we might make the better friends; but we'll make the most of what we have. Ye shall come on board my brig for half-an-hour, till the ebb sets, and drink a bowl with me."

Now, I longed to see the inside of a ship more than words can tell; but I was not going to put myself in jeopardy, and I told him my uncle and I had an appointment with a lawyer.

"Ay, ay," said he, "he passed me word of that. But, ye see, the boat'll set ye ashore at the town pier, and that's but a penny stone-cast from Rankeillor's house." And here he suddenly leaned down and whispered in my ear: "Take care of the old tod;[1] he means mischief. Come aboard till I can get a word with ye." And then, passing his arm through mine, he continued aloud, as he set off towards his boat: "But come, what can I bring ye from the Carolinas? Any friend of Mr. Balfour's can command. A roll of tobacco? Indian featherwork? a skin of a wild beast? a

[1]Fox.

stone pipe? the mockingbird that mews for all the world like a cat? the cardinal bird that is as red as blood?—take your pick and say your pleasure."

By this time we were at the boat-side, and he was handing me in. I did not dream of hanging back; I thought (the poor fool!) that I had found a good friend and helper, and I was rejoiced to see the ship. As soon as we were all set in our places, the boat was thrust off from the pier and began to move over the waters; and what with my pleasure in this new movement and my surprise at our low position, and the appearance of the shores, and the growing bigness of the brig as we drew near to it, I could hardly understand what the captain said, and must have answered him at random.

As soon as we were alongside (where I sat fairly gaping at the ship's height, the strong humming of the tide against its sides, and the pleasant cries of the seamen at their work) Hoseason, declaring that he and I must be the first aboard, ordered a tackle to be sent down from the main-yard. In this I was whipped into the air and set down again on the deck, where the captain stood ready waiting for me, and instantly slipped back his arm under mine. There I stood some while, a little dizzy with the unsteadiness of all around me, perhaps a little afraid, and yet vastly pleased with these strange sights; the captain meanwhile pointing out the strangest, and telling me their names and uses.

"But where is my uncle?" said I, suddenly.

"Ay," said Hoseason, with a sudden grimness, "that's the point."

I felt I was lost. With all my strength, I plucked myself clear of him and ran to the bulwarks. Sure enough, there was the boat pulling for the town, with my uncle sitting in the stern. I gave a piercing cry—"Help, help! Murder!" —so that both sides of the anchorage rang with it, and my uncle turned round where he was sitting, and showed me a face full of cruelty and terror.

It was the last I saw. Already strong hands had been plucking me back from the ship's side; and now a thunderbolt seemed to strike me; I saw a great flash of fire, and fell senseless.

Chapter 7

I GO TO SEA IN THE BRIG "COVENANT" OF DYSART

I came to myself in darkness, in great pain, bound hand and foot, and deafened by many unfamiliar noises. There sounded in my ears a roaring of water as of a huge mill-dam, the thrashing of heavy sprays, the thundering of the sails, and the shrill cries of seamen. The whole world now heaved giddily up, and now rushed giddily downward; and so sick and hurt was I in body, and my mind so much confounded, that it took me a long while, chasing my thoughts up and down, and ever stunned again by a fresh stab of pain, to realise that I must be lying somewhere bound in the belly of that unlucky ship, and that the wind must have strengthened to a gale. With the clear perception of my plight, there fell upon me a blackness of despair, a horror of remorse at my own folly, and a passion of anger at my uncle, that once more bereft me of my senses.

When I returned again to life, the same uproar, the same confused and violent movements, shook and deafened me; and presently, to my other pains and distresses, there was added the sickness of an unused landsman on the sea. In that time of my adventurous youth, I suffered many hardships; but none that was so crushing to my mind and body, or lit by so few hopes, as these first hours aboard the brig.

I heard a gun fire, and supposed the storm had proved too strong for us, and we were firing signals of distress. The thought of deliverance, even by death in the deep sea, was welcome to me. Yet it was no such matter; but (as I was afterwards told) a common habit of the captain's, which I here set down to show that even the worst man

may have his kindlier side. We were then passing, it
appeared, within some miles of Dysart, where the brig
was built, and where old Mrs. Hoseason, the captain's
mother, had come some years before to live; and whether
outward or inward bound, the *Covenant* was never suffered to go by that place by day, without a gun fired and
colours shown.

I had no measure of time; day and night were alike in
that ill-smelling cavern of the ship's bowels where I lay;
and the misery of my situation drew out the hours to
double. How long, therefore, I lay waiting to hear the ship
split upon some rock, or to feel her reel head foremost
into the depths of the sea, I have not the means of compu-
tation. But sleep at length stole from me the consciousness
of sorrow.

I was awakened by the light of a hand-lantern shining in
my face. A small man of about thirty, with green eyes and
a tangle of fair hair, stood looking down at me.

"Well," said he, "how goes it?"

I answered by a sob; and my visitor then felt my pulse
and temples, and set himself to wash and dress the wound
upon my scalp.

"Ay," said he, "a sore dunt.[1] What, man? Cheer up! The
world's no' done; you've made a bad start of it, but you'll
make a better. Have you had any meat?"

I said I could not look at it: and thereupon he gave me
some brandy and water in a tin pannikin, and left me once
more to myself.

The next time he came to see me, I was lying betwixt
sleep and waking, my eyes wide open in the darkness, the
sickness quite departed, but succeeded by a horrid giddiness and swimming that was almost worse to bear. I
ached, besides, in every limb, and the cords that bound
me seemed to be of fire. The smell of the hole in which I
lay seemed to have become a part of me; and during the
long interval since his last visit I had suffered tortures of
fear, now from the scurrying of the ship's rats, that sometimes pattered on my very face, and now from the dismal
imaginings that haunt the bed of fever.

[1]Stroke.

The glimmer of the lantern, as a trap opened, shone in like the heaven's sunlight; and though it only showed me the strong, dark beams of the ship that was my prison, I could have cried aloud for gladness. The man with the green eyes was the first to descend the ladder, and I noticed that he came somewhat unsteadily. He was followed by the captain. Neither said a word; but the first set to and examined me, and dressed my wound as before, while Hoseason looked me in my face with an odd, black look.

"Now, sir, you see for yourself," said the first: "a high fever, no appetite, no light, no meat: you see for yourself what that means."

"I am no conjurer, Mr. Riach," said the captain.

"Give me leave, sir," said Riach; "you've a good head upon your shoulders, and a good Scots tongue to ask with; but I will leave you no manner of excuse: I want that boy taken out of this hole and put in the forecastle."

"What ye may want, sir, is a matter of concern to nobody but yoursel'," returned the captain; "but I can tell ye that which is to be. Here he is; here he shall bide."

"Admitting that you have been paid in a proportion," said the other, "I will crave leave humbly to say that I have not. Paid I am, and none too much, to be the second officer of this old tub; and you ken very well if I do my best to earn it. But I was paid for nothing more."

"If ye could hold back your hand from the tin-pan, Mr. Riach, I would have no complaint to make of ye," returned the skipper; "and instead of asking riddles, I make bold to say that ye would keep your breath to cool your porridge. We'll be required on deck," he added, in a sharper note, and set one foot upon the ladder.

But Mr. Riach caught him by the sleeve.

"Admitting that you have been paid to do murder——" he began.

Hoseason turned upon him with a flash.

"What's that?" he cried. "What kind of talk is that?"

"It seems it is the talk that you can understand," said Mr. Riach, looking him steadily in the face.

"Mr. Riach, I have sailed with ye three cruises," replied the captain. "In all that time, sir, ye should have learned

to know me: I'm a stiff man, and a dour man; but for what
ye say the now—fie, fie!—it comes from a bad heart and a
black conscience. If ye say the lad will die—"

"Ay, will he!" said Mr. Riach.

"Well, sir, is not that enough?" said Hoseason. "Flit[1]
him where ye please!"

Thereupon the captain ascended the ladder; and I, who
had lain silent throughout this strange conversation, beheld Mr. Riach turn after him and bow as low as to his
knees in what was plainly a spirit of derision. Even in my
then state of sickness, I perceived two things: that the
mate was touched with liquor, as the captain hinted, and
that (drunk or sober) he was like to prove a valuable
friend.

Five minutes afterwards my bonds were cut, I was
hoisted on a man's back, carried up to the forecastle, and
laid in a bunk on some sea-blankets; where the first thing
that I did was to lose my senses.

It was a blessed thing indeed to open my eyes again
upon the daylight, and to find myself in the society of
men. The forecastle was a roomy place enough, set all
about with berths, in which the men of the watch below
were seated smoking, or lying down asleep. The day being
calm and the wind fair, the scuttle was open, and not only
the good daylight, but from time to time (as the ship
rolled) a dusty beam of sunlight shone in, and dazzled and
delighted me. I had no sooner moved, moreover, than one
of the men brought me a drink of something healing,
which Mr. Riach had prepared, and bade me lie still and I
should soon be well again. There were no bones broken,
he explained: "A clour[2] on the head was naething. Man,"
said he, "it was me that gave it ye!"

Here I lay for the space of many days a close prisoner,
and not only got my health again, but came to know my
companions. They were a rough lot indeed, as sailors
mostly are: being men rooted out of all the kindly parts of
life, and condemned to toss together on the rough seas,
with masters no less cruel. There were some among them
that had sailed with the pirates and seen things it would

[1]Take.   [2]Blow.

be a shame even to speak of; some were men that had run
from the king's ships, and went with a halter round their
necks, of which they made no secret; and all, as the saying
goes, were "at a word and a blow" with their best friends.
Yet I had not been many days shut up with them before I
began to be ashamed of my first judgment, when I had
drawn away from them at the Ferry pier, as though they
had been unclean beasts. No class of man is altogether
bad, but each has its own faults and virtues; and these
shipmates of mine were no exception to the rule. Rough
they were, sure enough; and bad, I suppose; but they had
many virtues. They were kind when it occurred to them,
simple even beyond the simplicity of a country lad like
me, and had some glimmerings of honesty.

There was one man, of maybe forty, that would sit on
my berthside for hours and tell me of his wife and child.
He was a fisher that had lost his boat, and thus been
driven to the deep-sea voyaging. Well, it is years ago now:
but I have never forgotten him. His wife (who was "young
by him," as he often told me) waited in vain to see her
man return; he would never again make the fire for her in
the morning, nor yet keep the bairn when she was sick.
Indeed, many of these poor fellows (as the event proved)
were upon their last cruise; the deep seas and cannibal
fish received them; and it is a thankless business to speak
ill of the dead.

Among other good deeds that they did, they returned
my money, which had been shared among them; and
though it was about a third short, I was very glad to get it,
and hoped great good from it in the land I was going to.
The ship was bound for the Carolinas; and you must not
suppose that I was going to that place merely as an exile.
The trade was even then much depressed; since that, and
with the rebellion of the colonies and the formation of the
United States, it has, of course, come to an end; but in
those days of my youth, white men were still sold into
slavery on the plantations, and that was the destiny to
which my wicked uncle had condemned me.

The cabin-boy Ransome (from whom I had first heard of
these atrocities) came in at times from the round-house,
where he berthed and served, now nursing a bruised limb

in silent agony, now raving against the cruelty of Mr. Shuan. It made my heart bleed; but the men had a great respect for the chief mate, who was as they said, "the only seaman of the whole jing-bang, and none such a bad man when he was sober." Indeed, I found there was a strange peculiarity about our two mates: that Mr. Riach was sullen, unkind, and harsh when he was sober, and Mr. Shuan would not hurt a fly except when he was drinking. I asked about the captain; but I was told drink made no difference upon that man of iron.

I did my best in the small time allowed me to make something like a man, or rather I should say something like a boy, of the poor creature, Ransome. But his mind was scarce truly human. He could remember nothing of the time before he came to sea; only that his father had made clocks, and had a starling in the parlour, which could whistle "The North Countrie"; all else had been blotted out in these years of hardship and cruelties. He had a strange notion of the dry land, picked up from sailors' stories: that it was a place where lads were put to some kind of slavery called a trade, and where apprentices were continually lashed and clapped into foul prisons. In a town, he thought every second person a decoy, and every third house a place in which seamen would be drugged and murdered. To be sure, I would tell him how kindly I had myself been used upon that dry land he was so much afraid of, and how well fed and carefully taught both by my friends and my parents: and if he had been recently hurt, he would weep bitterly and swear to run away; but if he was in his usual crack-brain humour, or (still more) if he had had a glass of spirits in the round-house, he would deride the notion.

It was Mr. Riach (Heaven forgive him!) who gave the boy drink; and it was, doubtless, kindly meant; but besides that it was ruin to his health, it was the pitifullest thing in life to see this unhappy, unfriended creature staggering, and dancing, and talking he knew not what. Some of the men laughed, but not all; others would grow as black as thunder (thinking, perhaps, of their own childhood or their own children) and bid him stop that nonsense, and think what he was doing. As for me, I felt ashamed to look at him, and the poor child still comes about me in my dreams.

All this time, you should know, the *Covenant* was meeting continual head-winds and tumbling up and down against head-seas, so that the scuttle was almost constantly shut, and the forecastle lighted only by a swinging lantern on a beam. There was constant labour for all hands; the sails had to be made and shortened every hour; the strain told on the men's temper; there was a growl of quarrelling all day long from berth to berth; and as I was never allowed to set my foot on deck, you can picture to yourselves how weary of my life I grew to be, and how impatient for a change.

And a change I was to get, as you shall hear; but I must first tell of a conversation I had with Mr. Riach, which put a little heart in me to bear my troubles. Getting him in a favourable stage of drink (for indeed he never looked near me when he was sober) I pledged him to secrecy, and told him my whole story.

He declared it was like a ballad; that he would do his best to help me; that I should have paper, pen, and ink, and write one line to Mr. Campbell and another to Mr. Rankeillor; and that if I had told the truth, ten to one he would be able (with their help) to pull me through and set me in my rights.

"And in the meantime," says he, "keep your heart up. You're not the only one, I'll tell you that. There's many a man hoeing tobacco over-seas that should be mounting his horse at his own door at home; many and many! And life is all a variorum, at the best. Look at me: I'm a laird's son and more than half a doctor, and here I am, man-Jack to Hoseason!"

I thought it would be civil to ask him for his story.

He whistled loud.

"Never had one," said he. "I liked fun, that's all." And he skipped out of the forecastle.

Chapter 8

THE ROUND-HOUSE

One night, about eleven o'clock, a man of Mr. Riach's watch (which was on deck) came below for his jacket; and instantly there began to go a whisper about the forecastle that "Shuan had done for him at last." There was no need of a name; we all knew who was meant; but we had scarce time to get the idea rightly in our heads, far less to speak of it, when the scuttle was again flung open, and Captain Hoseason came down the ladder. He looked sharply round the bunks in the tossing light of the lantern; and then, walking straight up to me, he addressed me, to my surprise, in tones of kindness.

"My man," said he, "we want ye to serve in the round-house. You and Ransome are to change berths. Run away aft with ye."

Even as he spoke, two seamen appeared in the scuttle, carrying Ransome in their arms; and the ship at that moment giving a great sheer into the sea, and the lantern swinging, the light fell direct on the boy's face. It was as white as wax, and had a look upon it like a dreadful smile. The blood in me ran cold, and I drew in my breath as if I had been struck.

"Run away aft; run away aft with ye!" cried Hoseason.

And at that I brushed by the sailors and the boy (who neither spoke nor moved), and ran up the ladder on deck.

The brig was sheering swiftly and giddily through a long, cresting swell. She was on the starboard tack, and on the left hand, under the arched foot of the foresail, I could see the sunset still quite bright. This, at such an hour of the night, surprised me greatly; but I was too ignorant to draw the true conclusion—that we were going north-about round Scotland, and were now on the high sea between the Orkney and Shetland Islands, having avoided the dangerous currents of the Pentland Firth. For my part, who had been so long shut in the dark and knew nothing of head-winds, I thought we might be half-way or more across the Atlantic. And indeed (beyond that I wondered a little at the lateness of the sunset light) I gave no heed to it, and pushed on across the decks, running between the seas, catching at ropes, and only saved from going overboard by one of the hands on deck, who had been always kind to me.

The round-house, for which I was bound, and where I was now to sleep and serve, stood some six feet above the decks, and considering the size of the brig, was of good dimensions. Inside were a fixed table and bench, and two berths, one for the captain and the other for the two mates, turn and turn about. It was all fitted with lockers from top to bottom, so as to stow away the officers' belongings and a part of the ship's stores; there was a second store-room underneath, which you entered by a hatchway in the middle of the deck; indeed, all the best of the meat and drink and the whole of the powder were collected in this place; and all the fire-arms, except the two pieces of brass ordnance, were set in a rack in the aftermost wall of the round-house. The most of the cutlasses were in another place.

A small window with a shutter on each side, and a skylight in the roof, gave it light by day; and after dark there was a lamp always burning. It was burning when I entered, not brightly, but enough to show Mr. Shuan sitting at the table, with the brandy-bottle and a tin pannikin in front of him. He was a tall man, strongly made and very black; and he stared before him on the table like one stupid.

He took no notice of my coming in; nor did he move when the captain followed and leant on the berth beside me, looking darkly at the mate. I stood in great fear of Hoseason, and had my reasons for it; but something told me I need not be afraid of him just then; and I whispered in his ear, "How is he?" He shook his head like one that does not know and does not wish to think, and his face was very stern.

Presently Mr. Riach came in. He gave the captain a glance that meant the boy was dead as plain as speaking, and took his place like the rest of us; so that we all three stood without a word, staring down at Mr. Shuan, and Mr. Shuan (on his side) sat without a word, looking hard upon the table.

All of a sudden he put out his hand to take the bottle; and at that Mr. Riach started forward and caught it away from him, rather by surprise than violence, crying out, with with an oath, that there had been too much of this work altogether, and that a judgment would fall upon the ship. And as he spoke (the weather sliding-doors standing open) he tossed the bottle into the sea.

Mr. Shuan was on his feet in a trice; he still looked dazed, but he meant murder, ay, and would have done it, for the second time that night, had not the captain stepped in between him and his victim.

"Sit down!" roars the captain. "Ye sot and swine, do ye know what ye've done? Ye've murdered the boy!"

Mr. Shuan seemed to understand; for he sat down again, and put up his hand to his brow.

"Well," he said, "he brought me a dirty pannikin!"

At that word, the captain and I and Mr. Riach all looked at each other for a second with a kind of frightened look; and then Hoseason walked up to his chief officer, took him by the shoulder, led him across to his bunk, and bade him lie down and go to sleep, as you might speak to a bad child. The murderer cried a little, but he took off his sea-boots and obeyed.

"Ah!" cried Mr. Riach, with a dreadful voice, "ye should have interfered lang syne. It's too late now."

"Mr. Riach," said the captain, "this night's work must never be kennt in Dysart. The boy went overboard, sir; that's what the story is; and I would give five pounds out of my pocket it was true!" He turned to the table. "What made ye throw the good bottle away?" he added. "There was nae sense in that, sir. Here, David, draw me another. They're in the bottom locker"; and he tossed me a key.

"Ye'll need a glass yourself, sir," he added to Riach. "Yon was an ugly thing to see."

So the pair sat down and hob-a-nobbed; and while they did so, the murderer, who had been lying and whimpering in his berth, raised himself upon his elbow and looked at them and at me.

That was the first night of my new duties; and in the course of the next day I had got well into the run of them. I had to serve at the meals, which the captain took at regular hours; sitting down with the officer who was off duty; all the day through I would be running with a dram to one or other of my three masters; and at night I slept on a blanket thrown on the deck boards at the aftermost end of the round-house, and right in the draught of the two doors. It was a hard and a cold bed; nor was I suffered to sleep without interruption; for some one would be always coming in from deck to get a dram, and when a fresh watch was to be set, two and sometimes all three would sit down and brew a bowl together. How they kept their health, I know not, any more than how I kept my own.

And yet in other ways it was an easy service. There was no cloth to lay; the meals were either of oatmeal porridge or salt junk, except twice a week, when there was duff:[1] and though I was clumsy enough and (not being firm on my sea-legs) sometimes fell with what I was bringing them, both Mr. Riach and the captain were singularly patient. I could not but fancy they were making up lee-way with their consciences, and that they would scarce have been so good with me if they had not been worse with Ransome.

As for Mr. Shuan, the drink, or his crime, or the two together, had certainly troubled his mind. I cannot say I ever saw him in his proper wits. He never grew used to my being there, stared at me continually (sometimes, I could have thought, with terror) and more than once drew back from my hand when I was serving him. I was pretty sure from the first that he had no clear mind of what he had done, and on my second day in the round-house I had the proof of it. We were alone, and he had been staring at me a long time, when, all at once, up he got, as pale as

[1]Flour pudding.

death, and came close up to me, to my great terror. But I had no cause to be afraid of him.

"You were not here before?" he asked.

"No, sir," said I.

"There was another boy?" he asked again; and when I had answered him, "Ah!" says he, "I thought that," and went and sat down, without another word, except to call for brandy.

You may think it strange, but for all the horror I had, I was still sorry for him. He was a married man, with a wife in Leith; but whether or no he had a family, I have now forgotten; I hope not.

Altogether it was no very hard life for the time it lasted, which (as you are to hear) was not long. I was as well fed as the best of them; even their pickles, which were the great dainty, I was allowed my share of; and had I liked I might have been drunk from morning to night, like Mr. Shuan. I had company, too, and good company of its sort. Mr. Riach, who had been to the college, spoke to me like a friend when he was not sulking, and told me many curious things, and some that were informing; and even the captain, though he kept me at the stick's end the most part of the time, would sometimes unbuckle a bit, and tell me of the fine countries he had visited.

The shadow of poor Ransome, to be sure, lay on all four of us, and on me and Mr. Shuan in particular, most heavily. And then I had another trouble of my own. Here I was, doing dirty work for three men that I looked down upon, and one of whom, at least, should have hung upon a gallows; that was for the present; and as for the future, I could only see myself slaving alongside of negroes in the tobacco-fields. Mr. Riach, perhaps from caution, would never suffer me to say another word about my story; the captain, whom I tried to approach, rebuffed me like a dog and would not hear a word; and as the days came and went, my heart sank lower and lower, till I was even glad of the work which kept me from thinking.

Chapter 9

THE MAN WITH THE BELT OF GOLD

More than a week went by, in which the ill-luck that had hitherto pursued the *Covenant* upon this voyage grew yet more strongly marked. Some days she made a little way; others, she was driven actually back. At last we were beaten so far to the south that we tossed and tacked to and fro the whole of the ninth day, within sight of Cape Wrath and the wild, rocky coast on either hand of it. There followed on that a council of the officers, and some decision which I did not rightly understand, seeing only the result: that we had made a fair wind of a foul one and were running south.

The tenth afternoon there was a falling swell and a thick, wet, white fog that hid one end of the brig from the other. All afternoon, when I went on deck, I saw men and officers listening hard over the bulwarks—"for breakers," they said; and though I did not so much as understand the word, I felt danger in the air, and was excited.

Maybe about ten at night, I was serving Mr. Riach and the captain at their supper, when the ship struck something with a great sound, and we heard voices singing out. My two masters leaped to their feet.

"She's struck!" said Mr. Riach.

"No, sir," said the captain. "We've only run a boat down."

And they hurried out.

The captain was in the right of it. We had run down a boat in the fog, and she had parted in the midst and gone to the bottom with all her crew but one. This man (as I heard afterwards) had been sitting in the stern as a passenger, while the rest were on the benches rowing. At the moment of the blow, the stern had been thrown into the air, and the man (having his hands free, and for all he was encumbered with a frieze overcoat that came below his knees) had leaped up and caught hold of the brig's bowsprit. It showed he had luck and much agility and unusual strength, that he should have thus saved himself from such a pass. And yet, when the captain brought him into the round-house, and I set eyes on him for the first time, he looked as cool as I did.

He was smallish in stature, but well set and as nimble as a goat; his face was of a good open expression, but sunburnt very dark, and heavily freckled and pitted with the small-pox; his eyes were unusually light and had a kind of dancing madness in them, that was both engaging and alarming; and when he took off his great-coat, he laid a pair of fine silver-mounted pistols on the table, and I saw that he was belted with a great sword. His manners, besides, were elegant, and he pledged the captain handsomely. Altogether I thought of him, at the first sight, that here was a man I would rather call my friend than my enemy.

The captain, too, was taking his observations, but rather of the man's clothes than his person. And to be sure, as soon as he had taken off the great-coat, he showed forth mighty fine for the round-house of a merchant brig: having a hat with feathers, a red waistcoat, breeches of black plush, and a blue coat with silver buttons and handsome silver lace; costly clothes, though somewhat spoiled with the fog and being slept in.

"I'm vexed, sir, about the boat," says the captain.

"There are some pretty men gone to the bottom," said the stranger, "that I would rather see on the dry land again than half a score of boats."

"Friends of yours?" said Hoseason.

"You have none such friends in your country," was the reply. "They would have died for me like dogs."

"Well, sir," said the captain, still watching him, "there are more men in the world than boats to put them in."

"And that's true, too," cried the other, "and ye seem to be a gentleman of great penetration."

"I have been in France, sir," says the captain, so that it

was plain he meant more by the words than showed upon the face of them.

"Well, sir," says the other, "and so has many a pretty man, for the matter of that."

"No doubt, sir," says the captain, "and fine coats."

"Oho!" says the stranger, "is that how the wind sets?" And he laid his hand quickly on his pistols.

"Don't be hasty," said the captain. "Don't do a mischief before ye see the need of it. Ye've a French soldier's coat upon your back and a Scots tongue in your head, to be sure; but so has many an honest fellow in these days, and I daresay none the worse of it."

"So?" said the gentleman in the fine coat: "are ye of the honest party?" (meaning, Was he a Jacobite? for each side, in these sort of civil broils, takes the name of honesty for its own).

"Why, sir," replied the captain, "I am a true-blue Protestant, and I thank God for it." (It was the first word of any religion I had ever heard from him, but I learnt afterwards he was a great church-goer while on shore.) "But, for all that," says he, "I can be sorry to see another man with his back to the wall."

"Can ye so, indeed?" asked the Jacobite. "Well, sir, to be quite plain with ye, I am one of those honest gentlemen that were in trouble about the years forty-five and six; and (to be still quite plain with ye) if I got into the hands of any of the red-coated gentry, it's like it would go hard with me. Now, sir, I was for France; and there was a French ship cruising here to pick me up; but she gave us the go-by in the fog—as I wish from the heart that ye had done yoursel'! And the best that I can say is this: If ye can set me ashore where I was going, I have that upon me will reward you highly for your trouble."

"In France?" says the captain. "No, sir; that I cannot do. But where ye come from—we might talk of that."

And then, unhappily, he observed me standing in my corner, and packed me off to the galley to get supper for the gentleman. I lost no time, I promise you; and when I came back into the round-house, I found the gentleman had taken a money-belt from about his waist, and poured out a guinea or two upon the table. The captain was looking at the guineas, and then at the belt, and then at the gentleman's face; and I thought he seemed excited.

"Half of it," he cried, "and I'm your man!"

The other swept back the guineas into the belt, and put it on again under his waistcoat. "I have told ye, sir," said he, "that not one doit of it belongs to me. It belongs to my chieftain," and here he touched his hat—"and while I would be but a silly messenger to grudge some of it that the rest might come safe, I should show myself a hound indeed if I bought my own carcass any too dear. Thirty guineas on the seaside, or sixty if ye set me on the Linnhe Loch. Take it, if ye will; if not, ye can do your worst."

"Ay," said Hoseason. "And if I give ye over to the soldiers?"

"Ye would make a fool's bargain," said the other. "My chief, let me tell you, sir, is forfeited, like every honest man in Scotland. His estate is in the hands of the man they call King George; and it is his officers that collect the rents, or try to collect them. But for the honour of Scotland, the poor tenant bodies take a thought upon their chief lying in exile; and this money is a part of that very rent for which King George is looking. Now, sir, ye seem to me to be a man that understands things: bring this money within the reach of Government, and how much of it'll come to you?"

"Little enough, to be sure," said Hoseason; and then, "if they knew," he added, dryly. "But I think, if I was to try, that I could hold my tongue about it."

"Ah, but I'll begowk[1] ye there!" cried the gentleman. "Play me false, and I'll play you cunning. If a hand is laid upon me, they shall ken what money it is."

"Well," returned the captain, "what must be must. Sixty guineas, and done. Here's my hand upon it."

"And here's mine," said the other.

And thereupon the captain went out (rather hurriedly, I thought), and left me alone in the round-house with the stranger.

At that period (so soon after the forty-five) there were

[1]Befool.

many exiled gentlemen coming back at the peril of their
lives, either to see their friends or to collect a little money;
and as for the Highland chiefs that had been forfeited, it
was a common matter of talk how their tenants would stint
themselves to send them money, and their clansmen outface the soldiery to get it in, and run the gauntlet of our
great navy to carry it across. All this I had, of course,
heard tell of; and now I had a man under my eyes whose
life was forfeit on all these counts and upon one more, for
he was not only a rebel and a smuggler of rents, but had
taken service with King Louis of France. And as if all this
were not enough, he had a belt full of golden guineas
round his loins. Whatever my opinions, I could not look
on such a man without a lively interest.

"And so you're a Jacobite?" said I, as I set meat before
him.

"Ay," said he, beginning to eat. "And you, by your long
face, should be a Whig?"[1]

"Betwixt and between," said I, not to annoy him; for
indeed I was as good a Whig as Mr. Campbell could make
me.

"And that's naething," said he. "But I'm saying, Mr.
Betwixt-and-Between," he added, "this bottle of yours is
dry; and it's hard if I'm to pay sixty guineas and be
grudged a dram upon the back of it."

"I'll go and ask for the key," said I, and stepped on
deck.

The fog was as close as ever, but the swell almost down.
They had laid the brig to, not knowing precisely where
they were, and the wind (what little there was of it) not
serving well for their true course. Some of the hands were
still hearkening for breakers; but the captain and the two
officers were in the waist with their heads together. It
struck me (I don't know why) that they were after no good;
and the first word I heard, as I drew softly near, more
than confirmed me.

It was Mr. Riach, crying out as if upon a sudden thought:
"Couldn't we wile him out of the round-house?"

[1]Whig or Whigamore was the name for those who were loyal to King George.
The Jacobites were descendants of those who had remained loyal to James II
and the Stewarts after the Revolution of 1688.

"He's better where he is," returned Hoseason; "he hasn't room to use his sword."

"Well, that's true," said Riach; "but he's hard to come at."

"Hut!" said Hoseason. "We can get the man in talk, one upon each side, and pin him by the two arms; or if that'll not hold, sir, we can make a run by both the doors and get him under hand before he has the time to draw."

At this hearing, I was seized with both fear and anger at these treacherous, greedy, bloody men that I sailed with. My first mind was to run away; my second was bolder.

"Captain," said I, "the gentleman is seeking a dram, and the bottle's out. Will you give me the key?"

They all started and turned about.

"Why, here's our chance to get the fire-arms!" Riach cried; and then to me: "Hark ye, David," he said, "do ye ken where the pistols are?"

"Ay, ay," put in Hoseason. "David kens; David's a good lad. Ye see, David my man, yon wild Hielandman is a danger to the ship, besides being a rank foe to King George, God bless him!"

I had never been so be-Davided since I came on board: but I said Yes, as if all I heard were quite natural.

"The trouble is," resumed the captain, "that all our firelocks, great and little, are in the round-house under this man's nose; likewise the powder. Now, if I, or one of the officers, was to go in and take them, he would fall to thinking. But a lad like you, David, might snap up a horn and a pistol or two without remark. And if ye can do it cleverly, I'll bear it in mind when it'll be good for you to have friends; and that's when we come to Carolina."

Here Mr. Riach whispered him a little.

"Very right, sir," said the captain; and then to myself: "And see here, David, yon man has a beltful of gold, and I give you my word that you shall have your fingers in it."

I told him I would do as he wished, though indeed I had scarce breath to speak with; and upon that he gave me the key of the spirit-locker, and I began to go slowly back to the round-house. What was I to do? They were dogs and thieves; they had stolen me from my own country; they had killed poor Ransome; and was I to hold the candle to another murder? But then, upon the other hand, there was the fear of death very plain before me; for what could a boy and a man, if they were as brave as lions, against a whole ship's company?

I was still arguing it back and forth, and getting no great clearness, when I came into the round-house and saw the Jacobite eating his supper under the lamp; and at that my mind was made up all in a moment. I have no credit by it; it was by no choice of mine, but as if by compulsion, that I walked right up to the table and put my hand on his shoulder.

"Do ye want to be killed?" said I.

He sprang to his feet, and looked a question at me as clear as if he had spoken.

"O!" cried I, "they're all murderers here; it's a ship full of them! They've murdered a boy already. Now it's you."

"Ay, ay," said he; "but they haven't got me yet." And then looking at me curiously, "Will ye stand with me?"

"That will I!" said I. "I am no thief, nor yet murderer. I'll stand by you."

"Why, then," said he, "what's your name?"

"David Balfour," said I; and then, thinking that a man with so fine a coat must like fine people, I added for the first time, "of Shaws."

It never occurred to him to doubt me, for a Highlander is used to see great gentlefolk in great poverty; but as he had no estate of his own, my words nettled a very childish vanity he had.

"My name is Stewart," he said, drawing himself up. "Alan Breck, they call me. A king's name is good enough for me, though I bear it plain and have the name of no farm-midden to clap to the hind-end of it."

And having administered this rebuke, as though it were something of a chief importance, he turned to examine our defences.

The round-house was built very strong, to support the breaching of the seas. Of its five apertures, only the sky-light and the two doors were large enough for the passage of a man. The doors, besides, could be drawn close; they were of stout oak, and ran in grooves, and were fitted with hooks to keep them either shut or open, as the need arose. The one that was already shut I secured in this fashion; but when I was proceeding to slide to the other, Alan stopped me.

"David," said he—"for I canna bring to mind the name of your landed estate, and so will make so bold as to call you David—that door, being open, is the best part of my defences."

"It would be yet better shut," says I.

"Not so, David," says he. "Ye see, I have but one face; but so long as the door is open and my face to it, the best part of my enemies will be in front of me, where I would aye wish to find them."

Then he gave me from the rack a cutlass (of which there were a few besides the fire-arms), choosing it with great care, shaking his head and saying he had never in all his life seen poorer weapons; and next he set me down to the table with a powder-horn, a bag of bullets and all the pistols, which he bade me charge.

"And that will be better work, let me tell you," said he, "for a gentleman of decent birth, than scraping plates and raxing[1] drams to a wheen tarry sailors."

Thereupon he stood up in the midst with his face to the door, and drawing his great sword, made trial of the room he had to wield it in.

"I must stick to the point," he said, shaking his head; "and that's a pity, too. It doesn't set my genius, which is all for the upper guard. And now," said he, "do you keep on charging the pistols, and give heed to me."

I told him I would listen closely. My chest was tight, my mouth dry, the light dark to my eyes; the thought of the numbers that were soon to leap in upon us kept my heart in a flutter; and the sea, which I heard washing round the brig, and where I thought my dead body would be cast ere morning, ran in my mind strangely.

"First of all," said he, "how many are against us?"

I reckoned them up; and such was the hurry of my mind, I had to cast the numbers twice. "Fifteen," said I.

Alan whistled. "Well," said he, "that can't be cured. And now follow me. It is my part to keep this door, where

[1]Reaching.

I look for the main battle. In that, ye have no hand. And mind and dinna fire to this side unless they get me down; for I would rather have ten foes in front of me than one friend like you cracking pistols at my back."

I told him, indeed I was no great shot.

"And that's very bravely said," he cried, in a great admiration of my candour. "There's many a pretty gentleman that wouldna dare to say it."

"But then, sir," said I, "there is the door behind you, which they may perhaps break in."

"Ay," said he, "and that is a part of your work. No sooner the pistols charged, than ye must climb up into yon bed where ye're handy at the window; and if they lift hand against the door, ye're to shoot. But that's not all. Let's make a bit of a soldier of ye, David. What else have ye to guard?"

"There's the skylight," said I. "But indeed, Mr. Stewart, I would need to have eyes upon both sides to keep the two of them; for when my face is at the one, my back is to the other."

"And that's very true," said Alan. "But have ye no ears to your head?"

"To be sure!" cried I. "I must hear the bursting of the glass!"

"Ye have some rudiments of sense," said Alan, grimly.

Chapter 10

THE SIEGE OF THE ROUND-HOUSE

But now our time of truce was come to an end. Those on deck had waited for my coming till they grew impatient; and scarce had Alan spoken, when the captain showed face in the open door.

"Stand!" cried Alan, and pointed his sword at him.

The captain stood, indeed; but he neither winced nor drew back a foot.

"A naked sword?" says he. "This is a strange return for hospitality."

"Do ye see me?" said Alan. "I am come of kings; I bear a king's name. My badge is the oak. Do ye see my sword? It has slashed the heads off mair Whigamores than you have toes upon your feet. Call upon your vermin to your back, sir, and fall on! The sooner the clash begins, the sooner ye'll taste this steel throughout your vitals."

The captain said nothing to Alan, but he looked over at me with an ugly look. "David," said he, "I'll mind this"; and the sound of his voice went through me with a jar.

Next moment he was gone.

"And now," said Alan, "let your hand keep your head, for the grip is coming."

Alan drew a dirk, which he held in his left hand in case they should run in under his sword. I, on my part, clambered up into the berth with an armful of pistols and something of a heavy heart, and set open the window where I was to watch. It was a small part of the deck that I could overlook, but enough for our purpose. The sea had gone down, and the wind was steady and kept the sails quiet; so that there was a great stillness in the ship, in which I made sure I heard the sound of muttering voices. A little after, and there came a clash of steel upon the deck, by which I knew they were dealing out the cutlasses and one had been let fall; and after that, silence again.

I do not know if I was what you call afraid; but my heart beat like a bird's, both quick and little; and there was a dimness came before my eyes which I continually rubbed away, and which continually returned. As for hope, I had none; but only a darkness of despair and a sort of anger against all the world that made me long to sell my life as dear as I was able. I tried to pray, I remember, but that same hurry of my mind, like a man running, would not suffer me to think upon the words; and my chief wish was to have the thing begin and be done with.

It came all of a sudden when it did, with a rush of feet and a roar, and then a shout from Alan, and a sound of blows and some one crying out as if hurt. I looked back over my shoulder, and saw Mr. Shuan in the doorway, crossing blades with Alan.

"That's him that killed the boy!" I cried.

"Look to your window!" said Alan; and as I turned back to my place, I saw him pass his sword through the mate's body.

It was none too soon for me to look to my own part; for my head was scarce back at the window, before five men, carrying a spare yard for a battering-ram, ran past me and took post to drive the door in. I had never fired with a pistol in my life, and not often with a gun; far less against a fellow-creature. But it was now or never; and just as they swang the yard, I cried out, "Take that!" and shot into their midst.

I must have hit one of them, for he sang out and gave back a step, and the rest stopped as if a little disconcerted. Before they had time to recover, I sent another ball over their heads; and at my third shot (which went as wide as the second) the whole party threw down the yard and ran for it.

Then I looked round again into the deck-house. The whole place was full of the smoke of my own firing, just as my ears seemed to be burst with the noise of the shots. But there was Alan, standing as before; only now his sword was running blood to the hilt, and himself so swelled with triumph and fallen into so fine an attitude, that he looked to be invincible. Right before him on the floor was Mr. Shuan, on his hands and knees; the blood was pouring from his mouth, and he was sinking slowly lower, with a terrible, white face; and just as I looked, some of those from behind caught hold of him by the heels and dragged him bodily out of the round-house. I believed he died as they were doing it.

"There's one of your Whigs for ye!" cried Alan; and then turning to me, he asked if I had done much execution.

I told him I had winged one, and thought it was the captain.

"And I've settled two," says he. "No, there's not enough blood let; they'll be back again. To your watch, David. This was but a dram before meat."

I settled back to my place, re-charging the three pistols I had fired, and keeping watch with both eye and ear.

Our enemies were disputing not far off upon the deck, and that so loudly that I could hear a word or two above the washing of the seas.

"It was Shuan bauchled[1] it," I heard one say.

And another answered him with a "Wheesht, man! He's paid the piper."

After that the voices fell again into the same muttering as before. Only now, one person spoke most of the time, as though laying down a plan, and first one and then another answered him briefly, like men taking orders. By this, I made sure they were coming on again, and told Alan.

"It's what we have to pray for," said he. "Unless we can give them a good distaste of us, and done with it, there'll be nae sleep for either you or me. But this time, mind, they'll be in earnest."

By this, my pistols were ready, and there was nothing to do but listen and wait. While the brush lasted, I had not the time to think if I was frighted; but now, when all was still again, my mind ran upon nothing else. The thought of the sharp swords and the cold steel was strong in me; and presently, when I began to hear stealthy steps

[1]Bungled.

and a brushing of men's clothes against the round-house wall, and knew they were taking their places in the dark, I could have found it in my mind to cry out aloud.

All this was upon Alan's side; and I had begun to think my share of the fight was at an end, when I heard some one drop softly on the roof above me.

Then there came a single call on the sea-pipe, and that was the signal. A knot of them made one rush of it, cutlass in hand, against the door; and at the same moment, the glass of the skylight was dashed in a thousand pieces, and a man leaped through and landed on the floor. Before he got his feet, I had clapped a pistol to his back, and might have shot him, too; only at the touch of him (and him alive) my whole flesh misgave me, and I could no more pull the trigger than I could have flown.

He had dropped his cutlass as he jumped, and when he felt the pistol, whipped straight round and laid hold of me, roaring out an oath; and at that either my courage came again, or I grew so much afraid as came to the same thing; for I gave a shriek and shot him in the midst of the body. He gave the most horrible, ugly groan and fell to the floor. The foot of a second fellow, whose legs were dangling through the skylight, struck me at the same time upon the head; and at that I snatched another pistol and shot this one through the thigh, so that he slipped through and tumbled in a lump on his companion's body. There was no talk of missing, any more than there was time to aim; I clapped the muzzle to the very place and fired.

I might have stood and stared at them for long, but I heard Alan shout as if for help, and that brought me to my senses.

He had kept the door so long; but one of the seamen, while he was engaged with others, had run in under his guard and caught him about the body. Alan was dirking him with his left hand, but the fellow clung like a leech. Another had broken in and had his cutlass raised. The door was thronged with their faces. I thought we were lost, and catching up my cutlass, fell on them in flank.

But I had not time to be of help. The wrestler dropped at last; and Alan, leaping back to get his distance, ran upon the others like a bull, roaring as he went. They broke before him like water, turning, and running, and falling one against another in their haste. The sword in his hands flashed like quicksilver into the huddle of our fleeing enemies; and at every flash there came the scream of a man hurt. I was still thinking we were lost, when lo! they were all gone, and Alan was driving them along the deck as a sheep-dog chases sheep.

Yet he was no sooner out than he was back again, being as cautious as he was brave; and meanwhile the seamen continued running and crying out as if he was still behind them; and we heard them tumble one upon another into the forecastle, and clap-to the hatch upon the top.

The round-house was like a shambles; three were dead inside, another lay in his death agony across the threshold; and there were Alan and I victorious and unhurt.

He came up to me with open arms. "Come to my arms!" he cried, and embraced and kissed me hard upon both cheeks. "David," said he, "I love you like a brother. And O, man," he cried in a kind of ecstasy, "am I no' a bonny fighter?"

Thereupon he turned to the four enemies, passed his sword clean through each of them, tumbled them out of doors one after the other. As he did so, he kept humming and singing and whistling to himself, like a man trying to recall an air; only what *he* was trying was to make one. All the while, the flush was in his face, and his eyes were as bright as a five-year-old child's with a new toy. And presently he sat down upon the table, sword in hand; the air that he was making all the time began to run a little clearer, and then clearer still; and then out he burst with a great voice into a Gaelic song.

I have translated it here, not in verse (of which I have no skill) but at least in the king's English. He sang it often afterwards, and the thing became popular; so that I have heard it, and had it explained to me, many's the time.

> This is the song of the sword of Alan;
> The smith made it,
> The fire set it;
> Now it shines in the hand of Alan Breck.

Their eyes were many and bright,
Swift were they to behold,
Many the hands they guided:
The sword was alone.

The dun deer troop over the hill,
They are many, the hill is one;
The dun deer vanish,
The hill remains.

Come to me from the hills of heather,
Come from the isles of the sea.
O far-beholding eagles,
Here is your meat.

Now this song which he made (both words and music) in the hour of our victory, is something less than just to me, who stood beside him in the tussle. Mr. Shuan and five more were either killed outright or thoroughly disabled; but of these, two fell by my hand, the two that came by the skylight. Four more were hurt, and of that number, one (and he not the least important) got his hurt from me. So that, altogether, I did my fair share both of the killing and the wounding, and might have claimed a place in Alan's verses. But poets have to think upon their rhymes; and in good prose talk, Alan always did me more than justice.

In the meanwhile, I was innocent of any wrong being done me. For not only I knew no word of the Gaelic; but what with the long suspense of the waiting, and the scurry and strain of our two spirits of fighting, and more than all, the horror I had of some of my own share in it, the thing was no sooner over than I was glad to stagger to a seat. There was that tightness on my chest that I could hardly breathe; the thought of the two men I had shot sat upon me like a nightmare; and all upon a sudden, and before I had a guess of what was coming, I began to sob and cry like any child.

Alan clapped my shoulder, and said I was a brave lad and wanted nothing but a sleep.

"I'll take the first watch," said he. "Ye've done well by

me, David, first and last; and I wouldn't lose you for all Appin—no, nor for Breadalbane."

So I made up my bed on the floor; and he took the first spell, pistol in hand and sword on knee, three hours by the captain's watch upon the wall. Then he roused me up, and I took my turn of three hours; before the end of which it was broad day, and a very quiet morning, with a smooth, rolling sea that tossed the ship and made the blood run to and fro on the round-house floor, and a heavy rain that drummed upon the roof. All my watch there was nothing stirring; and by the banging of the helm, I knew they had even no one at the tiller. Indeed (as I learned afterwards) there were so many of them hurt or dead, and the rest in so ill a temper, that Mr. Riach and the captain had to take turn and turn like Alan and me, or the brig might have gone ashore and nobody the wiser. It was a mercy the night had fallen so still, for the wind had gone down as soon as the rain began. Even as it was, I judged by the wailing of a great number of gulls that went crying and fishing round the ship, that she must have drifted pretty near the coast or one of the islands of the Hebrides; and at last, looking out of the door of the round-house, I saw the great stone hills of Skye on the right hand, and, a little more astern, the strange isle of Rum.

Chapter 11

THE CAPTAIN KNUCKLES UNDER

Alan and I sat down to breakfast about six of the clock.
The floor was covered with broken glass and in a horrid
mess of blood, which took away my hunger. In all other
ways we were in a situation not only agreeable but merry;
having ousted the officers from their own cabin, and having at command all the drink in the ship—both wine and
spirits—and all the dainty part of what was eatable, such
as the pickles and the fine sort of bread. This, of itself, was
enough to set us in good humour; but the richest part of it
was this, that the two thirstiest men that ever came out of
Scotland (Mr. Shuan being dead) were now shut in the
fore-part of the ship and condemned to what they hated
most—cold water.

"And depend upon it," Alan said, "we shall hear more
of them ere long. Ye may keep a man from the fighting
but never from his bottle."

We made good company for each other. Alan, indeed,
expressed himself most lovingly; and taking a knife from
the table, cut me off one of the silver buttons from his
coat.

"I had them," says he, "from my father, Duncan Stewart; and now give ye one of them to be a keepsake for last
night's work. And wherever ye go and show that button,
the friends of Alan Breck will come around you."

He said this as if he had been Charlemagne, and com-
manded armies; and indeed, much as I admired his courage, I was always in danger of smiling at his vanity: in
danger, I say, for had I not kept my countenance, I would
be afraid to think what a quarrel might have followed.

As soon as we were through with our meal he rummaged in the captain's locker till he found a clothes-brush; and then taking off his coat, began to visit his suit and brush away the stains, with such care and labour as I supposed to have been only usual with women. To be sure, he had no other; and, besides (as he said), it belonged to a king and so behoved to be royally looked after.

For all that, when I saw what care he took to pluck out the threads where the button had been cut away, I put a higher value on his gift.

He was still so engaged when we were hailed by Mr. Riach from the deck, asking for a parley; and I, climbing through the skylight and sitting on the edge of it, pistol in hand and with a bold front, though inwardly in fear of broken glass, hailed him back again and bade him speak out. He came to the edge of the round-house, and stood on a coil of rope, so that his chin was on a level with the roof; and we looked at each other a while in silence. Mr. Riach, as I do not think he had been very forward in the battle, so he had got off with nothing worse than a blow upon the cheek: but he looked out of heart and very weary, having been all night afoot, either standing watch or doctoring the wounded.

"This is a bad job," said he at last, shaking his head.

"It was none of our choosing," said I.

"The captain," says he, "would like to speak with your friend. They might speak at the window."

"And how do we know what treachery he means?" cried I.

"He means none, David," returned Mr. Riach, "and if he did, I'll tell ye the honest truth, we couldna get the men to follow."

"Is that so?" said I.

"I'll tell ye more than that," said he. "It's not only the men; it's me. I'm frich'ened, Davie." And he smiled across at me. "No," he continued, "what we want is to be shut of him."

Thereupon I consulted with Alan, and the parley was agreed to and parole given upon either side; but this was not the whole of Mr. Riach's business, and he now begged me for a dram with such instancy and such reminders of his former kindness, that at last I handed him a pannikin with about a gill of brandy. He drank a part, and then carried the rest down upon the deck, to share it (I suppose) with his superior.

A little after, the captain came (as was agreed) to one of the windows, and stood there in the rain, with his arm in a sling, and looking stern and pale, and so old that my heart smote me for having fired upon him.

Alan at once held a pistol in his face.

"Put that thing up!" said the captain. "Have I not passed my word, sir? or do ye seek to affront me?"

"Captain," says Alan, "I doubt your word is a breakable. Last night ye haggled and argle-bargled[1] like an apple-wife; and then passed me your word, and gave me your hand to back it; and ye ken very well what was the upshot. Be damned to your word!" says he.

"Well, well, sir," said the captain, "ye'll get little good by swearing." (And truly that was a fault of which the captain was quite free.) "But we have other things to speak," he continued, bitterly. "Ye've made a sore hash of my brig; I haven't hands enough left to work her; and my first officer (whom I could ill spare) has got your sword throughout his vitals, and passed without speech. There is nothing left me, sir, but to put back into the port of Glasgow after hands; and there (by your leave) ye will find them that are better able to talk to you."

"Ay?" said Alan; "and faith, I'll have a talk with them mysel'! Unless there's naebody speaks English in that town, I have a bonny tale for them. Fifteen tarry sailors upon the one side, and a man and a halfling boy upon the other! Oh, man, it's peetiful!"

Hoseason flushed red.

"No," continued Alan, "that'll no do. Ye'll just have to set me ashore as we agreed."

"Ay," said Hoseason, "but my first officer is dead—ye ken best how. There's none of the rest of us acquaint with this coast, sir; and it's one very dangerous to ships."

"I give ye your choice," says Alan. "Set me on dry ground in Appin, or Ardgour, or in Morven, or Arisaig, or

---

[1] Argued.

Morar; or, in brief, where ye please, within thirty miles of my own country; except in a country of the Campbells. That's a broad target. If ye miss that, ye must be as feckless at the sailoring as I have found ye at the fighting. Why, my poor country people in their bit cobles[1] pass from island to island in all weathers, ay, and by night too, for the matter of that."

"A coble's not a ship, sir," said the captain. "It has nae draught of water."

"Well, then, to Glasgow if ye list!" says Alan. "We'll have the laugh of ye at the least."

"My mind runs little upon laughing," said the captain. "But all this will cost money, sir."

"Well, sir," says Alan, "I am nae weathercock. Thirty guineas, if ye land me on the sea-side; and sixty, if ye put me in the Linnhe Loch."

"But see, sir, where we lie, we are but a few hours' sail from Ardnamurchan," said Hoseason. "Give me sixty, and I'll set ye there."

"And I'm to wear my brogues and run jeopardy of the red-coats to please you?" cries Alan. "No, sir; if ye want sixty guineas earn them, and set me in my own country."

"It's to risk the brig, sir," said the captain, "and your own lives along with her."

"Take it or want it," says Alan.

"Could ye pilot us at all?" asked the captain, who was frowning to himself.

"Well, it's doubtful," said Alan. "I'm more of a fighting man (as ye have seen for yoursel') than a sailor-man. But I have been often enough picked up and set down upon this coast, and should ken something of the lie of it."

The captain shook his head, still frowning.

"If I had lost less money on this unchancy cruise," says he, "I would see you in a rope's-end before I risked my brig, sir. But be it as ye will. As soon as I get a slant of wind (and there's some coming, or I'm the more mistaken) I'll put it in hand. But there's one thing more. We may meet in with a king's ship and she may lay us aboard, sir, with no blame of mine: they keep the cruisers thick upon

[1]Small fishing boats.

this coast, ye ken who for. Now, sir, if that was to befall, ye might leave the money."

"Captain," says Alan, "if ye see a pennant, it shall be your part to run away. And now, as I hear you're a little short of brandy in the fore-part, I'll offer ye a change: a bottle of brandy against two buckets of water."

That was the last clause of the treaty, and was duly executed on both sides; so that Alan and I could at last wash out the round-house and be quit of the memorials of those whom we had slain, and the captain and Mr. Riach could be happy again in their own way, the name of which was drink.

Chapter 12

I HEAR OF THE RED FOX

Before we had done cleaning out the round-house, a breeze sprang up from a little to the east of north. This blew off the rain and brought out the sun.

And here I must explain; and the reader would do well to look at a map. On the day when the fog fell and we ran down Alan's boat, we had been running through the Little Minch. At dawn after the battle, we lay becalmed to the east of the Isle of Canna or between that and Isle Eriska in the chain of the Long Island. Now to get from there to the Linnhe Loch, the straight course was through the narrows of the Sound of Mull. But the captain had no chart; he was afraid to trust his brig so deep among the islands; and the wind serving well, he preferred to go by west of Tiree and come up under the southern coast of the great Isle of Mull.

All day the breeze held in the same point, and rather freshened than died down; and towards afternoon, a swell began to set in from round the outer Hebrides. Our course, to go round about the inner isles, was to the west of south, so that at first we had this swell upon our beam, and were much rolled about. But after nightfall, when we had turned the end of Tiree and began to head more to the east, the sea came right astern.

Meanwhile, the early part of the day, before the swell came up, was very pleasant; sailing, as we were, in a bright sunshine and with many mountainous islands upon different sides. Alan and I sat in the round-house with the doors open on each side (the wind being straight astern), and smoked a pipe or two of the captain's fine tobacco. It was at this time we heard each other's stories, which was the more important to me, as I gained some knowledge of that wild Highland country on which I was so soon to land. In those days, so close on the back of the great rebellion, it was needful a man should know what he was doing when he went upon the heather.

It was I that showed the example, telling him all my misfortune; which he heard with great good-nature. Only, when I came to mention that good friend of mine, Mr. Campbell the minister, Alan fired up and cried out that he hated all that were of that name.

"Why," said I, "he is a man you should be proud to give your hand to."

"I know nothing I would help a Campbell to," says he, "unless it was a leaden bullet. I would hunt all of that name like blackcocks. If I lay dying, I would crawl upon my knees to my chamber window for a shot at one."

"Why, Alan," I cried, "what ails ye at the Campbells?"

"Well," says he, "ye ken very well that I am an Appin Stewart, and the Campbells have long harried and wasted those of my name; ay, and got lands of us by treachery—but never with the sword," he cried loudly, and with the word brought down his fist upon the table. But I paid the less attention to this, for I knew it was usually said by those who have the underhand. "There's more than that," he continued, "and all in the same story: lying words, lying papers, tricks fit for a peddler, and the show of what's legal over all, to make a man the more angry."

"You that are so wasteful of your buttons," said I, "I can hardly think you would be a good judge of business."

"Ah!" says he, falling again to smiling, "I got my wastefulness from the same man I got the buttons from; and that was my poor father, Duncan Stewart, grace be to him! He was the prettiest man of his kindred; and the best swordsman in the Hielands, David, and that is the same as to say, in all the world. I should ken, for it was him that taught me. He was in the Black Watch, when first it was mustered; and, like other gentlemen privates, had a gillie[1] at his back to carry his firelock for him on the march.

[1]Manservant.

Well, the King, it appears, was wishful to see Hieland swordsmanship; and my father and three more were chosen out and sent to London town, to let him see it at the best. So they were had into the palace and showed the whole art of the sword for two hours at a stretch, before King George and Queen Carline, and the Butcher Cumberland, and many more of whom I havena mind. And when they were through, the King (for all he was a rank usurper) spoke them fair and gave each man three guineas in his hand. Now, as they were going out of the palace, they had a porter's lodge to go by; and it came in on my father, as he was perhaps the first private Hieland gentleman that had ever gone by that door, it was right he should give the poor porter a proper notion of their quality. So he gives the King's three guineas into the man's hand, as if it was his common custom; the three others that came behind him did the same; and there they were on the street, never a penny the better for their pains. Some say it was one, that was the first to fee the King's porter; and some say it was another; but the truth of it is, that it was Duncan Stewart, as I am willing to prove with either sword or pistol. And that was the father that I had, God rest him!"

"I think he was not the man to leave you rich," said I.

"And that's true," said Alan. "He left me my breeks[1] to cover me, and little besides. And that was how I came to enlist, which was a black spot upon my character at the best of times, and would still be a sore job for me if I fell among the red-coats."

"What," cried I, "were you in the English army?"

"That was I," said Alan. "But I deserted to the right side at Prestonpans—and that's some comfort."

I could scarcely share this view: holding desertion under arms for an unpardonable fault in honour. But for all I was so young, I was wiser than say my thought. "Dear, dear," says I, "the punishment is death."

"Ay," said he, "if they got hands on me, it would be a short shrift and a lang tow for Alan! But I have the King of

[1] Trousers.

France's commission in my pocket, which would aye be some protection."

"I misdoubt it much," said I.

"I have doubts mysel'," said Alan, drily.

"And, good heaven, man," cried I, "you that are a condemned rebel, and a deserter, and a man of the French King's—what tempts ye back into this country? It's a braving of Providence."

"Tut!" says Alan, "I have been back every year since forty-six!"

"And what brings ye, man?" cried I.

"Well, ye see, I weary for my friends and country," said he. "France is a braw place, nae doubt; but I weary for the heather and the deer. And then I have bit things that I attend to. Whiles I pick up a few lads to serve the King of France: recruits, ye see; and that's aye a little money. But the heart of the matter is the business of my chief, Ardshiel."

"I thought they called your chief Appin," said I.

"Ay, but Ardshiel is the captain of the clan," said he, which scarcely cleared my mind. "Ye see, David, he that was all his life so great a man, and come of the blood and bearing the name of kings, is now brought down to live in a French town like a poor and private person. He that had four hundred swords at his whistle, I have seen, with these eyes of mine, buying butter in the market-place, and taking it home in a kale-leaf. This is not only a pain but a disgrace to us of his family and clan. There are the bairns forbye, the children and the hope of Appin, that must be learned their letters and how to hold a sword, in that far country. Now, the tenants of Appin have to pay a rent to King George; but their hearts are staunch, they are true to their chief; and what with love and a bit of pressure, and maybe a threat or two, the poor folk scrape up a second rent for Ardshiel. Well, David, I'm the hand that carries it." And he struck the belt about his body, so that the guineas rang.

"Do they pay both?" cried I.

"Ay, David, both," says he.

"What! two rents?" I repeated.

"Ay, David," said he. "I told a different tale to yon captain man; but this is the truth of it. And it's wonderful to me how little pressure is needed. But that's the handi-work of my good kinsman and my father's friend, James of the Glens; James Stewart, that is: Ardshiel's half-brother. He it is that gets the money in, and does the management."

This was the first time I heard the name of James Stewart, who was afterwards so famous at the time of his hanging. But I took little heed at the moment, for all my mind was occupied with the generosity of these poor Highlanders.

"I call it noble," I cried. "I'm a Whig, or little better; but I call it noble."

"Ay," said he, "ye're a Whig, but ye're a gentleman; and that's what does it. Now, if ye were one of the cursed race of Campbell, ye would gnash your teeth to hear tell of it. If ye were the Red Fox" . . . And at that name, his teeth shut together, and he ceased speaking. I have seen many a grim face, but never a grimmer than Alan's when he had named the Red Fox.

"And who is the Red Fox?" I asked, daunted, but still curious.

"Who is he?" cried Alan. "Well, and I'll tell you that. When the men of the clans were broken at Culloden, and the good cause went down, and the horses rode over the fetlocks in the best blood of the north, Ardshiel had to flee like a poor deer upon the mountains—he and his lady and his bairns. A sair[1] job we had of it before we got him shipped; and while he still lay in the heather, the English rogues, that couldna come at his life, were striking at his rights. They stripped him of his powers; they stripped him of his lands; they plucked the weapons from the hands of his clansmen, that had borne arms for thirty centuries; ay, and the very clothes off their backs—so that it's now a sin to wear a tartan plaid, and a man may be cast into a gaol if he has but a kilt about his legs. One thing they couldna kill. That was the love the clansmen bore their chief. These guineas are the proof of it. And now, in there steps a man, a Campbell, red-headed Colin of Glenure——"

"Is that him you call the Red Fox?" said I.

"Will ye bring me his brush?" cries Alan, fiercely. "Ay,

[1]Sad.

that's the man. In he steps, and gets papers from King George, to be so-called King's factor on the lands of Appin. And at first he sings small, and is hail-fellow-well-met with Sheamus—that's James of the Glens, my chieftain's agent. But by and by, that came to his ears that I have just told you; how the poor commons of Appin, the farmers and the crofters and the boumen, were wringing their very plaids to get a second rent, and send it over-seas for Ardshiel and his poor bairns. What was it ye called it, when I told ye?"

"I called it noble, Alan," said I.

"And you little better than a common Whig!" cries Alan. "But when it came to Colin Roy, the black Campbell blood in him ran wild. He sat gnashing his teeth at the wine-table. What! should a Stewart get a bite of bread, and him not be able to prevent it? Ah! Red Fox, if ever I hold you at a gun's end, the Lord have pity upon ye!" (Alan stopped to swallow down his anger.) "Well, David, what does he do? He declares all the farms to let. And, thinks he, in his black heart, 'I'll soon get other tenants that'll overbid these Stewarts, and Maccolls, and Macrobs' (for these are all names in my clan, David), 'and then,' thinks he, 'Ardshiel will have to hold his bonnet on a French roadside.'"

"Well," said I, "what followed?"

Alan laid down his pipe, which he had long since suffered to go out, and set his two hands upon his knees.

"Ay," said he, "ye'll never guess that! For these same Stewarts, and Maccolls, and Macrobs (that had two rents to pay, one to King George by stark force, and one to Ardshiel by natural kindness) offered him a better price than any Campbell in all broad Scotland; and far he sent seeking them—as far as to the sides of Clyde and the cross of Edinburgh—seeking, and fleeching,[1] and begging them to come, where there was a Stewart to be starved and a red-headed hound of a Campbell to be pleasured!"

"Well, Alan," said I, "that is a strange story, and a fine one, too. And Whig as I may be, I am glad the man was beaten."

"Him beaten?" echoed Alan. "It's little ye ken of Camp-

---

[1] Coaxing.

bells, and less of the Red Fox. Him beaten? No: nor will
be, till his blood's on the hill-side! But if the day comes,
David man, that I can find time and leisure for a bit of
hunting, there grows not enough heather in all Scotland to
hide him from my vengeance!"

"Man, Alan," said I, "ye are neither very wise nor very
Christian to blow off so many words of anger. They will do
the man ye call the Fox no harm, and yourself no good.
Tell me your tale plainly out. What did he next?"

"And that's a good observe, David," said Alan. "Troth
and indeed, they will do him no harm; the more's the pity!
And barring that about Christianity (of which my opinion
is quite otherwise, or I would be nae Christian), I am
much of your mind."

"Opinion here or opinion there," said I, "it's a kennt
thing that Christianity forbids revenge."

"Ay," said he, "it's well seen it was a Campbell taught
ye! It would be a convenient world for them and their
sort, if there was no such a thing as a lad and a gun behind
a heather bush! But that's nothing to the point. This is
what he did."

"Ay," said I, "come to that."

"Well, David," said he, "since he couldna be rid of the
loyal commons by fair means, he swore he would be rid of
them by foul. Ardshiel was to starve: that was the thing he
aimed at. And since them that fed him in his exile wouldna
be bought out—right or wrong, he would drive them out.
Therefore he sent for lawyers, and papers, and red-coats
to stand at his back. And the kindly folk of that country
must all pack and tramp, every father's son out of his
father's house, and out of the place where he was bred and
fed, and played when he was a callant.[1] And who are to
succeed them? Bare-leggit beggars! King George is to
whistle for his rents; he maun dow with less; he can
spread his butter thinner: what cares Red Colin? If he can
hurt Ardshiel, he has his wish; if he can pluck the meat
from my chieftain's table, and the bit toys out of his
children's hands, he will gang hame singing to Glenure!"

"Let me have a word," said I. "Be sure, if they take less

[1]Lad.

rents, be sure Government has a finger in the pie. It's not this Campbell's fault, man—it's his orders. And if ye killed this Colin to-morrow, what better would ye be? There would be another factor in his shoes, as fast as spur can drive."

"Ye're a good lad in a fight," said Alan; "but, man! ye have Whig blood in ye!"

He spoke kindly enough, but there was so much anger under his contempt that I thought it was wise to change the conversation. I expressed my wonder how, with the Highlands covered with troops, and guarded like a city in a siege, a man in his situation could come and go without arrest.

"It's easier than ye would think," said Alan. "A bare hill-side (ye see) is like all one road; if there's a sentry at one place, ye just go by another. And then the heather's a great help. And everywhere there are friends' houses and friends' byres and haystacks. And besides, when folk talk of a country covered with troops, it's but a kind of a byword at the best. A soldier covers nae mair of it than his boot-soles. I have fished a water with a sentry on the other side of the brae, and killed a fine trout; and I have sat in a heather bush within six feet of another, and learned a real bonny tune from his whistling. This was it," said he, and whistled me the air.

"And then, besides," he continued, "it's no' sae bad now as it was in forty-six. The Hielands are what they call pacified. Small wonder, with never a gun or a sword left from Cantyre to Cape Wrath, but what tenty[1] folk have hidden in their thatch! But what I would like to ken, David, is just how long? Not long, ye would think, with men like Ardshiel in exile and men like the Red Fox sitting birling[2] the wine and oppressing the poor at home. But it's a kittle[3] thing to decide what folk'll bear, and what they will not. Or why would Red Colin be riding his horse all over my poor country of Appin, and never a pretty lad to put a bullet in him?"

And with this Alan fell into a muse, and for a long time sate very sad and silent.

---

[1]Careful.   [2]Drinking.   [3]Difficult.

I will add the rest of what I have to say about my friend, that he was skilled in all kinds of music, but principally pipe-music; was a well-considered poet in his own tongue; had read several books both in French and English; was a dead shot, a good angler, and an excellent fencer with the small sword as well as with his own particular weapon. For his faults, they were on his face, and I now knew them all. But the worst of them, his childish propensity to take offence and to pick quarrels, he greatly laid aside in my case, out of regard for the battle of the round-house. But whether it was because I had done well myself, or because I had been a witness of his own much greater prowess, is more than I can tell. For though he had a great taste for courage in other men, yet he admired it most in Alan Breck.

Chapter 13

THE LOSS OF THE BRIG

It was already late at night, and as dark as it ever would be at that season of the year (and that is to say, it was still pretty bright), when Hoseason clapped his head into the round-house door.

"Here," said he, "come out and see if ye can pilot."

"Is this one of your tricks?" asked Alan.

"Do I look like tricks?" cries the captain. "I have other things to think of—my brig's in danger!"

By the concerned look of his face, and above all by the sharp tones in which he spoke of his brig, it was plain to both of us he was in deadly earnest; and so Alan and I, with no great fear of treachery, stepped on deck.

The sky was clear; it blew hard, and was bitter cold; a great deal of daylight lingered; and the moon, which was nearly full, shone brightly. The brig was close-hauled, so as to round the south-west corner of the Island of Mull, the hills of which (and Ben More above them all, with a wisp of mist upon the top of it) lay full upon the larboard bow. Though it was no good point of sailing for the *Covenant*, she tore through the seas at a great rate, pitching and straining, and pursued by the westerly swell.

Altogether it was no such ill night to keep the seas in; and I had begun to wonder what it was that sat so heavily upon the captain, when the brig rising suddenly on the top of a high swell, he pointed and cried to us to look. Away on the lee bow, a thing like a fountain rose out of the moonlit sea, and immediately after we heard a low sound of roaring.

"What do ye call that?" asked the captain, gloomily.

"The sea breaking on a reef," said Alan. "And now ye ken where it is; and what better would ye have?"

"Ay," said Hoseason, "if it was the only one."

And sure enough, just as he spoke there came a second fountain farther to the south.

"There!" said Hoseason. "Ye see for yourself. If I had kennt of these reefs, if I had had a chart, or if Shuan had been spared, it's not sixty guineas, no, nor six hundred, would have made me risk my brig in sic a stoneyard! But you, sir, that was to pilot us, have ye never a word?"

"I'm thinking," said Alan, "these'll be what they call the Torran Rocks."

"Are there many of them?" says the captain.

"Truly, sir, I am nae pilot," said Alan; "but it sticks in my mind there are ten miles of them."

Mr. Riach and the captain looked at each other.

"There's a way through them, I suppose?" said the captain.

"Doubtless," said Alan, "but where? But it somehow runs in my mind once more that it is clearer under the land."

"So?" said Hoseason. "We'll have to haul our wind then, Mr. Riach; we'll have to come as near in about the end of Mull as we can take her, sir; and even then we'll have the land to kep the wind off us, and that stoneyard on our lee. Well, we're in for it now, and may as well crack on."

With that he gave an order to the steersman, and sent Riach to the foretop. There were only five men on deck, counting the officers; these being all that were fit (or, at least, both fit and willing) for their work. So, as I say, it fell to Mr. Riach to go aloft, and he sat there looking out and hailing the deck with news of all he saw.

"The sea to the south is thick," he cried; and then, after a while, "it does seem clearer in by the land."

"Well, sir," said Hoseason to Alan, "we'll try your way of it. But I think I might as well trust to a blind fiddler. Pray God you're right."

"Pray God I am!" says Alan to me. "But where did I hear it? Well, well, it will be as it must."

As we got nearer to the turn of the land the reefs began

to be sown here and there on our very path; and Mr.
Riach sometimes cried down to us to change the course.
Sometimes, indeed, none too soon; for one reef was so
close on the brig's weather-board that when a sea burst
upon it the lighter sprays fell upon her deck and wetted us
like rain.

The brightness of the night showed us these perils as
clearly as by day, which was, perhaps, the more alarming.
It showed me, too, the face of the captain as he stood by
the steersman, now on one foot, now on the other, and
sometimes blowing in his hands, but still listening and
looking and as steady as steel. Neither he nor Mr. Riach
had shown well in the fighting; but I saw they were brave
in their own trade, and admired them all the more because I found Alan very white.

"Ochone, David," says he, "this is no' the kind of death
I fancy!"

"What, Alan!" I cried, "you're not afraid?"

"No," said he, wetting his lips, "but you'll allow yourself, it's a cold ending."

By this time, now and then sheering to one side or the
other to avoid a reef, but still hugging the wind and the
land, we had got round Iona and begun to come alongside
Mull. The tide at the tail of the land ran very strong, and
threw the brig about. Two hands were put to the helm,
and Hoseason himself would sometimes lend a help; and it
was strange to see three strong men throw their weight
upon the tiller, and it (like a living thing) struggle against
and drive them back. This would have been the greater
danger had not the sea been for some while free of obsta-
cles. Mr. Riach, besides, announced from the top that he
saw clear water ahead.

"Ye were right," said Hoseason to Alan. "Ye have saved
the brig, sir; I'll mind that when we come to clear accounts." And I believe he not only meant what he said,
but would have done it; so high a place did the *Covenant*
hold in his affections.

But this is matter only for conjecture, things having
gone otherwise than he forecast.

"Keep her away a point," sings out Mr. Riach. "Reef to
windward!"

And just at the same time the tide caught the brig, and threw the wind out of her sails. She came round into the wind like a top, and the next moment struck the reef with such a dunch as threw us all flat upon the deck, and came near to shake Mr. Riach from his place upon the mast.

I was on my feet in a minute. The reef on which we had struck was close in under the south-west end of Mull, off a little isle they call Earraid, which lay low and black upon the larboard. Sometimes the swell broke clean over us; sometimes it only ground the poor brig upon the reef, so that we could hear her beat herself to pieces; and what with the great noise of the sails, and the singing of the wind, and the flying of the spray in the moonlight, and the sense of danger, I think my head must have been partly turned, for I could scarcely understand the things I saw.

Presently I observed Mr. Riach and the seamen busy round the skiff, and still in the same blank, ran over to assist them; and as soon as I set my hand to work, my mind came clear again. It was no very easy task, for the skiff lay amidships and was full of hamper, and the breaking of the heavier seas continually forced us to give over and hold on; but we all wrought like horses while we could.

Meanwhile such of the wounded as could move came clambering out of the fore-scuttle and began to help; while the rest that lay helpless in their bunks harrowed me with screaming and begging to be saved.

The captain took no part. It seemed he was struck stupid. He stood holding by the shrouds, talking to himself and groaning out aloud whenever the ship hammered on the rock. His brig was like wife and child to him; he had looked on, day by day, at the mishandling of poor Ransome; but when it came to the brig, he seemed to suffer along with her.

All the time of our working at the boat, I remember only one other thing: that I asked Alan, looking across at the shore, what country it was; and he answered, it was the worst possible for him, for it was a land of the Campbells.

We had one of the wounded men told off to keep a watch upon the seas and cry us warning. Well, we had the boat about ready to be launched, when this man sang out pretty shrill: "For God's sake, hold on!" We knew by his tone that it was something more than ordinary; and sure enough, there followed a sea so huge that it lifted the brig right up and canted her over on her beam. Whether the cry came too late, or my hold was too weak, I know not; but at the sudden tilting of the ship I was cast clean over the bulwarks into the sea.

I went down, and drank my fill, and then came up, and got a blink of the moon, and then down again. They say a man sinks a third time for good. I cannot be made like other folk, then; for I would not like to write how often I went down, or how often I came up again. All the while, I was being hurled along, and beaten upon and choked, and then swallowed whole; and the thing was so distracting to my wits, that I was neither sorry nor afraid.

Presently I found I was holding to a spar, which helped me somewhat. And then all of a sudden I was in quiet water, and began to come to myself.

It was the spare yard I had got hold of, and I was amazed to see how far I had travelled from the brig. I hailed her, indeed; but it was plain she was already out of cry. She was still holding together; but whether or not they had yet launched the boat, I was too far off and too low down to see.

While I was hailing the brig, I spied a tract of water lying between us where no great waves came, but which yet boiled white all over and bristled in the moon with rings and bubbles. Sometimes the whole tract swung to one side, like the tail of a live serpent; sometimes, for a glimpse, it would all disappear and then boil up again. What it was I had no guess, which for the time increased my fear of it; but I now know it must have been the roost or tide race, which had carried me away so fast and tumbled me about so cruelly, and at last, as if tired of that play, had flung out me and the spare yard upon its landward margin.

I now lay quite becalmed, and began to feel that a man can die of cold as well as of drowning. The shores of Earraid were close in; I could see in the moonlight the dots of heather and the sparkling of the mica in the rocks.

"Well," thought I to myself, "if I cannot get as far as that, it's strange!"

I had no skill of swimming, Essen Water being small in our neighbourhood; but when I laid hold upon the yard with both arms, and kicked out with both feet, I soon began to find that I was moving. Hard work it was, and mortally slow; but in about an hour of kicking and splashing, I had got well in between the points of a sandy bay surrounded by low hills.

The sea was here quite quiet; there was no sound of any surf; the moon shone clear; and I thought in my heart I had never seen a place so desert and desolate. But it was dry land; and when at last it grew so shallow that I could leave the yard and wade ashore upon my feet, I cannot tell if I was more tired or more grateful. Both at least, I was: tired as I never was before that night; and grateful to God as I trust I have been often, though never with more cause.

Chapter 14

THE ISLET

With my stepping ashore I began the most unhappy part of my adventures. It was half-past twelve in the morning, and though the wind was broken by the land, it was a cold night. I dared not sit down (for I thought I should have frozen), but took off my shoes and walked to and fro upon the sand, barefoot, and beating my breast with infinite weariness. There was no sound of man or cattle; not a cock crew, though it was about the hour of their first waking; only the surf broke outside in the distance, which put me in mind of my perils and those of my friend. To walk by the sea at that hour of the morning, and in a place so desert-like and lonesome, struck me with a kind of fear.

As soon as the day began to break I put on my shoes and climbed a hill—the ruggedest scramble I ever undertook—falling, the whole way, between big blocks of granite, or leaping from one to another. When I got to the top the dawn was come. There was no sign of the brig, which must have lifted from the reef and sunk. The boat, too, was nowhere to be seen. There was never a sail upon the ocean; and in what I could see of the land was neither house nor man.

I was afraid to think what had befallen my shipmates, and afraid to look longer at so empty a scene. What with my wet clothes and weariness, and my belly that now began to ache with hunger, I had enough to trouble me without that. So I set off eastward along the south coast, hoping to find a house where I might warm myself, and perhaps get news of those I had lost. And at the worst, I considered the sun would soon rise and dry my clothes.

After a little, my way was stopped by a creek or inlet of the sea, which seemed to run pretty deep into the land; and as I had no means to get across, I must needs change my direction to go about the end of it. It was still the roughest kind of walking; indeed the whole, not only of Earraid, but of the neighbouring part of Mull (which they call the Ross) is nothing but a jumble of granite rocks with heather in among. At first the creek kept narrowing as I had looked to see; but presently to my surprise it began to widen out again. At this I scratched my head, but had still no notion of the truth: until at last I came to a rising ground, and it burst upon me all in a moment that I was cast upon a little barren isle, and cut off on every side by the salt seas.

Instead of the sun rising to dry me, it came on to rain, with a thick mist; so that my case was lamentable.

I stood in the rain, and shivered, and wondered what to do, till it occurred to me that perhaps the creek was fordable. Back I went to the narrowest point and waded in. But not three yards from shore, I plumped in head over ears; and if ever I was heard of more, it was rather by God's grace than my own prudence. I was no wetter (for that could hardly be), but I was all the colder for this mishap; and having lost another hope was the more unhappy.

And now, all at once, the yard came in my head. What had carried me through the roost would surely serve me to cross this little quiet creek in safety. With that I set off, undaunted, across the top of the isle, to fetch and carry it back. It was a weary tramp in all ways, and if hope had not buoyed me up, I must have cast myself down and given up. Whether with the sea salt, or because I was growing fevered, I was distressed with thirst, and had to stop, as I went, and drink the peaty water out of the hags.

I came to the bay at last, more dead than alive; and at the first glance, I thought the yard was something farther out than when I left it. In I went, for the third time into the sea. The sand was smooth and firm, and shelved gradually down, so that I could wade out till the water was almost to my neck and the little waves splashed into my face. But at that depth my feet began to leave me, and I durst venture in no farther. As for the yard, I saw it bobbing very quietly some twenty feet beyond.

I had borne up well until this last disappointment; but at that I came ashore, and flung myself down upon the sands and wept.

The time I spent upon the island is still so horrible a thought to me, that I must pass it lightly over. In all the books I have read of people cast away, they had either their pockets full of tools, or a chest of things would be thrown upon the beach along with them, as if on purpose. My case was very different. I had nothing in my pockets but money and Alan's silver button; and being inland bred, I was as much short of knowledge as of means.

I knew indeed that shell-fish were counted good to eat; and among the rocks of the isle I found a great plenty of limpets, which at first I could scarcely strike from their places, not knowing quickness to be needful. There were, besides, some of the little shells that we call buckies; I think periwinkle is the English name. Of these two I made my whole diet, devouring them cold and raw as I found them; and so hungry was I, that at first they seemed to me delicious.

Perhaps they were out of season, or perhaps there was something wrong in the sea about my island. But at least I had no sooner eaten my first meal than I was seized with giddiness and retching, and lay for a long time no better than dead. A second trial of the same food (indeed I had no other) did better with me, and revived my strength. But as long as I was on the island, I never knew what to expect when I had eaten; sometimes all was well, and sometimes I was thrown into a miserable sickness; nor could I ever distinguish what particular fish it was that hurt me.

All day it streamed rain; the island ran like a sop, there was no dry spot to be found; and when I lay down that night, between two boulders that made a kind of roof, my feet were in a bog.

The second day I crossed the island to all sides. There was no one part of it better than another; it was all desolate and rocky; nothing living on it but game birds which I lacked the means to kill, and the gulls which haunted the outlying rocks in a prodigious number. But the creek, or strait, that cut off the isle from the main land of the Ross, opened out on the north into a bay, and the bay again opened into the sound of Iona; and it was the neighbourhood of this place that I chose to be my home; though if I had thought upon the very name of home in such a spot, I must have burst out weeping.

I had good reasons for my choice. There was in this part of the isle a little hut of a house like a pig's hut, where fishers used to sleep when they came there upon their business; but the turf roof of it had fallen entirely in; so that the hut was of no use to me, and gave me less shelter than my rocks. What was more important, the shell-fish on which I lived grew there in great plenty; when the tide was out I could gather a peck at a time: and this was doubtless a convenience. But the other reason went deeper. I had become in no way used to the horrid solitude of the isle, but still looked round me on all sides (like a man that was hunted), between fear and hope that I might see some human creature coming. Now, from a little up the hill-side over the bay, I could catch a sight of the great, ancient church and the roofs of the people's houses in Iona. And on the other hand, over the low country of the Ross, I saw smoke go up, morning and evening, as if from a homestead in a hollow of the land.

I used to watch this smoke, when I was wet and cold, and had my head half turned with loneliness; and think of the fireside and the company, till my heart burned. It was the same with the roofs of Iona. Altogether, this sight I had of men's homes and comfortable lives, although it put a point on my own sufferings, yet it kept hope alive, and helped me to eat my raw shell-fish (which had soon grown to be a disgust) and saved me from the sense of horror I had whenever I was quite alone with dead rocks, and fowls, and the rain, and the cold sea.

I say it kept hope alive; and indeed it seemed impossible that I should be left to die on the shores of my own country, and within view of a church tower and the smoke of men's houses. But the second day passed; and though as long as the light lasted I kept a bright look-out for boats on the Sound or men passing on the Ross, no help came near me. It still rained, and I turned in to sleep, as wet as ever, and with a cruel sore throat, but a little comforted, perhaps, by having said good-night to my next neighbours, the people of Iona.

Charles the Second declared a man could stay outdoors more days in the year in the climate of England than in any other. This was very like a king, with a palace at his back and changes of dry clothes. But he must have had better luck on his flight from Worcester than I had on that miserable isle. It was the height of the summer; yet it rained for more than twenty-four hours, and did not clear until the afternoon of the third day.

This was the day of incidents. In the morning I saw a red deer, a buck with a fine spread of antlers, standing in the rain on the top of the island; but he had scarce seen me rise from under my rock, before he trotted off upon the other side. I supposed he must have swum the strait; though what should bring any creature to Earraid, was more than I could fancy.

A little after, as I was jumping about after my limpets, I was startled by a guinea-piece, which fell upon a rock in front of me and glanced off into the sea. When the sailors gave me my money again, they kept back not only about a third of the whole sum, but my father's leather purse; so that from that day out, I carried my gold loose in a pocket with a button. I now saw there must be a hole, and clapped my hand to the place in a great hurry. But this was to lock the stable-door after the steed was stolen. I had left the shore at Queen's Ferry with near on fifty pounds; now I found no more than two guinea-pieces and a silver shilling.

It is true I picked up a third guinea a little after, where it lay shining on a piece of turf. That made a fortune of three pounds and four shillings, English money, for a lad, the rightful heir of an estate, and now starving on an isle at the extreme end of the wild Highlands.

This state of my affairs dashed me still further; and indeed my plight on that third morning was truly pitiful. My clothes were beginning to rot; my stockings in particular were quite worn through, so that my shanks went naked; my hands had grown quite soft with the continual soaking; my throat was very sore, my strength had much abated, and my heart so turned against the horrid stuff I was condemned to eat, that the very sight of it came near to sicken me.

And yet the worst was not yet come.

There is a pretty high rock on the north-west of Earraid, which (because it had a flat top and overlooked the Sound) I was much in the habit of frequenting; not that ever I stayed in one place, save when asleep, my misery giving me no rest. Indeed, I wore myself down with continual and aimless goings and comings in the rain.

As soon, however, as the sun came out, I lay down on the top of that rock to dry myself. The comfort of the sunshine is a thing I cannot tell. It set me thinking hopefully of my deliverance, of which I had begun to despair; and I scanned the sea and the Ross with a fresh interest. On the south of my rock, a part of the island jutted out and hid the open ocean, so that a boat could thus come quite near me upon that side, and I be none the wiser.

Well, all of a sudden, a coble with a brown sail and a pair of fishers aboard of it, came flying round that corner of the isle, bound for Iona. I shouted out, and then fell on my knees on the rock and reached up my hands and prayed to them. They were near enough to hear—I could even see the colour of their hair; and there was no doubt but they observed me, for they cried out in the Gaelic tongue, and laughed. But the boat never turned aside, and flew on, right before my eyes, for Iona.

I could not believe such wickedness, and ran along the shore from rock to rock, crying on them piteously; even after they were out of reach of my voice, I still cried and waved to them; and when they were quite gone, I thought my heart would have burst. All the time of my troubles I wept only twice. Once, when I could not reach the yard, and now, the second time, when these fishers turned a deaf ear to my cries. But this time I wept and roared like a wicked child, tearing up the turf with my nails, and grinding my face in the earth. If a wish would kill men, those two fishers would never have seen morning, and I should likely have died upon my island.

When I was a little over my anger, I must eat again, but

with such loathing of the mess as I could now scarce
control. Sure enough, I should have done as well to fast,
for my fishes poisoned me again. I had all my first pains;
my throat was so sore I could scarce swallow; I had a fit of
strong shuddering, which clucked my teeth together; and
there came on me that dreadful sense of illness, which we
have no name for either in Scots or English. I thought I
should have died, and made my peace with God, forgiving
all men, even my uncle and the fishers; and as soon as I
had thus made up my mind to the worst, clearness came
upon me; I observed the night was falling dry; my clothes
were dried a good deal; truly, I was in a better case than
ever before, since I had landed on the isle; and so I got to
sleep at last, with a thought of gratitude.

The next day (which was the fourth of this horrible life
of mine) I found my bodily strength run very low. But the
sun shone, the air was sweet, and what I managed to eat
of the shell-fish agreed well with me and revived my
courage.

I was scarce back on my rock (where I went always the
first thing after I had eaten) before I observed a boat
coming down the Sound, and with her head, as I thought,
in my direction.

I began at once to hope and fear exceedingly; for I
thought these men might have thought better of their
cruelty and be coming back to my assistance. But another
disappointment, such as yesterday's, was more than I could
bear. I turned my back, accordingly, upon the sea, and
did not look again till I had counted many hundreds. The
boat was still heading for the island. The next time I
counted the full thousand, as slowly as I could, my heart
beating so as to hurt me. And then it was out of all
question! She was coming straight to Earraid!

I could no longer hold myself back, but ran to the
sea-side and out, from one rock to another, as far as I
could go. It is a marvel I was not drowned; for when I was
brought to a stand at last, my legs shook under me, and
my mouth was so dry, I must wet it with the sea-water
before I was able to shout.

All this time the boat was coming on; and now I was
able to perceive it was the same boat and the same two

men as yesterday. This I knew by their hair, which the one had of a bright yellow and the other black. But now there was a third man along with them, who looked to be of a better class.

As soon as they were come within easy speech, they let down their sail and lay quiet. In spite of my supplications, they drew no nearer in, and what frightened me most of all, the new man tee-hee'd with laughter as he talked and looked at me.

Then he stood up in the boat and addressed me a long while, speaking fast and with many wavings of his hand. I told him I had no Gaelic; and at this he became very angry, and I began to suspect he thought he was talking English. Listening very close, I caught the word "whateffer" several times; but all the rest was Gaelic and might have been Greek and Hebrew for me.

"Whatever," said I, to show him I had caught a word.

"Yes, yes—yes, yes," says he, and then he looked at the other men, as much as to say, "I told you I spoke English," and began again as hard as ever in the Gaelic.

This time I picked out another word, "tide." Then I had a flash of hope. I remembered he was always waving his hand towards the mainland of the Ross.

"Do you mean when the tide is out——?" I cried, and could not finish.

"Yes, yes," said he. "Tide."

At that I turned tail upon their boat (where my adviser had once more begun to tee-hee with laughter), leaped back the way I had come, from one stone to another, and set off running across the isle as I had never run before. In about half an hour I came out upon the shores of the creek; and, sure enough, it was shrunk into a little trickle of water through which I dashed, not above my knees, and landed with a shout on the main island.

A sea-bred boy would not have stayed a day on Earraid; which is only what they call a tidal islet, and except in the bottom of the neaps, can be entered and left twice in every twenty-four hours, either dry-shod, or at the most by wading. Even I, who had the tide going out and in before me in the bay, and even watched for the ebbs, the better to get my shell-fish—even I (I say) if I had sat down to think, instead of raging at my fate, must have soon guessed the secret, and got free. It was no wonder the fishers had not understood me. The wonder was rather that they had ever guessed my pitiful illusion, and taken the trouble to come back. I had starved with cold and hunger on that island for close upon one hundred hours. But for the fishers, I might have left my bones there, in pure folly. And even as it was, I had paid for it pretty dear, not only in past sufferings, but in my present case; being clothed like a beggar-man, scarce able to walk, and in great pain of my sore throat.

I have seen wicked men and fools, a great many of both; and I believe they both get paid in the end; but the fools first.

Chapter 15

THE LAD WITH THE SILVER BUTTON: THROUGH THE ISLE OF MULL

The Ross of Mull, which I had now got upon, was rugged and trackless, like the isle I had just left; being all bog, and briar, and big stone. There may be roads for them that know that country well; but for my part I had no better guide than my own nose, and no other landmark than Ben More.

I aimed as well as I could for the smoke I had seen so often from the island; and with all my great weariness and the difficulty of the way came upon the house in the bottom of a little hollow about five or six at night. It was low and longish, roofed with turf and built of unmortared stones; and on a mound in front of it, an old gentleman sat smoking his pipe in the sun.

With what little English he had, he gave me to understand that my shipmates had got safe ashore, and had broken bread in that very house on the day after.

"Was there one," I asked, "dressed like a gentleman?"

He said they all wore rough great-coats; but to be sure, the first of them, the one that came alone, wore breeches and stockings, while the rest had sailors' trousers.

"Ah," said I, "and he would have a feathered hat?"

He told me, no, that he was bareheaded like myself. At first I thought Alan might have lost his hat; and then the rain came in my mind, and I judged it more likely he had it out of harm's way under his great-coat. This set me smiling, partly because my friend was safe, partly to think of his vanity in dress.

And then the old gentleman clapped his hand to his

brow, and cried out that I must be the lad with the silver
button.

"Why, yes!" said I, in some wonder.

"Well, then," said the old gentleman, "I have a word for
you, that you are to follow your friend to his country, by
Torosay."

He then asked me how I had fared, and I told him my
tale. A south-country man would certainly have laughed;
but this old gentleman (I call him so because of his manners, for his clothes were dropping off his back) heard me
all through with nothing but gravity and pity. When I had
done, he took me by the hand, led me into his hut (it was
no better) and presented me before his wife, as if she had
been the Queen and I a duke.

The good woman set oat-bread before me and a cold
grouse, patting my shoulder and smiling to me all the
time, for she had no English; and the old gentleman (not
to be behind) brewed me a strong punch out of their
country spirit. All the while I was eating, and after that
when I was drinking the punch, I could scarce come to
believe in my good fortune; and the house, though it was
thick with the peat-smoke and as full of holes as a colan-
der, seemed like a palace.

The punch threw me in a strong sweat and a deep
slumber; the good people let me lie; and it was near noon
of the next day before I took the road, my throat already
easier and my spirits quite restored by good fare and good
news. The old gentleman, although I pressed him hard,
would take no money, and gave me an old bonnet for my
head; though I am free to own I was no sooner out of view
of the house, than I very jealously washed this gift of his in
a wayside fountain.

Thought I to myself: "If these are the wild Highlanders,
I could wish my own folk wilder."

I not only started late, but I must have wandered nearly
half the time. True, I met plenty of people, grubbing in
little miserable fields that would not keep a cat, or herding
little kine about the bigness of asses. The Highland dress
being forbidden by law since the rebellion, and the people
condemned to the Lowland habit, which they much disliked, it was strange to see the variety of their array.

Some went bare, only for a hanging cloak or great-coat, and carried their trousers on their backs like a useless burthen: some had made an imitation of the tartan with little parti-coloured stripes patched together like an old wife's quilt; others, again, still wore the Highland phila-beg,[1] but by putting a few stitches between the legs, transformed it into a pair of trousers like a Dutchman's. All those makeshifts were condemned and punished, for the law was harshly applied, in hopes to break up the clan spirit; but in that out-of-the-way, sea-bound isle, there were few to make remarks and fewer to tell tales.

They seemed in great poverty; which was no doubt natural, now that rapine was put down, and the chiefs kept no longer an open house; and the roads (even such a wandering, country by-track as the one I followed) were infested with beggars. And here again I marked a differ-ence from my own part of the country. For our Lowland beggars—even the gownsmen themselves, who beg by patent—had a louting, flattering way with them, and if you gave them a plack[2] and asked change, would very civilly return you a boddle.[3] But these Highland beggars stood on their dignity, asked alms only to buy snuff (by their account) and would give no change.

To be sure, this was no concern of mine, except in so far as it entertained me by the way. What was much more to the purpose, few had any English, and these few (unless they were of the brotherhood of beggars) not very anxious to place it at my service. I knew Torosay to be my destina-tion, and repeated the name to them and pointed; but instead of simply pointing in reply, they would give me a screed of the Gaelic that set me foolish; so it was small wonder if I went out of my road as often as I stayed in it.

At last, about eight at night, and already very weary, I came to a lone house, where I asked admittance, and was refused, until I bethought me of the power of money in so poor a country, and held up one of my guineas in my finger and thumb. Thereupon, the man of the house, who had hitherto pretended to have no English, and driven me from his door by signals, suddenly began to speak as

---

[1]Kilt.   [2]Four-penny coin.   [3]Two-penny coin.

clearly as was needful, and agreed for five shillings to give me a night's lodging and guide me the next day to Torosay.

I slept uneasily that night, fearing I should be robbed; but I might have spared myself the pain; for my host was no robber, only miserably poor and a great cheat. He was not alone in his poverty; for the next morning, we must go five miles about to the house of what he called a rich man to have one of my guineas changed. This was perhaps a rich man for Mull; he would have scarce been thought so in the south; for it took all he had—the whole house was turned upside down, and a neighbour brought under contribution, before he could scrape together twenty shillings in silver. The odd shilling he kept for himself, protesting he could ill afford to have so great a sum of money lying "locked up." For all that he was very courteous and well spoken, made us both sit down with his family to dinner, and brewed punch in a fine china bowl, over which my rascal guide grew so merry that he refused to start.

I was for getting angry, and appealed to the rich man (Hector Maclean was his name), who had been a witness to our bargain and to my payment of the five shillings. But Maclean had taken his share of the punch, and vowed that no gentleman should leave his table after the bowl was brewed; so there was nothing for it but to sit and hear Jacobite toasts and Gaelic songs, 'till all were tipsy and staggered off to the bed or the barn for their night's rest.

Next day (the fourth of my travels) we were up before five upon the clock; but my rascal guide got to the bottle at once, and it was three hours before I had him clear of the house, and then (as you shall hear) only for a worse disappointment.

As long as we went down a heathery valley that lay before Mr. Maclean's house, all went well; only my guide looked constantly over his shoulder, and when I asked him the cause, only grinned at me. No sooner, however, had we crossed the back of a hill, and got out of sight of the house windows, then he told me Torosay lay right in front, and that a hill-top (which he pointed out) was my best landmark.

"I care very little for that," said I, "since you are going with me."

The impudent cheat answered me in the Gaelic that he had no English.

"My fine fellow," I said, "I know very well your English comes and goes. Tell me what will bring it back? Is it more money you wish?"

"Five shillings mair," said he, "and hersel' will bring ye there."

I reflected a while and then offered him two, which he accepted greedily, and insisted on having in his hands at once— "for luck," as he said, but I think it was rather for my misfortune.

The two shillings carried him not quite as many miles; at the end of which distance, he sat down upon the way-side and took off his brogues from his feet, like a man about to rest.

I was now red-hot. "Ha!" said I, "have you no more English?"

He said impudently, "No."

At that I boiled over, and lifted my hand to strike him; and he, drawing a knife from his rags, squatted back and grinned at me like a wild-cat. At that, forgetting every-thing but my anger, I ran in upon him, put aside his knife with my left, and struck him in the mouth with the right. I was a strong lad and very angry, and he but a little man; and he went down before me heavily. By good luck, his knife flew out of his hand as he fell.

I picked up both that and his brogues, wished him a good-morning, and set off upon my way, leaving him barefoot and disarmed. I chuckled to myself as I went, being sure I was done with that rogue, for a variety of reasons. First, he knew he could have no more of my money; next, the brogues were worth in that country only a few pence; and lastly, the knife, which was really a dagger, it was against the law for him to carry.

In about half an hour of walk, I overtook a great, ragged man, moving pretty fast but feeling before him with a staff. He was quite blind, and told me he was a catechist, which should have put me at my ease. But his face went against me; it seemed dark and dangerous and secret; and presently, as we began to go on alongside, I saw the steel butt of a pistol sticking from under the flap of his coat-pocket. To carry such a thing meant a fine of fifteen pounds sterling upon a first offence, and transportation to the colonies upon a second. Nor could I quite see why a religious teacher should go armed, or what a blind man could be doing with a pistol.

I told him about my guide, for I was proud of what I had done, and my vanity for once got the heels of my prudence. At the mention of the five shillings he cried out so loud that I made up my mind I should say nothing of the other two, and was glad he could not see my blushes.

"Was it too much?" I asked, a little faltering.

"Too much!" cries he. "Why, I will guide you to Torosay myself for a dram of brandy. And give you the great pleasure of my company (me that is a man of some learning) in the bargain."

I said I did not see how a blind man could be a guide: but at that he laughed aloud, and said his stick was eyes enough for an eagle.

"In the Isle of Mull, at least," says he, "where I knew every stone and heather-bush by mark of head. See, now," he said, striking right and left, as if to make sure, "down there a burn is running; and at the head of it there stands a bit of a small hill with a stone cocked upon the top of that; and it's hard at the foot of the hill, that the way runs by to Torosay; and the way here, being for droves, is plainly trodden, and will show grassy through the heather."

I had to own he was right in every feature, and told my wonder.

"Ha!" says he, "that's nothing. Would ye believe me now, that before the Act came out, and when there were weapons in this country, I could shoot? Ay, could I!" cries he, and then with a leer: "If ye had such a thing as a pistol here to try with, I would show ye how it's done."

I told him I had nothing of the sort, and gave him a wider berth. If he had known, his pistol stuck at that time quite plainly out of his pocket, and I could see the sun twinkle on the steel of the butt. But by the better luck for me, he knew nothing, thought all was covered, and lied on in the dark.

He then began to question me cunningly, where I came from, whether I was rich, whether I could change a five-shilling piece for him (which he declared he had that moment in his sporran[1]), and all the time he kept edging up to me and I avoiding him. We were now upon a sort of green cattle-track which crossed the hills towards Torosay, and we kept changing sides upon that like dancers in a reel. I had so plainly the upper hand that my spirits rose, and indeed I took a pleasure in this game of blindman's buff; but the catechist grew angrier and angrier, and at last began to swear in Gaelic and to strike for my legs with his staff.

Then I told him that, sure enough, I had a pistol in my pocket as well as he, and if he did not strike across the hill due south I would even blow his brains out.

He became at once very polite; and after trying to soften me for some time, but quite in vain, he cursed me once more in Gaelic and took himself off. I watched him striding along, through bog and briar, tapping with his stick, until he turned the end of a hill and disappeared in the next hollow. Then I struck on again for Torosay, much better pleased to be alone than to travel with that man of learning. This was an unlucky day; and these two, of whom I had just rid myself, one after the other, were the two worst men I met with in the Highlands.

At Torosay, on the Sound of Mull and looking over to the mainland of Morven, there was an inn with an innkeeper, who was a Maclean, it appeared, of a very high family; for to keep an inn is thought even more genteel in the Highlands than it is with us, perhaps as partaking of hospitality, or perhaps because the trade is idle and drunken. He spoke good English, and finding me to be something of a scholar, tried me first in French, where he easily beat me, and then in the Latin, in which I don't know which of us did best. This pleasant rivalry put us at once upon friendly terms; and I sat up and drank punch with him (or to be more correct, sat up and watched him drink it), until he was so tipsy that he wept upon my shoulder.

I tried him, as if by accident, with a sight of Alan's button; but it was plain he had never seen or heard of it.

[1]Highland purse.

Indeed, he bore some grudge against the family and friends of Ardshiel, and before he was drunk he read me a lampoon, in very good Latin, but with a very ill meaning, which he had made in elegiac verses upon a person of that house.

When I told him of my catechist, he shook his head, and said I was lucky to have got clear off. "That is a very dangerous man," he said; "Duncan Mackiegh is his name; he can shoot by the ear at several yards, and has been often accused of highway robberies, and once of murder."

"The cream of it is," says I, "that he called himself a catechist."

"And why should he not?" says he, "when that is what he is. It was Maclean of Duart gave it to him because he was blind. But, perhaps it was a peety," says my host, "for he is always on the road, going from one place to another to hear the young folk say their religion; and, doubtless, that is a great temptation to the poor man."

At last, when my landlord could drink no more, he showed me to a bed, and I lay down in very good spirits; having travelled the greater part of that big and crooked Island of Mull, from Earraid to Torosay, fifty miles as the crow flies, and (with my wanderings) much nearer a hundred, in four days and with little fatigue. Indeed, I was by far in better heart and health of body at the end of that long tramp than I had been at the beginning.

Chapter 16

THE LAD WITH THE SILVER BUTTON: ACROSS MORVEN

There is a regular ferry from Torosay to Kinlochaline on the mainland. Both shores of the Sound are in the country of the strong clan of the Macleans, and the people that passed the ferry with me were almost all of that clan. The skipper of the boat, on the other hand, was called Neil Roy Macrob; and since Macrob was one of the names of Alan's clansmen, and Alan himself had sent me to that ferry, I was eager to come to private speech of Neil Roy.

In the crowded boat this was of course impossible, and the passage was a very slow affair. There was no wind, and as the boat was wretchedly equipped, we could pull but two oars on one side, and one on the other. The men gave way, however, with a good will, the passengers taking spells to help them, and the whole company giving the time in Gaelic boatsongs. And what with the songs, and the sea air, and the good-nature and spirit of all concerned, and the bright weather, the passage was a pretty thing to have seen.

But there was one melancholy part. In the mouth of Loch Aline we found a great seagoing ship at anchor; and this I supposed at first to be one of the King's cruisers which were kept along that coast, both summer and winter, to prevent communication with the French. As we got a little nearer, it became plain she was a ship of merchandise; and what still more puzzled me, not only her decks, but the seabeach also, were quite black with people, and skiffs were continually plying to and fro between them. Yet nearer, and there began to come to our ears a great sound of mourning, the people on board and those on the shore crying and lamenting one to another so as to pierce the heart.

Then I understood this was an emigrant ship bound for the American colonies.

We put the ferry-boat alongside, and the exiles leaned over the bulwarks, weeping and reaching out their hands to my fellow-passengers, among whom they counted some near friends. How long this might have gone on I do not know, for they seemed to have no sense of time: but at last the captain of the ship, who seemed near beside himself (and no great wonder) in the midst of this crying and confusion, came to the side and begged us to depart.

Thereupon Neil sheered off; and the chief singer in our boat struck into a melancholy air, which was presently taken up both by the emigrants and their friends upon the beach, so that it sounded from all sides like a lament for the dying. I saw the tears run down the cheeks of the men and women in the boat, even as they bent at the oars; and the circumstances and the music of the song (which is one called "Lochaber no more") were highly affecting even to myself.

At Kinlochaline I got Neil Roy upon one side of the beach, and said I made sure he was one of Appin's men.

"And what for no?" said he.

"I am seeking somebody," said I; "and it comes in my mind that you will have news of him. Alan Breck Stewart is his name." And very foolishly, instead of showing him the button, I sought to pass a shilling in his hand.

At this he drew back. "I am very much affronted," he said; "and this is not the way that one shentleman should behave to another at all. The man you ask for is in France; but if he was in my sporran," says he, "and your belly full of shillings, I would not hurt a hair upon his body."

I saw I had gone the wrong way to work, and without wasting time upon apologies, showed him the button lying in the hollow of my palm.

"Aweel, aweel," said Neil; "and I think ye might have begun with that end of the stick, whatever! But if ye are the lad with the silver button, all is well, and I have the word to see that ye come safe. But if ye will pardon me to speak plainly," says he, "there is a name that you should

never take into your mouth, and that is the name of Alan
Breck; and there is a thing that ye would never do, and
that is to offer your dirty money to a Hieland shentleman."

It was not very easy to apologise; for I could scarce tell
him (what was the truth) that I had never dreamed he
would set up to be a gentleman until he told me so. Neil
on his part had no wish to prolong his dealings with me,
only to fulfil his orders and be done with it; and he made
haste to give me my route. This was to lie the night in
Kinlochaline in the public inn; to cross Morven the next
day to Ardgour, and lie the night in the house of one John
of the Claymore, who was warned that I might come; the
third day, to be set across one loch at Corran and another
at Balachulish, and then ask my way to the house of James
of the Glens, at Aucharn in Duror of Appin. There was a
good deal of ferrying, as you hear; the sea in all this part
running deep into the mountains and winding about their
roots. It makes the country strong to hold and difficult to
travel, but full of prodigious wild and dreadful prospects.

I had some other advice from Neil: to speak with no one
by the way, to avoid Whigs, Campbells, and the "red-
soldiers"; to leave the road and lie in a bush if I saw any
of the latter coming, "for it was never chancy to meet in
with them"; and in brief, to conduct myself like a robber
or a Jacobite agent, as perhaps Neil thought me.

The inn at Kinlochaline was the most beggarly vile place
that ever pigs were styed in, full of smoke, vermin, and
silent Highlanders. I was not only discontented with my
lodging, but with myself for my mismanagement of Neil,
and thought I could hardly be worse off. But very wrong-
ly, as I was soon to see; for I had not been half an hour at
the inn (standing in the door most of the time, to ease my
eyes from the peat smoke) when a thunderstorm came
close by, the springs broke in a little hill on which the inn
stood, and one end of the house became a running water.
Places of public entertainment were bad enough all over
Scotland in those days; yet it was a wonder to myself,
when I had to go from the fireside to the bed in which I
slept, wading over the shoes.

Early in my next day's journey I overtook a little, stout,
solemn man, walking very slowly with his toes turned out,

sometimes reading in a book and sometimes marking the place with his finger, and dressed decently and plainly in something of a clerical style.

This I found to be another catechist, but of a different order from the blind man of Mull: being indeed one of those sent out by the Edinburgh Society for Propagating Christian Knowledge, to evangelise the more savage places of the Highlands. His name was Henderland; he spoke with the broad south-country tongue, which I was beginning to weary for the sound of; and besides common countryship, we soon found we had a more particular bond of interest. For my good friend, the minister of Essendean, had translated into the Gaelic in his by-time a number of hymns and pious books, which Henderland used in his work, and held in great esteem. Indeed, it was one of these he was carrying and reading when we met.

We fell in company at once, our ways lying together as far as to Kingairloch. As we went, he stopped and spoke with all the wayfarers and workers that we met or passed; and though of course I could not tell what they discoursed about, yet I judged Mr. Henderland must be well liked in the country-side, for I observed many of them to bring out their mulls[1] and share a pinch of snuff with him.

I told him as far in my affairs as I judged wise; as far, that is, as they were none of Alan's; and gave Balachulish as the place I was traveling to, to meet a friend; for I thought Aucharn, or even Duror, would be too particular, and might put him on the scent.

On his part, he told me much of his work and the people he worked among, the hiding priests and Jacobites, the Disarming Act, the dress, and many other curiosities of the time and place. He seemed moderate; blaming Parliament in several points, and especially because they had framed the Act more severely against those who wore the dress than against those who carried weapons.

This moderation put it in my mind to question him of the Red Fox and the Appin tenants; questions which, I thought, would seem natural enough in the mouth of one travelling to that country.

[1] Snuff boxes.

He said it was a bad business. "It's wonderful," said he, "where the tenants find the money, for their life is mere starvation. (Ye don't carry such a thing as snuff, do ye, Mr. Balfour? No. Well, I'm better wanting it.) But these tenants (as I was saying) are doubtless partly driven to it. James Stewart in Duror (that's him they call James of the Glens) is half-brother to Ardshiel, the captain of the clan; and he is a man much looked up to, and drives very hard. And then there's one they call Alan Breck—"

"Ah!" I cried, "what of him?"

"What of the wind that bloweth where it listeth?" said Henderland. "He's here and awa'; here to-day and gone to-morrow: a fair heather-cat. He might be glowering at the two of us out of yon whin-bush,[1] and I wouldna wonder! Ye'll no carry such a thing as snuff, will ye?"

I told him no, and that he had asked the same thing more than once.

"It's highly possible," said he, sighing. "But it seems strange ye shouldna carry it. However, as I was saying, this Alan Breck is a bold, desperate customer, and well kennt to be James's right hand. His life is forfeit already; he would boggle[2] at naething; and maybe, if a tenant-body was to hang back he would get a dirk in his wame.[3]"

"You make a poor story of it all, Mr. Henderland," said I. "If it is all fear upon both sides, I care to hear no more of it."

"Na," said Mr. Henderland, "but there's love too, and self-denial that should put the like of you and me to shame. There's something fine about it; no' perhaps Christian, but humanly fine. Even Alan Breck, by all that I hear, is a chield to be respected. There's many a lying sneck-draw[4] sits close in kirk in our own part of the country, and stands well in the world's eye, and maybe is a far worse man, Mr. Balfour, than yon misguided shedder of man's blood. Ay, ay, we might take a lesson by them. —Ye'll perhaps think I've been too long in the Hielands?" he added, smiling to me.

I told him not at all; that I had seen much to admire

---

[1]Gorse-bush (a spiny shrub).   [2]Take fright.   [3]Belly.   [4]Crafty fellow.

among the Highlanders; and if he came to that, Mr. Campbell himself was a Highlander.

"Ay," said he, "that's true. It's a fine blood."

"And what is the King's agent about?" I asked.

"Colin Campbell?" says Henderland. "Putting his head
in a bees' byke!"

"He is to turn the tenants out by force, I hear?" said I.

"Yes," says he, "but the business has gone back and
forth, as folk say. First, James of the Glens rode to Edinburgh, and got some lawyer (a Stewart, nae doubt—they
all hing together like bats in a steeple) and had the proceedings stayed. And then Colin Campbell cam' in again,
and had the upper hand before the Barons of Exchequer.
And now they tell me the first of the tenants are to flit
to-morrow. It's to begin at Duror under James's very
windows, which doesna seem wise by my humble way of
it."

"Do you think they'll fight?" I asked.

"Well," says Henderland, "they're disarmed—or supposed to be—for there's still a good deal of cold iron lying
by in quiet places. And then Colin Campbell has the
sogers coming. But for all that, if I was his lady wife, I
wouldna be well pleased till I got him home again. They're
queer customers, the Appin Stewarts."

I asked if they were worse than their neighbours.

"No they," said he. "And that's the worst part of it. For
if Colin Roy can get his business done in Appin, he has it
all to begin again in the next country, which they call
Mamore, and which is one of the countries of the Camerons. He's King's factor upon both, and from both he has
to drive out the tenants; and indeed, Mr. Balfour (to be
open with ye), it's my belief that if he escapes the one lot,
he'll get his death by the other."

So we continued talking and walking the great part of
the day; until at last, Mr. Henderland, after expressing his
delight in my company, and satisfaction at meeting with a
friend of Mr. Campbell's ("whom," says he, "I will make
bold to call that sweet singer of our covenanted Zion"),
proposed that I should make a short stage, and lie the
night in his house a little beyond Kingairloch. To say

truth, I was overjoyed; for I had no great desire for John of the Claymore, and since my double misadventure, first with the guide and next with the gentleman skipper, I stood in some fear of any Highland stranger. Accordingly we shook hands upon the bargain, and came in the afternoon to a small house, standing alone by the shore of the Linnhe Loch. The sun was already gone from the desert mountains of Ardgour upon the hither side, but shone on those of Appin on the farther; the loch lay as still as a lake, only the gulls were crying round the sides of it; and the whole place seemed solemn and uncouth.

We had no sooner come to the door of Mr. Henderland's dwelling, than to my great surprise (for I was now used to the politeness of Highlanders) he burst rudely past me, dashed into the room, caught up a jar and a small horn spoon, and began ladling snuff into his nose in most excessive quantities. Then he had a hearty fit of sneezing, and looked round upon me with a rather silly smile.

"It's a vow I took," says he. "I took a vow upon me that I wouldna carry it. Doubtless it's a great privation; but when I think upon the martyrs, not only to the Scottish Covenant but to other points of Christianity, I think shame to mind it."

As soon as we had eaten (and porridge and whey was the best of the good man's diet) he took a grave face and said he had a duty to perform by Mr. Campbell, and that was to inquire into my state of mind towards God. I was inclined to smile at him since the business of the snuff; but he had not spoken long before he brought the tears into my eyes. There are two things that men should never weary of: goodness and humility; we get none too much of them in this rough world among cold, proud people; but Mr. Henderland had their very speech upon his tongue. And though I was a good deal puffed up with my adventures and with having come off, as the saying is, with flying colours; yet he soon had me on my knees beside a simple, poor old man, and both proud and glad to be there.

Before we went to bed he offered me sixpence to help me on my way, out of a scanty store he kept in the turf wall of his house; at which excess of goodness I knew not what to do. But at last he was so earnest with me, that I thought it the more mannerly part to let him have his way, and so left him poorer than myself.

Chapter 17

THE DEATH OF THE RED FOX

The next day Mr. Henderland found for me a man who had a boat of his own and was to cross the Linnhe Loch that afternoon into Appin, fishing. Him he prevailed on to take me, for he was one of his flock; and in this way I saved a long day's travel and the price of the two public ferries I must otherwise have passed.

It was near noon before we set out; a dark day with clouds, and the sun shining upon little patches. The sea was here very deep and still, and had scarce a wave upon it; so that I must put the water to my lips before I could believe it to be truly salt. The mountains on either side were high, rough and barren, very black and gloomy in the shadow of the clouds, but all silver-laced with little water-courses where the sun shone upon them. It seemed a hard country, this of Appin, for people to care as much about as Alan did.

There was but one thing to mention. A little after we had started, the sun shone upon a little moving clump of scarlet close in along the waterside to the north. It was much of the same red as soldiers' coats; every now and then, too, there came little sparks and lightnings, as though the sun had struck upon bright steel.

I asked my boatman what it should be; and he answered he supposed it was some of the red soldiers coming from Fort William into Appin, against the poor tenantry of the country. Well, it was a sad sight to me; and whether it was because of my thoughts of Alan, or from something prophetic in my bosom, although this was but the second time I had seen King George's troops, I had no goodwill to them.

At last we came so near the point of land at the entering in of Loch Leven that I begged to be set on shore. My boatman (who was an honest fellow and mindful of his promise to the catechist) would fain have carried me on to Balachulish; but as this was to take me farther from my secret destination, I insisted, and was set on shore at last under the wood of Lettermore (or Lettervore, for I have heard it both ways) in Alan's country of Appin.

This was a wood of birches, growing on a steep, craggy side of a mountain that overhung the loch. It had many openings and ferny howes; and a road or bridle track ran north and south through the midst of it, by the edge of which, where was a spring, I sat down to eat some oat-bread of Mr. Henderland's, and think upon my situation.

Here I was not only troubled by a cloud of stinging midges, but far more by the doubts of my mind. What I ought to do, why I was going to join myself with an outlaw and a would-be murderer like Alan, whether I should not be acting more like a man of sense to tramp back to the south country direct, by my own guidance and at my own charges, and what Mr. Campbell or even Mr. Henderland would think of me if they should ever learn my folly and presumption: these were the doubts that now began to come in on me stronger than ever.

As I was so sitting and thinking, a sound of men and horses came to me through the wood; and presently after, at a turning of the road, I saw four travellers come into view. The way was in this part so rough and narrow that they came single and led their horses by the reins. The first was a great, red-headed gentleman, of an imperious and flushed face, who carried his hat in his hand and fanned himself, for he was in a breathing heat. The second, by his decent black garb and white wig, I correctly took to be a lawyer. The third was a servant, and wore some part of his clothes in tartan, which showed that his master was of a Highland family, and either an outlaw or else in singular good odour with the Government, since the wearing of tartan was against the Act. If I had been better versed in these things, I would have known the tartan to

be of the Argyle (or Campbell) colours. This servant had a
good-sized portmanteau strapped on his horse, and a net
of lemons (to brew punch with) hanging at the saddle bow;
as was often enough the custom with luxurious travellers
in that part of the country.

As for the fourth, who brought up the tail, I had seen
his like before, and knew him at once to be a sheriff's
officer.

I had no sooner seen these people coming than I made
up my mind (for no reason that I can tell) to go through
with my adventure; and when the first came alongside of
me, I rose up from the bracken and asked him the way to
Aucharn.

He stopped and looked at me, as I thought, a little
oddly; and then, turning to the lawyer, "Mungo," said he,
"there's many a man would think this more of a warning
than two pyats.[1] Here am I on my road to Duror on the
job ye ken; and here is a young lad starts up out of the
bracken, and speers[2] if I am on the way to Aucharn."

"Glenure," said the other, "this is an ill subject for
jesting."

These two had now drawn close up and were gazing at
me, while the two followers had halted about a stone-cast
in the rear.

"And what seek ye in Aucharn?" said Colin Roy Campbell of Glenure; him they called the Red Fox; for he it was
that I had stopped.

"The man that lives there," said I.

"James of the Glens," says Glenure, musingly; and then
to the lawyer: "Is he gathering his people, think ye?"

"Anyway," says the lawyer, "we shall do better to bide
where we are, and let the soldiers rally us."

"If you are concerned for me," said I, "I am neither of
his people nor yours, but an honest subject of King George,
owing no man and fearing no man."

"Why, very well said," replies the Factor. "But if I may
make so bold as ask, what does this honest man so far from
his country? and why does he come seeking the brother of
Ardshiel? I have power here, I must tell you. I am King's

---

[1]Magpies.   [2]Asks.

Factor upon several of these estates, and have twelve files of soldiers at my back."

"I have heard a waif word in the country," said I, a little nettled, "that you were a hard man to drive."

He still kept looking at me, as if in doubt.

"Well," said he, at last, "your tongue is bold; but I am no unfriend to plainness. If ye had asked me the way to the door of James Stewart on any other day but this, I would have set ye right and bidden ye God-speed. But to-day—eh, Mungo?" And he turned again to look at the lawyer.

But just as he turned there came the shot of a firelock from higher up the hill; and with the very sound of it Glenure fell upon the road.

"O, I am dead!" he cried, several times over.

The lawyer had caught him up and held him in his arms, the servant standing over and clasping his hands. And now the wounded man looked from one to another with scared eyes, and there was a change in his voice that went to the heart.

"Take care of yourselves," says he. "I am dead."

He tried to open his clothes as if to look for the wound, but his fingers slipped on the buttons. With that he gave a great sigh, his head rolled on his shoulder, and he passed away.

The lawyer said never a word, but his face was as sharp as a pen and as white as the dead man's; the servant broke out into a great noise of crying and weeping, like a child; and I, on my side, stood staring at them in a kind of horror. The sheriff's officer had run back at the first sound of the shot, to hasten the coming of the soldiers.

At last the lawyer laid down the dead man in his blood upon the road, and got to his own feet with a kind of stagger.

I believe it was his movement that brought me to my senses; for he had no sooner done so than I began to scramble up the hill, crying out, "The murderer! the murderer!"

So little a time had elapsed, that when I got to the top of the first steepness, and could see some part of the open mountain, the murderer was still moving away at no great distance. He was a big man, in a black coat, with metal buttons, and carried a long fowling-piece.

"Here!" I cried. "I see him!"

At that the murderer gave a little, quick look over his shoulder, and began to run. The next moment he was lost in a fringe of birches; then he came out again on the upper side, where I could see him climbing like a jackanapes, for that part was again very steep; and then he dipped behind a shoulder, and I saw him no more.

All this time I had been running on my side, and had got a good way up, when a voice cried upon me to stand.

I was at the edge of the upper wood, and so now, when I halted and looked back, I saw all the open part of the hill below me.

The lawyer and the sheriff's officer were standing just above the road, crying and waving on me to come back; and on their left, the red-coats, musket in hand, were beginning to struggle singly out of the lower wood.

"Why should I come back?" I cried. "Come you on!"

"Ten pounds if ye take that lad!" cried the lawyer. "He's an accomplice. He was posted here to hold us in talk."

At that word (which I could hear quite plainly, though it was to the soldiers and not to me that he was crying it) my heart came in my mouth with quite a new kind of terror. Indeed, it is one thing to stand the danger of your life, and quite another to run the peril of both life and character. The thing, besides, had come so suddenly, like thunder out of a clear sky, that I was all amazed and helpless.

The soldiers began to spread, some of them to run, and others to put up their pieces and cover me; and still I stood.

"Jouk[1] in here among the trees," said a voice, close by.

Indeed, I scarce knew what I was doing, but I obeyed; and as I did so, I heard the firelocks bang and the balls whistle in the birches.

Just inside the shelter of the trees I found Alan Breck standing, with a fishing-rod. He gave me no salutation; indeed it was no time for civilities; only "Come!" says he,

[1]Duck.

and set off running along the side of the mountain towards Balachulish; and I, like a sheep, to follow him.

Now we ran among the birches; now stooping behind low humps upon the mountain-side; now crawling on all fours among the heather. The pace was deadly: my heart seemed bursting against my ribs; and I had neither time to think nor breath to speak with. Only I remember seeing with wonder, that Alan every now and then would straighten himself to his full height and look back; and every time he did so, there came a great far-away cheering and crying of the soldiers.

Quarter of an hour later, Alan stopped, clapped down flat in the heather, and turned to me.

"Now," said he, "it's earnest. Do as I do, for your life."

And at the same speed, but now with infinitely more precaution, we traced back again across the mountain-side by the same way that we had come, only perhaps higher; till at last Alan threw himself down in the upper wood of Lettermore, where I had found him at the first, and lay, with his face in the bracken, panting like a dog.

My own sides so ached, my head so swam, my tongue so hung out of my mouth with heat and dryness, that I lay beside him like one dead.

Chapter 18

I TALK WITH ALAN IN THE WOOD OF LETTERMORE

Alan was the first to come round. He rose, went to the border of the wood, peered out a little, and then returned and sat down.

"Well," said he, "yon was a hot burst, David."

I said nothing, nor so much as lifted my face. I had seen murder done, and a great, ruddy, jovial gentleman struck out of life in a moment; the pity of that sight was still sore within me, and yet that was but a part of my concern. Here was murder done upon the man Alan hated; here was Alan skulking in the trees and running from the troops; and whether his was the hand that fired or only the head that ordered, signified but little. By my way of it, my only friend in that wild country was blood-guilty in the first degree; I held him in horror; I could not look upon his face; I would have rather lain alone in the rain on my cold isle, than in that warm wood beside a murderer.

"Are ye still wearied?" he asked again.

"No," said I, still with my face in the bracken; "no, I am not wearied now, and I can speak. You and me must twine,"[1] I said. "I liked you very well, Alan, but your ways are not mine, and they're not God's: and the short and the long of it is just that we must twine."

"I will hardly twine from ye, David, without some kind of reason for the same," said Alan, mighty gravely. "If ye ken anything against my reputation, it's the least thing that ye should do, for old acquaintance' sake, to let me hear

[1] Part.

119

the name of it; and if ye have only taken a distaste to my society, it will be proper for me to judge if I'm insulted."

"Alan," said I, "what is the sense of this? Ye ken very well yon Campbell man lies in his blood upon the road."

He was silent for a little; then says he, "Did ever ye hear tell of the story of the Man and the Good People?" —by which he meant the fairies.

"No," said I, "nor do I want to hear it."

"With your permission, Mr. Balfour, I will tell it you, whatever," says Alan. "The man, ye should ken, was cast upon a rock in the sea, where it appears the Good People were in use to come and rest as they went through to Ireland. The name of this rock is called the Skerryvore, and it's not far from where we suffered shipwreck. Well, it seems the man cried so sore, if he could just see his little bairn before he died! that at last the king of the Good People took peety upon him, and sent one flying that brought back the bairn in a poke[1] and laid it down beside the man where he lay sleeping. So when the man woke, there was a poke beside him and something into the inside of it that moved. Well, it seems he was one of these gentry that think aye the worst of things; and for greater security, he stuck his dirk throughout that poke before he opened it, and there was his bairn dead. I am thinking to myself, Mr. Balfour, that you and the man are very much alike."

"Do you mean you had no hand in it?" cried I, sitting up.

"I will tell you first of all, Mr. Balfour of Shaws, as one friend to another," said Alan, "that if I were going to kill a gentleman, it would not be in my own country, to bring trouble on my clan; and I would not go wanting sword and gun, and with a long fishing-rod upon my back."

"Well," said I, "that's true!"

"And now," continued Alan, taking out his dirk and laying his hand upon it in a certain manner, "I swear upon the Holy Iron I had neither art nor part, act nor thought in it."

[1]Bag.

"I thank God for that!" cried I, and offered him my hand.

He did not appear to see it.

"And here is a great deal of work about a Campbell!" said he. "They are not so scarce, that I ken!"

"At least," said I, "you cannot justly blame me, for you know very well what you told me in the brig. But the temptation and the act are different, I thank God again for that. We may all be tempted; but to take a life in cold blood, Alan!" And I could say no more for the moment. "And do you know who did it?" I added. "Do you know that man in the black coat?"

"I have nae clear mind about his coat," said Alan, cunningly; "but it sticks in my head that it was blue."

"Blue or black, did ye know him?" said I.

"I couldna just conscientiously swear to him," says Alan. "He gaed very close by me, to be sure, but it's a strange thing that I should just have been tying my brogues."

"Can you swear that you don't know him, Alan?" I cried, half angered, half in a mind to laugh at his evasions.

"Not yet," says he; "but I've a grand memory for forgetting, David."

"And yet there was one thing I saw clearly," said I; "and that was, that you exposed yourself and me to draw the soldiers."

"It's very likely," said Alan; "and so would any gentleman. You and me were innocent of that transaction."

"The better reason, since we were falsely suspected, that we should get clear," I cried. "The innocent should surely come before the guilty."

"Why, David," said he, "the innocent have aye a chance to get assoiled in court; but for the lad that shot the bullet, I think the best place for him will be the heather. Them that havena dipped their hands in any little difficulty, should be very mindful of the case of them that have. And that is the good Christianity. For if it was the other way round about, and the lad whom I couldna just clearly see had been in our shoes, and we in his (as might very well have been), I think we would be a good deal obliged to him oursel's if he would draw the soldiers."

When it came to this, I gave Alan up. But he looked so

innocent all the time, and was in such clear good faith in what he said, and so ready to sacrifice himself for what he deemed his duty, that my mouth was closed. Mr. Henderland's words came back to me: that we ourselves might take a lesson by these wild Highlanders. Well, here I had taken mine. Alan's morals were all tail-first; but he was ready to give his life for them, such as they were.

"Alan," said I, "I'll not say it's the good Christianity as I understand it, but it's good enough. And here I offer ye my hand for the second time."

Whereupon he gave me both of his, saying surely I had cast a spell upon him, for he could forgive me anything. Then he grew very grave, and said we had not much time to throw away, but must both flee that country; he, because he was a deserter, and the whole of Appin would now be searched like a chamber, and every one obliged to give a good account of himself; and I, because I was certainly involved in the murder.

"O!" says I, willing to give him a little lesson, "I have no fear of the justice of my country."

"As if this was your country!" said he. "Or as if ye would be tried here, in a country of Stewarts!"

"It's all Scotland," said I.

"Man, I whiles wonder at ye," said Alan. "This is a Campbell that's been killed. Well, it'll be tried in Inverara, the Campbell's head place; with fifteen Campbells in the jury-box, and the biggest Campbell of all (and that's the Duke) sitting cocking on the bench. Justice, David? The same justice, by all the world, as Glenure found a while ago at the road-side."

This frighted me a little, I confess, and would have frighted me more if I had known how nearly exact were Alan's predictions; indeed it was but in one point that he exaggerated, there being but eleven Campbells on the jury; though as the other four were equally in the Duke's dependence, it mattered less than might appear. Still, I cried out that he was unjust to the Duke of Argyle who (for all he was a Whig) was yet a wise and honest nobleman.

"Hoot!" said Alan, "the man's a Whig, nae doubt; but I would never deny he was a good chieftain to his clan. And what would the clan think if there was a Campbell shot,

and naebody hanged, and their own chief the Justice
General? But I have often observed," says Alan, "that
you Low-country bodies have no clear idea of what's right
and wrong."

At this I did at last laugh out aloud; when to my surprise, Alan joined in, and laughed as merrily as myself.

"Na, na," said he, "we're in the Hielands, David; and
when I tell ye to run, take my word and run. Nae doubt
it's a hard thing to skulk and starve in the heather, but it's
harder yet to lie shackled in a red-coat prison."

I asked him whither we should flee; and as he told me
"to the Lowlands," I was a little better inclined to go with
him; for, indeed, I was growing impatient to get back and
have the upper hand of my uncle. Besides, Alan made so
sure there would be no question of justice in the matter,
that I began to be afraid he might be right. Of all deaths, I
would truly like least to die by the gallows; and the
picture of that uncanny instrument came into my head
with extraordinary clearness (as I had once seen it en-
graved at the top of a peddler's ballad) and took away my
appetite for courts of justice.

"I'll chance it, Alan," said I. "I'll go with you."

"But mind you," said Alan, "it's no small thing. Ye
maun lie bare and hard, and brook many an empty belly.
Your bed shall be the muircock's, and your life shall be
like the hunted deer's, and ye shall sleep with your hand
upon your weapons. Ay, man, ye shall taigle many a weary
foot, or we get clear! I tell ye this at the start, for it's a life
that I ken well. But if ye ask what other chance ye have, I
answer: Nane. Either take to the heather with me, or else
hang."

"And that's a choice very easily made," said I; and we
shook hands upon it.

"And now let's take another keek at the red-coats," says
Alan, and he led me to the north-eastern fringe of the
wood.

Looking out between the trees, we could see a great
side of mountain, running down exceeding steep into the
waters of the loch. It was a rough part, all hanging stone,
and heather, and bit scrogs of birchwood; and away at the
far end towards Balachulish, little wee red soldiers were

dipping up and down over hill and howe, and growing smaller every minute. There was no cheering now, for I think they had other uses for what breath was left them; but they still stuck to the trail, and doubtless thought that we were close in front of them.

Alan watched them, smiling to himself.

"Ay," said he, "they'll be gey[1] weary before they've got to the end of that employ! And so you and me, David, can sit down and eat a bite, and breathe a bit longer, and take a dram from my bottle. Then we'll strike for Aucharn, the house of my kinsman, James of the Glens, where I must get my clothes, and my arms, and money to carry us along; and then, David, we'll cry 'Forth, Fortune!' and take a cast among the heather."

So we sat again and ate and drank, in a place whence we could see the sun going down into a field of great, wild and houseless mountains, such as I was now condemned to wander in with my companion. Partly as we so sat, and partly afterwards, on the way to Aucharn, each of us narrated his adventures; and I shall here set down so much of Alan's as seems either curious or needful.

It appears he ran to the bulwarks as soon as the wave was passed; saw me, and lost me, and saw me again, as I tumbled in the roost; and at last had one glimpse of me clinging on the yard. It was this that put him in some hope I would maybe get to land after all, and made him leave those clues and messages which had brought me (for my sins) to that unlucky country of Appin.

In the meanwhile, those still on the brig had got the skiff launched, and one or two were on board of her already, when there came a second wave greater than the first, and heaved the brig out of her place, and would certainly have sent her to the bottom, had she not struck and caught on some projection of the reef. When she had struck first, it had been bows-on, so that the stern had hitherto been lowest. But now her stern was thrown in the air, and the bows plungèd under the sea; and with that, the water began to pour into the fore-scuttle like the pouring of a mill-dam.

[1]Very.

It took the colour out of Alan's face, even to tell what followed. For there were still two men lying impotent in their bunks; and these, seeing the water pour in and thinking the ship had foundered, began to cry out aloud, and that with such harrowing cries that all who were on deck tumbled one after another into the skiff and fell to their oars. They were not two hundred yards away, when there came a third great sea; and at that the brig lifted clean over the reef; her canvas filled for a moment, and she seemed to sail in chase of them, but settling all the while; and presently she drew down and down, as if a hand was drawing her; and the sea closed over the *Covenant* of Dysart.

Never a word they spoke as they pulled ashore, being stunned with the horror of that screaming; but they had scarce set foot upon the beach when Hoseason woke up, as if out of a muse, and bade them lay hands upon Alan. They hung back indeed, having little taste for the employment; but Hoseason was like a fiend, crying that Alan was alone, that he had a great sum about him, that he had been the means of losing the brig and drowning all their comrades, and that here was both revenge and wealth upon a single cast. It was seven against one; in that part of the shore there was no rock that Alan could set his back to; and the sailors began to spread out and come behind him.

"And then," said Alan, "the little man with the red head—I havena mind of the name that he is called—"

"Riach," said I.

"Ay," said Alan, "Riach! Well, it was him that took up the clubs for me, asked the men if they werena feared of a judgment, and, says he, 'Dod, I'll put my back to the Hielandman's mysel'.' That's none such an entirely bad little man, yon little man with the red head," said Alan. "He has some spunks of decency."

"Well," said I, "he was kind to me in his way."

"And so he was to Alan," said he; "and by my troth, I found his way a very good one! But ye see, David, the loss of the ship, and the cries of these poor lads sat very ill upon the man; and I'm thinking that would be the cause of it."

"Well, I would think so," says I; "for he was as keen as any of the rest at the beginning. But how did Hoseason take it?"

"It sticks in my mind that he would take it very ill," says Alan. "But the little man cried to me to run, and indeed I thought it was a good observe, and ran. The last that I saw they were all in a knot upon the beach, like folk that were not agreeing very well together."

"What do you mean by that?" said I.

"Well, the fists were going," said Alan; "and I saw one man go down like a pair of breeks. But I thought it would be better no' to wait. Ye see there's a strip of Campbells in that end of Mull, which is no good company for a gentleman like me. If it hadna been for that I would have waited and looked for ye mysel', let alone giving a hand to the little man." (It was droll how Alan dwelt on Mr. Riach's stature, for, to say the truth, the one was not much smaller than the other.) "So," says he, continuing, "I set my best foot forward, and whenever I met in with any one I cried out there was a wreck ashore. Man, they didna stop to fash[1] with me! Ye should have seen them linking for the beach! And when they got there they found they had had the pleasure of a run, which is aye good for a Campbell. I'm thinking it was a judgment on the clan that the brig went down in the lump and didna break. But it was a very unlucky thing for you, that same; for if any wreck had come ashore they would have hunted high and low, and would soon have found ye."

[1]Trouble.

Chapter 19

THE HOUSE OF FEAR

Night fell as we were walking, and the clouds, which had broken up in the afternoon, settled in and thickened, so that it fell, for the season of the year, extremely dark. The way we went was over rough mountain sides; and though Alan pushed on with an assured manner, I could by no means see how he directed himself.

At last, about half-past ten of the clock, we came to the top of a brae, and saw lights below us. It seemed a house-door stood open and let out a beam of fire and candle-light; and all round the house and steading five or six persons were moving hurriedly about, each carrying a lighted brand.

"James must have tint[1] his wits," said Alan. "If this was the soldiers instead of you and me, he would be in a bonny mess. But I dare say he'll have a sentry on the road, and he would ken well enough no soldiers would find the way that we came."

Hereupon he whistled three times, in a particular manner. It was strange to see how, at the first sound of it, all the moving torches came to a stand, as if the bearers were affrighted; and how, at the third, the bustle began again as before.

Having thus set folks' minds at rest, we came down the brae, and were met at the yard gate (for this place was like a well-doing farm) by a tall, handsome man of more than fifty, who cried out to Alan in the Gaelic.

"James Stewart," said Alan, "I will ask ye to speak in

[1]Lost.

127

Scots, for here is a young gentleman with me that has nane of the other. This is him," he added, putting his arm through mine, "a young gentleman of the Lowlands, and a laird in his country too, but I am thinking it will be the better for his health if we give his name the go-by."

James of the Glens turned to me for a moment, and greeted me courteously enough; the next he had turned to Alan.

"This has been a dreadful accident," he cried. "It will bring trouble on the country." And he wrung his hands.

"Hoots!" said Alan, "ye must take the sour with the sweet, man. Colin Roy is dead, and be thankful for that!"

"Ay," said James, "and by my troth, I wish he was alive again! It's all very fine to blow and boast beforehand; but now it's done, Alan; and who's to bear the wyte[1] of it? The accident fell out in Appin—mind ye that, Alan; it's Appin that must pay; and I am a man that has a family."

While this was going on I looked about me at the servants. Some were on ladders, digging in the thatch of the house or the farm buildings, from which they brought out guns, swords, and different weapons of war; others carried them away; and by the sound of mattock blows from somewhere farther down the brae, I suppose they buried them. Though they were all so busy, there prevailed no kind of order in their efforts; men struggled together for the same gun and ran into each other with their burning torches; and James was continually turning about from his talk with Alan, to cry out orders which were apparently never understood. The faces in the torch-light were like those of people overborne with hurry and panic; and though none spoke above his breath, their speech sounded both anxious and angry.

It was about this time that a lassie came out of the house carrying a pack or bundle; and it has often made me smile to think how Alan's instinct awoke at the mere sight of it.

"What's that the lassie has?" he asked.

"We're just setting the house in order, Alan," said James, in his frightened and somewhat fawning way. "They'll search Appin with candles, and we must have all things

---

[1]Blame.

straight. We're digging the bit guns and swords into the moss, ye see; and these, I am thinking, will be your ain French clothes. We'll be to bury them, I believe."

"Bury my French clothes!" cried Alan. "Troth, no!" And he laid hold upon the packet and retired into the barn to shift himself, recommending me in the meanwhile to his kinsman.

James carried me accordingly into the kitchen and sat down with me at table, smiling and talking at first in a very hospitable manner. But presently the gloom returned upon him; he sat frowning and biting his fingers; only remembered me from time to time; and then gave me but a word or two and a poor smile, and back into his private terrors. His wife sat by the fire and wept, with her face in her hands; his eldest son was crouched upon the floor, running over a great mass of papers and now and again setting one alight and burning it to the bitter end; all the while a servant lass with a red face was rummaging about the room, in a blind hurry of fear, and whimpering as she went; and every now and again one of the men would thrust in his face from the yard, and cry for orders.

At last James could keep his seat no longer, and begged my permission to be so unmannerly as walk about. "I am but poor company altogether, sir," says he, "but I can think of nothing but this dreadful accident, and the trouble it is like to bring upon quite innocent persons."

A little after he observed his son burning a paper which he thought should have been kept; and at that his excitement burst out so that it was painful to witness. He struck the lad repeatedly.

"Are you gone gyte?"[1] he cried. "Do you wish to hang your father?" and forgetful of my presence, carried on at him a long time together in the Gaelic, the young man answering nothing; only the wife, at the name of hanging, throwing her apron over her face and sobbing out louder than before.

This was all wretched for a stranger like myself to hear and see; and I was right glad when Alan returned, looking like himself in his fine French clothes, though (to be sure)

[1]Mad.

they were now grown almost too battered and withered to deserve the name of fine. I was then taken out in my turn by another of the sons, and given that change of clothing of which I had stood so long in need, and a pair of Highland brogues made of deer-leather, rather strange at first, but after a little practice very easy to the feet.

By the time I came back Alan must have told his story; for it seemed understood that I was to fly with him, and they were all busy upon our equipment. They gave us each a sword and pistols, though I professed my inability to use the former; and with these, and some ammunition, a bag of oatmeal, an iron pan, and a bottle of right French brandy, we were ready for the heather. Money, indeed, was lacking. I had about two guineas left; Alan's belt having been despatched by another hand, that trusty messenger had no more than seventeen-pence to his whole fortune; and as for James, it appears he had brought himself so low with journeys to Edinburgh and legal expenses on behalf of the tenants, that he could only scrape together three-and-fivepence-halfpenny, the most of it in coppers.

"This'll no' do," said Alan.

"Ye must find a safe bit somewhere near by," said James, "and get word sent to me. Ye see, ye'll have to get this business prettily off, Alan. This is no time to be stayed for a guinea or two. They're sure to get wind of ye, sure to seek ye, and by my way of it, sure to lay on ye the wyte of this day's accident. If it falls on you, it falls on me that am your near kinsman and harboured ye while ye were in the country. And if it comes on me——" he paused, and bit his fingers, with a white face. "It would be a painful thing for our friends if I was to hang," said he.

"It would be an ill day for Appin," says Alan.

"It's a day that sticks in my throat," said James. "O man, man, man—man Alan! you and me have spoken like two fools!" he cried, striking his hand upon the wall so that the house rang again.

"Well, and that's true, too," said Alan; "and my friend from the Lowlands here" (nodding at me) "gave me a good word upon that head, if I would only have listened to him."

"But see here," said James, returning to his former manner, "if they lay me by the heels, Alan, it's then that you'll be needing the money. For with all that I have said and that you have said, it will look very black against the two of us; do ye mark that? Well, follow me out, and ye'll see that I'll have to get a paper out against ye mysel'; I'll have to offer a reward for ye; ay, will I! It's a sore thing to do between such near friends; but if I get the dirdun[1] of this dreadful accident, I'll have to fend for myself, man. Do ye see that?"

He spoke with a pleading earnestness, taking Alan by the breast of the coat.

"Ay," said Alan, "I see that."

"And ye'll have to be clear of the country, Alan—ay, and clear of Scotland—you and your friend from the Lowlands, too. For I'll have to paper your friend from the Lowlands. Ye see that, Alan—say that ye see that!"

I thought Alan flushed a bit. "This is unco hard on me that brought him here, James," said he, throwing his head back. "It's like making me a traitor!"

"Now, Alan man!" cried James. "Look things in the face! He'll be papered anyway; Mungo Campbell 'll be sure to paper him; what matters if I paper him too? And then, Alan, I am a man that has a family." And then, after a little pause on both sides: "And, Alan, it'll be a jury of Campbells," said he.

"There's one thing," said Alan, musingly, "that naebody kens his name."

"Nor yet they shallna, Alan! There's my hand on that," cried James, for all the world as if he had really known my name and was foregoing some advantage. "But just the habit he was in, and what he looked like, and his age, and the like? I couldna well do less."

"I wonder at your father's son," cried Alan, sternly. "Would ye sell the lad with a gift? Would ye change his clothes and then betray him?"

"No, no, Alan," said James. "No, no: the habit he took off—the habit Mungo saw him in." But I thought he seemed crestfallen; indeed, he was clutching at every

[1]Blame.

straw, and all the time, I daresay, saw the faces of his hereditary foes on the bench, and in the jury-box, and the gallows in the background.

"Well, sir," says Alan, turning to me, "what say ye to that? Ye are here under the safeguard of my honour; and it's my part to see nothing done but what shall please you."

"I have but one word to say," said I; "for to all this dispute I am a perfect stranger. But the plain common-sense is to set the blame where it belongs, and that is on the man that fired the shot. Paper him, as ye call it, set the hunt on him; and let honest, innocent folk show their faces in safety."

But at this both Alan and James cried out in horror; bidding me hold my tongue, for that was not to be thought of; and asking me what the Camerons would think? (which confirmed me, it must have been a Cameron from Mamore that did the act) and if I did not see that the lad might be caught? "Ye havena surely thought of that?" said they, with such innocent earnestness, that my hands dropped at my side and I despaired of argument.

"Very well, then," said I, "paper me, if you please, paper Alan, paper King George! We're all three innocent, and that seems to be what's wanted. But at least, sir," said I to James, recovering from my little fit of annoyance, "I am Alan's friend, and if I can be helpful to friends of his, I will not stumble at the risk."

I thought it best to put a fair face on my consent, for I saw Alan troubled; and, besides (thinks I to myself), as soon as my back is turned, they will paper me, as they call it, whether I consent or not. But in this I saw I was wrong; for I had no sooner said the words, than Mrs. Stewart leaped out of her chair, came running over to us, and wept first upon my neck and then on Alan's, blessing God for our goodness to her family.

"As for you, Alan, it was no more than your bounden duty," she said. "But for this lad that has come here and seen us at our worst, and seen the goodman fleeching like a suitor, him that by rights should give his commands like any king—as for you, my lad," she says, "my heart is wae not to have your name, but I have your face; and as long as my heart beats under my bosom, I will keep it, and think of it, and bless it." And with that she kissed me, and burst once more into such sobbing, that I stood abashed.

"Hoot, hoot," said Alan, looking mighty silly. "The day comes unco soon in this month of July; and to-morrow there'll be a fine to-do in Appin, a fine riding of dragoons, and crying of 'Cruachan!'[1] and running of red-coats; and it behoves you and me to the sooner be gone."

Thereupon we said farewell, and set out again, bending somewhat eastwards, in a fine mild dark night, and over much the same broken country as before.

[1]The rallying-word of the Campbells.

Chapter 20

THE FLIGHT IN THE HEATHER: THE ROCKS

Sometimes we walked, sometimes ran; and as it drew on to morning, walked ever the less and ran the more. Though, upon its face, that country appeared to be a desert, yet there were huts and houses of the people, of which we must have passed more than twenty, hidden in quiet places of the hills. When we came to one of these, Alan would leave me in the way, and go himself and rap upon the side of the house and speak a while at the window with some sleeper awakened. This was to pass the news; which, in that country, was so much of a duty that Alan must pause to attend to it even while fleeing for his life; and so well attended to by others, that in more than half of the houses where we called they had heard already of the murder. In the others, as well as I could make out (standing back at a distance and hearing a strange tongue), the news was received with more of consternation than surprise.

For all our hurry, day began to come in while we were still far from any shelter. It found us in a prodigious valley, strewn with rocks and where ran a foaming river. Wild mountains stood around it; there grew there neither grass nor trees; and I have sometimes thought since then, that it may have been the valley called Glencoe, where the massacre was in the time of King William. But for the details of our itinerary, I am all to seek; our way lying now by short cuts, now by great detours; our pace being so hurried, our time of journeying usually by night; and the names of such places as I asked and heard being in the Gaelic tongue and the more easily forgotten.

The first peep of morning, then, showed us this horrible place, and I could see Alan knit his brow.

"This is no fit place for you and me," he said. "This is a place they're bound to watch."

And with that he ran harder than ever down to the water-side, in a part where the river was split in two among three rocks. It went through with a horrid thundering that made my belly quake; and there hung over the lynn[1] a little mist of spray. Alan looked neither to the right nor to the left, but jumped clean upon the middle rock and fell there on his hands and knees to check himself, for that rock was small and he might have pitched over on the far side. I had scarce time to measure the distance or to understand the peril before I had followed him, and he had caught and stopped me.

So there we stood, side by side upon a small rock slippery with spray, a far broader leap in front of us, and the river dinning upon all sides. When I saw where I was, there came on me a deadly sickness of fear, and I put my hand over my eyes. Alan took me and shook me; I saw he was speaking, but the roaring of the falls and the trouble of my mind prevented me from hearing; only I saw his face was red with anger, and that he stamped upon the rock. The same look showed me the water raging by, and the mist hanging in the air; and with that I covered my eyes again and shuddered.

The next minute Alan had set the brandy bottle to my lips, and forced me to drink about a gill, which sent the blood into my head again. Then, putting his hands to his mouth, and his mouth to my ear, he shouted, "Hang or drown!" and turning his back upon me, leaped over the farther branch of the stream, and landed safe.

I was now alone upon the rock, which gave me the more room; the brandy was singing in my ears; I had this good example fresh before me, and just wit enough to see that if I did not leap at once, I should never leap at all. I bent low on my knees and flung myself forth, with that kind of anger of despair that has sometimes stood me in stead of courage. Sure enough, it was but my hands that

[1]Waterfall.

reached the full length; these slipped, caught again, slipped again; and I was sliddering back into the lynn, when Alan seized me, first by the hair, then by the collar, and with a great strain dragged me into safety.

Never a word he said, but set off running again for his life, and I must stagger to my feet and run after him. I had been weary before, but now I was sick and bruised, and partly drunken with the brandy; I kept stumbling as I ran, I had a stitch that came near to overmaster me; and when at last Alan paused under a great rock that stood there among a number of others, it was none too soon for David Balfour.

A great rock I have said; but by rights it was two rocks leaning together at the top, both some twenty feet high, and at the first sight inaccessible. Even Alan (though you may say he had as good as four hands) failed twice in an attempt to climb them; and it was only at the third trial, and then by standing on my shoulders and leaping up with such force as I thought must have broken my collar bone, that he secured a lodgment. Once there, he let down his leathern girdle; and with the aid of that and a pair of shallow footholds in the rock, I scrambled up beside him.

Then I saw why we had come there; for the two rocks, being both somewhat hollow on the top and sloping one to the other, made a kind of dish or saucer, where as many as three or four men might have lain hidden.

All this while Alan had not said a word, and had run and climbed with such a savage, silent frenzy of hurry, that I knew that he was in mortal fear of some miscarriage. Even now we were on the rock he said nothing, nor so much as relaxed the frowning look upon his face; but clapped flat down, and keeping only one eye above the edge of our place of shelter scouted all round the compass. The dawn had come quite clear; we could see the stony sides of the valley, and its bottom which was bestrewed with rocks, and the river which went from one side to another, and made white falls; but nowhere the smoke of a house, nor any living creature but some eagles screaming round a cliff.

Then at last Alan smiled.

"Ay," said he, "now we have a chance"; and then looking at me with some amusement, "Ye're no very gleg[1] at the jumping," said he.

At this I suppose I coloured with mortification for he added at once, "Hoots! small blame to ye! To be feared of a thing and yet to do it, is what makes the prettiest kind of a man. And then there was water there, and water's a thing that dauntons even me. No, no," said Alan, "it's no' you that's to blame, it's me."

I asked him why.

"Why," said he, "I have proved myself a gomeril[2] this night. For first of all I take a wrong road, and that in my own country of Appin; so that the day has caught us where we should never have been; and thanks to that, we lie here in some danger and mair discomfort. And next (which is the worst of the two, for a man that has been so much among the heather as myself) I have come wanting a water-bottle, and here we lie for a long summer's day with naething but neat spirit. Ye may think that a small matter; but before it comes night, David, ye'll give me news of it."

I was anxious to redeem my character, and offered, if he would pour out the brandy, to run down and fill the bottle at the river.

"I wouldna waste the good spirit either," says he. "It's been a good friend to you this night; or in my poor opinion, ye would still be cocking on yon stone. And what's mair," says he, "ye may have observed (you that's a man of so much penetration) that Alan Breck Stewart was perhaps walking quicker than his ordinar'."

"You!" I cried, "you were running fit to burst."

"Was I so?" said he. "Well, then, ye may depend upon it, there was nae time to be lost. And now here is enough said; gang you to your sleep, lad, and I'll watch."

Accordingly, I lay down to sleep; a little peaty earth had drifted in between the top of the two rocks, and some bracken grew there, to be a bed to me; the last thing I heard was still the crying of the eagles.

I daresay it would be nine in the morning when I was

---

[1]Brisk.   [2]Fool.

roughly awakened, and found Alan's hand pressed upon my mouth.

"Wheesht!" he whispered. "Ye were snoring."

"Well," said I, surprised at his anxious and dark face, "and why not?"

He peered over the edge of the rock, and signed to me to do the like.

It was now high day, cloudless, and very hot. The valley was as clear as in a picture. About half a mile up the water was a camp of red-coats; a big fire blazed in their midst, at which some were cooking; and near by, on the top of a rock about as high as ours, there stood a sentry, with the sun sparkling on his arms. All the way down along the river-side were posted other sentries; here near together, there widelier scattered; some planted like the first, on places of command, some on the ground level and marching and counter-marching, so as to meet half way. Higher up the glen, where the ground was more open, the chain of posts was continued by horse-soldiers, whom we could see in the distance riding to and fro. Lower down, the infantry continued; but as the stream was suddenly swelled by the confluence of a considerable burn, they were more widely set, and only watched the fords and stepping-stones.

I took but one look at them, and ducked again into my place. It was strange indeed to see this valley, which had lain so solitary in the hour of dawn, bristling with arms and dotted with the red-coats and breeches.

"Ye see," said Alan, "this was what I was afraid of, Davie: that they would watch the burn-side. They began to come in about two hours ago, and, man! but ye're a grand hand at the sleeping! We're in a narrow place. If they get up the sides of the hill, they could easy spy us with a glass; but if they'll only keep in the foot of the valley, we'll do yet. The posts are thinner down the water; and, come night, we'll try our hand at getting by them."

"And what are we to do till night?" I asked.

"Lie here," says he, "and birstle."[1]

That one good Scots word, "birstle," was indeed the most of the story of the day that we had now to pass.

[1]Toast.

You are to remember that we lay on the bare top of a rock, like scones upon a girdle; the sun beat upon us cruelly; the rock grew so heated, a man could scarce endure the touch of it; and the little patch of earth and fern, which kept cooler, was only large enough for one at a time. We took turn about to lie on the naked rock, which was indeed like the position of that saint that was martyred on a gridiron; and it ran in my mind how strange it was, that in the same climate and at only a few days' distance, I should have suffered so cruelly, first from cold upon my island and now from heat upon this rock.

All the while we had no water, only raw brandy for a drink, which was worse than nothing; but we kept the bottle as cool as we could, burying it in the earth, and got some relief by bathing our breasts and temples.

The soldiers kept stirring all day in the bottom of the valley, now changing guard, now in patrolling parties hunting among the rocks. These lay round in so great a number, that to look for men among them was like looking for a needle in a bottle of hay; and being so hopeless a task, it was gone about with the less care. Yet we could see the soldiers pike their bayonets among the heather, which sent a cold thrill into my vitals; and they would sometimes hang about our rock, so that we scarce dared to breathe.

It was in this way that I first heard the right English speech; one fellow as he went by actually clapping his hand upon the sunny face of the rock on which we lay, and plucking it off again with an oath. "I tell you it's 'ot," says he; and I was amazed at the clipping tones and the odd sing-song in which he spoke, and no less at that strange trick of dropping out the letter "h." To be sure, I had heard Ransome; but he had taken his ways from all sorts of people, and spoke so imperfectly at the best, that I set down the most of it to childishness. My surprise was all the greater to hear that manner of speaking in the mouth of a grown man; and indeed I have never grown used to it; nor yet altogether with the English grammar, as perhaps a very critical eye might here and there spy out even in these memoirs.

The tediousness and pain of these hours upon the rock grew only the greater as the day went on; the rock getting still the hotter and the sun fiercer. There were giddiness, and sickness, and sharp pangs like rheumatism, to be supported. I minded then, and have often minded since, on the lines in our Scots psalm:—

> "The moon by night thee shall not smite,
>   Nor yet the sun by day";

and indeed it was only by God's blessing that we were neither of us sun-smitten.

At last, about two, it was beyond men's bearing, and there was now temptation to resist, as well as pain to thole.[1] For the sun being now got a little into the west, there came a patch of shade on the east side of our rock, which was the side sheltered from the soldiers.

"As well one death as another," said Alan, and slipped over the edge and dropped on the ground on the shadowy side.

I followed him at once, and instantly fell all my length, so weak was I and so giddy with that long exposure. Here, then, we lay for an hour or two, aching from head to foot, as weak as water, and lying quite naked to the eye of any soldier who should have strolled that way. None came, however, all passing by on the other side; so that our rock continued to be our shield even in this new position.

Presently we began again to get a little strength; and as the soldiers were now lying closer along the river-side, Alan proposed that we should try a start. I was by this time afraid of but one thing in the world; and that was to be set back upon the rock; anything else was welcome to me; so we got ourselves at once in marching order, and began to slip from rock to rock one after the other, now crawling flat on our bellies in the shade, now making a run for it, heart in mouth.

The soldiers, having searched this side of the valley after a fashion, and being perhaps somewhat sleepy with the sultriness of the afternoon, had now laid by much of their vigilance, and stood dozing at their posts or only kept a lookout along the banks of the river; so that in this

---

[1] Endure.

way, keeping down the valley and at the same time towards the mountains, we drew steadily away from their neighbourhood. But the business was the most wearing I had ever taken part in. A man had need of a hundred eyes in every part of him, to keep concealed in that uneven country and within cry of so many and scattered sentries. When we must pass an open place, quickness was not all, but a swift judgment not only of the lie of the whole country, but of the solidity of every stone on which we must set foot; for the afternoon was now fallen so breathless that the rolling of a pebble sounded abroad like a pistol-shot, and would start the echo calling among the hills and cliffs.

By sundown we had made some distance, even by our slow rate of progress, though to be sure the sentry on the rock was still plainly in our view. But now we came on something that put all fears out of season; and that was a deep, rushing burn that tore down, in that part, to join the glen river. At the sight of this we cast ourselves on the ground and plunged head and shoulders in the water; and I cannot tell which was the more pleasant, the great shock as the cool stream went over us, or the greed with which we drank of it.

We lay there (for the banks hid us), drank again and again, bathed our chests, let our wrists trail in the running water till they ached with the chill; and at last, being wonderfully renewed, we got out the meal-bag and made drammach in the iron pan. This, though it is but cold water mingled with oatmeal, yet makes a good enough dish for a hungry man; and where there are no means of making fire, or (as in our case) good reason for not making one, it is the chief stand-by of those who have taken to the heather.

As soon as the shadow of the night had fallen, we set forth again, at first with the same caution, but presently with more boldness, standing our full height and stepping out at a good pace of walking. The way was very intricate, lying up the steep sides of mountains and along the brows of cliffs; clouds had come in with the sunset, and the night was dark and cool; so that I walked without much fatigue, but in continual fear of falling and rolling down the mountains, and with no guess at our direction.

The moon rose at last and found us still on the road; it was in its last quarter, and was long beset with clouds; but after a while shone out and showed me many dark heads of mountains, and was reflected far underneath us on the narrow arm of a sea-loch.

At this sight we both paused: I struck with wonder to find myself so high and walking (as it seemed to me) upon clouds: Alan to make sure of his direction.

Seemingly he was well pleased, and he must certainly have judged us out of ear-shot of all our enemies; for throughout the rest of our night-march he beguiled the way with whistling of many tunes, warlike, merry, plaintive; reel tunes that made the foot go faster; tunes of my own south country that made me fain to be home from my adventures; and all these, on the great, dark, desert mountains, making company upon the way.

Chapter 21

THE FLIGHT IN THE HEATHER: THE HEUGH OF CORRYNAKIEGH

Early as day comes in the beginning of July, it was still dark when we reached our destination, a cleft in the head of a great mountain, with a water running through the midst, and upon the one hand a shallow cave in a rock. Birches grew there in a thin, pretty wood, which a little farther on was changed into a wood of pines. The burn was full of trout; the wood of cushat-doves; on the open side of the mountain beyond, whaups would be always whistling, and cuckoos were plentiful. From the mouth of the cleft we looked down upon a part of Mamore, and on the sea-loch that divides that country from Appin; and this from so great a height as made it my continual wonder and pleasure to sit and behold them.

The name of the cleft was the Heugh of Corrynakiegh; and although from its height and being so near upon the sea, it was often beset with clouds, yet it was on the whole a pleasant place, and the five days we lived in it went happily.

We slept in the cave, making our bed of heather bushes which we cut for that purpose, and covering ourselves with Alan's great-coat. There was a low concealed place, in a turning of the glen, where we were so bold as to make fire: so that we could warm ourselves when the clouds set in, and cook hot porridge, and grill the little trouts that we caught with our hands under the stones and overhanging banks of the burn. This was indeed our chief pleasure and business; and not only to save our meal against worse times, but with a rivalry that much amused us, we spent a great part of our days at the water-side, stripped to the waist and groping about or (as they say) guddling for these fish. The largest we got might have been a quarter of a pound; but they were of good flesh and flavour, and when broiled upon the coals, lacked only a little salt to be delicious.

In any by-time Alan must teach me to use my sword, for my ignorance had much distressed him; and I think besides, as I had sometimes the upper hand of him in the fishing, he was not sorry to turn to an exercise where he had so much the upper hand of me. He made it somewhat more of a pain than need have been, for he stormed at me all through the lessons in a very violent manner of scolding, and would push me so close that I made sure he must run me through the body. I was often tempted to turn tail, but held my ground for all that, and got some profit of my lessons; if it was but to stand on guard with an assured countenance, which is often all that is required. So, though I could never in the least please my master, I was not altogether displeased with myself.

In the meanwhile, you are not to suppose that we neglected our chief business, which was to get away.

"It will be many a long day," Alan said to me on our first morning, "before the red-coats think upon seeking Corrynakiegh; so now we must get word sent to James, and he must find the siller for us."

"And how shall we send that word?" says I. "We are here in a desert place, which yet we dare not leave; and unless ye get the fowls of the air to be your messengers, I see not what we shall be able to do."

"Ay?" said Alan. "Ye're a man of small contrivance, David."

Thereupon he fell in a muse, looking in the embers of the fire; and presently, getting a piece of wood, he fashioned it in a cross, the four ends of which he blackened on the coals. Then he looked at me a little shyly.

"Could ye lend me my button?" says he. "It seems a strange thing to ask a gift again, but I own I am laith to cut another."

I gave him the button; whereupon he strung it on a strip of his great-coat which he had used to bind the cross;

and tying in a little sprig of birch and another of fir, he looked upon his work with satisfaction.

"Now," said he, "there is a little clachan" (what is called a hamlet in the English) "not very far from Corrynakiegh, and it has the name of Koalisnacoan. There there are living many friends of mine whom I could trust with my life, and some that I am no' just so sure of. Ye see, David, there will be money set upon our heads; James himsel' is to set money on them; and as for the Campbells, they would never spare siller where there was a Stewart to be hurt. If it was otherwise, I would go down to Koalisnacoan whatever, and trust my life into these people's hands as lightly as I would trust another with my glove."

"But being so?" said I.

"Being so," said he, "I would as lief they didna see me. There's bad folk everywhere, and what's far worse, weak ones. So when it comes dark again, I will steal down into that clachan, and set this that I have been making in the window of a good friend of mine, John Breck Maccoll, a bouman[1] of Appin's."

"With all my heart," says I; "and if he finds it, what is he to think?"

"Well," says Alan, "I wish he was a man of more penetration, for by my troth I am afraid he will make little enough of it! But this is what I have in my mind. This cross is something in the nature of the crosstarrie, or fiery cross, which is the signal of gathering in our clans; yet he will know well enough the clan is not to rise, for there it is standing in his window, and no word with it. So he will say to himsel', *The clan is not to rise, but there is something*. Then he will see my button, and that was Duncan Stewart's. And then he will say to himsel', *The son of Duncan is in the heather, and has need of me*."

"Well," said I, "it may be. But even supposing so, there is a good deal of heather between here and the Forth."

"And that is a very true word," says Alan. "But then John Breck will see the sprig of birch and the sprig of pine; and he will say to himsel' (if he is a man of any penetration at

---

[1]Tenant who takes stock from the landlord and shares with him the increase.

all, which I misdoubt), *Alan will be lying in a wood which is both of pines and birches*. Then he will think to himsel', *That is not so very rife hereabout*; and then he will come and give us a look up in Corrynakiegh. And if he does not, David, the devil may fly away with him, for what I care; for he will no' be worth the salt to his porridge."

"Eh, man," said I, drolling with him a little, "you're very ingenious! But would it not be simpler for you to write him a few words in black and white?"

"And that is an excellent observe, Mr. Balfour of Shaws," says Alan, drolling with me; "and it would certainly be much simpler for me to write to him, but it would be a sore job for John Breck to read it. He would have to go to the school for two-three years; and it's possible we might be wearied waiting on him."

So that night Alan carried down his fiery cross and set it in the bouman's window. He was troubled when he came back; for the dogs had barked and the folk run out from their houses; and he thought he had heard a clatter of arms and seen a red-coat come to one of the doors. On all accounts we lay the next day in the borders of the wood and kept a close look-out, so that if it was John Breck that came we might be ready to guide him, and if it was the red-coats we should have time to get away.

About noon a man was to be spied, straggling up the open side of the mountain in the sun, and looking round him as he came, from under his hand. No sooner had Alan seen him than he whistled; the man turned and came a little towards us: then Alan would give another "peep!" and the man would come still nearer; and so by the sound of whistling, he was guided to the spot where we lay.

He was a ragged, wild, bearded man, about forty, grossly disfigured with the small-pox, and looked both dull and savage. Although his English was very bad and broken, yet Alan (according to his very handsome use, whenever I was by) would suffer him to speak no Gaelic. Perhaps the strange language made him appear more backward than he really was; but I thought he had little good-will to serve us, and what he had was the child of terror.

Alan would have had him carry a message to James; but the bouman would hear of no message. "She was forget it," he said in his screaming voice; and would either have a letter or wash his hands of us.

I thought Alan would be gravelled at that, for we lacked the means of writing in that desert. But he was a man of more resources than I knew; searched the wood until he found the quill of a cushat-dove, which he shaped into a pen; made himself a kind of ink with gunpowder from his horn and water from the running stream; and tearing a corner from his French military commission (which he carried in his pocket, like a talisman to keep him from the gallows), he sat down and wrote as follows:

"DEAR KINSMAN,—Please send the money by the bearer to the place he kens of.

"Your affectionate cousin,
"A. S."

This he entrusted to the bouman, who promised to make what manner of speed he best could, and carried it off with him down the hill.

He was three full days gone, but about five in the evening of the third, we heard a whistling in the wood, which Alan answered; and presently the bouman came up the water-side, looking for us, right and left. He seemed less sulky than before, and indeed he was no doubt well pleased to have got to the end of such a dangerous commission.

He gave us the news of the country: that it was alive with red-coats; that arms were being found, and poor folk brought in trouble daily; and that James and some of his servants were already clapped in prison at Fort William, under strong suspicion of complicity. It seemed it was noised on all sides that Alan Breck had fired the shot; and there was a bill issued for both him and me, with one hundred pounds reward.

This was all as bad as could be; and the little note the bouman had carried us from Mrs. Stewart was of a miserable sadness. In it she besought Alan not to let himself be captured, assuring him, if he fell in the hands of the troops, both he and James were no better than dead men. The money she had sent was all that she could beg or borrow, and she prayed heaven we could be doing with it. Lastly, she said, she enclosed us one of the bills in which we were described.

This we looked upon with great curiosity and not a little fear, partly as a man may look in a mirror, partly as he might look into the barrel of an enemy's gun to judge if it be truly aimed. Alan was advertised as "a small, pock-marked, active man of thirty-five or thereby, dressed in a feathered hat, a French side-coat of blue with silver buttons, and lace a great deal tarnished, a red waistcoat and breeches of black shag"; and I as "a tall strong lad of about eighteen, wearing an old blue coat, very ragged, an old Highland bonnet, a long home-spun waistcoat, blue breeches; his legs bare, low-country shoes, wanting the toes; speaks like a Lowlander, and has no beard."

Alan was well enough pleased to see his finery so fully remembered and set down; only when he came to the word tarnish, he looked upon his lace like one a little mortified. As for myself, I thought I cut a miserable figure in the bill; and yet was well enough pleased too, for since I had changed these rags, the description had ceased to be a danger and become a source of safety.

"Alan," said I, "you should change your clothes."

"Na, troth!" said Alan, "I have nae others. A fine sight I would be, if I went back to France in a bonnet!"

This put a second reflection in my mind: that if I were to separate from Alan and his tell-tale clothes I should be safe against arrest, and might go openly about my business. Nor was this all; for suppose I was arrested when I was alone, there was little against me; but suppose I was taken in company with the reputed murderer, my case would begin to be grave. For generosity's sake I dare not speak my mind upon this head; but I thought of it none the less.

I thought of it all the more, too, when the bouman brought out a green purse with four guineas in gold, and the best part of another in small change. True, it was more than I had. But then Alan, with less than five guineas, had to get as far as France; I, with my less than two, not beyond Queensferry; so that taking things in their proportion, Alan's society was not only a peril to my life, but a burden on my purse.

But there was no thought of the sort in the honest head of my companion. He believed he was serving, helping, and protecting me. And what could I do but hold my peace, and chafe, and take my chance of it?

"It's little enough," said Alan, putting the purse in his pocket, "but it'll do my business: And now, John Breck, if ye will hand me over my button, this gentleman and me will be for taking the road."

But the bouman, after feeling about in a hairy purse that hung in front of him in the Highland manner (though he wore otherwise the Lowland habit, with sea-trousers), began to roll his eyes strangely, and at last said, "Her nainsel' will loss it," meaning he thought he had lost it.

"What!" cried Alan, "you will lose my button, that was my father's before me? Now I will tell you what is in my mind, John Breck: it is in my mind this is the worst day's work that ever ye did since ye were born."

And as Alan spoke, he set his hands on his knees and looked at the bouman with a smiling mouth, and that dancing light in his eyes that meant mischief to his enemies.

Perhaps the bouman was honest enough; perhaps he had meant to cheat and then, finding himself alone with two of us in a desert place, cast back to honesty as being safer; at least, and all at once, he seemed to find that button and handed it to Alan.

"Well, and it is a good thing for the honour of the Maccolls," said Alan, and then to me, "Here is my button back again, and I thank you for parting with it, which is of a piece with all your friendships to me." Then he took the warmest parting of the bouman.

"For," says he, "ye have done very well by me, and set your neck at a venture, and I will always give you the name of a good man."

Lastly, the bouman took himself off by one way; and Alan and I (getting our chattels together) struck into another to resume our flight.

Chapter 22

THE FLIGHT IN THE HEATHER: THE MOOR

Some seven hours' incessant, hard travelling brought us early in the morning to the end of a range of mountains. In front of us there lay a piece of low, broken, desert land, which we must now cross. The sun was not long up, and shone straight in our eyes; a little, thin mist went up from the face of the moorland like a smoke; so that (as Alan said) there might have been twenty squadron of dragoons there and we none the wiser.

We sat down, therefore, in a howe[1] of the hillside till the mist should have risen, and made ourselves a dish of drammach, and held a council of war.

"David," said Alan, "this is the kittle bit. Shall we lie here till it comes night, or shall we risk it, and stave on ahead?"

"Well," said I, "I am tired indeed, but I could walk as far again, if that was all."

"Ay, but it isna," said Alan, "nor yet the half. This is how we stand: Appin's fair death to us. To the south it's all Campbells, and no' to be thought of. To the north; well, there's no muckle to be gained by going north; neither for you, that wants to get to Queensferry, nor yet for me, that wants to get to France. Well then, we'll can strike east."

"East be it!" says I, quite cheerily; but I was thinking, in to myself: "O, man, if you would only take one point of the compass and let me take any other, it would be the best for both of us."

"Well, then, east, ye see, we have the muirs," said

[1]Hollow.

Alan. "Once there, David, it's mere pitch-and-toss. Out on yon bald, naked, flat place, where can a body turn to? Let the red-coats come over a hill, they can spy you miles away; and the sorrow's in their horses' heels, they would soon ride you down. It's no good place, David; and I'm free to say, it's worse by daylight than by dark."

"Alan," said I, "hear my way of it. Appin's death for us; we have none too much money, nor yet meal; the longer they seek, the nearer they may guess where we are; it's all a risk; and I give my word to go ahead until we drop."

Alan was delighted. "There are whiles," said he, "when ye are altogether too canny and Whiggish to be company for a gentleman like me; but there come other whiles when ye show yoursel' a mettle spark; and it's then, David, that I love ye like a brother."

The mist rose and died away, and showed us that country lying as waste as the sea; only the moorfowl and the peewees crying upon it, and far over to the east, a herd of deer, moving like dots. Much of it was red with heather; much of the rest broken up with bogs and hags and peaty pools; some had been burnt black in a heath fire; and in another place there was quite a forest of dead firs, standing like skeletons. A wearier-looking desert man never saw; but at least it was clear of troops, which was our point.

We went down accordingly into the waste, and began to make our toilsome and devious travel towards the eastern verge. There were the tops of mountains all round (you are to remember) from whence we might be spied at any moment; so it behoved us to keep in the hollow parts of the moor, and when these turned aside from our direction to move upon its naked face with infinite care. Sometimes, for half an hour together, we must crawl from one heather bush to another, as hunters do when they are hard upon the deer. It was a clear day again, with a blazing sun; the water in the brandy bottle was soon gone; and altogether, if I had guessed what it would be to crawl half the time upon my belly and to walk much of the rest stooping nearly to the knees, I should certainly have held back from such a killing enterprise.

Toiling and resting and toiling again, we wore away the morning; and about noon lay down in a thick bush of heather to sleep. Alan took the first watch; and it seemed to me I had scarce closed my eyes before I was shaken up to take the second. We had no clock to go by; and Alan stuck a sprig of heath in the ground to serve instead; so that as soon as the shadow of the bush should fall so far to the east, I might know to rouse him. But I was by this time so weary that I could have slept twelve hours at a stretch; I had the taste of sleep in my throat; my joints slept even when my mind was waking; the hot smell of the heather, and the drone of the wild bees, were like possets to me; and every now and again I would give a jump and find I had been dozing.

The last time I woke I seemed to come back from farther away, and thought the sun had taken a great start in the heavens. I looked at the sprig of heath, and at that I could have cried aloud: for I saw I had betrayed my trust. My head was nearly turned with fear and shame; and at what I saw, when I looked out around me on the moor, my heart was like dying in my body. For sure enough, a body of horse-soldiers had come down during my sleep, and were drawing near to us from the south-east, spread out in the shape of a fan and riding their horses to and fro in the deep parts of the heather.

When I waked Alan, he glanced first at the soldiers, then at the mark and the position of the sun, and knitted his brows with a sudden, quick look, both ugly and anxious, which was all the reproach I had of him.

"What are we to do now?" I asked.

"We'll have to play at being hares," said he. "Do ye see yon mountain?" pointing to one on the north-eastern sky.

"Ay," said I.

"Well then," says he, "let us strike for that. Its name is Ben Alder; it is a wild, desert mountain full of hills and hollows, and if we can win to it before the morn, we may do yet."

"But, Alan," cried I, "that will take us across the very coming of the soldiers!"

"I ken that fine," said he; "but if we are driven back on Appin, we are two dead men. So now, David man, be brisk!"

With that he began to run forward on his hands and

knees with an incredible quickness, as though it were his natural way of going. All the time, too, he kept winding in and out in the lower parts of the moorland where we were the best concealed. Some of these had been burned or at least scathed with fire; and there rose in our faces (which were close to the ground) a blinding, choking dust as fine as smoke. The water was long out; and this posture of running on the hands and knees brings an overmastering weakness and weariness, so that the joints ache and the wrists faint under your weight.

Now and then, indeed, where was a big bush of heather, we lay a while, and panted, and putting aside the leaves, looked back at the dragoons. They had not spied us, for they held straight on; a half-troop, I think, covering about two miles of ground, and beating it mighty thoroughly as they went. I had awakened just in time; a little later, and we must have fled in front of them, instead of escaping on one side. Even as it was, the least misfortune might betray us; and now and again, when a grouse rose out of the heather with a clap of wings, we lay as still as the dead and were afraid to breathe.

The aching and faintness of my body, the labouring of my heart, the soreness of my hands, and the smarting of my throat and eyes in the continual smoke of dust and ashes, had soon grown to be so unbearable that I would gladly have given up. Nothing but the fear of Alan lent me enough of a false kind of courage to continue. As for himself (and you are to bear in mind that he was cumbered with a great-coat) he had first turned crimson, but as time went on the redness began to be mingled with patches of white; his breath cried and whistled as it came; and his voice, when he whispered his observations in my ear during our halts, sounded like nothing human. Yet he seemed in no way dashed in spirits, nor did he at all abate in his activity; so that I was driven to marvel at the man's endurance.

At length, in the first gloaming of the night, we heard a trumpet sound, and looking back from among the heather, saw the troop beginning to collect. A little after, they had built a fire and camped for the night, about the middle of the waste.

At this I begged and besought that we might lie down and sleep.

"There shall be no sleep the night!" said Alan. "From now on, these weary dragoons of yours will keep the crown of the muirland, and none will get out of Appin but winged fowls. We got through in the nick of time, and shall we jeopard what we've gained? Na, na, when the day comes, it shall find you and me in a fast place on Ben Alder."

"Alan," I said, "it's not the want of will: it's the strength that I want. If I could, I would; but as sure as I'm alive, I cannot."

"Very well, then," said Alan. "I'll carry ye."

I looked to see if he were jesting; but no, the little man was in dead earnest; and the sight of so much resolution shamed me.

"Lead away!" said I. "I'll follow."

He gave me one look as much as to say, "Well done, David!" and off he set again at his top speed.

It grew cooler and even a little darker (but not much) with the coming of the night. The sky was cloudless; it was still early in July, and pretty far north; in the darkest part of that night, you would have needed pretty good eyes to read, but for all that, I have often seen it darker in a winter mid-day. Heavy dew fell and drenched the moor like rain; and this refreshed me for a while. When we stopped to breathe, and I had time to see all about me, the clearness and sweetness of the night, the shapes of the hills like things asleep, and the fire dwindling away behind us, like a bright spot in the midst of the moor, anger would come upon me in a clap that I must still drag myself in agony and eat the dust like a worm.

By what I have read in books, I think few that have held a pen were ever really wearied, or they would write of it more strongly. I had no care of my life, neither past nor future, and I scarce remembered there was such a lad as David Balfour; I did not think of myself, but just of each fresh step which I was sure would be my last, with despair— and of Alan, who was the cause of it, with hatred. Alan was in the right trade as a soldier; this is the officer's part to make men continue to do things, they know not where-

fore, and when, if the choice was offered, they would lie
down where they were and be killed. And I daresay I
would have made a good enough private; for in these last
hours, it never occurred to me that I had any choice but
just to obey as long as I was able, and die obeying.

Day began to come in, after years, I thought; and by
that time we were past the greatest danger, and could
walk upon our feet like men, instead of crawling like
brutes. But, dear heart have mercy! what a pair we must
have made, going double like old grandfathers, stumbling
like babes, and as white as dead folk. Never a word passed
between us; each set his mouth and kept his eyes in front
of him, and lifted up his foot and set it down again, like
people lifting weights at a country play;[1] all the while,
with the moorfowl crying "peep!" in the heather, and the
light coming slowly clearer in the east.

I say Alan did as I did. Not that ever I looked at him,
for I had enough ado to keep my feet; but because it
is plain he must have been as stupid with weariness
as myself, and looked as little where we were going,
or we should not have walked into an ambush like blind
men.

It fell in this way. We were going down a heathery
brae, Alan leading and I following a pace or two behind,
like a fiddler and his wife; when upon a sudden the
heather gave a rustle, three or four ragged men leaped
out, and the next moment we were lying on our backs,
each with a dirk at his throat.

I don't think I cared; the pain of this rough handling was
quite swallowed up by the pains of which I was already
full; and I was too glad to have stopped walking to mind
about a dirk. I lay looking up in the face of the man that
held me; and I mind his face was black with the sun and
his eyes very light, but I was not afraid of him. I heard
Alan and another whispering in the Gaelic; and what they
said was all one to me.

Then the dirks were put up, our weapons were taken
away, and we were set face to face, sitting in the heather.

[1]Village fair.

"They are Cluny's men," said Alan. "We couldna have fallen better. We're just to bide here with these, which are his out-sentries, till they can get word to the chief of my arrival."

Now Cluny Macpherson, the chief of the clan Vourich, had been one of the leaders of the great rebellion six years before; there was a price on his life; and I had supposed him long ago in France, with the rest of the heads of that desperate party. Even tired as I was, the surprise of what I heard half wakened me.

"What," I cried, "is Cluny still here?"

"Ay, is he so!" said Alan. "Still in his own country and kept by his own clan. King George can do no more."

I think I would have asked farther, but Alan gave me the put-off. "I am rather wearied," he said, "and I would like fine to get a sleep." And without more words, he rolled on his face in a deep heather bush, and seemed to sleep at once.

There was no such thing possible for me. You have heard grasshoppers whirring in the grass in the summer-time? Well, I had no sooner closed my eyes, than my body, and above all my head, belly, and wrists, seemed to be filled with whirring grasshoppers; and I must open my eyes again at once, and tumble and toss, and sit up and lie down; and look at the sky which dazzled me, or at Cluny's wild and dirty sentries, peering out over the top of the brae and chattering to each other in the Gaelic.

That was all the rest I had, until the messenger returned; when, as it appeared that Cluny would be glad to receive us, we must get once more upon our feet and set forward. Alan was in excellent good spirits, much refreshed by his sleep, very hungry, and looking pleasantly forward to a dram and a dish of hot collops,[1] of which, it seems, the messenger had brought him word. For my part, it made me sick to hear of eating. I had been dead-heavy before, and now I felt a kind of dreadful lightness, which would not suffer me to walk. I drifted like a gossamer; the ground seemed to me a cloud, the hills a feather-weight, the air to have a current, like a running burn, which

---

[1]Thick slices of meat.

carried me to and fro. With all that, a sort of horror of despair sat on my mind, so that I could have wept at my own helplessness.

I saw Alan knitting his brows at me, and supposed it was in anger; and that gave me a pang of light-headed fear, like what a child may have. I remember, too, that I was smiling, and could not stop smiling, hard as I tried; for I thought it was out of place at such a time. But my good companion had nothing in his mind but kindness; and the next moment, two of the gillies had me by the arms, and I began to be carried forward with great swiftness (or so it appeared to me, although I daresay it was slowly enough in truth), through a labyrinth of dreary glens and hollows and into the heart of that dismal mountain of Ben Alder.

Chapter 23

CLUNY'S CAGE

We came at last to the foot of an exceeding steep wood, which scrambled up a craggy hill-side, and was crowned by a naked precipice.

"It's here," said one of the guides, and we struck up hill.

The trees clung upon the slope, like sailors on the shrouds of a ship; and their trunks were like the rounds of a ladder, by which we mounted.

Quite at the top, and just before the rocky face of the cliff sprang above the foliage, we found that strange house which was known in the country as "Cluny's Cage." The trunks of several trees had been wattled across, the intervals strengthened with stakes, and the ground behind this barricade levelled up with earth to make the floor. A tree, which grew out from the hill-side, was the living centre-beam of the roof. The walls were of wattle and covered with moss. The whole house had something of an egg-shape; and it half hung, half stood in that steep, hill-side thicket, like a wasps' nest in a green hawthorn.

Within, it was large enough to shelter five or six persons with some comfort. A projection of the cliff had been cunningly employed to be the fireplace; and the smoke rising against the face of the rock, and being not dissimilar in colour, readily escaped notice from below.

This was but one of Cluny's hiding-places; he had caves, besides, and underground chambers in several parts of his country; and following the reports of his scouts, he moved from one to another as the soldiers drew near or moved away. By this manner of living, and thanks to the affection of his clan, he had not only stayed all this time in safety, while so many others had fled or been taken and slain: but stayed four or five years longer, and only went to France at last by the express command of his master. There he soon died; and it is strange to reflect that he may have regretted his Cage upon Ben Alder.

When we came to the door he was seated by his rock chimney, watching a gillie about some cookery. He was mighty plainly habited, with a knitted nightcap drawn over his ears, and smoked a foul cutty[1] pipe. For all that he had the manners of a king, and it was quite a sight to see him rise out of his place to welcome us.

"Well, Mr. Stewart, come awa', sir!" said he, "and bring in your friend that as yet I dinna ken the name of."

"And how is yourself, Cluny?" said Alan. "I hope ye do brawly, sir. And I am proud to see ye, and to present to ye my friend the Laird of Shaws, Mr. David Balfour."

Alan never referred to my estate without a touch of a sneer, when we were alone; but with strangers, he rang the words out like a herald.

"Step in by, the both of ye, gentlemen," says Cluny. "I make ye welcome to my house, which is a queer, rude place for certain, but one where I have entertained a royal personage, Mr. Stewart—ye doubtless ken the personage I have in my eye. We'll take a dram for luck, and as soon as this handless man of mine has the collops ready, we'll dine and take a hand at the cartes as gentlemen should. My life is a bit driegh,"[2] says he, pouring out the brandy; "I see little company, and sit and twirl my thumbs, and mind upon a great day that is gone by, and weary for another great day that we all hope will be upon the road. And so here's a toast to ye: The Restoration!"

Thereupon we all touched glasses and drank. I am sure I wished no ill to King George; and if he had been there himself in proper person, it's like he would have done as I did. No sooner had I taken out the dram than I felt hugely better, and could look on and listen, still a little mistily

[1]Short.   [2]Dull.

perhaps, but no longer with the same groundless horror and distress of mind.

It was certainly a strange place, and we had a strange host. In his long hiding, Cluny had grown to have all manner of precise habits, like those of an old maid. He had a particular place where no one else must sit; the Cage was arranged in a particular way, which none must disturb; cookery was one of his chief fancies, and even while he was greeting us in, he kept an eye to the collops.

It appears, he sometimes visited or received visits from his wife and one or two of his nearest friends, under the cover of night; but for the more part lived quite alone, and communicated only with his sentinels and the gillies that waited on him in the Cage. The first thing in the morning, one of them, who was a barber, came and shaved him, and gave him the news of the country, of which he was immoderately greedy. There was no end to his questions; he put them as earnestly as a child; and at some of the answers, laughed out of all bounds of reason, and would break out again laughing at the mere memory, hours after the barber was gone.

To be sure, there might have been a purpose in his questions; for though he was thus sequestered, and like the other landed gentlemen of Scotland, stripped by the late Act of Parliament of legal powers, he still exercised a patriarchal justice in his clan. Disputes were brought to him in his hiding-hole to be decided; and the men of his country, who would have snapped their fingers at the Court of Session, laid aside revenge and paid down money at the bare word of this forfeited and hunted outlaw. When he was angered, which was often enough, he gave his commands and breathed threats of punishment like any king; and his gillies trembled and crouched away from him like children before a hasty father. With each of them, as he entered, he ceremoniously shook hands, both parties touching their bonnets at the same time in a military manner. Altogether, I had a fair chance to see some of the inner workings of a Highland clan; and this with a proscribed, fugitive chief; his country conquered; the troops riding upon all sides in quest of him, sometimes within a mile of where he lay; and when the least of the ragged fellows whom he rated and threatened, could have made a fortune by betraying him.

On that first day, as soon as the collops were ready, Cluny gave them with his own hand a squeeze of a lemon (for he was well supplied with luxuries) and bade us draw in to our meal.

"They," said he, meaning the collops, "are such as I gave His Royal Highness in this very house; bating the lemon juice, for at that time we were glad to get the meat and never fashed for kitchen.[1] Indeed, there were mair dragoons than lemons in my country in the year forty-six."

I do not know if the collops were truly very good, but my heart rose against the sight of them, and I could eat but little. All the while Cluny entertained us with stories of Prince Charlie's stay in the Cage, giving us the very words of the speakers, and rising from his place to show us where they stood. By these, I gathered the Prince was a gracious, spirited boy, like the son of a race of polite kings, but not so wise as Solomon. I gathered, too, that while he was in the Cage, he was often drunk; so the fault that has since, by all accounts, made such a wreck of him, had even then begun to show itself.

We were no sooner done eating than Cluny brought out an old, thumbed, greasy pack of cards, such as you may find in a mean inn; and his eyes brightened in his face as he proposed that we should fall to playing.

Now this was one of the things I had been brought up to eschew like disgrace; it being held by my father neither the part of a Christian nor yet of a gentleman to set his own livelihood and fish for that of others, on the cast of painted pasteboard. To be sure, I might have pleaded my fatigue, which was excuse enough; but I thought it behoved that I should bear a testimony. I must have got very red in the face, but I spoke steadily, and told them I had no call to be a judge of others, but for my own part, it was a matter on which I had no clearness.

Cluny stopped mingling the cards. "What in the deil's

[1]Condiment.

name is this?" says he. "What kind of Whiggish, canting
talk is this, for the house of Cluny Macpherson?"

"I will put my hand in the fire for Mr. Balfour," says
Alan. "He is an honest and a mettle gentleman, and I
would have ye bear in mind who says it. I bear a king's
name," says he, cocking his hat; "and I and any that I call
friend are company for the best. But the gentleman is
tired, and should sleep; if he has no mind to the cartes, it
will never hinder you and me. And I'm fit and willing, sir,
to play ye any game that ye can name."

"Sir," says Cluny, "in this poor house of mine I would
have you to ken that any gentleman may follow his pleasure. If your friend would like to stand on his head, he is
welcome. And if either he, or you, or any other man, is
not preceesely satisfied, I will be proud to step outside
with him."

I had no will that these two friends should cut their
throats for my sake.

"Sir," said I, "I am very wearied, as Alan says; and
what's more, as you are a man that likely has sons of your
own, I may tell you it was a promise to my father."

"Say nae mair, say nae mair," said Cluny, and pointed
me to a bed of heather in a corner of the Cage. For all that
he was displeased enough, looked at me askance, and
grumbled when he looked. And indeed it must be owned
that both my scruples and the words in which I declared
them, smacked somewhat of the Covenanter, and were
little in their place among wild Highland Jacobites.

What with the brandy and the venison, a strange heavi-
ness had come over me; and I had scarce lain down upon
the bed before I fell into a kind of trance, in which I
continued almost the whole time of our stay in the Cage.
Sometimes I was broad awake and understood what passed;
sometimes I only heard voices, of men snoring, like the
voice of a silly river; and the plaids upon the wall dwin-
dled down and swelled out again, like firelight shadows on
the roof. I must sometimes have spoken or cried out, for I
remember I was now and then amazed at being answered;
yet I was conscious of no particular nightmare, only of a
general, black, abiding horror—a horror of the place I was

in, and the bed I lay in, and the plaids on the wall, and the voices, and the fire, and myself.

The barber-gillie, who was a doctor too, was called in to prescribe for me; but as he spoke in the Gaelic, I understood not a word of his opinion, and was too sick even to ask for a translation. I knew well enough I was ill, and that was all I cared about.

I paid little heed while I lay in this poor pass. But Alan and Cluny were most of the time at the cards, and I am clear that Alan must have begun by winning; for I remember sitting up, and seeing them hard at it, and a great glittering pile of as much as sixty or a hundred guineas on the table. It looked strange enough, to see all this wealth in a nest upon a cliff-side, wattled about growing trees. And even then, I thought it seemed deep water for Alan to be riding, who had no better battle-horse than a green purse and a matter of five pounds.

The luck, it seems, changed on the second day. About noon I was wakened as usual for dinner, and as usual refused to eat, and was given a dram with some bitter infusion which the barber had prescribed. The sun was shining in at the open door of the Cage, and this dazzled and offended me. Cluny sat at the table, biting the pack of cards. Alan had stooped over the bed, and had his face close to my eyes; to which, troubled as they were with the fever, it seemed of the most shocking bigness.

He asked me for a loan of my money.

"What for?" said I.

"O, just for a loan," said he.

"But why?" I repeated. "I don't see."

"Hut, David!" said Alan, "ye wouldna grudge me a loan?"

I would, though, if I had had my senses! But all I thought of then was to get his face away, and I handed him my money.

On the morning of the third day, when we had been forty-eight hours in the Cage, I awoke with a great relief of spirits, very weak and weary indeed, but seeing things of the right size and with their honest, everyday appearance. I had a mind to eat, moreover, rose from bed of my own movement, and as soon as we had breakfasted, stepped to the entry of the Cage and sat down outside in the top of the wood. It was a grey day with a cool, mild air: and I sat in a dream all morning, only disturbed by the passing by of Cluny's scouts and servants coming with provisions and reports; for as the coast was at that time clear, you might almost say he held court openly.

When I returned, he and Alan had laid the cards aside, and were questioning a gillie; and the chief turned about and spoke to me in the Gaelic.

"I have no Gaelic, sir," said I.

Now since the card question, everything I said or did had the power of annoying Cluny. "Your name has more sense than yourself, then," said he, angrily; "for it's good Gaelic. But the point is this. My scout reports all clear in the south, and the question is, have ye the strength to go?"

I saw cards on the table, but no gold; only a heap of little written papers, and these all on Cluny's side. Alan, besides, had an odd look, like a man not very well content; and I began to have a strong misgiving.

"I do not know if I am as well as I should be," said I, looking at Alan; "but the little money we have has a long way to carry us."

Alan took his under-lip into his mouth, and looked upon the ground.

"David," says he at last, "I've lost it; there's the naked truth."

"My money too?" said I.

"Your money too," says Alan, with a groan. "Ye shouldna have given it me. I'm daft when I get to the cartes."

"Hoot-toot! hoot-toot!" said Cluny. "It was all daffing; it's all nonsense. Of course you'll have your money back again, and the double of it, if ye'll make so free with me. It would be a singular thing for me to keep it. It's not to be supposed that I would be any hindrance to gentlemen in your situation; that would be a singular thing!" cries he, and began to pull gold out of his pocket with a mighty red face.

Alan said nothing, only looked on the ground.

"Will you step to the door with me, sir?" said I.

Cluny said he would be very glad, and followed me readily enough, but he looked flustered and put out.

"And now, sir," says I, "I must first acknowledge your generosity."

"Nonsensical nonsense!" cries Cluny. "Where's the generosity? This is just a most unfortunate affair; but what would ye have me do—boxed up in this bee-skep[1] of a cage of mine—but just set my friends to the cartes, when I can get them? And if they lose, of course, it's not to be supposed——" And here he came to a pause.

"Yes," said I, "if they lose, you give them back their money; and if they win, they carry away yours in their pouches! I have said before that I grant your generosity; but to me, sir, it's a very painful thing to be placed in this position."

There was a little silence, in which Cluny seemed always as if he was about to speak, but said nothing. All the time he grew redder and redder in the face.

"I am a young man," said I, "and I ask your advice. Advise me as you would your son. My friend fairly lost his money, after having fairly gained a far greater sum of yours; can I accept it back again? Would that be the right part for me to play? Whatever I do, you can see for yourself it must be hard upon a man of any pride."

"It's rather hard on me, too, Mr. Balfour," said Cluny, "and ye give me very much the look of a man that has entrapped poor people to their hurt. I wouldna have my friends come to any house of mine to accept affronts; no," he cried, with a sudden heat of anger, "nor yet to give them!"

"And so you see, sir," said I, "there is something to be said upon my side; and this gambling is a very poor employ for gentlefolks. But I am still waiting your opinion."

I am sure if ever Cluny hated any man it was David Balfour. He looked me all over with a warlike eye, and I saw the challenge at his lips. But either my youth disarmed him or perhaps his own sense of justice. Certainly

---

[1]Beehive.

it was a mortifying matter for all concerned, and not least Cluny; the more credit that he took it as he did.

"Mr. Balfour," said he, "I think you are too nice and covenanting, but for all that you have the spirit of a very pretty gentleman. Upon my honest word, ye may take this money—it's what I would tell my son—and here's my hand along with it!"

Chapter 24

THE FLIGHT IN THE HEATHER: THE QUARREL

Alan and I were put across Loch Errocht under cloud of night, and went down its eastern shore to another hiding-place near the head of Loch Rannoch, whither we were led by one of the gillies from the Cage. This fellow carried all our luggage and Alan's great-coat in the bargain, trotting along under the burthen, far less than the half of which used to weigh me to the ground, like a stout hill-pony with a feather; yet he was a man that, in plain contest, I could have broken on my knee.

Doubtless it was a great relief to walk disencumbered; and perhaps without that relief, and the consequent sense of liberty and lightness, I could not have walked at all. I was but new risen from a bed of sickness; and there was nothing in the state of our affairs to hearten me for much exertion; travelling, as we did, over the most dismal deserts in Scotland, under a cloudy heaven, and with divided hearts among the travellers.

For long we said nothing; marching alongside or one behind the other, each with a set countenance; I, angry and proud, and drawing what strength I had from these two violent and sinful feelings: Alan angry and ashamed, —ashamed that he had lost my money, angry that I should take it so ill.

The thought of a separation ran always the stronger in my mind; and the more I approved of it, the more ashamed I grew of my approval. It would be a fine, handsome, generous thing, indeed, for Alan to turn round and say to me: "Go, I am in the most danger, and my company only increases yours." But for me to turn to the friend who certainly loved me, and say to him: "You are in great danger, I am in but little; your friendship is a burden; go, take your risks and bear your hardships alone——" no, that was impossible; and even to think of it privily to myself made my cheeks to burn.

And yet Alan had behaved like a child, and (what is worse) a treacherous child. Wheedling my money from me while I lay half-conscious was scarce better than theft; and yet here he was trudging by my side, without a penny to his name, and by what I could see, quite blithe to sponge upon the money he had driven me to beg. True, I was ready to share it with him; but it made me rage to see him count upon my readiness.

These were the two things uppermost in my mind; and I could open my mouth upon neither without black ungenerosity. So I did the next worst, and said nothing, nor so much as looked once at my companion, save with the tail of my eye.

At last, upon the other side of Loch Errocht, going over a smooth, rushy place, where the walking was easy, he could bear it no longer, and came close to me.

"David," says he, "this is no way for two friends to take a small accident. I have to say that I'm sorry; and so that's said. And now if you have anything, ye'd better say it."

"O," says I, "I have nothing."

He seemed disconcerted; at which I was meanly pleased.

"No," said he, with rather a trembling voice, "but when I say I was to blame?"

"Why, of course, ye were to blame," said I, coolly; "and you will bear me out that I have never reproached you."

"Never," says he; "but ye ken very well that ye've done worse. Are we to part? Ye said so once before. Are ye to say it again? There's hills and heather enough between here and the two seas, David; and I will own I'm no' very keen to stay where I'm no' wanted."

This pierced me like a sword, and seemed to lay bare my private disloyalty.

"Alan Breck!" I cried; and then: "Do you think I am one to turn my back on you in your chief need? You dursn't say it to my face. My whole conduct's there to give the lie to it. It's true, I fell asleep upon the muir; but that was from weariness, and you do wrong to cast it up to me——"

"Which is what I never did," said Alan.

"But aside from that," I continued, "what have I done that you should even me to dogs by such a supposition? I never yet failed a friend, and it's not likely I'll begin with you. There are things between us that I can never forget, even if you can."

"I will only say this to ye, David," said Alan, very quietly, "that I have long been owing ye my life, and now I owe ye money. Ye should try to make that burden light for me."

This ought to have touched me, and in a manner it did, but the wrong manner. I felt I was behaving badly; and was now not only angry with Alan, but angry with myself in the bargain; and it made me the more cruel.

"You asked me to speak," said I. "Well, then, I will. You own yourself that you have done me a disservice; I have had to swallow an affront: I have never reproached you, I never named the thing till you did. And now you blame me," cried I, "because I canna laugh and sing as if I was glad to be affronted. The next thing will be that I'm to go down upon my knees and thank you for it! You should think more of others, Alan Breck. If ye thought more of others, ye would perhaps speak less about yourself; and when a friend that likes you very well has passed over an offence without a word, you would be blithe to let it lie, instead of making it a stick to break his back with. By your own way of it, it was you that was to blame; then it shouldna be you to seek the quarrel."

"Aweel," said Alan, "say nae mair."

And we fell back into our former silence; and came to our journey's end, and supped, and lay down to sleep, without another word.

The gillie put us across Loch Rannoch in the dusk of the next day, and gave us his opinion as to our best route. This was to get us up at once into the tops of the mountains: to go round by a circuit, turning the heads of Glen Lyon, Glen Lochay, and Glen Dochart, and come down upon the Lowlands by Kippen and the upper waters of the Forth. Alan was little pleased with a route which led us

through the country of his blood-foes, the Glenorchy Campbells. He objected that by turning to the east, we should
come almost at once among the Athole Stewarts, a race of
his own name and lineage, although following a different
chief, and come besides by a far easier and swifter way to
the place whither we were bound. But the gillie, who was
indeed the chief man of Cluny's scouts, had good reasons
to give him on all hands, naming the force of troops in
every district, and alleging finally (as well as I could understand) that we should nowhere be so little troubled as
in a country of the Campbells.

Alan gave way at last, but with only half a heart. "It's
one of the dowiest[1] countries in Scotland," said he. "There's
naething there that I ken, but heath, and crows, and
Campbells. But I see that ye're a man of some penetration; and be it as ye please!"

We set forth accordingly by this itinerary; and for the
best part of three nights travelled on eerie mountains and
among the well-heads of wild rivers; often buried in mist,
almost continually blown and rained upon, and not once
cheered by any glimpse of sunshine. By day, we lay and
slept in the drenching heather; by night, incessantly clambered upon break-neck hills and among rude crags. We
often wandered; we were often so involved in fog, that we
must lie quiet till it lightened. A fire was never to be
thought of. Our only food was drammach and a portion of
cold meat that we had carried from the Cage; and as for
drink, Heaven knows we had no want of water.

This was a dreadful time, rendered the more dreadful
by the gloom of the weather and the country. I was never
warm; my teeth chattered in my head; I was troubled with
a very sore throat, such as I had on the isle; I had a painful
stitch in my side, which never left me; and when I slept in
my wet bed, with the rain beating above and the mud
oozing below me, it was to live over again in fancy the
worst part of my adventures—to see the tower of Shaws lit
by lightning, Ransome carried below on the men's backs,
Shuan dying on the round-house floor, or Colin Campbell
grasping at the bosom of his coat. From such broken

_____
[1]Most dismal.

slumbers, I would be aroused in the gloaming, to sit up in the same puddle where I had slept, and sup cold drammach; the rain driving sharp in my face or running down my back in icy trickles; the mist enfolding us like as in a gloomy chamber—or, perhaps, if the wind blew, falling suddenly apart and showing us the gulf of some dark valley where the streams were crying aloud.

The sound of an infinite number of rivers came up from all round. In this steady rain the springs of the mountain were broken up; every glen gushed water like a cistern; every stream was in high spate, and had filled and over-flowed its channel. During our night tramps, it was sol-emn to hear the voice of them below in the valleys, now booming like thunder, now with an angry cry. I could well understand the story of the Water Kelpie, that demon of the streams, who is fabled to keep wailing and roaring at the ford until the coming of the doomed traveller. Alan I saw believed it, or half believed it; and when the cry of the river rose more than usually sharp, I was little sur-prised (though, of course, I would still be shocked) to see him cross himself in the manner of the Catholics.

During all these horrid wanderings we had no familiari-ty, scarcely even that of speech. The truth is that I was sickening for my grave, which is my best excuse. But besides that I was of an unforgiving disposition from my birth, slow to take offence, slower to forget it, and now incensed both against my companion and myself. For the best part of two days he was unweariedly kind; silent, indeed, but always ready to help, and always hoping (as I could very well see) that my displeasure would blow by. For the same length of time I stayed in myself, nursing my anger, roughly refusing his services, and passing him over with my eyes as if he had been a bush or a stone.

The second night, or rather the peep of the third day, found us upon a very open hill, so that we could not follow our usual plan and lie down immediately to eat and sleep. Before we had reached a place of shelter, the grey had come pretty clear, for though it still rained, the clouds ran higher; and Alan, looking in my face, showed some marks of concern.

"Ye had better let me take your pack," said he, for

perhaps the ninth time since we had parted from the scout beside Loch Rannoch.

"I do very well, I thank you," said I, as cold as ice.

Alan flushed darkly. "I'll not offer it again," he said. "I'm not a patient man, David."

"I never said you were," said I, which was exactly the rude, silly speech of a boy of ten.

Alan made no answer at the time, but his conduct answered for him. Henceforth, it is to be thought, he quite forgave himself for the affair at Cluny's; cocked his hat again, walked jauntily, whistled airs, and looked at me upon one side with a provoking smile.

The third night we were to pass through the western end of the country of Balquhidder. It came clear and cold, with a touch in the air like frost, and a northerly wind that blew the clouds away and made the stars bright. The streams were full, of course, and still made a great noise among the hills; but I observed that Alan thought no more upon the Kelpie, and was in high good spirits. As for me, the change of weather came too late; I had lain in the mire so long that (as the Bible has it) my very clothes "abhorred me"; I was dead weary, deadly sick and full of pains and shiverings; the chill of the wind went through me, and the sound of it confused my ears. In this poor state I had to bear from my companion something in the nature of a persecution. He spoke a good deal, and never without a taunt. "Whig" was the best name he had to give me. "Here," he would say, "here's a dub for ye to jump, my Whiggie! I ken you're a fine jumper!" And so on; all the time with a gibing voice and face.

I knew it was my own doing, and no one else's; but I was too miserable to repent. I felt I could drag myself but little farther; pretty soon, I must lie down and die on these wet mountains like a sheep or a fox, and my bones must whiten there like the bones of a beast. My head was light, perhaps, but I began to love the prospect; I began to glory in the thought of such a death, alone in the desert, with the wild eagles besieging my last moments. Alan would repent then, I thought; he would remember, when I was dead, how much he owed me, and the remembrance would be torture. So I went like a sick, silly, and bad-hearted schoolboy, feeding my anger against a fellow-man, when I would have been better on my knees, crying on God for mercy. And at each of Alan's taunts, I hugged myself. "Ah!" thinks I to myself, "I have a better taunt in readiness; when I lie down and die, you will feel it like a buffet in your face; ah, what a revenge! ah, how you will regret your ingratitude and cruelty!"

All the while, I was growing worse and worse. Once I had fallen, my leg simply doubling under me, and this had struck Alan for the moment; but I was afoot so briskly, and set on again with such a natural manner, that he soon forgot the incident. Flushes of heat went over me, and then spasms of shuddering. The stitch in my side was hardly bearable. At last I began to feel that I could trail myself no farther: and with that, there came on me all at once the wish to have it out with Alan, let my anger blaze, and be done with my life in a more sudden manner. He had just called me "Whig." I stopped.

"Mr. Stewart," said I, in a voice that quivered like a fiddle-string, "you are older than I am, and should know your manners. Do you think it either very wise or very witty to cast my politics in my teeth? I thought, where folk differed, it was the part of gentlemen to differ civilly; and if I did not, I may tell you I could find a better taunt than some of yours."

Alan had stopped opposite to me, his hat cocked, his hands in his breeches-pockets, his head a little on one side. He listened, smiling evilly, as I could see by the starlight; and when I had done he began to whistle a Jacobite air. It was the air made in mockery of General Cope's defeat at Prestonpans:—

> "Hey, Johnnie Cope, are ye waukin' yet?
> And are your drums a-beatin' yet?"

And it came in my mind that Alan, on the day of that battle, had been engaged upon the royal side.

"Why do ye take that air, Mr. Stewart?" said I. "Is that to remind me you have been beaten on both sides?"

The air stopped on Alan's lips. "David!" said he.

"But it's time these manners ceased," I continued; "and

I mean you shall henceforth speak civilly of my King and my good friends the Campbells."

"I am a Stewart——" began Alan.

"O!" says I, "I ken ye bear a king's name. But you are to remember, since I have been in the Highlands, I have seen a good many of those that bear it; and the best I can say of them is this, that they would be none the worse of washing."

"Do you know that you insult me?" said Alan, very low.

"I am sorry for that," said I, "for I am not done; and if you distaste the sermon, I doubt the pirliecue[1] will please you as little. You have been chased in the field by the grown men of my party; it seems a poor kind of pleasure to outface a boy. Both the Campbells and the Whigs have beaten you; you have run before them like a hare. It behoves you to speak of them as of your betters."

Alan stood quite still, the tails of his great-coat clapping behind him in the wind.

"This is a pity," he said at last. "There are things said that cannot be passed over."

"I never asked you to," said I. "I am as ready as yourself."

"Ready?" said he.

"Ready," I repeated. "I am no blower and boaster like some that I could name. Come on!" And drawing my sword, I fell on guard as Alan himself had taught me.

"David!" he cried. "Are ye daft? I canna draw upon ye, David. It's fair murder."

"That was your look-out when you insulted me," said I.

"It's the truth!" cried Alan, and he stood for a moment, wringing his mouth in his hand like a man in sore perplexity. "It's the bare truth," he said, and drew his sword. But before I could touch his blade with mine, he had thrown it from him and fallen to the ground. "Na, na," he kept saying, "na, na—I canna, I canna."

At this the last of my anger oozed all out of me; and I found myself only sick, and sorry, and blank, and wondering at myself. I would have given the world to take back what I had said; but a word once spoken, who can recapture it? I minded me of all Alan's kindness and courage in

---

[1] A second sermon.

the past, how he had helped and cheered and borne with me in our evil days; and then recalled my own insults, and saw that I had lost for ever that doughty friend. At the same time, the sickness that hung upon me seemed to redouble, and the pang in my side was like a sword for sharpness. I thought I must have swooned where I stood.

This it was that gave me a thought. No apology could blot out what I had said; it was needless to think of one, none could cover the offence; but where an apology was vain, a mere cry for help might bring Alan back to my side. I put my pride away from me.

"Alan!" I said; "if ye canna help me, I must just die here."

He started up sitting, and looked at me.

"It's true," said I. "I'm by with it. O, let me get into the bield[1] of a house—I'll can die there easier." I had no need to pretend; whether I chose or not, I spoke in a weeping voice that would have melted a heart of stone.

"Can ye walk?" asked Alan.

"No," said I, "not without help. This last hour my legs have been fainting under me; I've a stitch in my side like a red-hot iron; I canna breathe right. If I die, ye'll can forgive me, Alan? In my heart, I liked ye fine—even when I was the angriest."

"Wheesht, wheesht!" cried Alan. "Dinna say that! David man, ye ken——" He shut his mouth upon a sob. "Let me get my arm about ye," he continued; "that's the way! Now lean upon me hard. Gude kens where there's a house! We're in Balwhidder, too; there should be no want of houses, no, nor friends' houses here. Do ye gang easier so, Davie?"

"Ay," said I, "I can be doing this way"; and I pressed his arm with my hand.

Again he came near sobbing. "Davie," said he, "I'm no' a right man at all; I have neither sense nor kindness; I couldna remember ye were just a bairn, I couldna see ye were dying on your feet; Davie, ye'll have to try and forgive me."

"O man, let's say no more about it!" said I. "We're

---

[1]Shelter.

neither one of us to mend the other—that's the truth! We must just bear and forbear, man Alan.—O, but my stitch is sore! Is there nae house?"

"I'll find a house to ye, David," he said, stoutly. "We'll follow down the burn, where there's bound to be houses. My poor man, will ye no' be better on my back?"

"O, Alan," says I, "and me a good twelve inches taller?"

"Ye're no such a thing," cried Alan, with a start. "There may be a trifling matter of an inch or two; I'm no' saying; I'm just exactly what ye would call a tall man, whatever; and I dare say," he added, his voice tailing off in a laughable manner, "now when I come to think of it, I dare say ye'll be just about right. Ay, it'll be a foot, or near-hand; or may be even mair!"

It was sweet and laughable to hear Alan eat his words up in the fear of some fresh quarrel. I could have laughed, had not my stitch caught me so hard; but if I had laughed, I think I must have wept too.

"Alan," cried I, "what makes ye so good to me? What makes ye care for such a thankless fellow?"

"'Deed, and I don't know," said Alan. "For just precisely what I thought I liked about ye was that ye never quarrelled:—and now I like ye better!"

Chapter 25

IN BALQUHIDDER

At the door of the first house we came to, Alan knocked, which was no very safe enterprise in such a part of the Highlands as the Braes of Balquhidder. No great clan held rule there; it was filled and disputed by small septs, and broken remnants, and what they call "chiefless folk," driven into the wild country about the springs of Forth and Teith by the advance of the Campbells. Here were Stewarts and Maclarens, which came to the same thing, for the Maclarens followed Alan's chief in war, and made but one clan with Appin. Here, too, were many of that old, proscribed, nameless, red-handed clan of the Macgregors. They had always been ill-considered, and now worse than ever, having credit with no side or party in the whole country of Scotland. Their chief, Macgregor of Macgregor, was in exile; the more immediate leader of that part of them about Balquhidder, James More, Rob Roy's eldest son, lay waiting his trial in Edinburgh Castle; they were in ill-blood with Highlander and Lowlander, with the Grahames, the Maclarens, and the Stewarts; and Alan, who took up the quarrel of any friend, however distant, was extremely wishful to avoid them.

Chance served us very well; for it was a household of Maclarens that we found, where Alan was not only welcome for his name's sake but known by reputation. Here then I was got to bed without delay, and a doctor fetched, who found me in a sorry plight. But whether because he was a very good doctor, or I a very young, strong man, I lay bedridden for no more than a week, and before a month, I was able to take the road again with a good heart.

All this time Alan would not leave me, though I often pressed him, and indeed his foolhardiness in staying was a common subject of outcry with the two or three friends that were let into the secret. He hid by day in a hole of the braes under a little wood; and at night, when the coast was clear, would come into the house to visit me. I need not say if I was pleased to see him; Mrs. Maclaren, our hostess, thought nothing good enough for such a guest; and as Duncan Dhu (which was the name of our host) had a pair of pipes in his house, and was much of a lover of music, the time of my recovery was quite a festival, and we commonly turned night into day.

The soldiers let us be; although once a party of two companies and some dragoons went by in the bottom of the valley, where I could see them through the window as I lay in bed. What was much more astonishing, no magistrate came near me, and there was no question put of whence I came or whither I was going; and in that time of excitement, I was as free of all inquiry as though I had lain in a desert. Yet my presence was known before I left to all the people in Balquhidder and the adjacent parts; many coming about the house on visits and these (after the custom of the country) spreading the news among their neighbours. The bills, too, had now been printed. There was one pinned near the foot of my bed, where I could read my own not very flattering portrait and, in larger characters, the amount of the blood-money that had been set upon my life. Duncan Dhu and the rest that knew that I had come there in Alan's company, could have entertained no doubt of who I was; and many others must have had their guess. For though I had changed my clothes, I could not change my age or person; and Lowland boys of eighteen were not so rife in these parts of the world, and above all about that time, that they could fail to put one thing with another, and connect me with the bill. So it was, at least. Other folk keep a secret among two or three near friends, and somehow it leaks out; but among these clansmen, it is told to a whole country-side, and they will keep it for a century.

There was but one thing happened worth narrating; and that is the visit I had of Robin Oig, one of the sons of the notorious Rob Roy. He was sought upon all sides on a charge of carrying a young woman from Balfron and marrying her (as was alleged) by force; yet he stepped about Balquhidder like a gentleman in his own walled policy. It was he who had shot James Maclaren at the plough-stilts, a quarrel never satisfied; yet he walked into the house of his blood enemies as a rider[1] might into a public inn.

Duncan had time to pass me word of who it was; and we looked at one another in concern. You should understand, it was then close upon the time of Alan's coming, the two were little likely to agree; and yet if we sent word or sought to make a signal, it was sure to arouse suspicion in a man under so dark a cloud as the Macgregor.

He came in with a great show of civility, but like a man among inferiors; took off his bonnet to Mrs. Maclaren, but clapped it on his head again to speak to Duncan; and having thus set himself (as he would have thought) in a proper light, came to my bedside and bowed.

"I am given to know, sir," says he, "that your name is Balfour."

"They call me David Balfour," said I, "at your service."

"I would give ye my name in return, sir," he replied, "but it's one somewhat blown upon of late days; and it'll perhaps suffice if I tell ye that I am own brother to James More Drummond or Macgregor, of whom ye will scarce have failed to hear."

"No, sir," said I, a little alarmed; "nor yet of your father, Macgregor-Campbell." And I sat up and bowed in bed; for I thought best to compliment him, in case he was proud of having had an outlaw to his father.

He bowed in return. "But what I am come to say, sir," he went on, "is this. In the year '45, my brother raised a part of the 'Gregara,' and marched six companies to strike a stroke for the good side; and the surgeon that marched with our clan and cured my brother's leg when it was broken in the brush at Prestonpans, was a gentleman of the same name precisely as yourself. He was brother to

---

[1]Salesman.

Balfour of Baith; and if you are in any reasonable degree of nearness one of that gentleman's kin, I have come to put myself and my people at your command."

You are to remember that I knew no more of my descent than any cadger's dog; my uncle, to be sure, had prated of some of our high connections, but nothing to the present purpose; and there was nothing left me but that bitter disgrace of owning that I could not tell.

Robin told me shortly he was sorry he had put himself about, turned his back upon me without a sign of salutation, and as he went towards the door, I could hear him telling Duncan that I was "only some kinless loon that didn't know his own father." Angry as I was at these words, and ashamed of my own ignorance, I could scarce keep from smiling that a man who was under the lash of the law (and was indeed hanged some three years later) should be so nice as to the descent of his acquaintances.

Just in the door, he met Alan coming in; and the two drew back and looked at each other like strange dogs. They were neither of them big men, but they seemed fairly to swell out with pride. Each wore a sword, and by a movement of his haunch, thrust clear the hilt of it, so that it might be the more readily grasped and the blade drawn.

"Mr. Stewart, I am thinking," says Robin.

"Troth, Mr. Macgregor, it's not a name to be ashamed of," answered Alan.

"I did not know ye were in my country, sir," says Robin.

"It sticks in my mind that I am in the country of my friends the Maclarens," says Alan.

"That's a kittle point," returned the other. "There may be two words to say to that. But I think I will have heard that you are a man of your sword?"

"Unless ye were born deaf, Mr. Macgregor, ye will have heard a good deal more than that," says Alan. "I am not the only man that can draw steel in Appin; and when my kinsman and captain, Ardshiel, had a talk with a gentleman of your name, not so many years back, I could never hear that the Macgregor had the best of it."

"Do ye mean my father, sir?" says Robin.

"Well, I wouldna wonder," said Alan. "The gentleman I

have in my mind had the ill-taste to clap Campbell to his name."

"My father was an old man," returned Robin. "The match was unequal. You and me would make a better pair, sir."

"I was thinking that," said Alan.

I was half out of bed, and Duncan had been hanging at the elbow of these fighting cocks ready to intervene upon the least occasion. But when that word was uttered, it was a case of now or never; and Duncan, with something of a white face to be sure, thrust himself between.

"Gentlemen," said he, "I will have been thinking of a very different matter, whateffer. Here are my pipes, and here are you two gentlemen who are baith acclaimed pipers. It's an auld dispute which one of ye's the best. Here will be a braw chance to settle it."

"Why, sir," said Alan, still addressing Robin, from whom indeed he had not so much as shifted his eyes, nor yet Robin from him, "why, sir," says Alan, "I think I will have heard some sough[1] of the sort. Have ye music, as folk say? Are ye a bit of a piper?"

"I can pipe like a Macrimmon!" cries Robin.

"And that is a very bold word," quoth Alan.

"I have made bolder words good before now," returned Robin, "and that against better adversaries."

"It is easy to try that," says Alan.

Duncan Dhu made haste to bring out the pair of pipes that was his principal possession, and to set before his guests a mutton-ham and a bottle of that drink which they call Atholebrose, and which is made of old whisky, strained honey and sweet cream, slowly beaten together in the right order and proportion. The two enemies were still on the very breach of a quarrel; but down they sat, one upon each side of the peat fire, with a mighty show of politeness. Maclaren pressed them to taste his mutton-ham and "the wife's brose," reminding them the wife was out of Athole and had a name far and wide for her skill in that confection. But Robin put aside these hospitalities as bad for the breath.

[1] Rumour.

"I would have ye to remark, sir," said Alan, "that I havena broken bread for near upon ten hours, which will be worse for the breath than any brose in Scotland."

"I will take no advantages, Mr. Stewart," replied Robin. "Eat and drink; I'll follow you."

Each ate a small portion of the ham and drank a glass of the brose to Mrs. Maclaren; and then, after a great number of civilities, Robin took the pipes and played a little spring in a very ranting[1] manner.

"Ay, ye can blow," said Alan, and taking the instrument from his rival, he first played the same spring in a manner identical with Robin's and then wandered into variations, which, as he went on, he decorated with a perfect flight of grace-notes, such as pipers love, and call the "warblers."

I had been pleased with Robin's playing; Alan's ravished me.

"That's no' very bad, Mr. Stewart," said the rival, "but ye show a poor device in your warblers."

"Me!" cried Alan, the blood starting to his face. "I give ye the lie."

"Do ye own yourself beaten at the pipes, then," said Robin, "that ye seek to change them for the sword?"

"And that's very well said, Mr. Macgregor," returned Alan; "and in the meantime" (laying a strong accent on the word) "I take back the lie. I appeal to Duncan."

"Indeed, ye need appeal to naebody," said Robin. "Ye're a far better judge than any Maclaren in Balquhidder: for it's a God's truth that you're a very creditable piper for a Stewart. Hand me the pipes."

Alan did as he asked; and Robin proceeded to imitate and correct some part of Alan's variations, which it seemed that he remembered perfectly.

"Ay, ye have music," said Alan, gloomily.

"And now be the judge yourself, Mr. Stewart," said Robin; and taking up the variations from the beginning, he worked them throughout to so new a purpose, with such ingenuity and sentiment, and with so odd a fancy and so quick a knack in the grace-notes, that I was amazed to hear him.

[1]Lively.

As for Alan, his face grew dark and hot, and he sat and gnawed his fingers, like a man under some deep affront. "Enough!" he cried. "Ye can blow the pipes—make the most of that." And he made as if to rise.

But Robin only held out his hand as if to ask for silence, and struck into the slow measure of a pibroch. It was a fine piece of music in itself, and nobly played; but it seems, besides, it was a piece peculiar to the Appin Stewarts and a chief favourite with Alan. The first notes were scarce out, before there came a change in his face; when the time quickened, he seemed to grow restless in his seat; and long before that piece was at an end, the last signs of his anger died from him, and he had no thought but for the music.

"Robin Oig," he said, when it was done, "ye are a great piper. I am not fit to blow in the same kingdom with ye. Body of me! ye have mair music in your sporran than I have in my head! And though it still sticks in my mind that I could maybe show ye another of it with the cold steel, I warn ye beforehand—it'll no' be fair! It would go against my heart to haggle a man that can blow the pipes as you can!"

Thereupon that quarrel was made up; all night long the brose was going and the pipes changing hands; and the day had come pretty bright, and the three men were none the better for what they had been taking, before Robin as much as thought upon the road.

Chapter 26

END OF THE FLIGHT: WE PASS THE FORTH

The month, as I have said, was not yet out but it was already far through August, and beautiful warm weather, with every sign of an early and great harvest, when I was pronounced able for my journey. Our money was now run to so low an ebb that we must think first of all on speed; for if we came not soon to Mr. Rankeillor's, or if when we came there he should fail to help me, we must surely starve. In Alan's view, besides, the hunt must have now greatly slackened; and the line of the Forth and even Stirling Bridge, which is the main pass over that river, would be watched with little interest.

"It's a chief principle in military affairs," said he, "to go where ye are least expected. Forth is our trouble; ye ken the saying, 'Forth bridles the wild Hielandman.' Well, if we seek to creep round about the head of that river and come down by Kippen or Balfron, it's just precisely there that they'll be looking to lay hands on us. But if we stave on straight to the auld Brig of Stirling, I'll lay my sword they let us pass unchallenged."

The first night, accordingly, we pushed to the house of a Maclaren in Strathire, a friend of Duncan's, where we slept the twenty-first of the month, and whence we set forth again about the fall of night to make another easy stage. The twenty-second we lay in a heather bush on the hill-side in Uam Var, within view of a herd of deer, the happiest ten hours of sleep in a fine, breathing sunshine and on bone-dry ground, that I have ever tasted. That night we struck Allan Water, and followed it down; and coming to the edge of the hills saw the whole Carse of

Stirling underfoot, as flat as a pancake, with the town and castle on a hill in the midst of it, and the moon shining on the Links of Forth.

"Now," said Alan, "I kenna if ye care, but ye're in your own land again. We passed the Hieland Line in the first hour; and now if we could but pass yon crooked water, we might cast our bonnets in the air."

In Allan Water, near by where it falls into the Forth, we found a little sandy islet, overgrown with burdock, butterbur, and the like low plants, that would just cover us if we lay flat. Here it was we made our camp, within plain view of Stirling Castle, whence we could hear the drums beat as some part of the garrison paraded. Shearers worked all day in a field on one side of the river, and we could hear the stones going on the hooks and the voices and even the words of the men talking. It behoved to lie close and keep silent. But the sand of the little isle was sun-warm, the green plants gave us shelter for our heads, we had food and drink in plenty; and to crown all, we were within sight of safety.

As soon as the shearers quit their work and the dusk began to fall, we waded ashore and struck for the Bridge of Stirling, keeping to the fields and under the field fences.

The bridge is close under the castle hill, an old, high, narrow bridge with pinnacles along the parapet; and you may conceive with how much interest I looked upon it, not only as a place famous in history, but as the very doors of salvation to Alan and myself. The moon was not yet up when we came there; a few lights shone along the front of the fortress, and lower down a few lighted windows in the town; but it was all mighty still, and there seemed to be no guard upon the passage.

I was for pushing straight across; but Alan was more wary.

"It looks unco quiet," said he; "but for all that we'll lie down here cannily behind a dyke, and make sure."

So we lay for about a quarter of an hour, whiles whispering, whiles lying still and hearing nothing earthly but the washing of the water on the piers. At last there came by an old, hobbling woman with a crutch stick; who first stopped a little, close to where we lay, and bemoaned

herself and the long way she had travelled; and then set
forth again up the steep spring of the bridge. The woman
was so little, and the night still so dark, that we soon lost
sight of her; only heard the sound of her steps, and her
stick, and a cough that she had by fits, draw slowly farther
away.

"She's bound to be across now," I whispered.

"Na," said Alan, "her foot still sounds boss[1] upon the
bridge."

And just then—"Who goes?" cried a voice, and we
heard the butt of a musket rattle on the stones. I must
suppose the sentry had been sleeping, so that had we
tried, we might have passed unseen; but he was awake
now, and the chance forfeited.

"This'll never do," said Alan. "This'll never, never do
for us, David."

And without another word, he began to crawl away
through the fields; and a little after, being well out of
eye-shot, got to his feet again, and struck along a road that
led to the eastward. I could not conceive what he was
doing; and indeed I was so sharply cut by the disappointment, that I was little likely to be pleased with anything.
A moment back and I had seen myself knocking at Mr.
Rankeillor's door to claim my inheritance, like a hero in a
ballad; and here was I back again, a wandering, hunted
blackguard, on the wrong side of Forth.

"Well?" said I.

"Well," said Alan, "what would ye have? They're none
such fools as I took them for. We have still the Forth to
pass, Davie—weary fall the rains that fed and the hill-
sides that guided it!"

"And why go east?" said I.

"Ou, just upon the chance!" said he. "If we canna pass
the river, we'll have to see what we can do for the firth."

"There are fords upon the river, and none upon the
firth," said I.

"To be sure there are fords, and a bridge forbye," quoth
Alan; "and of what service, when they are watched?"

[1] Hollow.

"Well," said I, "but a river can be swum."

"By them that have the skill of it," returned he; "but I have yet to hear that either you or me is much of a hand at that exercise; and for my own part, I swim like a stone."

"I'm not up to you in talking back, Alan," I said; "but I can see we're making bad worse. If it's hard to pass a river, it stands to reason it must be worse to pass a sea."

"But there's such a thing as a boat," says Alan, "or I'm the more deceived."

"Ay, and such a thing as money," says I. "But for us that have neither one nor other, they might just as well not have been invented."

"Ye think so?" said Alan.

"I do that," said I.

"David," says he, "ye're a man of small invention and less faith. But let me set my wits upon the hone, and if I canna beg, borrow, nor yet steal a boat, I'll make one!"

"I think I see ye!" said I. "And what's more than all that: if ye pass a bridge, it can tell no tales; but if we pass the firth, there's the boat on the wrong side—somebody must have brought it—the countryside will all be in a bizz——"

"Man!" cried Alan, "if I make a boat, I'll make a body to take it back again! So deave[1] me with no more of your nonsense, but walk (for that's what you've got to do)—and let Alan think for ye."

All night, then, we walked through the north side of the Carse under the high line of the Ochil mountains; and by Alloa and Clackmannan and Culross, all of which we avoided: and about ten in the morning, mighty hungry and tired, came to the little clachan of Limekilns. This is a place that sits near in by the water-side, and looks across the Hope to the town of the Queen's Ferry. Smoke went up from both of these, and from other villages and farms upon all hands. The fields were being reaped; two ships lay anchored, and boats were coming and going on the Hope. It was altogether a right pleasant sight to me; and I could not take my fill of gazing at these comfortable,

[1]Deafen.

green, cultivated hills and the busy people both of the field and sea.

For all that, there was Mr. Rankeillor's house on the south shore, where I had no doubt wealth awaited me; and here was I upon the north, clad in poor enough attire of an outlandish fashion, with three silver shillings left to me of all my fortune, a price set upon my head, and an outlawed man for my sole company.

"O, Alan!" said I, "to think of it! Over there, there's all that heart could want waiting me; and the birds go over, and the boats go over—all that please can go, but just me only! O, man, but it's a heart-break!"

In Limekilns we entered a small change-house, which we only knew to be a public by the wand over the door, and bought some bread and cheese from a good-looking lass that was the servant. This we carried with us in a bundle, meaning to sit and eat it in a bush of wood on the sea-shore, that we saw some third part of a mile in front. As we went, I kept looking across the water and sighing to myself; and though I took no heed of it, Alan had fallen into a muse. At last he stopped in the way.

"Did ye take heed of the lass we bought this of?" says he, tapping on the bread and cheese.

"To be sure," said I, "and a bonny lass she was."

"Ye thought that?" cries he. "Man, David, that's good news."

"In the name of all that's wonderful, why so?" says I. "What good can that do?"

"Well," said Alan, with one of his droll looks, "I was rather in hopes it would maybe get us that boat."

"If it were the other way about, it would be liker it," said I.

"That's all that you ken, ye see," said Alan. "I don't want the lass to fall in love with ye, I want her to be sorry for ye, David; to which end there is no manner of need that she should take you for a beauty. Let me see" (looking me curiously over). "I wish ye were a wee thing paler; but apart from that ye'll do fine for my purpose—ye have a fine, hang-dog, rag-and-tatter, clappermaclaw[1] kind of a

[1] Ragamuffin.

look to ye, as if ye had stolen the coat from a potato-bogle.[1] Come; right about, and back to the change-house for that boat of ours."

I followed him, laughing.

"David Balfour," said he, "ye're a very funny gentleman by your way of it, and this is a very funny employ for ye, no doubt. For all that, if ye have any affection for my neck (to say nothing of your own) ye will perhaps be kind enough to take this matter responsibly. I am going to do a bit of play-acting, the bottom ground of which is just exactly as serious as the gallows for the pair of us. So bear it, if ye please, in mind, and conduct yourself according."

"Well, well," said I, "have it as you will."

As we got near the clachan, he made me take his arm and hang upon it like one almost helpless with weariness; and by the time he pushed open the change-house door, he seemed to be half carrying me. The maid appeared surprised (as well she might be) at our speedy return; but Alan had no words to spare for her in explanation, helped me to a chair, called for a tass[2] of brandy with which he fed me in little sips, and then breaking up the bread and cheese helped me to eat it like a nursery-lass; the whole with that grave, concerned, affectionate countenance, that might have imposed upon a judge. It was small wonder if the maid were taken with the picture we presented, of a poor, sick, over-wrought lad and his most tender comrade. She drew quite near, and stood leaning with her back on the next table.

"What's like wrong with him?" said she at last.

Alan turned upon her, to my great wonder, with a kind of fury. "Wrong?" cries he. "He's walked more hundreds of miles than he has hairs upon his chin, and slept oftener in wet heather than dry sheets. Wrong, quo' she! Wrong enough, I would think! Wrong, indeed!" and he kept grumbling to himself as he fed me, like a man ill-pleased.

"He's young for the like of that," said the maid.

"Ower young," said Alan, with his back to her.

"He would be better riding," says she.

"And where could I get a horse to him?" cried Alan,

[1]Scarecrow.   [2]Glass.

turning on her with the same appearance of fury. "Would ye have me steal?"

I thought this roughness would have sent her off in dudgeon, as indeed it closed her mouth for the time. But my companion knew very well what he was doing; and for as simple as he was in some things of life, had a great fund of roguishness in such affairs as these.

"Ye needna tell me," she said at last—"ye're gentry."

"Well," said Alan, softened a little (I believe against his will) by this artless comment, "and suppose we were? Did ever you hear that gentrice put money in folk's pockets?"

She sighed at this, as if she were herself some disinherited great lady. "No," says she, "that's true indeed."

I was all this while chafing at the part I played, and sitting tongue-tied between shame and merriment; but somehow at this I could hold in no longer, and bade Alan let me be, for I was better already. My voice stuck in my throat for I ever hated to take part in lies; but my very embarrassment helped on the plot, for the lass no doubt set down my husky voice to sickness and fatigue.

"Has he nae friends?" said she, in a tearful voice.

"That has he so!" cried Alan, "if we could but win to them!—friends and rich friends, beds to lie in, food to eat, doctors to see to him—and here he must tramp in the dubs[1] and sleep in the heather like a beggar-man."

"And why that?" says the lass.

"My dear," said Alan, "I canna very safely say; but I'll tell ye what I'll do instead," says he, "I'll whistle ye a bit tune." And with that he leaned pretty far over the table, and in a mere breath of a whistle, but with a wonderful pretty sentiment, gave her a few bars of "Charlie is my darling."

"Wheesht," says she, and looked over her shoulder to the door.

"That's it," said Alan.

"And him so young!" cries the lass.

"He's old enough to——" and Alan struck his forefinger on the back part of his neck, meaning that I was old enough to lose my head.

---

[1] Puddles.

"It would be a black shame," she cried, flushing high.

"It's what will be, though," said Alan, "unless we manage the better."

At this the lass turned and ran out of that part of the house, leaving us alone together.—Alan in high good humour at the furthering of his schemes, and I in bitter dudgeon at being called a Jacobite and treated like a child.

"Alan," I cried, "I can stand no more of this."

"Ye'll have to sit it, then, Davie," said he. "For if ye upset the pot now, ye may scrape your own life out of the fire, but Alan Breck is a dead man."

This was so true that I could only groan; and even my groan served Alan's purpose, for it was overheard by the lass as she came flying in again with a dish of white puddings and a bottle of strong ale.

"Poor lamb!" says she and had no sooner set the meat before us, than she touched me on the shoulder with a little friendly touch, as much as to bid me cheer up. Then she told us to fall-to, and there would be no more to pay; for the inn was her own, or at least her father's, and he was gone for the day to Pittencrieff. We waited for no second bidding, for bread and cheese is but cold comfort and the puddings smelt excellently well; and while we sat and ate, she took up that same place by the next table, looking on, and thinking, and frowning to herself, and drawing the string of her apron through her hand.

"I'm thinking ye have rather a long tongue," she said at last to Alan.

"Ay," said Alan; "but ye see I ken the folk I speak to."

"I would never betray ye," said she, "if ye mean that."

"No," said he, "ye're not that kind. But I'll tell ye what ye would do, ye would help."

"I couldna," said she, shaking her head. "No, I couldna."

"No," said he, "but if ye could?"

She answered him nothing.

"Look here, my lass," said Alan, "there are boats in the kingdom of Fife, for I saw two (no less) upon the beach, as I came in by your town's end. Now if we could have the use of a boat to pass under cloud of night into Lothian, and some secret, decent kind of a man to bring that boat back again and keep his counsel, there would be two souls

saved—mine to all likelihood—his to a dead surety. If we
lack that boat, we have but three shillings left in this wide
world; and where to go, and how to do, and what other
place there is for us except the chains of a gibbet—I give
you my naked word, I kenna! Shall we go wanting, lassie?
Are ye to lie in your warm bed and think upon us, when
the wind growls in the chimney and the rain tirls on the
roof? Are ye to eat your meat by the cheeks of a red fire,
and think upon this poor sick lad of mine, biting his
finger-ends on a blae muir for cauld and hunger? Sick or
sound, he must aye be moving; with the death-grapple at
his throat he must aye be trailing in the rain on the lang
roads; and when he gants[1] his last on a rickle[2] of cauld
stanes, there will be nae friends near him but only me and
God."

At this appeal, I could see the lass was in great trouble
of mind, being tempted to help us, and yet in some fear
she might be helping malefactors; and so now I determined to step in myself and to allay her scruples with a
portion of the truth.

"Did ever you hear," said I, "of Mr. Rankeillor of the
Ferry?"

"Rankeillor the writer?" said she. "I daursay that!"

"Well," said I, "it's to his door that I am bound, so you
may judge by that if I am an ill-doer; and I will tell you
more, that though I am indeed, by a dreadful error, in
some peril of my life, King George has no truer friend in
all Scotland than myself."

Her face cleared up mightily at this, although Alan's
darkened.

"That's more than I would ask," said she. "Mr. Rankeillor
is a kennt man." And she bade us finish our meat, get
clear of the clachan as soon as might be, and lie close in
the bit wood on the sea beach. "And ye can trust me,"
says she, "I'll find some means to put you over."

At this we waited for no more, but shook hands with her
upon the bargain, made short work of the puddings, and
set forth again from Limekilns as far as to the wood. It was
a small piece of perhaps a score of elders and hawthorns

---

[1]Gasps.   [2]Pile.

and a few young ashes, not thick enough to veil us from passers-by upon the road or beach. Here we must lie, however, making the best of the brave warm weather and the good hopes we now had of a deliverance, and planning more particularly what remained for us to do.

We had but one trouble all day; when a strolling piper came and sat in the same wood with us; a red-nosed, blear-eyed, drunken dog, with a great bottle of whisky in his pocket, and a long story of wrongs that had been done him by all sorts of persons, from the Lord President of the Court of Session, who had denied him justice, down to the Bailies of Inverkeithing, who had given him more of it than he desired. It was impossible but he should conceive some suspicion of two men lying all day concealed in a thicket and having no business to allege. As long as he stayed there, he kept us in hot water with prying questions; and after he was gone, as he was a man not very likely to hold his tongue, we were in the greater impatience to be gone ourselves.

The day came to an end with the same brightness; the night fell quiet and clear; lights came out in houses and hamlets and then, one after another, began to be put out; but it was past eleven, and we were long since, strangely tortured with anxieties, before we heard the grinding of oars upon the rowing pins. At that, we looked out and saw the lass herself coming rowing to us in a boat. She had trusted no one with our affairs, not even her sweetheart, if she had one; but as soon as her father was asleep, had left the house by a window, stolen a neighbour's boat, and come to our assistance single-handed.

I was abashed how to find expression for my thanks; but she was no less abashed at the thought of hearing them; begged us to lose no time and to hold our peace, saying (very properly) that the heart of our matter was in haste and silence; and so, what with one thing and another, she had set us on the Lothian shore not far from Carriden, had shaken hands with us, and was out again at sea and rowing for Limekilns, before there was one word said either of her service or our gratitude.

Even after she was gone, we had nothing to say, as

indeed nothing was enough for such a kindness. Only Alan stood a great while upon the shore shaking his head.

"It is a very fine lass," he said at last. "David, it is a very fine lass." And a matter of an hour later, as we were lying in a den on the sea-shore and I had been already dozing, he broke out again in commendations of her character. For my part, I could say nothing, she was so simple a creature that my heart smote me both with remorse and fear; remorse because we had traded upon her ignorance; and fear lest we should have anyway involved her in the dangers of our situation.

Chapter 27

I COME TO MR. RANKEILLOR

The next day it was agreed that Alan should fend for
himself till sunset; but as soon as it began to grow dark, he
should lie in the fields by the roadside near to Newhalls,
and stir for naught until he heard me whistling. At first I
proposed I should give him for a signal the "Bonnie House
of Airlie," which was a favourite of mine; but he objected
that as the piece was very commonly known, any ploughman
might whistle it by accident; and taught me instead a little
fragment of a Highland air, which has run in my head
from that day to this, and will likely run in my head when
I lie dying. Every time it comes to me, it takes me off to
that last day of my uncertainty, with Alan sitting up in the
bottom of the den, whistling and beating the measure with
a finger, and the grey of the dawn coming on his face.

I was in the long street of Queen's Ferry before the sun
was up. It was a fairly built burgh, the houses of good
stone, many slated; the town-hall not so fine, I thought, as
that of Peebles, nor yet the street so noble; but take it
altogether, it put me to shame for my foul tatters.

As the morning went on, and the fires began to be
kindled, and the windows to open, and the people to
appear out of the houses, my concern and despondency
grew ever the blacker. I saw now that I had no grounds to
stand upon; and no clear proof of my rights, nor so much
as of my own identity. If it was all a bubble, I was indeed
sorely cheated and left in a sore pass. Even if things were
as I conceived, it would in all likelihood take time to
establish my contentions; and what time had I to spare
with less than three shillings in my pocket, and a con-

demned, hunted man upon my hands to ship out of the country? Truly, if my hope broke with me, it might come to the gallows yet for both of us. And as I continued to walk up and down, and saw people looking askance at me upon the street or out of windows, and nudging or speaking one to another with smiles, I began to take a fresh apprehension: that it might be no easy matter even to come to speech of the lawyer, far less to convince him of my story.

For the life of me I could not muster up the courage to address any of these reputable burghers; I thought shame even to speak with them in such a pickle of rags and dirt; and if I had asked for the house of such a man as Mr. Rankeillor, I suppose they would have burst out laughing in my face. So I went up and down and through the street, and down to the harbour-side, like a dog that has lost its master, with a strange gnawing in my inwards, and every now and then a movement of despair. It grew to be high day at last, perhaps nine in the fore-noon; and I was worn with these wanderings, and chanced to have stopped in front of a very good house on the landward side, a house with beautiful, clear glass windows, flowering knots upon the sills, the walls new-harled[1] and a chase-dog sitting yawning on the step like one that was at home. Well, I was even envying this dumb brute, when the door fell open and there issued forth a shrewd, ruddy, kindly, consequential man in a well-powdered wig and spectacles. I was in such a plight that no one set eyes on me once, but he looked at me again; and this gentleman, as it proved, was so much struck with my poor appearance that he came straight up to me and asked me what I did.

I told him I was come to the Queen's Ferry on business, and taking heart of grace, asked him to direct me to the house of Mr. Rankeillor.

"Why," said he, "that is his house that I have just come out of; and for a rather singular chance, I am that very man."

"Then, sir," said I, "I have to beg the favour of an interview."

[1]Newly rough-cast.

"I do not know your name," said he, "nor yet your face."

"My name is David Balfour," said I.

"David Balfour?" he repeated, in rather a high tone, like one surprised. "And where have you come from, Mr. David Balfour?" he asked, looking me pretty drily in the face.

"I have come from a great many strange places, sir," said I; "but I think it would be as well to tell you where and how in a more private manner."

He seemed to muse a while, holding his lip in his hand, and looking now at me and now upon the causeway of the street.

"Yes," says he, "that will be the best, no doubt." And he led me back with him into his house, cried out to some one whom I could not see that he would be engaged all morning, and brought me into a little dusty chamber full of books and documents. Here he sat down, and bade me be seated; though I thought he looked a little ruefully from his clean chair to my muddy rags. "And now," says he, "if you have any business, pray be brief and come swiftly to the point. *Nec gemino bellum Trojanum orditur ab ovo*—do you understand that?" says he, with a keen look.

"I will even do as Horace says, sir," I answered, smiling, "and carry you *in medias res*." He nodded as if he was well pleased, and indeed his scrap of Latin had been set to test me. For all that, and though I was somewhat encouraged, the blood came in my face when I added: "I have reason to believe myself some rights on the estate of Shaws."

He got a paper book out of a drawer and set it before him open. "Well?" said he.

But I had shot my bolt and sat speechless.

"Come, come, Mr. Balfour," said he, "you must continue. Where were you born?"

"In Essendean, sir," said I, "the year 1733, the 12th of March."

He seemed to follow this statement in his paper book; but what that meant I knew not. "Your father and mother?" said he.

"My father was Alexander Balfour, school-master of that place," said I, "and my mother Grace Pitarrow; I think her people were from Angus."

"Have you any papers proving your identity?" asked Mr. Rankeillor.

"No, sir," said I, "but they are in the hands of Mr. Campbell, the minister, and could be readily produced. Mr. Campbell, too, would give me his word; and for that matter, I do not think my uncle would deny me."

"Meaning Mr. Ebenezer Balfour?" says he.

"The same," said I.

"Whom you have seen?" he asked.

"By whom I was received into his own house," I answered.

"Did you ever meet a man of the name of Hoseason?" asked Mr. Rankeillor.

"I did so, sir, for my sins," said I; "for it was by his means and the procurement of my uncle, that I was kidnapped within sight of this town, carried to sea, suffered shipwreck and a hundred other hardships, and stand before you to-day in this poor accoutrement."

"You say you were shipwrecked," said Rankeillor; "where was that?"

"Off the south end of the Isle of Mull," said I. "The name of the isle on which I was cast up is the Island Earraid."

"Ah!" says he, smiling, "you are deeper than me in the geography. But so far, I may tell you, this agrees pretty exactly with other informations that I hold. But you say you were kidnapped; in what sense?"

"In the plain meaning of the word, sir," said I. "I was on my way to your house, when I was trepanned on board the brig, cruelly struck down, thrown below, and knew no more of anything till we were far at sea. I was destined for the plantations; a fate that, in God's providence, I have escaped."

"The brig was lost on June the 27th," says he, looking in his book, "and we are now at August the 24th. Here is a considerable hiatus, Mr. Balfour, of near upon two months. It has already caused a vast amount of trouble to your friends; and I own I shall not be very well contented until it is set right."

"Indeed, sir," said I, "these months are very easily filled up; but yet before I told my story, I would be glad to know that I was talking to a friend."

"This is to argue in a circle," said the lawyer. "I cannot be convinced till I have heard you. I cannot be your friend till I am properly informed. If you were more trustful, it would better befit your time of life. And you know, Mr. Balfour, we have a proverb in the country that evil-doers are aye evil-dreaders."

"You are not to forget, sir," said I, "that I have already suffered by my trustfulness; and was shipped off to be a slave by the very man that (if I rightly understand) is your employer."

All this while I had been gaining ground with Mr. Rankeillor, and in proportion as I gained ground, gaining confidence. But at this sally, which I made with something of a smile myself, he fairly laughed aloud.

"No, no," said he, "it is not so bad as that. *Fui, non sum*. I *was* indeed your uncle's man of business; but while you (*imberbis juvenis custode remoto*) were gallivanting in the west, a good deal of water has run under the bridges; and if your ears did not sing, it was not for lack of being talked about. On the very day of your sea disaster, Mr. Campbell stalked into my office, demanding you from all the winds. I had never heard of your existence; but I had known your father; and from matters in my competence (to be touched upon hereafter) I was disposed to fear the worst. Mr. Ebenezer admitted having seen you; declared (what seemed improbable) that he had given you considerable sums; and that you had started for the continent of Europe, intending to fulfil your education, which was probable and praiseworthy. Interrogated how you had come to send no word to Mr. Campbell, he deponed that you had expressed a great desire to break with your past life. Further interrogated where you now were, protested ignorance, but believed you were in Leyden. That is a close sum of his replies. I am not exactly sure that any one believed him," continued Mr. Rankeillor with a smile; "and in particular he so much disrelished some expres-

sions of mine that (in a word) he showed me to the door.
We were then at a full stand; for whatever shrewd suspicions we might entertain, we had no shadow of probation.
In the very article, comes Captain Hoseason with the
story of your drowning; whereupon all fell through; with
no consequences but concern to Mr. Campbell, injury to
my pocket, and another blot upon your uncle's character,
which could very ill afford it. And now, Mr. Balfour," said
he, "you understand the whole process of these matters,
and can judge for yourself to what extent I may be trusted."

Indeed he was more pedantic than I can represent him,
and placed more scraps of Latin in his speech; but it was
all uttered with a fine geniality of eye and manner which
went far to conquer my distrust. Moreover, I could see he
now treated me as if I was myself beyond a doubt; so that
first point of my identity seemed fully granted.

"Sir," said I, "if I tell you my story, I must commit a
friend's life to your discretion. Pass me your word it shall
be sacred; and for what touches myself, I will ask no
better guarantee than just your face."

He passed me his word very seriously. "But," said he,
"these are rather alarming prolocutions; and if there are in
your story any little jostles to the law, I would beg you to
bear in mind that I am a lawyer, and pass lightly."

Thereupon I told him my story from the first, he listening with his spectacles thrust up and his eyes closed, so
that I sometimes feared he was asleep. But no such matter! he heard every word (as I found afterward) with such
quickness of hearing and precision of memory as often
surprised me. Even strange outlandish Gaelic names, heard
for that time only, he remembered and would remind me
of, years after. Yet when I called Alan Breck in full, we
had an odd scene. The name of Alan had of course rung
through Scotland, with the news of the Appin murder and
the offer of the reward; and it had no sooner escaped me
than the lawyer moved in his seat and opened his eyes.

"I would name no unnecessary names, Mr. Balfour,"
said he; "above all of Highlanders, many of whom are
obnoxious to the law."

"Well, it might have been better not," said I, "but since
I have let it slip, I may as well continue."

"Not at all," said Mr. Rankeillor. "I am somewhat dull of hearing, as you may have remarked; and I am far from sure I caught the name exactly. We will call your friend, if you please, Mr. Thomson—that there may be no reflections. And in future, I would take some such way with any Highlander that you may have to mention—dead or alive."

By this, I saw he must have heard the name all too clearly, and had already guessed I might be coming to the murder. If he chose to play this part of ignorance, it was no matter of mine; so I smiled, said it was no very Highland-sounding name, and consented. Through all the rest of my story Alan was Mr. Thomson; which amused me the more, as it was a piece of policy after his own heart. James Stewart, in like manner, was mentioned under the style of Mr. Thomson's kinsman; Colin Campbell passed as a Mr. Glen; and to Cluny, when I came to that part of my tale, I gave the name of "Mr. Jameson, a Highland chief." It was truly the most open farce, and I wondered that the lawyer should care to keep it up; but, after all, it was quite in the taste of that age, when there were two parties in the state, and quiet persons, with no very high opinions of their own, sought out every cranny to avoid offence to either.

"Well, well," said the lawyer, when I had quite done, "this is a great epic, a great Odyssey of yours. You must tell it, sir, in a sound Latinity when your scholarship is riper; or in English if you please, though for my part I prefer the stronger tongue. You have rolled much; *quæ regio in terris*—what parish in Scotland (to make a homely translation) has not been filled with your wanderings? You have shown, besides, a singular aptitude for getting into false positions; and, yes, upon the whole, for behaving well in them. This Mr. Thomson seems to me a gentleman of some choice qualities, though perhaps a trifle bloody-minded. It would please me none the worse, if (with all his merits) he were soused in the North Sea, for the man, Mr. David, is a sore embarrassment. But you are doubtless quite right to adhere to him; indubitably, he adhered to you. *It comes*—we may say—he was your true companion; nor less *paribus curis vestigia figit*, for I daresay you would both take an orra[1] thought upon the gallows. Well, well, these days are fortunately by; and I think (speaking humanly) that you are near the end of your troubles."

As he thus moralised on my adventures, he looked upon me with so much humour and benignity that I could scarce contain my satisfaction. I had been so long wandering with lawless people, and making my bed upon the hills and under the bare sky, that to sit once more in a clean, covered house, and to talk amicably with a gentleman in broadcloth, seemed mighty elevations. Even as I thought so, my eye fell on my unseemly tatters, and I was once more plunged in confusion. But the lawyer saw and understood me. He rose, called over the stair to lay another plate, for Mr. Balfour would stay to dinner, and led me into a bedroom in the upper part of the house. Here he set before me water and soap, and a comb; and laid out some clothes that belonged to his son; and here, with another apposite tag, he left me to my toilet.

[1]Extra.

Chapter 28

I GO IN QUEST OF MY INHERITANCE

I made what change I could in my appearance; and blithe was I to look in the glass and find the beggar-man a thing of the past, and David Balfour come to life again. And yet I was ashamed of the change too, and, above all, of the borrowed clothes. When I had done, Mr. Rankeillor caught me on the stair, made me his compliments, and had me again into the cabinet.

"Sit ye down, Mr. David," said he, "and now that you are looking a little more like yourself, let me see if I can find you any news. You will be wondering, no doubt, about your father and your uncle? To be sure it is a singular tale; and the explanation is one that I blush to have to offer you. For," says he, really with embarrassment, "the matter hinges on a love-affair."

"Truly," said I, "I cannot very well join that notion with my uncle."

"But your uncle, Mr. David, was not always old," replied the lawyer, "and what may perhaps surprise you more, not always ugly. He had a fine, gallant air; people stood in their doors to look after him, as he went by on a mettle horse. I have seen it with these eyes, and I ingenuously confess, not altogether without envy; for I was a plain lad myself and a plain man's son; and in those days it was a case of *Odi te, qui bellus es, Sabelle*."

"It sounds like a dream," said I.

"Ay, ay," said the lawyer, "that is how it is with youth and age. Nor was that all, but he had a spirit of his own that seemed to promise great things in the future. In 1715, what must he do but run away to join the rebels? It

was your father that pursued him, found him in a ditch,
and brought him back *multum gementem*; to the mirth of
the whole country. However, *majora canamus*—the two
lads fell in love, and that with the same lady. Mr. Ebenezer,
who was the admired and the beloved, and the spoiled
one, made, no doubt, mighty certain of the victory; and
when he found he had deceived himself, screamed like a
peacock. The whole country heard of it; now he lay sick at
home, with his silly family standing round the bed in
tears; now he rode from public-house to public-house, and
shouted his sorrows into the lug[1] of Tom, Dick, and Harry.
Your father, Mr. David, was a kind gentleman; but he was
weak, dolefully weak; took all this folly with a long countenance; and one day—by your leave!—resigned the lady.
She was no such fool, however; it's from her you must
inherit your excellent good sense; and she refused to be
bandied from one to another. Both got upon his knees to
her; and the upshot of the matter for that while was that
she showed both of them the door. That was in August;
dear me! the same year I came from college. The scene
must have been highly farcical."

I thought myself it was a silly business, but I could not
forget my father had a hand in it. "Surely, sir, it had some
note of tragedy," said I.

"Why, no, sir, not at all," returned the lawyer. "For
tragedy implies some ponderable matter in dispute, some
dignus vindice nodus; and this piece of work was all about
the petulance of a young ass that had been spoiled, and
wanted nothing so much as to be tied up and soundly
belted. However, that was not your father's view; and the
end of it was, that from concession to concession on your
father's part, and from one height to another of squalling,
sentimental selfishness upon your uncle's, they came at
last to drive a sort of bargain, from whose ill results you
have recently been smarting. The one man took the lady,
the other the estate. Now, Mr. David, they talk a great
deal of charity and generosity; but in this disputable state
of life, I often think the happiest consequences seem to
flow when a gentleman consults his lawyer, and takes all

[1]Ear.

the law allows him. Anyhow, this piece of Quixotry on your father's part, as it was unjust in itself, has brought forth a monstrous family of injustices. Your father and mother lived and died poor folk; you were poorly reared; and in the meanwhile, what a time it has been for the tenants on the estate of Shaws! And I might add (if it was a matter I cared much about) what a time for Mr. Ebenezer!"

"And yet that is certainly the strangest part of all," said I, "that a man's nature should thus change."

"True," said Mr. Rankeillor. "And yet I imagine it was natural enough. He could not think that he had played a handsome part. Those who knew the story gave him the cold shoulder; those who knew it not, seeing one brother disappear, and the other succeed in the estate, raised a cry of murder; so that upon all sides he found himself evited.[1] Money was all he got by his bargain; well, he came to think the more of money. He was selfish when he was young, he is selfish now that he is old; and the latter end of all these pretty manners and fine feelings you have seen for yourself."

"Well, sir," said I, "and in all this, what is my position?"

"The estate is yours beyond a doubt," replied the lawyer. "It matters nothing what your father signed, you are the heir of entail. But your uncle is a man to fight the indefensible; and it would be likely your identity that he would call in question. A lawsuit is always expensive, and a family lawsuit always scandalous; besides which, if any of your doings with your friend Mr. Thomson were to come out, we might find that we had burned our fingers. The kidnapping, to be sure, would be a court card upon our side, if we could only prove it. But it may be difficult to prove; and my advice (upon the whole) is to make a very easy bargain with your uncle, perhaps even leaving him at Shaws where he has taken root for a quarter of a century, and contenting yourself in the meanwhile with a fair provision."

I told him I was very willing to be easy, and that to carry family concerns before the public was a step from which I was naturally much averse. In the meantime

[1]Shunned.

(thinking to myself) I began to see the outlines of that scheme on which we afterwards acted.

"The great affair," I asked, "is to bring home to him the kidnapping?"

"Surely," said Mr. Rankeillor, "and if possible, out of court. For mark you here, Mr. David: we could no doubt find some men of the *Covenant* who would swear to your reclusion; but once they were in the box, we could no longer check their testimony, and some word of your friend Mr. Thomson must certainly crop out—which (from what you have let fall) I cannot think to be desirable."

"Well, sir," said I, "here is my way of it." And I opened my plot to him.

"But this would seem to involve my meeting the man Thomson?" says he, when I had done.

"I think so, indeed, sir," said I.

"Dear doctor!" cries he, rubbing his brow. "Dear doctor! No, Mr. David, I am afraid your scheme is inadmissible. I say nothing against your friend, Mr. Thomson: I know nothing against him; and if I did—mark this, Mr. David!—it would be my duty to lay hands on him. Now I put it to you: is it wise to meet? He may have matters to his charge. He may not have told you all. His name may not be even Thomson!" cries the lawyer, twinkling; "for some of these fellows will pick up names by the roadside as another would gather haws."[1]

"You must be the judge, sir," said I.

But it was clear my plan had taken hold upon his fancy, for he kept musing to himself till we were called to dinner and the company of Mrs. Rankeillor; and that lady had scarce left us again to ourselves and a bottle of wine, ere he was back harping on my proposal. When and where was I to meet my friend Mr. Thomson; was I sure of Mr. T.'s discretion; supposing we could catch the old fox tripping, would I consent to such and such a term of an agreement—these and the like questions he kept asking at long intervals, while he thoughtfully rolled his wine upon his tongue. When I had answered all of them, seemingly

---

[1]Hawthorne berries.

to his contentment, he fell into a still deeper muse, even the claret being now forgotten. Then he got a sheet of paper and a pencil, and set to work writing and weighing every word; and at last touched a bell and had his clerk into the chamber.

"Torrance," said he, "I must have this written out fair against to-night; and when it is done, you will be so kind as put on your hat and be ready to come along with this gentleman and me, for you will probably be wanted as a witness."

"What, sir," cried I, as soon as the clerk was gone, "are you to venture it?"

"Why, so it would appear," says he, filling his glass. "But let us speak no more of business. The very sight of Torrance brings in my head a little droll matter of some years ago, when I had made a tryst with the poor oaf at the cross of Edinburgh. Each had gone his proper errand; and when it came four o'clock, Torrance had been taking a glass and did not know his master, and I, who had forgot my spectacles, was so blind without them, that I give you my word I did not know my own clerk." And thereupon he laughed heartily.

I said it was an odd chance, and smiled out of politeness; but what held me all the afternoon in wonder, he kept returning and dwelling on this story, and telling it again with fresh details and laughter; so that I began at last to be quite put out of countenance and feel ashamed for my friend's folly.

Towards the time I had appointed with Alan, we set out from the house, Mr. Rankeillor and I arm in arm, and Torrance following behind with the deed in his pocket and a covered basket in his hand. All through the town, the lawyer was bowing right and left, and continually being button-holed by gentlemen on matters of burgh or private business; and I could see he was one greatly looked up to in the county. At last we were clear of the houses, and began to go along the side of the haven and towards the Hawes Inn and the ferry pier, the scene of my misfortune. I could not look upon the place without emotion, recalling how many that had been there with me that day were now no more: Ransome taken I could hope, from the evil to come; Shuan passed where I dared not follow him; and the poor souls that had gone down with the brig in her last plunge. All these, and the brig herself, I had outlived; and come through these hardships and fearful perils without scathe. My only thought should have been of gratitude; and yet I could not behold the place without sorrow for others and a chill of recollected fear.

I was so thinking when, upon a sudden, Mr. Rankeillor cried out, clapped his hand to his pockets, and began to laugh.

"Why," he cries, "if this be not a farcical adventure! After all that I said, I have forgot my glasses!"

At that, of course, I understood the purpose of his anecdote, and knew that if he had left his spectacles at home, it had been done on purpose, so that he might have the benefit of Alan's help without the awkwardness of recognising him. And indeed it was well thought upon; for now (suppose things to go the very worst) how could Rankeillor swear to my friend's identity, or how be made to bear damaging evidence against myself? For all that, he had been a long while of finding out his want, and had spoken to and recognised a good few persons as we came through the town; and I had little doubt myself that he saw reasonably well.

As soon as we were past the Hawes (where I recognised the landlord smoking his pipe in the door, and was amazed to see him look no older) Mr. Rankeillor changed the order of march, walking behind with Torrance and sending me forward in the manner of a scout. I went up the hill, whistling from time to time my Gaelic air; and at length I had the pleasure to hear it answered and to see Alan rise from behind a bush. He was somewhat dashed in spirits, having passed a long day alone skulking in the county, and made but a poor meal in an alehouse near Dundas. But at the mere sight of my clothes, he began to brighten up; and as soon as I had told him in what a forward state our matters were, and the part I looked to him to play in what remained, he sprang into a new man.

"And that is a very good notion of yours," says he; "and

I dare to say that you could lay your hands upon no better man to put it through than Alan Breck. It is not a thing (mark ye) that any one could do, but takes a gentleman of penetration. But it sticks in my head your lawyer-man will be somewhat wearying to see me," says Alan.

Accordingly I cried and waved on Mr. Rankeillor, who came up alone and was presented to my friend, Mr. Thomson.

"Mr. Thomson, I am pleased to meet you," said he. "But I have forgotten my glasses; and our friend Mr. David here" (clapping me on the shoulder) "will tell you that I am little better than blind, and that you must not be surprised if I pass you by to-morrow."

This he said, thinking that Alan would be pleased; but the Highlandman's vanity was ready to startle at a less matter than that.

"Why, sir," says he, stiffly, "I would say it mattered the less as we are met here for a particular end, to see justice done to Mr. Balfour; and by what I can see, not very likely to have much else in common. But I accept your apology, which was a very proper one to make."

"And that is more than I could look for, Mr. Thomson," said Rankeillor, heartily. "And now as you and I are the chief actors in this enterprise, I think we should come into a nice agreement; to which end, I propose that you should lend me your arm, for (what with the dusk and the want of my glasses) I am not very clear as to the path; and as for you, Mr. David, you will find Torrance a pleasant kind of body to speak with. Only let me remind you, it's quite needless he should hear more of your adventures or those of—ahem—Mr. Thomson."

Accordingly these two went on ahead in very close talk, and Torrance and I brought up the rear.

Night was quite come when we came in view of the house of Shaws. Ten had been gone some time; it was dark and mild, with a pleasant, rustling wind in the south-west that covered the sound of our approach; and as we drew near we saw no glimmer of light in any portion of the building. It seemed my uncle was already in bed, which was indeed the best thing for our arrangements. We made

our last whispered consultations some fifty yards away;
and then the lawyer and Torrance and I crept quietly up
and crouched down beside the corner of the house; and as
soon as we were in our places, Alan strode to the door
without concealment and began to knock.

Chapter 29

I COME INTO MY KINGDOM

For some time Alan volleyed upon the door, and his knocking only roused the echoes of the house and neighbourhood. At last, however, I could hear the noise of a window gently thrust up, and knew that my uncle had come to his observatory. By what light there was, he would see Alan standing, like a dark shadow, on the steps; the three witnesses were hidden quite out of his view; so that there was nothing to alarm an honest man in his own house. For all that, he studied his visitor a while in silence, and when he spoke his voice had a quaver of misgiving.

"What's this?" says he. "This is nae kind of time of night for decent folk; and I hae nae trokings[1] wi' night-hawks. What brings ye here? I have a blunderbush."

"Is that yoursel', Mr. Balfour?" returned Alan, stepping back and looking up into the darkness. "Have a care of that blunderbuss; they're nasty things to burst."

"What brings ye here? and whae are ye?" says my uncle angrily.

"I have no manner of inclination to rowt out my name to the country-side," said Alan; "but what brings me here is another story, being more of your affairs than mine; and if ye're sure it's what ye would like, I'll set it to a tune and sing it to you."

"And what is't?" asked my uncle.

"David," says Alan.

[1] Dealings.

"What was that?" cried my uncle, in a mighty changed voice.

"Shall I give ye the rest of the name, then?" said Alan.

There was a pause; and then, "I'm thinking I'll better let ye in," says my uncle, doubtfully.

"I daresay that," said Alan; "but the point is, Would I go? Now I will tell you what I am thinking. I am thinking that it is here upon this doorstep that we must confer upon this business; and it shall be here or nowhere at all whatever; for I would have you to understand that I am as stiffnecked as yoursel', and a gentleman of better family."

This change of note disconcerted Ebenezer; he was a little while digesting it, and then says he, "Weel, weel, what must be must," and shut the window. But it took him a long time to get down-stairs, and a still longer to undo the fastenings, repenting (I daresay) and taken with fresh claps of fear at every second step and every bolt and bar. At last, however, we heard the creak of the hinges, and it seems my uncle slipped gingerly out and (seeing that Alan had stepped back a pace or two) sate him down on the top doorstep with the blunderbuss ready in his hands.

"And now," says he, "mind I have my blunderbush, and if ye take a step nearer ye're as good as deid."

"And a very civil speech," says Alan, "to be sure."

"Na," says my uncle, "but this is no' a very chancy kind of a proceeding, and I'm bound to be prepared. And now that we understand each other, ye'll can name your business."

"Why," says Alan, "you that are a man of so much understanding, will doubtless have perceived that I am a Hieland gentleman. My name has nae business in my story; but the county of my friends is no' very far from the Isle of Mull, of which ye will have heard. It seems there was a ship lost in those parts; and the next day a gentleman of my family was seeking wreck-wood for his fire along the sands, when he came upon a lad that was half drowned. Well, he brought him to; and he and some other gentlemen took and clapped him in an auld, ruined castle, where from that day to this he has been a great expense to my friends. My friends are a wee wild-like, and not so particular about the law as some that I could name; and finding that the lad owned some decent folk, and was your born nephew, Mr. Balfour, they asked me to give ye a bit call and confer upon the matter. And I may tell ye at the off-go, unless we can agree upon some terms, ye are little likely to set eyes upon him. For my friends," added Alan, simply, "are no' very well off."

My uncle cleared his throat. "I'm no' very caring," says he. "He wasna a good lad at the best of it, and I've nae call to interfere."

"Ay, ay," said Alan, "I see what ye would be at: pretending ye don't care, to make the ransom smaller."

"Na," said my uncle, "it's the mere truth. I take nae manner of interest in the lad, and I'll pay nae ransom, and ye can make a kirk and a mill of him for what I care."

"Hoot, sir," says Alan. "Blood's thicker than water, in the deil's name! Ye canna desert your brother's son for the fair shame of it; and if ye did, and it came to be kennt, ye wouldna be very popular in your country-side, or I'm the more deceived."

"I'm no' just very popular the way it is," returned Ebenezer; "and I dinna see how it would come to be kennt. No by me, onyway; nor yet by you or your friends. So that's idle talk, my buckie," says he.

"Then it'll have to be David that tells it," said Alan.

"How that?" says my uncle, sharply.

"Ou, just this way," says Alan. "My friends would doubtless keep your nephew as long as there was any likelihood of siller to be made of it, but if there was nane, I am clearly of opinion they would let him gang where he pleased, and be damned to him!"

"Ay, but I'm no' very caring about that either," said my uncle. "I wouldna be muckle made up with that."

"I was thinking that," said Alan.

"And what for why?" asked Ebenezer.

"Why, Mr. Balfour," replied Alan, "by all that I could hear, there were two ways of it: either ye liked David and would pay to get him back; or else ye had very good reasons for not wanting him, and would pay for us to keep him. It seems it's not the first; well then, it's the second;

and blythe am I to ken it, for it should be a pretty penny in my pocket and the pockets of my friends."

"I dinna follow ye there," said my uncle.

"No?" said Alan. "Well, see here: you dinna want the lad back; well, what do ye want done with him, and how much will ye pay?"

My uncle made no answer, but shifted uneasily on his seat.

"Come, sir," cried Alan. "I would have you to ken that I am a gentleman; I bear a king's name; I am nae rider to kick my shanks at your hall-door. Either give me an answer in civility, and that out of hand; or, by the top of Glencoe, I will ram three feet of iron through your vitals."

"Eh, man," cried my uncle, scrambling to his feet, "give me a meenit! What's like wrong with ye? I'm just a plain man and nae dancing-master; and I'm trying to be as ceevil as it's morally possible. As for that wild talk, it's fair disrepitable. Vitals, says you! And where would I be with my blunderbush?" he snarled.

"Powder and your auld hands are but as the snail to the swallow against the bright steel in the hands of Alan," said the other. "Before your jottering finger could find the trigger, the hilt would dirl[1] on your breast bane."

"Eh, man, whae's denying it?" said my uncle. "Pit it as ye please, ha'e't your ain way; I'll do naething to cross ye. Just tell me what like ye'll be wanting, and ye'll see that we'll can agree fine."

"Troth, sir," said Alan, "I ask for nothing but plain dealing. In two words: do ye want the lad killed or kept?"

"O sirs!" cried Ebenezer. "O sirs, me! that's no kind of language!"

"Killed or kept!" repeated Alan.

"O, keepit, keepit!" wailed my uncle. "We'll have nae bloodshed, if you please."

"Well," says Alan, "as ye please; that'll be the dearer."

"The dearer?" cries Ebenezer. "Would ye fyle your hands wi' crime?"

"Hoot!" said Alan, "they're baith crime, whatever! And

[1]Quiver.

the killing's easier, and quicker, and surer. Keeping the lad'll be a fashious[1] job, a fashious, kittle business."

"I'll have him keepit, though," returned my uncle. "I never had naething to do with onything morally wrong; and I'm no gaun to begin, to pleasure a wild Hielandman."

"Ye're unco scrupulous," sneered Alan.

"I'm a man o' principle," said Ebenezer simply; "and if I have to pay for it, I'll have to pay for it. And besides," says he, "ye forget the lad's my brother's son."

"Well, well," said Alan, "and now about the price. It's no' very easy for me to set a name upon it; I would first have to ken some small matters. I would have to ken, for instance, what ye gave Hoseason at the first off-go?"

"Hoseason!" cries my uncle, struck aback. "What for?"

"For kidnapping David," says Alan.

"It's a lee, it's a black lee!" cried my uncle. "He was never kidnapped. He leed in his throat that tauld ye that. Kidnapped? He never was!"

"That's no fault of mine nor yet of yours," said Alan; "nor yet of Hoseason's, if he's a man that can be trusted."

"What do ye mean?" cried Ebenezer. "Did Hoseason tell ye?"

"Why, ye donnered auld runt, how else would I ken?" cried Alan. "Hoseason and me are partners; we gang shares; so ye can see for yoursel' what good ye can do leeing. And I must plainly say ye drove a fool's bargain when ye let a man like the sailor-man so far forward in your private matters. But that's past praying for; and ye must lie on your bed the way ye made it. And the point in hand is just this: what did ye pay him?"

"Has he tauld ye himsel'?" asked my uncle.

"That's my concern," said Alan.

"Weel," said my uncle, "I dinna care what he said, he lee'd, and the solemn God's truth is this, that I gave him twenty pound. But I'll be perfec'ly honest with ye: forbye that, he was to have the selling of the lad in Caroliny, whilk would be as muckle mair, but no' from my pocket, ye see."

"Thank you, Mr. Thomson. That will do excellently

---

[1]Troublesome.

well," said the lawyer, stepping forward; and then mighty
civilly, "Good-evening, Mr. Balfour," said he.

And, "Good-evening, Uncle Ebenezer," said I.

And, "It's a braw nicht, Mr. Balfour," added Torrance.

Never a word said my uncle, neither black nor white;
but just sat where he was on the top doorstep and stared
upon us like a man turned to stone. Alan filched away his
blunderbuss; and the lawyer, taking him by the arm,
plucked him up from the doorstep, led him into the kitch-
en, whither we all followed, and set him down in a chair
beside the hearth, where the fire was out and only a
rushlight burning.

There we all looked upon him for a while, exulting
greatly in our success, but yet with a sort of pity for the
man's shame.

"Come, come, Mr. Ebenezer," said the lawyer, "you
must not be down-hearted, for I promise you we shall
make easy terms. In the meanwhile give us the cellar key,
and Torrance shall draw us a bottle of your father's wine in
honour of the event." Then, turning to me and taking me
by the hand, "Mr. David," says he, "I wish you all joy in
your good fortune, which I believe to be deserved." And
then to Alan, with a spice of drollery, "Mr. Thomson, I
pay you my compliment; it was most artfully conducted;
but in one point you somewhat outran my comprehension.
Do I understand your name to be James? or Charles? or is
it George, perhaps?"

"And why should it be any of the three, sir?" quoth
Alan, drawing himself up, like one who smelt an offence.

"Only, sir, that you mentioned a king's name," replied
Rankeillor; "and as there has never yet been a King Thomson, or his fame at least has never come my way, I judged
you must refer to that you had in baptism."

This was just the stab that Alan would feel keenest, and
I am free to confess he took it very ill. Not a word would
he answer, but stepped off to the far end of the kitchen,
and sat down and sulked; and it was not till I stepped after
him, and gave him my hand and thanked him by title as
the chief spring of my success, that he began to smile a
bit, and was at last prevailed upon to join our party.

By that time we had the fire lighted, and a bottle of

wine uncorked; a good supper came out of the basket, to
which Torrance and I and Alan set ourselves down; while
the lawyer and my uncle passed into the next chamber to
consult. They stayed there closeted about an hour; at the
end of which period they had come to a good understanding, and my uncle and I set our hands to the agreement in
a formal manner. By the terms of this, my uncle bound
himself to satisfy Rankeillor as to his intromissions, and to
pay me two clear thirds of the yearly income of Shaws.

So the beggar in the ballad had come home; and when I
lay down that night on the kitchen chests, I was a man of
means and had a name in the country. Alan and Torrance
and Rankeillor slept and snored on their hard beds; but for
me who had lain out under heaven and upon dirt and
stones so many days and nights, and often with an empty
belly, and in fear of death, this good change in my case
unmanned me more than any of the former evil ones; and
I lay till dawn, looking at the fire on the roof and planning
the future.

Chapter 30

GOOD-BYE

So far as I was concerned myself, I had come to port; but I had still Alan, to whom I was so much beholden, on my hands; and I felt besides a heavy charge in the matter of the murder and James of the Glens. On both these heads I unbosomed to Rankeillor the next morning, walking to and fro about six of the clock before the house of Shaws, and with nothing in view but the fields and woods that had been my ancestors' and were now mine. Even as I spoke on these grave subjects, my eye would take a glad bit of a run over the prospect, and my heart jump with pride.

About my clear duty to my friend, the lawyer had no doubt: I must help him out of the country at whatever risk; but in the case of James he was of a different mind.

"Mr. Thomson," says he, "is one thing, Mr. Thomson's kinsman quite another. I know little of the facts, but I gather that a great noble (whom we will call, if you like, the D. of A.[1]) has some concern and is even supposed to feel some animosity in the matter. The D. of A. is doubtless an excellent nobleman; but, Mr. David, *timeo qui nocuere deos*. If you interfere to baulk his vengeance, you should remember there is one way to shut your testimony out; and that is to put you in the dock. There you would be in the same pickle as Mr. Thomson's kinsman. You will object that you are innocent; well, but so is he. And to be tried for your life before a Highland jury, on a Highland quarrel, and with a Highland judge upon the bench, would be a brief transition to the gallows."

[1]The Duke of Argyle.

Now I had made all these reasonings before and found no very good reply to them; so I put on all the simplicity I could. "In that case, sir," said I, "I would just have to be hanged—would I not?"

"My dear boy," cries he, "go in God's name and do what you think is right. It is a poor thought that at my time of life I should be advising you to choose the safe and shameful; and I take it back with an apology. Go and do your duty; and be hanged, if you must, like a gentleman. There are worse things in the world than to be hanged."

"Not many, sir," said I, smiling.

"Why, yes, sir," he cried, "very many. And it would be ten times better for your uncle (to go no farther afield) if he were dangling decently upon a gibbet."

Thereupon he turned into the house (still in a great fervour of mind, so that I saw I had pleased him heartily) and there he wrote me two letters, making his comments on them as he wrote.

"This," says he, "is to my bankers, the British Linen Company, placing a credit to your name. Consult Mr. Thomson, he will know of ways; and you, with this credit, can supply the means. I trust you will be a good husband of your money; but in the affair of a friend like Mr. Thomson, I would be even prodigal. Then for his kinsman, there is no better way than that you should seek the Advocate, tell him your tale, and offer testimony; whether he may take it or not, is quite another matter, and will turn on the D. of A. Now, that you may reach the Lord Advocate well recommended, I give you here a letter to a namesake of your own, the learned Mr. Balfour of Pilrig, a man whom I esteem. It will look better that you should be presented by one of your own name; and the laird of Pilrig is much looked up to in the Faculty and stands well with Lord Advocate Grant. I would not trouble him, if I were you, with any particulars; and (do you know?) I think it would be needless to refer to Mr. Thomson. Form yourself upon the laird, he is a good model; when you deal with the Advocate, be discreet; and in all these matters, may the Lord guide you, Mr. David!"

Thereupon he took his farewell, and set out with Torrance for the Ferry, while Alan and I turned our faces for the city of Edinburgh. As we went by the footpath and beside the gateposts and the unfinished lodge, we kept looking back at the house of my fathers. It stood there, bare and great and smokeless, like a place not lived in; only in one of the top windows, there was the peak of a nightcap bobbing up and down, and back and forward, like the head of a rabbit from a burrow. I had little welcome when I came, and less kindness while I stayed; but at least I was watched as I went away.

Alan and I went slowly forward upon our way, having little heart either to walk or speak. The same thought was uppermost in both, that we were near the time of our parting; and remembrance of all the bygone days sate upon us sorely. We talked indeed of what should be done; and it was resolved that Alan should keep to the country, biding now here, now there, but coming once in the day to a particular place where I might be able to communicate with him, either in my own person or by messenger. In the meanwhile, I was to seek out a lawyer, who was an Appin Stewart, and a man therefore to be wholly trusted; and it should be his part to find a ship and to arrange for Alan's safe embarkation. No sooner was this business done, than the words seemed to leave us; and though I would seek to jest with Alan under the name of Mr. Thomson, and he with me on my new clothes and my estate, you could feel very well that we were nearer tears than laughter.

We came the by-way over the hill of Corstorphine; and when we got near to the place called Rest-and-be-Thankful, and looked down on Corstorphine bogs and over to the city and the castle on the hill, we both stopped, for we both knew without a word said that we had come to where our ways parted. Here he repeated to me once again what had been agreed upon between us: the address of the lawyer, the daily hour at which Alan might be found, and the signals that were to be made by any that came seeking him. Then I gave him what money I had (a guinea or two of Rankeillor's) so that he should not starve in the meanwhile; and then we stood a space, and looked over at Edinburgh in silence.

"Well, good-bye," said Alan, and held out his left hand.

"Good-bye," said I, and gave the hand a little grasp, and went off down hill.

Neither one of us looked the other in the face, nor so long as he was in my view did I take one back glance at the friend I was leaving. But as I went on my way to the city, I felt so lost and lonesome, that I could have found it in my heart to sit down by the dyke, and cry and weep like any baby.

It was coming near noon when I passed in by the West Kirk and the Grassmarket into the streets of the capital. The huge height of the buildings, running up to ten and fifteen stories, the narrow arched entries that continually vomited passengers, the wares of the merchants in their windows, the hubbub and endless stir, the foul smells and the fine clothes, and a hundred other particulars too small to mention, struck me into a kind of stupor of surprise, so that I let the crowd carry me to and fro; and yet all the time what I was thinking of was Alan at Rest-and-be-Thankful; and all the time (although you would think I would not choose but be delighted with these braws and novelties) there was a cold gnawing in my inside like a remorse for something wrong.

The hand of Providence brought me in my drifting to the very doors of the British Linen Company's bank.

Bibliography

OTHER WORKS BY ROBERT LOUIS STEVENSON

Novels and Tales

New Arabian Nights (1882)
Treasure Island (1883)
Prince Otto (1885)
The Strange Case of Dr. Jekyll and Mr. Hyde (1886)
The Merry Men and Other Tales and Fables (1887)
The Black Arrow: A Tale of Two Roses (1888)
The Master of Ballantrae (1889)
The Wrong Box (with Lloyd Osbourne, 1889)
David Balfour (also called *Catriona*, 1893)
The Ebb-Tide (with Lloyd Osbourne, 1894)
The Weir of Herminston (unfinished, 1896)
St. Ives (completed by Arthur Quiller-Couch, 1897)

Poetry

A Child's Garden of Verses (1885)
Underwoods (1887)
Ballads (1890)
Songs of Travel and Other Verses (1896)

Essays and Travel Books

An Inland Voyage (1878)
Travels with a Donkey in the Cevennes (1879)
Virginibus Puerisque (1881)
Familiar Studies of Men and Books (1882)
Memories and Portraits (1887)
Vailima Letters (to Sidney Colvin, 1895)

There is no complete modern edition of Stevenson's writings, but there are several good collected editions. Notable are the Pentland edition, ed. Edmund Gosse (20 vols, 1906–7) and the Vailima edition, ed. Lloyd Osbourne with Fanny Van de Grift Stevenson (26 vols, 1922–23). The standard edition of Stevenson's poetry is *Collected Poems*, ed. Janet Adam Smith, 2nd ed. (New York: Viking, 1971).

BIOGRAPHICAL AND CRITICAL WORKS

The official biography of Stevenson is *The Life of Robert Louis Stevenson* by Graham Balfour (New York: Scribner, 1901), and the standard modern biography is *Voyage to Windward: The Life of Robert Louis Stevenson* by J.C. Furnas (New York: Sloane, 1951). Also of special interest are *The Letters of Robert Louis Stevenson to His Family and Friends*, ed. Sidney Colvin, 2nd ed. (New York: Scribner, 1911); *RLS: Letters to Charles Baxter*, ed. De Lancey Ferguson and Marshall Waingrow (New Haven: Yale University Press, 1956); *Our Samoan Adventure*, ed. Charles Neider (New York: Harper, 1955); *From Scotland to Silverado*, ed. James D. Hart (Cambridge: Harvard University Press, 1966); *Henry James and Robert Louis Stevenson: A Record of Friendship and Criticism*, ed. Janet Adam Smith (London: Hart-Davis, 1948).

Aldington, Richard. *Portrait of a Rebel: The Life and Work of Robert Louis Stevenson*. London: Evans. 1957.

Baildon, Henry B. *Robert Louis Stevenson: A Life Study in Criticism*. London: Chatto & Windus, 1901.

Chesterton, G.K. *Robert Louis Stevenson*. London: Hodder & Stoughton, 1902.

Cooper, Lettice. *Robert Louis Stevenson*. London: Home & Van Thal, 1947.

Daiches, David. *Robert Louis Stevenson*. Norfolk, CT: New Directions, 1947.

—. *Robert Louis Stevenson and His World*. London: Thames and Hudson, 1973.

Eigner, Edwin M. *Robert Louis Stevenson and Romantic Tradition*. Princeton: Princeton University Press, 1966.

Elliot, Nathaniel. "Robert Louis Stevenson and Scottish Literature." *English Literature in Transition (1880–1920)* 12 (1969): 79–85.

Elwin, Malcolm. *The Strange Case of Robert Louis Stevenson*. London: Macdonald, 1950.

Fowler, Alistair. "Parables of Adventure: The Debatable Novels of Robert Louis Stevenson" *Nineteenth-Century Scottish Fiction: Critical Essays*, ed. Ian Campbell. Totowa, NJ: Barnes & Noble, 1979.

Hellman, George S. *The True Stevenson: A Study in Clarification*. Boston: Little, Brown, 1925.

Kelman, John, Jr. *The Faith of Robert Louis Stevenson*. New York: Revell, 1903.

Kiely, Robert. *Robert Louis Stevenson and the Fiction of Adventure*. Cambridge: Harvard University Press, 1964.

Mackay, Margaret. *The Violent Friend: The Story of Mrs. Robert Louis Stevenson 1840–1914*. Garden City, NY: Doubleday, 1968.

Masson, Rosaline. *The Life of Robert Louis Stevenson*. Edinburgh: Chambers, 1923.

Osbourne, Lloyd. *An Intimate Portrait of R.L.S.* New York: Scribner, 1924.

Pope-Hennessy, James. *Robert Louis Stevenson*. New York: Simon & Schuster, 1975.

Rice, Edward. *Journey to Upolu: Robert Louis Stevenson, Victorian Rebel*. New York: Dodd, Mead, 1974.

Saposnik, Irving S. *Robert Louis Stevenson*. New York: Twayne, 1974.

Smith, Janet Adam. *R. L. Stevenson*. London: Duckworth, 1937.

Steuart, J.A. *Robet Louis Stevenson: A Critical Biography*, 2 vols. Boston: Little, Brown, 1924.

Strong, Isobel and Lloyd Osbourne. *Memories of Vailima*. New York: Scribner, 1902.

Swinnerton, Frank. *R. L. Stevenson: A Critical Study*. London: Secker, 1914.

GREAT BOOKS FROM GREAT BRITAIN

The English literary heroes and heroines you've adored are now available from Bantam Classics in specially low-priced editions. These beautifully designed books feature the characters of Jane Eyre, Sydney Carton from *A Tale of Two Cities* and Pip from *Great Expectations*. All these Bantam Classics bring you the best in English Literature at affordable prices.

☐	21019	**EMMA** Jane Austen	$1.75
☐	21051	**DAVID COPPERFIELD** Charles Dickens	$2.50
☐	21015	**GREAT EXPECTATIONS** Charles Dickens	$1.95
☐	21017	**A TALE OF TWO CITIES** Charles Dickens	$1.50
☐	21026	**HEART OF DARKNESS** and **THE SECRET SHARER** Joseph Conrad	$1.50
☐	21027	**LORD JIM** Joseph Conrad	$1.95
☐	21020	**JANE EYRE** Charlotte Bronte	$1.75
☐	21059	**THE TURN OF THE SCREW AND OTHER SHORT FICTION** Henry James	$1.95

Titles by Thomas Hardy:

☐	21023	**JUDE THE OBSCURE**	$1.75
☐	21024	**THE MAYOR OF CASTERBRIDGE**	$1.95
☐	21025	**THE RETURN OF THE NATIVE**	$1.75
☐	21061	**TESS OF THE D'URBERVILLES**	$2.25

☐	21021	**WUTHERING HEIGHTS** Emily Bronte	$1.75
